LSAT
LAW
SCHOOL
ADMISSION
TEST

Thomas H. Martinson, J.D.

ARCO
New York

Third Edition

 ARCO

Simon & Schuster, Inc.
Gulf+Western Building
One Gulf+Western Plaza
New York, NY 10023

DISTRIBUTED BY PRENTICE HALL TRADE

Manufactured in the United States of America

1 2 3 4 5 6 7 8 9 10

Library of Congress Cataloging in Publication Data

Martinson, Thomas H.
    LSAT, law school admission test / Thomas H. Martinson. — 3rd ed.
      p.   cm.
   ISBN 0-13-526476-6
   1. Law School Admission Test. 2. Law schools—United States-
-Entrance examinations. I. Title. II. Title: Law school admission
test.
KF285.Z9M365 1989   89-98
340′.076—dc19   CIP

To Lynn Simonson
A Teacher Par Excellence

CONTENTS

PART I: GENERAL TEST-TAKING INFORMATION

How to Use This Book 3
    Why This Book Is Best 3
    The Importance of the LSAT Score 3
    Why and How Preparation Is Effective 3
    What You Need to Do 4
    Measuring Progress 5
About the LSAT 7
    Purpose of the LSAT 7
    Format of the LSAT 7
    Scoring of the LSAT 8
    Use of the Writing Sample by Law Schools 8
    Registration for the LSAT and LSDAS 9
    Special LSAT Administrations 9

PART II: TEST BUSTERS

General Test-taking Tactics 13
Logical Reasoning 19
Reading Comprehension 47
Analytical Reasoning 59
Writing Sample 82

PART III: APPLYING TO LAW SCHOOL

The Law School Admission Process 93
    The Numbers Game 93
    Other Factors 94
    Persuading the Admission Committee 95
    Letters of Recommendation 96
    Concluding Advice 97

PART IV: FOUR FULL-LENGTH PRACTICE EXAMINATIONS

Practice Examination 1
    Answer Sheet 101
    Examination Forecast 103
    Writing Sample 103
    Section I 105
    Section II 113
    Section III 117
    Section IV 125

Answer Key 129
Explanatory Answers 130
Practice Examination 2
Answer Sheet 157
Examination Forecast 159
Writing Sample 159
Section I 161
Section II 165
Section III 173
Section IV 178
Answer Key 186
Explanatory Answers 187
Practice Examination 3
Answer Sheet 211
Examination Forecast 213
Writing Sample 213
Section I 215
Section II 223
Section III 227
Section IV 235
Answer Key 243
Explanatory Answers 244
Practice Examination 4
Answer Sheet 271
Examination Forecast 273
Writing Sample 273
Section I 275
Section II 279
Section III 287
Section IV 295
Answer Key 303
Explanatory Answers 304

Part I

General Test-Taking Information

HOW TO USE THIS BOOK

WHY THIS BOOK IS BEST

The book that you hold in your hand is different from other preparation books in several ways that will help you get a better LSAT score.

First, there is much more instructional material in this book than in other, comparable preparation books. Our special Test Busters section offers substantial reviews of what each question type is all about and how to master it. This section is not filled out with just more drill work. It really teaches you something.

Second, the answer explanations are not only longer than usual, they discuss all the answer choices—explaining why the wrong choices were attractive. There are no one-sentence explanations. There are, after all, four wrong answers to cope with for every right answer.

Third, this book offers a complete program of preparation including general test-taking hints and specific hints for each type of question in the Test Busters review and in the answer explanations, many of which are longer than the questions they explain.

Fourth, there is a separate attack strategy for each question type, including detailed timing recommendations on sections and question types where students have had trouble in the past.

Fifth, the treatment of the Writing Sample section not only reviews some of the basic rules of good writing, it gives you a fail-safe method of making sure that you will have something to write about.

Sixth, the problems in the four practice tests are just like those in the test. There will be no surprises.

Seventh, there is nothing in the book that is not going to be on the test. There are no "extras" that only fill up the book without helping your score. Everything you need is here, while anything you don't is not.

For all these reasons we want to tell you how to get the full value of this book towards getting the best possible LSAT score.

THE IMPORTANCE OF THE LSAT SCORE

You know the LSAT score is important. It is used both as a cutoff and as one of two major criteria in evaluating your application. Consult the *Prelaw Handbook* published by the Association of American Law Schools. Law school by law school, the charts showing the LSAT scores and grade point averages of all their applicants and which ones were admitted are more eloquent than we could ever be.

WHY AND HOW PREPARATION IS EFFECTIVE

The LSAT is intended by its makers to test mental and academic skills that they regard as taking a long time to develop. These skills are usually referred to as "the ability to read, understand, and reason'' but are somewhat narrower than that designation might imply. There are three separate ways that preparation can raise your score.

1. UNDERSTANDING THE TEST: Good preparation will help you to know what each section of the test is about, and to analyze each subtype of question and explain what it is asking. Also included in this area of benefit are such technical matters as knowing whether to guess (yes, on the LSAT), how the timing works, etc.

2. IMPROVING YOUR TEST-TAKING SKILLS: Good test-taking skills improve the efficiency of your other academic and mental skills. There are many different test-taking skills. One of the most difficult to master is knowing just which other skills should be used for different question types. That skill is fully explained in this book. Other test-taking skills include the order in which parts of the section should be read and the emphasis to be given to each, how to tell the answer choices apart, key words to be aware of, what you DON'T have to worry about, and how to avoid various simple errors.

3. IMPROVING YOUR ''ABILITY TO READ, UNDERSTAND, AND REASON'': Or at least the mental and academic skills that go by that name on the LSAT. Reading, reasoning, and problem solving are skills that you use every day, and which, like all skills, can be improved. One of the most effective ways of improving any skill, and the one used in this book, is clear identification of errors and the appropriate times to use various subparts of these skills.

Perhaps an analogy to a ''physical'' skill will help (no skill is purely physical; there is always a major mental element). A tennis player may have a dozen excellent shots, but still play poorly because he or she does not know when to use them to best advantage or lacks one critical shot.

You may be in a similiar position. You have spent years learning a large number of mental and academic skills, but if you don't know which ones to use on which parts of the test, you won't do as well as you should. Similarly, you can probably benefit from brushing up, or perhaps learning in the first place, some of the skills needed for the LSAT.

We won't pretend that a five-year-old could pick up this book and then get a perfect score on the LSAT. But you are not five years old and you don't need a perfect score, just a better one. A better score is just what you will get if you master the skills presented in this book.

WHAT YOU NEED TO DO

How then shall you use this book? We will give you guidance in three areas: how to evaluate your needs and resources, how to set up a workable study plan, and how to study this sort of material effectively. Naturally there is some overlap between these three areas.

The first and most important thing that you need to do is take this book seriously. If you are just going to read a page here and there, casually do some problems without regard to timing, and never read the explanations—well, in that case, you are not going to benefit nearly as much as you could. It takes work and commitment—YOUR work and YOUR commitment.

Now, having been stirred to action, here is what you do.

Evaluating Your Needs and Resources

The most valuable resource you have in this work is your time. You may have a great deal of time or you may have only a little. You need to set priorities so that you can get the most return for the time invested.

Actually, your needs are not too complicated to evaluate. You should assume that you need to study closely each Test Busters section, unless you are previously both familiar AND successful with the kinds of questions it treats. If you think you don't need to study one or two of the Test Busters question reviews, do the appropriate sections in the first practice test as a check. Unless you get over 85% right, study the Overview. By the way, as a first exercise in logical reasoning, note that the use of 85% as a criterion in this context does not mean you should expect to get 85% of every section right on the test. As is explained in the next chapter, the LSAT scoring doesn't require that criterion. Even if you can get 85% right without help, you could still probably benefit from further study.

That leaves the practice tests. You must take at least one test as a full-dress rehearsal. That is the highest priority after the instructional material. It is good to do all of the practice tests, but if time does not permit, you can do extra sections of the question types that give you difficulty. The Writing Sample, while not unimportant, is not as important as the other sections, as explained in the next chapter and the Writing Sample Instructional Overview.

As you study and do the practice tests, you will develop a list of your problem areas, which will direct your further studying. The development of this list is described later, in the section on effective studying.

Now consider your time. Do not overestimate how much time you have. If you think you have four hours every day, say instead that you have two hours five days a week. If you actually have the extra time, you can always do more studying, but if you plan on more than you actually do, you will feel bad and your priorities may become distorted. Be conservative.

Even if it is just 45 minutes a day, that is fine. Just make sure that it is actually 45 minutes and not 20 minutes of telephone calls and only 25 minutes of study. Regular study in small amounts is much better than occasional larger periods. The practice tests that you take as complete tests should be done in one sitting.

Take a piece of paper right now and write down all the time you want to dedicate to studying for the LSAT between now and the test date. If you don't know the test date, consult the official LSAT bulletin.

Setting Up a Workable Study Plan

Once you know how much time you have, you are halfway to having a plan that will work. Each week, you should plan exactly on which topics or tests you will work. You cannot plan the entire process at the beginning because you won't know how long things take until you have done some of them. Allow TWICE as much time as your best estimate of the time it really takes. If you actually do finish quicker, you'll feel good and there is no harm done. You will find your margin used up very quickly.

Never plan two things for the same time. For the best results, your study time must be totally dedicated to study. If you can do some extra review of your notes while commuting, so much the better, but make that extra time, not prime time.

In sum, then, the keys to setting up a workable plan are dedicated time, conservative estimation, and advance planning in writing. Aside from helping you to remember when you are to study for the LSAT, putting the plan in writing will remind you to reschedule the hours that will inevitably be superseded by some "emergency" or special event.

MEASURING PROGRESS

We should make one final note about studying with this book. Although you will almost surely gain in confidence and ability to attack exam items, it will not be possible to supply you with an objective measure of your improvement. This is because it is impossible for us to administer the practice tests included in this book over a large enough population to get results that we could then compare with those obtained from a similar population on previously administered LSATs. We are sure that you can understand why that is not possible. "But," you ask, "can I not use the scoring formula from some old exam?" The answer is no!

The scoring formula for an LSAT is unique to that particular exam, and it includes adjustment factors to keep the level of difficulty the same from administration to administration. (See "Scoring of the New LSAT," page 8.) Although the test developers attempt to keep the level of difficulty fairly constant, their efforts are never perfect. The Analytical Reasoning section in June may be unexpectedly easier than that given in February of that year, or more difficult than that given in October of the previous year. To avoid possible scoring inequities, the scoring formula is designed to even out this "lumpiness." Since the scoring formula varies from actual test to actual test, it would be highly inappropriate for you to attempt to use such a formula for the practice tests in this book——not even to get a rough idea of your score.

You must remember that a very small change in the number of questions you answer correctly can mean a very large change in your score. In the middle ranges of the scoring scale, a difference of as few as two questions per section (totaling eight for the entire test) can mean a difference of 10 percentile points on your exam score (again, see "Scoring," page 8). Obviously, then, using an inappropriate scoring formula should be discouraged.

We might add further that we consider this to be a serious fault of those other preparation books which gratuitously supply scoring formulas. It would, of course, have been easy enough for us to have inserted a scoring formula in this book, but that would have been intellectually dishonest. Insofar as we are aware, no one, except the test developers themselves, has the sophisticated statistical data needed to support such a conclusion about scoring.

Finally, this analysis has an important implication for your study. Aside from a general feeling of increased confidence and ability, you will not be able to chart your progress——not even by comparing numbers of questions answered correctly. You must remember that test sections vary in level of difficulty. Thus it would not be appropriate for you to make a judgment such as: "Well, I answered 20 out of 30 questions on this section in Practice Test 1, and only 19 out of 30 questions on the same subject in Practice Test 2; therefore, I have not made any progress." A difference in performance of this sort is likely the result of a variation in the level of difficulty; that is, the second section mentioned is more difficult than the first section. So even if you do not see a steady improvement in the number of questions answered correctly per section, this does not necessarily mean that you are not improving.

In a way, then, you have to take it as a sort of article of faith that conscientious study will result in a better LSAT score, but that is not a difficult belief to accept. After all, it is our, and surely your own, experience that conscientious preparation leaves you better able to handle any task you may be undertaking, whether it be a history exam, a sales presentation, a tennis match, or even the LSAT.

GOOD LUCK AND GOOD STUDYING!

ABOUT THE LSAT

PURPOSE OF THE LSAT

The LSAT is a standardized test intended to assist law schools in making admissions decisions by giving a standard assessment of mental skills considered to be important to the study of law. The LSAT scores are designed to be a measure of the "ability to read, understand, and reason" according to the Law School Admissions Council, the consortium of law schools which owns and controls the LSAT.

The purpose of a standard measure is to permit the law school admissions decisions to be based, at least in part, on an "objective" comparison of all the candidates—no matter what their college or background. There has been some controversy about the degree to which the laudable goal of "objectivity and total evenhandedness" has been met. There is no similar disagreement about the importance that the law schools place on the LSAT scores in making their admissions decisions.

At base, the purpose of the LSAT is to be part of the criteria for law school admissions, and your purpose in taking it is to do as well as you can so you will have the best possible chance of getting into the law school of your choice.

FORMAT OF THE NEW LSAT

Starting with the June 1989 administration of the test, LSATs have a new look. The sections are now 45 minutes long and there are only three types of questions—Reading Comprehension, Logical Reasoning, and Analytical Reasoning. (A brief description of each question type follows. For more details, see the specific chapters devoted to each.) There is also a Writing Sample, which is discussed in detail later in the Writing Sample Instructional Overview. The scoring system now runs from a low score of 10 to a high score of 48. Your score is still based solely on the number of questions you answer correctly, with no deduction for incorrect answers.

Here is a very brief description of each question type.

READING COMPREHENSION questions are based on a reading passage and ask you to demonstrate your understanding of the passage by answering questions about the structure, meaning, and implications of the passage. This type of question has been used on the LSAT for many years. Similar questions appear on several other standardized exams, such as the SAT, GMAT, and GRE.

LOGICAL REASONING questions are based on very short arguments. You are asked to demonstrate your understanding of the arguments by choosing answers that describe the argument, weaken or strengthen it, identify its premises, or state its conclusions or implications.

ANALYTICAL REASONING questions are based on a set of information which you must organize in order to answer the questions. Diagrams of various sorts are helpful. This is also referred to as "logical games" and is not dissimilar to games found in various magazines. A similar version of this question type appears on the GRE.

As with previous LSATs, not every section of the test administered to you will actually be used to compute your LSAT score. Your score will be based on the sum of your answers to three of the four sections——one section of each of the three question types just described. Your work on the other section is only your contribution to the research and development of future LSATs. Unfortunately, you will not be able to tell which sections are to be counted in your case and which is not.

Furthermore, LSATs will now present ''operational'' and ''nonoperational'' sections (as they are called) in any order whatsoever and in different orders for different students. Thus, your test booklet may be ordered like this:

1. reading, 2. logic, 3. logic, 4. analytic.

Another student's test booklet may be like this:

1. logic, 2. reading, 3. analytic, 4. reading.

And the two booklets might have none of the same sections in the same places——even though the same three sections that count will appear somewhere on every version of the test booklet used at a particular administration.

The bottom line is that you must do all the sections.

The three operational sections of the LSAT will have a total of approximately 100 questions that count towards your score. While some format variation will occur, a typical test would be:

Reading Comprehension	35 questions, 5 passages
Logical Reasoning	35 questions
Analytical Reasoning	30 questions, 5–6 problem sets

SCORING OF THE LSAT

As previously noted, LSAT scores are reported on a scale ranging from 10 to 48. (Initially, the designers of the test contemplated a range of 10 to 50, but unforeseen complications required that it be adjusted.) Scaled scores are based on what is called a raw score, which is simply the number of questions you have answered correctly. So the scoring of your exam proceeds as follows.

First, the grading machine ''reads'' your answer sheet grid, totaling the number of questions you have answered correctly, ignoring incorrect answers, omissions, and miscoded responses (e.g., multiple answers to a single question). In other words, there is no ''penalty'' for an incorrect answer; the score is based solely on the number of questions answered correctly.

Second, the computer converts this raw score into a scaled score by using a formula uniquely designed for each administration of the exam. For example:

$$(\text{Raw Score} \times .5984) - 7.7149 = \text{Scaled Score}$$

Thus, raw scores of 60, 70, 80, and 90 (out of 100 total) might result in scaled scores of 28, 34, 40, and 46, respectively. The test developer also provides a table that allows you and the law schools to convert these scores to percentile rankings. You will find a copy of this information in the bulletins distributed as part of the LSAT registration packet.

USE OF THE WRITING SAMPLE BY LAW SCHOOLS

Usually at the beginning of the test, you will be asked to do a writing sample based on a vacuous question that will be given to you. The sole purpose of this writing sample is to give the law schools an idea of your spontaneous writing abilities, done in a situation where it is definitely your work alone. The writing sample is not looked at by the testing service, but only photocopied and sent directly to all the law schools who are receiving your LSAT scores.

As will be discussed in the Writing Sample Overview, a rough survey of law school admissions officers indicates that the writing sample will usually be used as a ''tie-breaker'' or secondary credential of much less importance than the LSAT score. However, a very poor writing sample could seriously undermine an otherwise strong application at many schools. While a very strong writing sample will not equally redeem an otherwise weak application, it may be the deciding factor where your application is approximately as strong as someone else's.

REGISTRATION FOR THE LSAT AND LSDAS

You can obtain registration materials for both the LSAT and the Law School Data Assembly Service (LSDAS) required by most law schools in the same package, either from your college's prelaw advisor or dean or by writing to:

Law School Admissions Services
Box 2000
Newtown, PA 18940

You should register well in advance of the test and should get your materials as soon as possible. The registration booklet also contains a full-length sample test which you should do as part of your preparation. While this test lacks answer explanations, it is very useful in the later stages of your preparation.

SPECIAL LSAT ADMINISTRATIONS

Special arrangements can be made for the physically and visually handicapped, for persons whose religious beliefs forbid taking the test on a Saturday, and for some other persons with special needs. The key to making satisfactory arrangements is time. If you want to make any special arrangements for taking the LSAT, communicate immediately with the Law School Admissions Services at the address just given.

Part II
Test Busters

TEST BUSTERS

GENERAL TEST-TAKING TACTICS

Even though the LSAT uses three different question types, there are some tactics that are applicable to the test as a whole.

Starting to Work

 Take a brief overview of each section before beginning to work on it.

This is just a matter of caution. Some small adjustments in test format are always possible, so do not get caught off guard. When time is announced for you to begin work on a section, take five to ten seconds to look through the pages of that section. If there are unexpected changes, you can readily adjust your plan of attack.

 Don't stop to ask directions.

Your allotted 45 minutes is all the time you get for a section. No additional time is given for reading instructions. If you spend 30 seconds reading directions each time you begin a new question type, you could lose a question in each section.

The solution to this problem is to be thoroughly familiar with the directions for each question type and the format in which it is presented *before* the exam. Then you will recognize the format and already know what is required without having to review the directions for that part.

Covering Ground

The scoring mechanism for the LSAT is the simple formula "score = correct answers." No points are awarded for near misses, and no extra points are given for accuracy. This means you have got to cover as much ground as possible.

 Move as quickly as possible without unnecessarily sacrificing accuracy.

On the one hand you have to answer as many questions as you can in the 45 minutes; on the other hand, you cannot afford to be so careful that you begin to beat yourself by not answering enough questions to get a good score. There is a trade-off between speed and accuracy, one that you can find only through practice.

To demonstrate the necessity of the trade-off, consider the cases of three hypothet-

13

ical students: Timmy Toocareful, Carl Careless, and Terry Testwise.

On his exam, Timmy Toocareful attempted only 65 questions, but he was very accurate. Of the 65, Timmy answered 60 correctly, missing only 5. Additionally, he guessed at the remaining 35 questions, getting ⅕ of those right (as expected) for another 7 points.

Carl Careless used the opposite strategy. He worked very quickly to ensure that he attempted all 100 questions, and he paid the price. Of the 100, he answered only 70 correctly.

Terry Testwise used the proper strategy of working as quickly as possible without unnecessarily sacrificing accuracy. Of the 100, she attempted 85, missing 10. And she guessed at the other 15 questions, hitting ⅕ of them (as expected) for another 3 points.

The score reports would show:

Timmy Toocareful: Raw Score: 67   Scaled Score: 32

Carl Careless: Raw Score: 70   Scaled Score: 34

Terry Testwise: Raw Score: 78   Scaled Score: 39

Most students are probably prone to err on the side of caution. In this case, Timmy, fearful of answering incorrectly, doesn't attempt enough questions to get his best score. Since there is no penalty for answering incorrectly, don't be overly worried about mistakes. Of course, you don't want to be needlessly careless, but it's probably better to go too quickly than too slowly.

The following Test Buster will help you find the right tradeoff:

Don't spend too much time on any question.

All questions are given equal weight. No extra credit is given for a difficult question. So there is no reason to keep working on a question after you have given it your best shot. Instead, once you realize that you are spinning your wheels, make the decision to make a guess and move on to the next question.

Beat the Clock

Many years ago, there was a program on television called "Beat the Clock." Contestants were given silly things to do within a certain time limit. For example, a contestant might be asked to stack 100 paper cups on top of each other in 30 seconds—while blindfolded! (The LSAT is a lot like this.) On the television studio wall was a large clock with a single hand so contestants could keep track of the passing time. You need a similar device.

Bring your own watch to the test.

The proctors in charge of administering the test are supposed to keep you advised of the passing time, for example, by writing on a blackboard how many minutes remain. But you should not rely on their diligence. In the first place, it's easy for a proctor to forget to mark the passing time at exactly the right moment. So when you see the proctor write "5 minutes left," you might have only 4 minutes left or as much as 6 minutes left. Further, the proctor might mark the correct time at the right moment without your knowledge. When you look up from your work you see "5 minutes left," but when did the proctor write that down?

The solution is to have a watch with you. If you have a digital watch with a stopwatch function, you can use that. If your digital watch does not have a stopwatch function, write down the starting time for the section when you begin. Quickly add 45 minutes to that and write down the time you must finish. Circle that number for easy reference. If you have a watch with hands, adjust the minute hand to quarter-past any hour (the 3). The hour is irrelevant. If you begin work with the minute hand on the 3, your time will be up when the minute hand reaches the 12.

Keeping track of the time is not an end unto itself. You keep track of the time in order to use it to answer questions.

Concentrate intensely. If you find that your mind does begin to wander, stop briefly and regather your concentration.

The LSAT is an arduous task. There is no way that you can maintain your concentration throughout all four of the forty-five-minute sections plus the thirty-minute writing sample. There will be times when your attention begins to flag. Learn to recognize this. For example, if you find that you are reading and rereading the same line without understanding, put down your pencil, close your eyes, take a deep breath or two (or rub your eyes or whatever), and then get back to work.

Don't become obsessed with time.

Although time is an important part of the test, don't become preoccupied with the passing seconds. There are convenient points in each section to stop and check the remaining time, for example, as you turn a page.

Busting the Multiple-Choice Format

Because of the multiple-choice format, you have a real advantage over the LSAT. The correct answer is always right there on the page. To be sure, it's surrounded by wrong choices, but it may be possible to eliminate one or more of those other choices as non-answers. Look at the following reading comprehension question:

The author argues that the evidence supporting the new theory is

(A) hypothetical
(B) biased
(C) empirical
(D) speculative
(E) fragmentary

You might think that it is impossible to make any progress on a reading comprehension question without the reading selection, but you can eliminate three of the five answers in this question as non-answers.

Study the question stem. We can infer that the author of the selection has at least implicitly passed judgment on the evidence supporting the new theory. What kind of judgment might someone make about the evidence adduced to support a theory? (A), (C), and (D) all seem extremely unlikely. As for (A), while the theory is itself a hypothesis, the evidence supporting the theory would not be hypothetical. As for (C), evidence is empirical by definition. So it is unlikely that anyone would argue "This evidence is empirical." And (D) can be eliminated for the same reason as (A). Admittedly, this leaves you with a choice of (B) or (E), a choice that depends on the content of the reading selection; but at least you have a 50–50 chance of getting the question correct—even without reading the selection.

This brings us to the question of guessing.

Leave no stone unturned.

Unlike some other standardized exams you might have taken (such as the SAT), no points are deducted for incorrect answers. Since there is no penalty for taking a guess, and since there is always a chance you will hit on the right answer, don't leave any answer space blank. For those questions on which you can eliminate choices, make an educated guess. But even if you don't get to some questions, at least make a random guess on your answer sheet. You can't lose; you can only win.

The arrangement of answer choice letters is random. There is one exception to this general rule.

Strings of three letters are used. Strings of four or more letters are not used.

Although strings of four or more of one letter are theoretically possible, they just don't occur. This is because the testwriters break them up. So you will not find a string of four (A)s in a row. If you do, at least one of your four answers will be wrong. Which one is it? There is no way of knowing for sure without checking your work.

Care and Feeding of the Answer Sheet

Your test materials come in two parts: a booklet of thirty-odd pages containing the test questions and an answer sheet covered with rows of lettered spaces for your responses. The space for marking your answers to a section will look something like this:

15	Ⓐ Ⓑ Ⓒ Ⓓ Ⓔ	22	Ⓐ Ⓑ Ⓒ Ⓓ Ⓔ	29	Ⓐ Ⓑ Ⓒ Ⓓ Ⓔ
16	Ⓐ Ⓑ Ⓒ Ⓓ Ⓔ	23	Ⓐ Ⓑ Ⓒ Ⓓ Ⓔ	30	Ⓐ Ⓑ Ⓒ Ⓓ Ⓔ
17	Ⓐ Ⓑ Ⓒ Ⓓ Ⓔ	24	Ⓐ Ⓑ Ⓒ Ⓓ Ⓔ	31	Ⓐ Ⓑ Ⓒ Ⓓ Ⓔ
18	Ⓐ Ⓑ Ⓒ Ⓓ Ⓔ	25	Ⓐ Ⓑ Ⓒ Ⓓ Ⓔ	32	Ⓐ Ⓑ Ⓒ Ⓓ Ⓔ
19	Ⓐ Ⓑ Ⓒ Ⓓ Ⓔ	26	Ⓐ Ⓑ Ⓒ Ⓓ Ⓔ	33	Ⓐ Ⓑ Ⓒ Ⓓ Ⓔ
20	Ⓐ Ⓑ Ⓒ Ⓓ Ⓔ	27	Ⓐ Ⓑ Ⓒ Ⓓ Ⓔ	34	Ⓐ Ⓑ Ⓒ Ⓓ Ⓔ
21	Ⓐ Ⓑ Ⓒ Ⓓ Ⓔ	28	Ⓐ Ⓑ Ⓒ Ⓓ Ⓔ	35	Ⓐ Ⓑ Ⓒ Ⓓ Ⓔ

Your answer sheet is graded by a machine that "reads" the marks you have made.

Code your answers neatly, filling completely the answer space with a dark pencil mark. Leave no stray marks on the answer sheet. Enter one, and only one, answer per question. Don't worry if the answer sheet has more blanks than your booklet has questions. Leave the extra spaces blank.

Perhaps a visual aid will help explain the importance of this Test Buster:

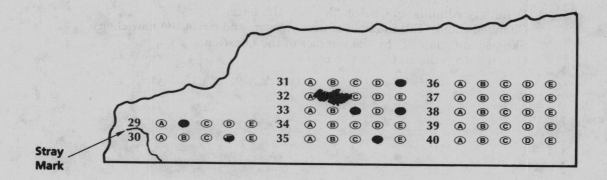

The answers to questions 29 and 35 are correctly entered. The answer to question 30, however, is incomplete; the machine might not see it. The answer to question 31 is too light; again, the machine might miss it. The mark for question 32 is messy; the machine might read (A), (B), or (C) as the intended response. Question 33 will be treated as incorrect since more than one space is darkened (no credit, no penalty). Question 34 will be treated in the same way since it has been left blank. (Leaving it blank was a mistake. It should have been answered even with a guess.)

The most common error in answer sheet management is misplacing an entire block of answers. This occurs when a test-taker skips a question in the test booklet but fails to skip a corresponding space on the answer sheet. The result is that the intended pattern of response is there, but it is displaced by one or more spaces. Unfortunately, the machine that grades the paper reads what actually is on the answer sheet—not what the test-taker intended. Here are some Test Busters to help you avoid this unpleasant problem.

Code your answers in groups.

Most test-takers code their response to each question just after they have answered the question. They work in the rhythm: solve, code, solve, code, solve, code, and so on. It is this rhythm that can trip them up if they skip a question. Instead, of coding your responses one by one, try coding them in groups.

Work problems for a while (noting your choices). Then find an appropriate moment to enter your responses on your answer sheet. You might wait until you have reached the end of a page. As time for a section draws to a close, you should make sure you are current with your coding, so you will probably want to go to the one-by-one method. You don't want to run out of time on a section without the opportunity to enter answers to every question that you have worked.

Even if you are coding in groups, there is the ever-present danger of an error. If you find that you have made a mistake, what do you do? You erase the wrong responses and enter the correct ones.

Keep a separate record of your progress in your test booklet, including correct responses, skipped questions, and doubtful questions.

There is no single record keeping system that is good for everyone, so develop your own. You might consider using some of the following:

Correct Answer: Circle the letter of the choice.
Definitely Eliminated Choice: "X" over the letter.
Changed choice: Fill in circle of first answer, and circle the new choice.
Skipped question: "?" by the number of the question.
Question to recheck: Circle the number.

LOGICAL REASONING

A Logical Reasoning section on the LSAT will contain 35 or 36 questions and have a time limit of 45 minutes. You may have a test form which includes more than one Logical Reasoning section, in which case only one of the two Logical Reasoning sections will be scored. The other will contain trial questions being tested for validity so they can be used on future exams. Once again, we stress that since you have absolutely no way of determining which questions, if any, are trial questions, you must treat each and every question as though it is vital to your test's scores. The Logical Reasoning section or sections can appear as any of the exam's four sections.

Now, the very title of this section—*Logical* Reasoning—causes some students to worry, for it suggests to them that they will be tested on the formal rules of logic. They imagine that they will encounter problems using Latin terms and mathematical symbols and notations. Fortunately, this is not the case. Doing well in this section does not depend upon having had any official instruction in logic, such as a college course in symbolic logic.

Instead, the section is actually a test of two skills—reading ability and reasoning power—both of which are essential to the practice of law. Of course, it cannot be denied that a student who has had formal training in logic, for example, the standard introduction to logic offered by most college philosophy departments, may find occasion to put that training to use in this section, but many brilliant thinkers have never received so much as a single hour of instruction in the rules of thinking.

The value of a course in logic is not so much that it teaches a student anything new—after all, we all *do think* even if we do not *know how* it is that we think. Rather, the value of a logic course is that it brings some order or structure to what we do quite naturally. Perhaps an analogy drawn from athletics might make the point clear. Some people are natural sprinters and can run very fast. Nonetheless, a good coach can show even the most gifted runners how they can improve their performances. The same is true of thinking. Some people are naturally brilliant thinkers, others are not; but whatever the level of natural ability, everyone could definitely benefit from "coaching" in this area. In this Instructional Overview, we will try to offer some hints on how to sharpen up your analytical abilities. It must be emphasized, however, that the material we present is not new. This is not like a course in organic chemistry where a student can get a good grade simply by memorizing all the formulas. Instead, we are just trying to make you *aware* of what you have always done—to put you in touch with your thought processes.

As you read, pay careful attention to details.

We may use a newspaper ad to illustrate the danger of not attending to detail.

Seventy-three percent of the doctors surveyed said they would, if asked by a patient, recommend Lite Cigarettes with their low tar and nicotine for patients who smoke.

Does the ad claim that many *doctors* are encouraging people to smoke Lite Cigarettes? Not exactly, for the claim made by the ad is carefully qualified in several respects. First, the ad speaks of a certain *percentage* of doctors without saying how many doctors were questioned. Second, the doctors who did respond did not say they *do* recommend Lite Cigarettes; the ad says specifically they *would* recommend Lite Cigarettes *if* a patient asked them about cigarette smoking. And third, the final phrase of the ad also makes a very important qualification: The doctors would make such a recommendation for those patients who *do* smoke already. We can see from this very simple illustration that there is a great difference between the general impression created by this advertisement and what the advertisement really says. And this is one skill you need to develop: careful reading with attention to detail.

It should be obvious, then, that it does absolutely no good to memorize the instruction: Read carefully! Instead, as you study these materials, make cross-connections to similar material you have encountered—for example, another advertisement. Also, you should practice being alert. Someone who is really aware of the importance of careful reading is always attending to detail. This is not to suggest that good thinkers are paranoid about people trying to trick or deceive them, and the *LSAT Bulletin* is explicit on this point as well. The problems do not involve cute tricks. But careful thinkers are always paying attention. Learning to be a careful thinker involves practice. We would never imagine that an athlete could learn to run faster or jump higher by just listening to a lecture on muscle structure. We know very well that the athlete has to take that information and incorporate it into his training regimen. Fortunately, the practice field for logical thinking is everyday life. Think carefully about everything your hear or read.

Our approach here will not concentrate on classifying actual LSAT logical reasoning problems. The kinds of questions used are too numerous for simple classification. Instead, we will try to give a highly condensed course in logic, pointing out the most common argument forms and fallacies that appear on the LSAT. Then, in our answer explanations to the practice tests that follow, we will study the question stems used in the Logical Reasoning section to test whether a candidate can recognize these forms and fallacies. If you feel you would benefit from further reading in logic and have the time to pursue these studies, we recommend the standard college textbook on elementary logic: *Introduction to Logic,* Irving M. Copi (Macmillan Publishing Co.: NY, 1978), particularly chapters one through seven.

 ## Analyze arguments into three parts: conclusion, premises, inference.

An *argument* is a group of statements or assertions one of which, the *conclusion,* is supposed to follow from the others, the *premises*. Some arguments are very short and simple:

Premise: No fish are mammals.
Conclusion: No mammals are fish.

Others are extremely lengthy and complex, taking up entire volumes. Some arguments are good, some are bad. Scientists use arguments to justify a conclusion regarding the cause of some natural phenomenon; politicians use arguments to reach conclusions about the desirability of government policies. But even given this wide variety of structures and uses, arguments fall into one or two general categories, depending on the kind of *inference* which is required to get *from the premises to the conclusion*. An inference which depends solely on the meanings of the terms used in the argument is called a *deductive* argument. All other arguments are termed *inductive*. So all arguments have three parts—premise(s), inference, conclusion; and the difference between deduction and induction is the kind of inference. Let us take a look at some examples.

A *deductive* argument is one in which the inference is guaranteed by the meanings of the terms:

> Premises: All bats are mammals.
> All mammals are warm-blooded.
> Conclusion: Therefore, all bats are warm-blooded.

We know that this argument has to be correct just by looking at it. No research is necessary to show us that the conclusion *follows automatically* from the premises. This argument is what the logicians call a *valid argument,* by which they mean that the conclusion does follow from the premises; or more precisely, *if* the premises are true, then the conclusion must also be true. We must be careful to distinguish "truth" from "validity." Logic is an "arm-chair" science. The logician is concerned with the *connection* between the assertions. He is concerned only incidentally, if at all, with the ultimate truth of those assertions.

We might think of logic, then, as analogous in function to a computer. The computer generates outputs on the basis of inputs; if the input is correct (and the computer is functioning properly), then the output will also be correct. But if the input is wrong, then the output will be correct only as a matter of luck. So, too, the logical thinker takes the input which is given to him and he processes it; he says, in effect, "I myself know nothing about bats personally; but if the information you have given me is correct, then the conclusion is also correct." In deductive logic, we speak of arguments as being logical or illogical, or, using the more technical terms, we speak of them as being "valid" or "invalid." We never refer to an *argument* as being "true" or "false." The statements used in making the argument may be true or false, but the deductive argument itself—the inference from premises to conclusion—can only be valid or invalid, logical or illogical, good or bad, but never true or false.

An *inductive* argument also moves from premises to a conclusion, but it uses a different kind of inference: a probable inference. For example:

> Premise: My car will not start; and the fuel gauge reads "empty."
> Conclusion: Therefore, the car is probably out of gas.

Notice that here, unlike our deductive argument, the conclusion does not follow with certainty; it is not guaranteed. The conclusion does seem to be likely or probable, but there are some gaps in the argument. It is possible, for example, that the fuel gauge is broken, or that there is fuel in the tank and the car will not start because something else is wrong. Since we have used the terms "valid" and "invalid" to apply to deductive arguments, we will not want to use them to apply to inductive arguments. Instead, we will speak of inductive inferences as being "strong" or "weak," and we realize that no conclusion which follows inductively is guaranteed. Some inductive conclusions are very strong:

> Premise: This is an ordinary coin I am tossing.
> Conclusion: Therefore, it will not come to rest on its edge.

It is of course possible that the coin will land on its edge—but very, very unlikely. Some inductive conclusions are very weak:

> Premise: This year the July Fourth picnic was rained out.
> Conclusion: Therefore, every year the July Fourth picnic is rained out.

But regardless of the relative strength of the argument, both of these examples have the same inductive form. The conclusions do not follow from the premises as a matter of logic.

CONCLUSIONS

Begin by locating the conclusion of the argument.

Locating the conclusion of an argument and defining its exact scope is the first step in evaluating the strength of any argument. You cannot begin to look for fallacies or other weaknesses in a line of reasoning or even find the line of reasoning until you have clearly identifed the point the author wishes to prove. Any attempt to skip over this important step can only result in misunderstanding and confusion. We have all had the experience of discussing a point for some length of time only to say finally, "Oh, now I see what you were saying, and I agree with you." Of course, sometimes such misunderstandings are the fault of the speaker, who perhaps did not clearly state his position in the first place. This is particularly true in less formal discourse, such as conversation, where we have not carefully prepared our remarks before the discussion begins; but it can also occur in writing, though in the case of writing the proponent of a claim generally has the opportunity to consider his words carefully, and is therefore, one would hope, less likely to misstate his point. Often, however, the misunderstanding cannot be charged to the speaker or writer and the blame must be placed on the listener or the reader.

Careful thinkers will obviously want to know precisely what is being claimed in an argument they are examining. They know it is a waste of their mental energy to attack a point which has not been advanced by their opponents but is only the product of their own failure to pay careful attention. In order to help you become more sensitive to the importance of finding the exact point of an argument, we will discuss conclusions in two steps: (1) locating the main point of an argument, and (2) defining exactly the main point of any argument.

The logical structure of an argument is not necessarily dependent on the order in which sentences appear.

Sometimes the main point of an argument is fairly easy to find—it is the last statement in the paragraph:

> Since this watch was manufactured in Switzerland, and all Swiss watches are reliable, <u>this watch must be reliable</u>.

Here the conclusion or the point of the line of reasoning is the part that is underlined. The argument also contains two premises: "this watch was manufactured in Switzerland" and "all Swiss watches are reliable." The same argument could be made, however, with the statements presented in a different order:

> <u>This watch must be reliable</u> since it was manufactured in Switzerland and all Swiss watches are reliable.
>
> or
>
> <u>This watch must be reliable</u> since all Swiss watches are reliable and it was manufactured in Switzerland.

or

Since this watch was manufactured in Switzerland, <u>it must be reliable</u> because all Swiss watches are reliable.

So we cannot always count on the conclusion of the argument being the last sentence of the paragraph even though sometimes it is.

Look for words that signal the conclusion.

It is always necessary to ask, "What is the main point of this argument?" Or perhaps, "What is the author trying to prove here?" If the conclusion is not the last statement in a passage, it may be *signaled* by indicator words. We often use transitional words or phrases such as *therefore, hence, thus, so, it follows that, as a result,* and *consequently* to announce to the reader or listener that we are making an inference, that is, that we are moving from our premise(s) to our conclusion. For example:

> Ms. Slote has a Masters in Education, and she has 20 years of teaching experience, therefore (hence, thus, etc.) she is a good teacher.

Here the conclusion is "she is a good teacher," and the premises are "Ms. Slote has a Masters in Education" and "she has 20 years of teaching experience."

Look for words that signal premises.

In some arguments the premises rather than the conclusion are signaled. Words which signal premises include *since, because, for,* and others which normally connect a dependent clause to an independent one. For example:

> Since Rex has been with the company 20 years and does such a good job, <u>he will probably receive a promotion</u>.
>
> or
>
> <u>Rex will probably receive a promotion</u> because he has been with the company 20 years and he does such a good job.
>
> or
>
> If Rex has been with the company 20 years and has done a good job, <u>he will probably receive a promotion</u>.

In each of the three examples just presented, the conclusion is "Rex will probably receive a promotion" and the premise is that "he has been with the company 20 years and does a good job."

Ask yourself, "What is the author or speaker trying to prove?"

Not all arguments, however, are broken down by the numbers, so to speak. Sometimes inattention on the part of the author or speaker, or sometimes matters of style, result in an argument which does not include a prominent signal of any sort. In such a case, the readers or listeners must use their judgments to answer the question, "What is the author or speaker trying to prove?" For example:

> We must reduce the amount of money we spend on space exploration. Right now, the Soviet Union is launching a massive military buildup, and

we need the additional money to purchase military equipment to match the anticipated increase in Soviet strength.

In this argument there are no key words to announce the conclusion, nor is the conclusion the last sentence or statement made in the passage. Instead, the reader must ask, "What is the author trying to prove?" Is the author trying to *prove* that the Soviet Union is beginning a military buildup? No, because that statement is used as a premise in the larger argument, so it cannot be the conclusion. Is the main point that we must match the Soviet buildup? Again the answer is "no," because that, too, is an intermediate step on the way to some other conclusion. Is the author trying to prove that we must cut back on the budget for space exploration? The answer is "yes, that is the author's point." The other two statements are premises which lead the author to conclude that a cutback in space exploration is necessary.

Sometimes an argument may contain arguments within the main argument. Thus, the argument about the need for military expenditures might have included this subargument:

> The Soviets are now stockpiling titanium, a metal which is used in building airplanes. And each time the Soviet Union has stockpiled titanium it has launched a massive military buildup. So, right now, the Soviet Union is launching a massive military buildup.

Notice that now one of the premises of an earlier argument is the conclusion of a subargument. The conclusion of the subargument is "the Soviet Union is launching a massive military buildup," which has two explicit premises: "The Soviets are now stockpiling titanium" and "a stockpiling of titanium means a military buildup." So in trying to find the main point of argument, one must also be alert to the possibility that an intermediate conclusion may also function as a premise in the main argument.

Define precisely the conclusion of the argument.

Once the main point of the argument has been isolated, it is necessary to take the second step of exactly defining that point. In particular, one must be attentive to any qualifying remarks made by the author. In this regard it will be helpful to ask three questions: (1) How great a claim (or limited a claim) is the author making? (2) Precisely what is the author talking about? And (3), what is the author's intention in making the claim?

Pay careful attention to quantifiers.

The first of these questions reminds us that authors will frequently qualify their claims by using words such as *some, none, never, always, everywhere,* and *sometimes.* Thus, there is a big difference in the claims:

> All mammals live on land.
> Most mammals live on land.

The first is false; the second is true. Compare also:

> The United States and the Soviet Union have never been allies.
> For the past 30 years, the United States and the Soviet Union have not been allies.

Again, the first statement is false and the second is true. Finally, compare:

> It is raining and the temperature is predicted to drop below 32°F, therefore it will <u>surely</u> snow.
>
> It is raining and the temperature is predicted to drop below 32°F, therefore it will <u>probably</u> snow.

The first is a much less cautious claim than the second, and it if failed to snow the first claim would have been proved false, though not the second. The second statement claims only that it is probable that snow will follow, not that it definitely will. So someone could make the second claim and defend it when the snow failed to materialize by saying, "Well, I allowed for that in my original statement."

 ## Pay careful attention to descriptive phrases.

The second group of elements to pay attention to are the descriptive words used in a passage. Here we cannot even hope to provide a list, so the best we can do is present some examples.

> In nations which have a bicameral legislature, the speed with which legislation is passed is largely a function of the strength of executive leadership.

Notice here that the author makes a claim about "nations," so (at least without further information to license such an extension) it would be wrong to apply the author's reasoning to *states* (such as New York) which also have bicameral legislatures. Further, we would not want to conclude that the author believes that bicameral legislatures pass different laws from those passed by unicameral legislatures. The author mentions only the "speed" with which the laws are passed—not their content. Let us take another example:

> All of the passenger automobiles manufactured by Detroit auto makers since 1975 have been equipped with seat belts.

We would not want to conclude from this statement that all *trucks* have also been equipped with seat belts since the author makes a claim only about "passenger automobiles," nor would we want to conclude that *imported cars* have seat belts, for the author mentions Detroit-made cars only. Finally, here is yet another example in which the descriptive terms in the claim are intended to restrict the claim:

> No other major department store offers you a low price and a 75-day warranty on parts and labor on this special edition of the XL-30 color television.

The tone of the ad is designed to create a very large impression on the hearer, but the precise claim made is fairly limited. First, the ad's claim is specifically restricted to a comparison of "department" stores, and "major" department stores at that. It is possible that some non-major department store offers a similar warranty and price; also it may be that another type of retail store, say, an electronics store, makes a similar offer. Second, other stores, department or otherwise, may offer a better deal on the product, say, a low price with a three-month warranty, and still the claim would stand—so long as no one else offered exactly a "75-day" warranty. Finally, the ad is restricted to a "special edition" of the television, so, depending on what that means, the ad may be even more restrictive in its claim.

Do not confuse "fact" with "recommendation."

The final point in understanding the conclusion is to be careful to distinguish between claims of fact and proposals of change. Do not assume that if an author claims to have found a problem, he also knows how to solve it. An author can make a claim about the cause of some event without believing that the event can be prevented or even that it ought to be prevented. For example, from the argument:

> Since the fifth ward vote is crucial to Gordon's campaign, if Gordon fails to win over the ward leaders he will be defeated in the election.

you cannot conclude that the author believes Gordon should or should not be elected. The author gives only a factual analysis without endorsing or condemning either possible outcome. Also, from the argument:

> Each year the rotation of the Earth slows a few tenths of a second. In several million years, it will have stopped altogether, and life as we know it will no longer be able to survive on Earth.

you cannot conclude that the author wants to find a solution for the slowing of Earth's rotation. For all we know, the author thinks the process is inevitable, or even desirable.

To summarize this discussion of conclusions, remember that you must find the conclusion the author is aiming at by uncovering the structure of the argument. (Did the author try to prove this, and if so, did he use this as a premise of a further argument?) Then pay careful attention to the precise claim made by the conclusion.

THE LOGICAL FUNCTION OF PREMISES

The conclusion of an argument rests upon the premises.

In our discussion of conclusions, we implicitly treated the problem of finding the premises of an argument, for in separating the conclusion from the remainder of the paragraph, we also isolated those premises explicitly used by the author in constructing his chain of reasoning. In this section, we do not need to redo that analysis, but it will be useful if we describe three important kinds of assumptions an author might make—value judgments, factual assumptions, and definitional assumptions. Then we will discuss the significance of assumptions.

One very important kind of assumption is the *value judgment*. For example, if we argue that the city government should spend money to hire a crossing guard to protect schoolchildren walking to school, we have implicitly assumed that the lives of schoolchildren are important and, further, that protecting these lives is a proper function of city government. Another kind of assumption is the *factual assumption*. For example, "The ball struck the window and the glass shattered. So the person who threw the ball broke the window." Here the explanation uses the factual assumption that it was the ball that broke the glass—and not some super ray fired by a Martian at the same time. Finally, a third group of assumptions, *definitional assumptions,* are those called into play when we use vague terms. For example, the person who threw the ball is to blame for the broken window, because a person is responsible for his misdeeds. Here the conclusion rests upon the assumption that throwing the ball is, by definition (at least under the circumstances), a misdeed.

With this in mind, we can turn to a discussion of the importance of assumptions in evaluating an argument. In our discussion of conclusions, we noticed that the conclusion of one argument may function as a premise of yet a further argument. With a little imagination, we could construct an argument in which there might be 20, 30, or even more intermediate links in the chain of reasoning joining the initial premise and the final conclusion. Of course, in practice our arguments are hardly ever so complicated. Usually, we require only three or four steps. For example, we may reason:

> Since there is snow on the ground, it must have snowed last night. If it snowed last night, then the temperature must have dropped below 32°F. The temperature drops below 32°F only in the winter. So, since there is snow on the ground, it must be winter here.

We can easily imagine also extending this string of situational assumptions in either direction. Instead of starting with "there is snow on the ground," we might have backed up one further step and reasoned, "If there is a snowman on the front lawn, it must be because there is snow on the ground"; and from the presence of the snowman on the front lawn we could have reached the conclusion that it is winter here. Or we might extend the argument to yet another conclusion. Using the additional premise "If it is winter here, it is summer in Australia," we could reason from "there is a snowman on the front lawn" to "it is summer in Australia."

In practice, however, we do not extend our arguments indefinitely in either direction. We stop at the conclusion we had hoped to prove, and we begin from what seems to us to be a convenient and secure starting point: "If there is snow on the ground, then it must have snowed last night." Now it is obvious that the strength of an argument depends in a very important way upon the legitimacy of its assumptions; in fact, defeating an assumption is the most effective way of attacking any argument. Let us consider examples of arguments using our three types of assumptions.

 ## Determine whether the argument makes any unwarranted factual assumptions.

A very simple factual assumption is the following:

Premises: If there is gasoline in the tank, my car will start.
            I checked and there is gasoline in the tank.
Conclusion: Therefore, my car will start.

A very effective attack on this argument can be aimed at the first premise. One would want to object that the situational premise "if gas, then car starts" is unacceptable because it ignores the fact that there are other reasons the car may fail to start, e.g., the battery is dead, the distributor cap is wet, the engine was stolen. Now the conclusion "my car will start" no longer has any support. Of course it is possible that the car will start, but whether it does or not will not be determinable from the specific argument we have just defeated.

An example of a value judgment is the following:

Premises: The government should help people who might hurt themselves.
Cigarette smoking is harmful to people.
Conclusion: Therefore, the government ought to prevent people from smoking.

One way of attacking this argument is to attack the value judgment that the government ought to protect people from themselves. That might be done by talking about freedom or individual rights, and it will not be possible to clearly *defeat* the assumption of value. In our first argument, the assumption was a question of fact—causal laws in the physical universe—and could be resolved by empirical evidence. In arguments resting on value judgments, it may never be possible to get final agreement. But for purposes of evaluating the strength of an argument, one way of *pursuing the issue,* which is to say, one way of objecting to the argument, is to reject the value judgment upon which it rests.

Determine whether the argument uses unacceptable definitional assumptions.

Finally, a definitional assumption is similar to a valuational one:

Premises: An inexperienced person will not make an effective Supreme Court Justice.
A person with only ten years of legal practice is inexperienced.
Conclusion: Therefore, a person with only ten years of legal practice will not make an effective Supreme Court Justice.

This argument is a valid deductive argument, but that does not mean it is unassailable as it applies to the real world. One way of attacking the argument is to question its second premise by insisting that ten years is long enough to make a person experienced. Of course, that might be disputed, but at least that is a possible line of attack on the argument. After all, if it could be *proved* that ten years of practice makes one experienced, then the conclusion of the argument must be considered to have been defeated.

Look for hidden premises.

In each of our three examples, the attack on the argument was fairly easy to find. To be sure, there were others available to us; but at the very least we knew one way of attacking the argument would be to question the assumptions on which it rested. Unfortunately, the attack is not always this easy to find because many times arguments are built upon hidden or concealed assumptions, and this is not necessarily because the proponent of the argument is intentionally hiding something which he knows will weaken his argument. Since an argument could be extended backward indefinitely (But why do you believe that? So why do you think that? What is your reason for that?), the starting point of an argument is always a bit arbitrary. Even someone who is giving what he thinks to be a correct and honest argument will make some assumptions which he does not explicitly acknowledge.

Argument:	The ground is damp, so it must have rained last night.
Hidden premise:	Rain is the only thing which causes the ground to become damp.
Argument:	Homosexuality is a sin; therefore, there should be laws against such practices.
Hidden premise:	The government ought to enforce morality.
Argument:	John is the perfect husband; he never cheats on his wife.
Hidden premise:	Any husband who does not cheat on his wife is a perfect husband.

So, in evaluating an argument, it is always important to be aware of the possibility of hidden assumptions which might be open to attack. This is particularly true if one finds an argument which on the surface appears to be logically correct, but reaches a conclusion that seems factually impossible, or one that seems valuationally or judgmentally absurd. In such a situation, it is a good idea to look for a hidden assumption that makes the argument work. Of course, even though the conclusion seems strange, it might just be correct, in which case careful thinkers admit that their initial reactions to the argument were wrong, and they change their minds. Similarly, a reasonable-appearing conclusion can be based on inadequate or wrong argumentation.

With regard to premises, then, we have learned that every argument rests upon them. An explanation of events usually rests upon factual premises, and a proposal for action rests upon value judgments. And both kinds of arguments will make definitional assumptions. It should also be kept in mind that since a complex argument is made of subarguments, a final factual conclusion may ultimately have a value judgment somewhere in the argument supporting it, and by the same token a final value judgment may have a factual premise somewhere in the argument supporting it. Many times the assumptions of an argument will not be explicitly mentioned by the author; they may be hidden. But whether an assumption is explicit or just implicit, it is of critical importance to the argument, and for this reason attacks on premises can be very powerful.

EVALUATING INFERENCES (INDUCTIVE)

In the preceding two sections, we describe the importance of finding the conclusion and the premises of an argument. We now turn our attention to techniques for evaluating the inference that is supposed to link the conclusion to the premises. Our discussion of inductive inferences is a checklist of the most important kinds of fallacies that appear on the LSAT. You should not, however, allow yourself to think that you can memorize the list and apply it mechanically to logical reasoning problems. The classification we present is somewhat artificial, and discretion is required in using it. We will discuss seven fallacies: The *ad hominem* attack, circular reasoning, appeals to irrelevant considerations, false cause, hasty generalization, ambiguity, and false analogy.

An *ad hominem* attack is aimed at the person.

This is any argument which is directed against the source of the claim rather than the claim itself. Since there are times when such attacks are useful, as when the credibility of the speaker is at issue, we must be careful to distinguish the illegitimate *ad hominem* attack from the legitimate attack on a person's credibility. An illegitimate *ad hominem* argument is one which ignores the merits of the issue in favor of an attempt to discredit the source of the argument where the credibility of the speaker is not at issue. For example:

> We should not accept Professor Smith's analysis of the causes of traffic accidents because we know that she has been unfaithful to her husband.

Setting aside such outlandish speculations as the possibility that Professor Smith has killed her husband in a fake accident (and the *LSAT Bulletin* specifically warns against such speculation), we can see that there is no connection between Smith's analysis of accidents and her infidelity to her husband. So this is an illegitimate attack. A student who wants to see further examples of such attacks need only read the daily newspaper with particular attention to any political campaign or other political struggle. On the other hand, there are attacks on the credibility of speakers which are legitimate. We are all suspicious of the claims made by salespersons, and rightly so! More generally, it is legitimate to take account of any possible self-interest in making a statement. For example:

> General: The Army needs more and bigger tanks. Even though they are expensive, they are vital to the nation's security.
>
> Politician: And if I am elected governor, I will cut taxes and put an end to crime.

In these cases it is not wrong to point out that the speaker's vision may be clouded by his own interest in the outcome of the matter.

A circular argument (begging the question) is an argument in which the conclusion to be proved appears also as a premise.

A second fallacy commonly used on the LSAT is that of circular reasoning. Any argument which includes the conclusion it hopes to prove as one of its premises is fallacious because it is circular. For example:

> Beethoven was the greatest composer of all time, because he wrote the greatest music of any composer, and he who composes the greatest music must be the greatest composer.

The conclusion of this argument is that Beethoven was the greatest composer of all time, but one of the premises of the argument is that he composed the greatest music, and the other premise states that that is the measure of greatness. The argument is fallacious, for there is really no argument for the conclusion at all, just a restatement of the conclusion.

Determine whether the premises provide adequate support for the conclusion.

A third type of fallacy you might encounter in a Logical Reasoning section is any appeal to irrelevant considerations. For example, an argument which appeals to the popularity of a position to prove the position is fallacious. For example:

Frederick must be the best choice for chairman because most people believe that he is the best person for the job.

That many people hold an opinion obviously does not guarantee its correctness—after all, many people once thought airplanes couldn't fly. Another appeal to an irrelevant consideration might be an illegitimate appeal to authority. For example:

The theory of evolution is only so much hogwash, and this is clearly proved by the fact that Professor Edwards, who got an M.A. in French Literature from Yale University, says so.

In this case, the authority is not an authority on the topic for which authority is needed. Now, there may be legitimate appeals to authority. For example:

Inflation erodes the standard of living of those person who are retired and have fixed incomes such as savings or pensions; and Professor Jones, an economist who did a study on the harms of inflation, concluded that over 75% of retired people live on fixed incomes.

In this case, the appeal to authority is legitimate. We often just defer to the expertise of others, but we must be careful to select our sources of authority so that we find ones that are unbiased and truly expert.

When analyzing a causal explanation, look for alternative explanations.

A fourth type of fallacy, and one of which the LSAT is fond, is the fallacy of the false cause. An argument that commits this error attributes a causal relationship between two events where none exists—or at least the relationship is misidentified. For example:

Every time the doorbell rings I find there is someone at the door. Therefore, it must be the case that the doorbell calls these people to my door.

Obviously, the casual link suggested here is backwards. It is the presence of the person at the door which then leads to the ringing of the bell, not vice versa. A more serious example of the fallacy of the false cause is:

There were more air traffic fatalities in 1979 than there were in 1969; therefore, the airways are more dangerous today than they were ten years ago.

The difficulty with this argument is that it attributes the increase to a lack of safety when, in fact, it is probably attributable to an increase in air travel generally.

A generalization is only as strong as the sample on which it is based.

A fifth fallacy is that of hasty generalization. In our discussion about the structure of an argument, where we distinguished inductive from deductive arguments, we remarked that the best one can hope for in an inductive argument is that it will *probably* be true. We pointed out that some arguments are very strong, while some are weak. A common weakness in an inductive argument is the hasty generalization, that is, basing a large conclusion on too little data. For example:

> All four times I have visited Chicago it has rained; therefore, Chicago probably gets very little sunshine.

The rather obvious difficulty with the argument is that it moves from a small sample—four visits—to a very broad conclusion, Chicago gets little sunshine. Of course, generalizing on the basis of a sample or limited experience can be legitimate:

> All five of the buses manufactured by Gutmann which we inspected have defective wheel mounts; therefore, some other buses manufactured by Gutmann probably have similar defects.

Admittedly this argument is not airtight. Perhaps the other uninspected buses do not have the same defect, but this second argument is much stronger than the first.

Determine whether the argument is consistent in its use of terms.

A sixth fallacy which the LSAT has used in the past is that of ambiguity. Anytime there is a shifting in the meaning of terms used in an argument, the argument has committed a fallacy of ambiguity. For example:

> Man is only one million years old. John is a man. Therefore, John is only one million years old.

The error of the argument is that it uses the word *man* as two different meanings. In the first occurrence *man* is used as a group; in the second occurrence *man* designates a particular individual. Another, less playful, example:

> Sin occurs only when man fails to follow the will of God. But since God is all-powerful, what He wills must actually be. Therefore, it is impossible to deviate from the will of God, so there can be no sin in the world.

The equivocation here is in the word *will*. The first time it is used, the author intends that the will of God is God's wish and implies that it *is* possible to fail to comply with those wishes. In the second instance, the author uses the word *will* in a way that implies that such deviation is *not* possible. The argument reaches the conclusion that there is no sin in the world only by playing on these two senses of "will of God."

An argument from analogy is only as strong as the similarity of the two situations.

A seventh fallacy which might appear on the LSAT is that of false analogy. We do sometimes present legitimate arguments from analogy. For example:

The government should pay more to its diplomats who work in countries with unstable governments. The work is more dangerous there than in stable countries. This is very similar to paying soldiers combat premiums if they are stationed in a war zone.

The argument here relies on an analogy between diplomats in a potentially dangerous country and soldiers in combat areas. Of course, the analogy is not perfect—no analogy can be more than an analogy. But some analogies are clearly so imperfect that they have no persuasive force. For example:

People should have to be licensed before they are allowed to have children. After all, we require people who operate automobiles to be licensed.

In this case, the two situations—driving and having children—are so dissimilar that we would probably want to say they are not analogous at all—having children has nothing to do with driving.

While the ingenuity of the test makers can result in logical reasoning problems that do not precisely fit these fallacies of induction, there will be very few problems on the test which have any other sort of inductive reasoning errors. The practice tests in this book contain many illustrations of each kind of problem with full explanations. There are also problems that show how these different errors can be combined in one problem.

EVALUATING INFERENCES (DEDUCTIVE)

In the last section, we discussed some common inductive fallacies; in this section, we turn our attention to deductive reasoning. You will recall from the first section that a deductive inference differs from an inductive inference in that the deductive inference—if it is valid—is guaranteed by the meanings of the terms used in the argument. The argument form we most often associate with the study of logic is the syllogism, a term that will be familiar to anyone who has studied basic logic:

All trees are plants.
All redwoods are trees.
Therefore, all redwoods are plants.

Ancient and medieval thinkers devoted a great deal of study to the various forms of syllogisms and other logical structures, and their treatments are full of technicalities—technicalities we can safely ignore. All that one requires for the LSAT is a working knowledge of the forms without all the jargon. Thus, although we have employed some technical terms in these materials, this was strictly for purposes of organization, and you need not commit these to memory. Our discussion will treat four groups of deductive arguments: direct inferences, syllogisms, implications, and relational sequences.

Direct Inferences

By a direct inference, we mean a conclusion which follows from a single premise. For example, from the statement "no birds are mammals" we can conclude "no mammals are birds," since there is no individual which is a member of both the group bird and the group mammal. From "no birds are mammals" we could also reach the conclusion that "all birds are not mammals," but this is really nothing more than a grammatical restructuring of the original form, whereas the statement "no mammals are birds" is actually an inference (it is a totally new claim).

Setting aside possible variations in grammatical structure ("no B are M" = "all B are not M," "some B are M" = "some B are not non-M," etc.), we may organize such assertions into four groups, depending on whether they make a claim about "some" on the one hand or, on the other hand, either "all" or "no" members of groups and whether they are "affirmative" or "negative." In order to save space and also to show that our techniques are generally applicable—that is, not dependent on any particular content—we will find it convenient to use capital letters as substitutes for terms. Thus, "all birds are mammals" becomes "all B are M," which could also stand for "all bats are myopic," but nothing is lost in the translation since we are concerned with the formal relations and not the actual substantive or content relations between sentences. Using capital letters, we set up the following scheme so that we have sentences which make affirmative claims about all of a group, negative claims about all of a group, affirmative claims about part of a group, and negative claims about part of a group.

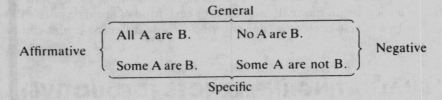

General

Affirmative {
All A are B.   No A are B.

Some A are B.   Some A are not B.
} Negative

Specific

The word "some" means only "at least one."

Before we proceed any further, there is one very important point regarding use of the word *some* which we must make. The LSAT follows the logician in using the word *some* to mean only "at least one." So a statement of the sort "some A are B" means *only* that there is at least one A which is also a B. The statement does *not* imply as well that there are some A's which are not B's. Similarly, the statement "some A are not B" means that there is at least one A which is not a B; it does *not* imply that there are also some A's which are B's. Notice that this is at variance with our ordinary conversational usage of the word *some*. In conversation a person who states, "Some of the students have not turned in their term papers," probably wants us to understand that some students have turned in their papers, but this additional implication depends upon the context in which the statement is made. Strictly speaking, as a matter of logic, the statement "some students have not turned in their term papers" means just that—"some students have not turned in their term papers"—and does not mean further that some students have turned in their term papers. It is conceivable that no student has turned in a term paper; still, the statement "some students have not turned in their term papers" would be accurate. Even though it only partially describes the situation—*some* as opposed to *all*—it does give an accurate description of that part it describes.

Perhaps a little thought experiment will clarify the point. Imagine that you are standing in front of an opaque container with marbles in it, and you are asked to pick marbles blindly from the container. You pick a marble which happens to be red. At that point, we ask you to describe the color or colors of the marbles in the container. You can say, "Some of the marbles are red" (setting aside the difficulty that the red marble is no longer in the container, for we are talking about the marble population without regard to such technicalities). This statement is obviously true since you hold the proof in your hand. Now, if you draw the remaining marbles from the container, one of two situations will develop. Either all of the remaining marbles will prove to be red, in which case you can say, "All of the marbles are red," or not all of the remaining marbles will prove to be red, in which case you can say, "Some of the marbles are not red." But since our first statement, "Some of the marbles are red," was proven to be true by the fact that you held a red marble in your hand, and since a true statement does not become false with the passing of time (again, setting aside such difficulties as demonstrative pronouns, such as "this is a live cat"—ten years later it is dead—and time-dependent statements, such as "Bush is *now* President"), the statement "some marbles are red" remains true even if it should turn out that "all marbles are red." What this shows is that the statement "some marbles are red" is not logically inconsistent with—does not contradict—the statement "all marbles are red." Similarly, "all M are R" not only does not contradict "some M are R," but the latter statement must actually follow from the former. A moment's reflection will also show that a similar relationship exists between the statements of the negative form, "some M are not R" and "no M are R." The only possible exception would be a logically reasoning question that consists of a discussion between two persons in the form of a transcript. If the tone is *very* conversational, one of the speakers *might* mean *some* in its everyday sense.

Use Venn or circle diagrams to analyze deductive arguments.

It is also fairly apparent that there are interrelationships among all the statement forms. For example, if "all A are B" is true, then both "no A are B" and "some A are not B" must be false. One way of exhibiting these relationships is through the use of Venn or circle diagrams. (These are also used in analytical reasoning problems.) We will use a circle to mark off a "logical area." So a circle which we label "A" separates the field of the page into two spaces, A and not-A. The interior of the circle is the space where all A's are located, and anything located outside the circle is not an A (it is a non-A):

Diagram 1:

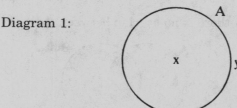

In Diagram 1, *x* is an A, but *y* is not an A, which is to say *y* is a non-A. Now, if we draw two overlapping circles, we can represent not only two groups, A and B, but also the intersection of those groups:

Diagram 2:

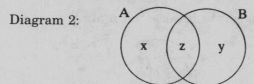

In Diagram 2, *x* is an A, which is not, however, a B; *y* is a B, which is not, however, an A; and *z* is something which is both A and B.

If it is true that "all A are B," then it is not possible for something to be an "A but not also a B," so we blot out that portion of our circle diagram which contains the area "A but not also B":

Diagram 3:

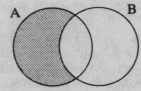

Now if it is true that "all A are B," then:
"no A are B" is false. (All the A are B.)
"some A are B" is true. (All the A are within the B circle.)
"some A are not B" is false. (That area is eliminated.)
If it is false that "all A are B," that might be because "no A are B":

Diagram 4:

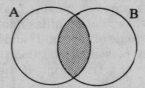

However, it might also be because "some, though not all, A are not B":

Diagram 5:

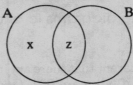

Both situations are consistent with "all A are B" being a false statement. So, if it is false that "all A are B," then:
"no A are B" might be true or false. (We cannot choose between Diagram 4 and Diagram 5.)
"some A are B" might be true or false. (We have no basis for choice.)
"some A are not B" is true. (This is the case with both Diagram 4 and Diagram 5.)
If it is true that "no A are B," then there is no overlap between the two:

Diagram 6:

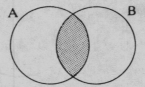

So, "all A are B" is false. (There is no overlap.)
"some A are B" is false. (There is no overlap.)
"some A are not B" is true. (That part is left open.)

But if "no A are B" is false, that might be because "all A are B":

Diagram 7:

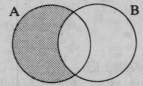

But it might equally well be because "some, though not all, A are B":

Diagram 8:

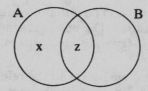

Therefore, "all A are B" might be true or false. (There is no basis for choice.)
    "some A are B" is true. (See Diagrams 7 and 8).
    "some A are not B" might be true or false. (There is no basis for choice between diagrams.)

If it is true that "some A are B,"

Diagram 9:

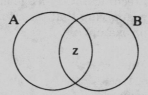

then "all A are B" might be true or false. (See discussion of *some*.)
    "no A are B" is false. (See Diagram 9.)
    "some A are not B" might be true or false. (See discussion of *some*.)
If it is false that "some A are B," this can only be because there is no overlap between the two circles:

Diagram 10:

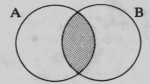

Therefore, "all A are B" is false. (There is no overlap at all.)
    "no A are B" is true. (As shown by Diagram 10.)
    "some A are not B" is true. (That area is left open.)

If it is true that "some A are not B":

Diagram 11:

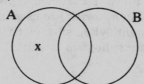

then "all A are B" is false. (Shown by the *x* in Diagram 11.)
    "no A are B" might be true or false. (The *x* does not close off the overlap of A and B, but then again we do not know that there are individuals with the characteristic A and B.)
    "some A are B" might be true or false. (See the reasoning just given for "no A are B.")
If it is false that "some A are not B":

Diagram 12:

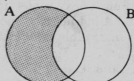

then the area of the A circle which does not overlap the B circle is empty, as shown by Diagram 12. Therefore:

"all A are B" is true. (The one is contained in the other.)
"no A are B" is false. (The one is contained in the other.)
"some A are B" is true. (In fact, all are, but see our discussion of *some*.)

A word of caution: Do not memorize all the relationships just presented. The circle diagrams will provide an aid for thought and practice, and they will also prove useful in our study of the second form of deductive inference: the syllogism.

Syllogisms. Technically, a syllogism is supposed to be constructed from three statements, two of which are assumptions, and the third the conclusion. However, since the LSAT is not a test of technical knowledge of logical forms, it may use the term *syllogism* in a looser way, applying that term to an argument with four, or perhaps even five, statements. For example:

All trees are plants.
All redwoods are trees.
This tree is a redwood.
Therefore, this tree is a plant.

If we analyzed this argument in a technical way, we would say it includes not one, but two syllogisms—the conclusion of the first forming a premise of the second:

All trees are plants.
All redwoods are trees.
Therefore, all redwoods are plants.

All redwoods are plants.
This tree is a redwood.
Therefore, this tree is a plant.

But for purposes of the LSAT, you can call the first argument a syllogism as well.

Of course, a syllogism can be constructed using negative statements as well. Now, depending on which statement forms are used and how the terms are arranged, we can construct many different syllogisms. Not all of these, however, would be valid. For example, the following syllogism is valid.

All A are B.
No B are C.
Therefore, no A are C.

We can show its validity by using a variation on our circle diagrams. Now we have three terms rather than two terms. Remember that two terms or groups might be related in three ways: An A which is not a B, a B which is not an A, and something which is both A and B. When we add our third term, C, we have to allow for something which is a C but not an A or B; something which is a C and B but not an A; something which is a C and A but not a B; and something which is C, B, and A. In other words, there are seven possible combinations.

1. an A, but not a B or C
2. a B, but not an A or C
3. an A and B, but not a C
4. a C, but not an A or B

5. an A and C, but not a B
6. a B and C, but not an A
7. an A, B, and C

These seven possibilities can be shown on a three-circle diagram:

Diagram 13: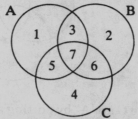

Using our three-circle diagrams, we can show the validity of the syllogism constructed at the beginning of this paragraph. Since our first premise states that "all A are B," we can eliminate the areas of the diagram that are within the A circle but not within the B circle. This corresponds to areas 1 and 5 in Diagram 13.

Diagram 14:

Our second premise states that "no B are C," so we must eliminate those areas, corresponding to 6 and 7 on Diagram 13, which allow that something might be a B and a C. (Notice that something which is an A, B, and C—area 7—is automatically something which is a B and a C.)

Diagram 15: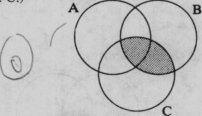

Now if we enter both premises one and two on the same diagram, we have:

Diagram 16: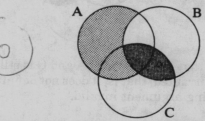

The conclusion of our syllogism asserts that "no A are C," and our diagram confirms this. The only area of A left open is within the B circle; all A but non-B areas have been erased.

Another example of a valid syllogism is:

All A are B.
Some C are A.
Therefore, some C are B.

In a syllogism in which one of the propositions uses "some" and the other proposition uses "all" or "no," it is a good idea to enter the "all" or "no" information first. So we enter first "all A are B":

Diagram 17:

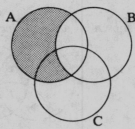

Then we enter "some C are A" by putting an *x* in the area of C and A. Since there is only one such area left, the *x* must be placed so:

Diagram 18:

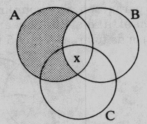

Now the diagram shows the validity of our syllogism: There is at least one C which is also a B.

An example of an *invalid* deductive argument is the syllogism that has the form:

No A are B.
No B are C.
Therefore, no A are C.

We enter the first and second premises:

Diagram 19:

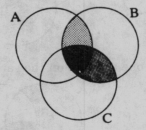

But then we observe that the overlap of A and C is still open, so our conclusion that "no A are C" is not warranted, that is, it does not definitely follow from our premises. So, too, is the following argument invalid.

Some A are B.
Some B are not C.
Therefore, some A are not C.

Since there is no premise which begins with "all" or "no," we are forced to start with a premise which begins with "some." We take premise number one first—"Some A are B"—but we have no way of determining whether or not the A's which are B's are also C's. So we will leave open those possibilities:

Diagram 20:

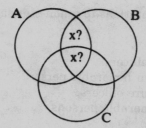

Now we add the information "some B are not C," again keeping open the possibility that something might be a B and an A, or a B but not an A:

Diagram 21:

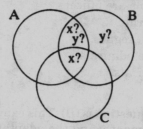

Diagram 21 shows that the conclusion, "some A are not C," does not follow from our premises because we do not definitely know the locations of our *x*'s or *y*'s, as indicated by the question marks.

Adapt the Venn diagram technique to solve problems.

Of course, you cannot expect that every logical reasoning problem on the exam with a form similar to the syllogism will fit this form exactly. To be sure, in the past we have seen exact syllogisms, but more often the problems involve more terms and more statements. Still, it is possible to adapt the pure Venn diagram to the non-standard syllogism:

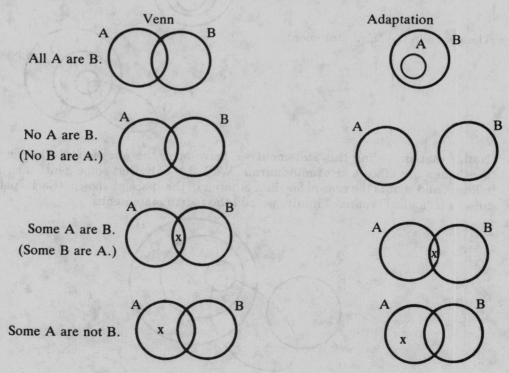

We can apply these adaptations to a non-standard problem of the sort that could appear on the exam:

All admirals are officers.
No officer is not an honorable person.
Some gentlemen are officers.
No rogues are honorable persons.

Which of the following conclusions can be drawn from the statements above?

(A) All honorable persons are officers.
(B) No rogues are admirals.
(C) Some gentlemen are rogues.
(D) Some gentlemen are admirals.
(E) All officers are admirals.

The correct answer to this question is (B). This can be demonstrated using diagrams. We diagram our first statement using the adaptation:

Then we add our second statement (which is equivalent to saying "All officers are honorable persons.").

Then we add the third statement:

Notice that in adding this statement we leave open the question of whether all gentlemen are officers or even admirals. We know only that some gentlemen are officers, and that is the reason for the *x* entered in the space as shown. (Each spatial area is a "logical" space.) Finally, we add the fourth statement:

Notice that we leave open the question of whether a rogue might be a gentleman in the same way we have left open the question of whether all gentlemen are honorable.

From the diagram we see that (A) and (E) commit the same error. We cannot conclude from a statement such as "all A are B" that "all B are A." The "admiral" circle is within the "officer" circle and the "officer" circle is within the "honorable" circle. Then (C) and (D) commit the same error. It is possible that some gentlemen are rogues, for that is an area left open on the diagram. It is also possible that some gentlemen are admirals, but that is not necessarily true. It is true, however, as the diagram shows, that no rogues are admirals. The logical space for rogues, represented by the "R" circle, is completely outside the logical space for admirals, the "A" circle, which is completely contained within the "honorable," or "H," circle.

Let us conclude our discussion of Venn diagrams by emphasizing that this is just one of many ways of solving such problems. Some students remark that they find it easier to solve these problems "verbally," that is, without the assistance of any diagram. That is fine. We offer these diagrams as a suggestion; we certainly do not intend to prescribe. If you find them useful, then you have yet another way of attacking such problems on the exam. If you do not find them to be helpful, then, after at least making an effort to understand how they work, you may rely on some other strategy.

Use capital letters for concepts to analyze the argument's logical structure.

Thus far, we have treated deductive inferences that involved relationships among terms. Now we treat a group of deductive arguments, which we will call implications, that are based on the connections of *sentences* as opposed to *terms*. An example of an implication argument is:

> If John is elected president, Mary is elected vice-president, and if Mary is elected vice-president, Paul is elected secretary. Therefore, if John is elected president, Paul is elected secretary.

If we employ our capital letters again, this time using each letter to stand for a clause (or sentence), we can see that our argument has the form:

> If J, then M.
> If M, then P.
> Therefore, if J, then P.

Notice that our entire argument is phrased in the conditional. Our conclusion does not state that "Paul is elected secretary." It states rather that "*if* J, then P," and that entire conditional statement is the conclusion of the argument.

Another common form of implication is illustrated by the argument:

> If John is elected president, Mary is elected vice-president. John is elected president. Therefore, Mary is elected vice-president.

The form of the argument is:

> If J, then M.
> J.
> Therefore, M.

Notice that this argument differs from our conditional argument, for our second premise definitely asserts, "John is elected president." Now, since the validity of an argument is dependent only upon its form, it is clear that any argument which has this form is valid. This form of argument must not, however, be confused with the superficially similar but invalid form:

> If A, then B.
> B.
> Therefore, A.

The first premise asserts only that A is followed by B; it does not assert that an occurrence of situation B is necessarily preceded by an occurrence of situation A. For example, the following argument is not valid.

> If an object is made of clay, it will not burn. This object will not burn. Therefore, this object is made of clay.

There are many objects that will not burn and that are not made of clay—those made of steel, for example. So *any* argument which has this form is invalid.

Another common form of implication which is valid is illustrated by the argument:

> If John is elected president, then Mary is elected vice-president. Mary is not elected vice-president. Therefore, John is not elected president.

It has the form:

> If J, then M.
> Not M.
> Therefore, not J.

Since the first premise states that an occurrence of situation J will be followed by an occurrence of situation M, and since the second premise tells us that situation M did not occur, we can logically conclude that situation J did not occur, for if J had occurred, so, too, would M have occurred. A similar but invalid argument form is illustrated by the argument:

> If John is elected president, then Mary is elected vice-president. John is not elected president. Therefore, Mary is not elected vice-president.

That this argument is invalid is demonstrated by the consideration that the first premise states only that an occurrence of J is followed by an occurrence of M. The premises do not establish that M can occur *only* if J also occurs. The first premise says, "*if* J, then M," not "M only if J." So any argument of the form "If A, then B. Not A. Therefore, not B." is *invalid*.

Not all valid implicational forms have been shown; our illustrations are intended to illustrate the technique of substituting capital letters for sentences. This allows us to isolate the general *form* of an argument, which makes analyzing or comparing that form easier.

Use a diagram to analyze relational sequences.

There is a final group of deductive arguments which we call relational sequences. A simple example is provided by the argument:

A is greater than B.
B is greater than C.
Therefore, A is greater than C.

These arguments are susceptible to treatment by using pictorial devices.

A is greater than B:

B A
Less   More

B is greater than C:

C B A
Less   More

The conclusion is shown by the diagram to be correct.

LOGICAL REASONING ATTACK STRATEGIES

As we indicated earlier, the difficulty with the Logical Reasoning section of the LSAT is that there is such a variety of question stems that it is difficult to provide a mechanical procedure for approaching such problems. The following tips, however, may help make our somewhat abstract discussion of logic easier to apply to actual LSAT-type problems. In any event, you should keep in mind that the materials presented thus far are merely an overview. There is much more detailed discussion of specific problems in the practice tests contained in this book.

Preview question stems.

The first point of attack in the Logical Reasoning section is to read the question stem (the part to which the question mark is attached) before reading the paragraph or sample argument. The reason for this suggestion is easily explained. There are many different questions that one might ask about an argument: "How can it be strengthened?" "How can it be weakened?" "What are its assumptions?" "How is the argument developed?" and so on. If you read an argument without focusing your attention on some aspect of it, all of these aspects of argumentation (and even more) are likely to come to mind. Unfortunately, this is distracting. The most efficient way to handle the logical reasoning questions is to read the stem of the question first. Let that guide you in what to look for as you read.

Attack the answer choices.

The differences between the answer choices often help you isolate the issues in the problem. Attack the answer choices by:

1. always reading all the answer choices

2. eliminating obviously incorrect choices

3. contrasting remaining choices to isolate the relevant issues

Remember that you are only trying to choose the best answer. The best is often not perfect and the less than best (incorrect) answers often have some merit.

Special Logical Reasoning Questions

Many of the logical reasoning questions are straightforward questions about how to attack and defend arguments. Some questions, however, involve special twists of thinking.

Logical similarity questions.

For a question that asks, "Which of the following arguments is most similar?" remember that you are not supposed to correct the argument. You are supposed to find an answer choice with a similar structure—even if the original argument contains a fallacy. Also, be careful to notice exactly what is to be paralleled—all of an argument, one speaker, or whatever.

Statement reliability questions.

For a question that asks, "Which of the following statements is the most reliable?" look carefully at the qualifications of the author in relation to the topic on which he is writing, and also look for elements of self-interest in the statement.

Completion questions.

For a question that requires you to complete a paragraph, keep in mind that you must complete the structure of the argument as a whole as well as the particular sentence. This means that an answer choice which repeats something already said is not correct. The correct answer must be the *completion* of the thought.

Assumption questions.

When the question stem asks for the identification of assumptions, it is seeking implicit or unstated premises that—like all premises—are necessary to the argument.

When the question stem asks for weakening ideas, it is usually a matter of attacking implicit assumptions which justify the application of the evidence to the conclusion(s).

When the question stem asks for strengthening ideas, the correct answer might be merely an explicit statement of a previously implicit premise.

Verbal exchange questions.

When the question stem asks what the second person in an exchange has interpreted the first person to mean, two things are important: (1) The second person has *mis*-interpreted the first person and, thus, (2) the correct answer must relate to the second person's comments, not to those of the first.

Reading Comprehension

The reading selections that you will find on the LSAT are unlike the material you are accustomed to reading in three respects: topic, format, and density. First, you are not likely to be familiar with the topics of all the reading selections.

The LSAT assumes that you are not familiar with the content of the reading selections.

The test writers go out of their way to find material that test-takers will not have seen before, since they want to avoid giving anyone an advantage over other candidates. If you do encounter a topic you have studied before, that is an unusual stroke of luck. Rest assured, however, that everything you need to answer the questions is included in the selection itself.

LSAT reading selections always begin in the middle of nowhere.

When you begin, you will have no advance warning of the topic discussed in the selection. As a result, the selection seems to begin in the middle of nowhere. Imagine that you encounter the following as the opening sentence of a reading comprehension selection on your LSAT:

> Of the wide variety of opinions on which evolutionary factors were responsible for the growth of hominid intelligence, a theory currently receiving consideration is that intraspecific warfare played an important role by encouraging strategy sessions requiring a sort of verbal competition.

An appropriate reaction to this might be "What the . . . !" But in reality the topic introduced by the sentence above is not that bizarre. Let's give the sentence a context, say a scholarly journal.

PRIMITIVE BATTLE PLANS: A NEW THEORY ABOUT THE GROWTH OF HUMAN INTELLIGENCE

Of the wide variety of opinions on which evolutionary factors were responsible for the growth of hominid intelligence, a theory currently receiving consideration is that intraspecific warfare played an important role by encouraging strategy sessions requiring a sort of verbal competition.

The title summarizes the main point of the article and alerts you to the topic that will be introduced in the opening sentence. Unfortunately, on the LSAT you will not be shown this courtesy. The selections will start rather abruptly, in the middle of nowhere.

A third factor tends to make LSAT reading selections tiresome:

The style of LSAT reading comprehension selections is dry, compact, and often tedious.

To be suitable for the LSAT, the selection must not be too long or too short. So the selections, which are taken from previously published material, are carefully edited. Even when the topic of the selection is itself interesting, the selection that emerges from the editing can be deadly boring.

These three features, unusual topic, abrupt beginning, and dense style, all work together to cause trouble for you.

Don't let the reading comprehension selections intimidate you.

Many students are simply overawed by the reading selections. They begin to think "I've never even heard of this; I'll never be able to answer any questions." And when you start thinking like that, you're already beaten. Keep in mind that the passages are chosen so that you will be surprised, but remember that the selections are written so that they contain everything you need to answer the questions.

What about the questions? Every reading comprehension question asked on an LSAT can be put into one of six categories.

TYPES OF READING COMPREHENSION QUESTIONS

Main Idea Questions

Every reading selection is edited so that it discusses some central theme, that is, it makes a main point. Main idea questions ask about this central theme or main point. They are most often phrased:

> The primary purpose of the passage is to . . . .
> The author is primarily concerned with . . . .
> Which of the following best describes the main point of the passage?
> Which of the following titles best summarizes the content of the passage?

Supporting Idea Questions

These questions ask not about the main point of the selection but about details included by the author to support or to develop the main theme of the selection. These questions may be worded as follows:

> According to the passage, . . .
> The author mentions . . . .
> Which of the following does the author discuss?

Implied Idea Questions

These questions ask about ideas that are not explicitly stated in the selection but are strongly implied. They are often worded as follows:

> It can be inferred from the passage that . . . .
> The author implies that . . . .
> Which of the following can be inferred from the passage?

Logical Structure Questions

These questions ask about the organization of the passage. They may ask about the overall development of the selection, such as:

> The author develops the thesis primarily by . . .
> Which of the following best describes the author's method?

Or they may ask about the role played by a detail:

> The author mentions . . . in order to . . . .
> The author introduces . . . primarily to . . . .

Further Application Questions

These questions ask that you take what you have learned from the passage and apply it to a new situation. To answer this type of question you must go beyond what is explicitly stated or even strongly implied and comment on a situation not even discussed in the passage. These questions are phrased as:

> With which of the following conclusions would the author most likely agree?
> Which of the following statements, if true, would most weaken the conclusion . . . ?

Attitude Questions

These questions ask you to identify the overall tone of the passage or the author's attitude toward something discussed in the passage:

> The tone of the passage can best be described as . . . .
> The author's attitude toward . . . is one of . . . .

Later we will study specific examples of each type of question. For the present, you should just realize that reading selections are written in such a way as to be the vehicle for these six types of questions.

HOW TO READ AN LSAT READING COMPREHENSION SELECTION

Each LSAT reading selection is in a sense an "excuse" to ask one of the six types of questions just mentioned. So the six types give you some idea of what the LSAT thinks is good reading.

According to the LSAT, good reading involves three levels of understanding and evaluation. First, you must be able to grasp the overall idea or main point of the selection along with its general organization. Second, you must be able to subject the specific details to greater scrutiny and explain what something means and why it was introduced. Finally, you should be able to evaluate what the author has written, determining what further conclusions might be drawn and judging whether the argument is good or bad.

The first and most general level of understanding is the most important in a sense, for you cannot appreciate the details of a selection unless you understand the overall structure. And the second level must come before the third, because you will not be able to evaluate the selection unless you know exactly what it says. This priority of levels dictates the strategy you should follow in reading the selection.

Begin your attack on a selection by previewing the first sentence of each paragraph.

Your first task is to grasp the overall point of the selection. The first sentence of a paragraph is often the topic sentence, so a quick preview of first sentences should give you a rough idea of the subject of the selection.

As you read, consciously ask yourself, "What is the main point of this discussion?"

Keeping in mind what you have learned by previewing topic sentences, begin your reading. As you read, try to summarize the main topic of discussion. Once you can articulate the main point of the selection, it will be easier to place the specific details into the overall organization.

As you read, consciously ask yourself, "Why has the author introduced this idea?"

Once you have the main idea in mind, you must try to relate specific details to it, placing them in the overall framework.

Bracket, manually or mentally, material that is very technical or otherwise difficult to understand.

You don't need to have a full understanding of every single detail to appreciate the organization of the selection and most of its detail. If you encounter material that is overly technical and difficult to understand, draw a box around it with a pencil and leave it. You will already understand what "place" it occupies in the overall argument; having marked its location, you can easily find it if you need to study it more carefully in order to answer a question.

 At the end of your reading, pause and quickly review the structure of the passage.

This does not mean you should try to recall all of the details you have read. However, you should be able to explain to yourself, at least vaguely, the main point of the selection and the most important features of the argument.

ANSWERING THE QUESTIONS

 On a main idea question, choose an answer that refers to all of the important elements of the passage without going beyond the scope of the passage.

The correct answer to a main idea question will summarize the main point of the passage. The wrong answers are too broad or too narrow. Some will be too broad and attribute too much to the author. Others will be too narrow and focus on one small element of the selection, thereby ignoring the overall point.

Some main idea questions are phrased as sentence completions.

 With a main idea question in sentence completion form, be sure to test the suitability of the first word of each choice.

EXAMPLE:

The author's primary purpose is to

(A) argue for . . . .   (D) persuade . . . .
(B) criticize . . . .   (E) denounce . . . .
(C) describe . . . .

Make sure that the first word or phrase is truly descriptive of the passage. In the example just given, if the selection is neutral in tone, providing nothing more than a description of some phenomenon, you could safely eliminate (A), (B), (D), and (E).

 On a supporting idea question, find the part of the passage that is intended to be the basis for that question.

A supporting idea question basically asks "What did the author say?" This means that the answer to the question has to be stated explicitly in the passage. The best way to handle such a question is to make sure that you find the correct reference. Watch out! Wrong answers can refer you to other parts of the selection. In this way they do cite something specifically mentioned in the selection, but the citation is not an answer to the question asked. Wrong answers can also refer to things never mentioned in the selection.

On a supporting idea question, eliminate answer choices referring to something not mentioned in the passage or going beyond the scope of the passage.

One way the test writers have of preparing wrong answers is to mention things related to the general topic of the selection but not specifically discussed there. An answer to an explicit question will appear in the selection.

Sometimes the test writer will use a thought-reverser. For example:

The author mentions all of the following EXCEPT:

If a supporting idea question contains a thought-reverser, the wrong answers can be found in the selection. The correct answer is not mentioned.

This is implicit in what was said above. Sometimes an explicit idea question will include a thought-reverser. In that case, it is asking for what is not mentioned in the selection. Out of the five choices, therefore, four will actually appear in the selection. The fifth, and wrong, choice will not.

Some questions ask about what can be inferred from the passage:

The correct answer to an implied idea question will be only a short step removed from what is explicitly stated in the text of the selection.

A question that asks about what can be inferred from a selection does not require a long chain of deductive reasoning. It is usually a one-step inference. For example, the selection might make a statement to the effect that "X only occurs in the presence of Y." The question might ask, "In the absence of Y, which should occur?" The correct answer would be: "X does not occur."

Some questions ask about the overall logical structure of a passage.

The correct answer to a question that asks about the overall logical structure of a selection should correctly describe in general terms the overall development of the selection.

This kind of logical structure question is very much like a main idea question. Whereas a main idea question asks about the *content* of the selection, this type of question asks about the *logical structure* of the selection.

Other questions ask about the logical function of specific details.

 On a question that asks about the logical function of a detail, find the appropriate reference and determine why the author introduced the detail at just that point.

This kind of question is related to the supporting details questions. Here, however, the question stem states specifically that the detail has been mentioned but asks why. What role does it play in the overall argument?

Further application questions are the most difficult of all, for they require you to work in that third and most difficult level of reading comprehension.

 On a further application question, find the answer choice that has the most connection with the text of the selection.

You will see many examples of further applications question in the practice materials that follow. For the moment, accept the fact that the correct answer will be the one most clearly supported by the text.

 On an attitude or tone question, try to create a continuum of the answer choices and locate the author's attitude or tone on that continuum.

EXAMPLE

The tone of the passage is best described as one of

(A) outrage   **(D)** alarm
(B) approval   **(E)** enthusiasm
(C) objectivity

Arrange these attitudes in a line, from the most negative to the most positive:

(−) . . outrage . . alarm . . objectivity . . approval . . enthusiasm . . (+)

An Example of Reading Comprehension

Directions: Read the passage below, and answer the questions that follow based on your understanding of the passage.

A fundamental principle of pharmacology is that all drugs have multiple actions. Actions that are desirable in the treatment of disease are considered therapeutic, while those that are undesirable or pose risks to the patient are called "effects." Adverse drug effects range from the triv-
5 ial, e.g., nausea or dry mouth, to the serious, e.g., massive gastrointestinal bleeding or thromboembolism; and some drugs can be lethal. Therefore, an effective system for the detection of adverse drug effects is an important component of the health care system of any advanced nation. Much of the research conducted on new drugs aims at identifying the

10 conditions of use that maximize beneficial effects and minimize the risk of
    adverse effects. The intent of drug labeling is to reflect this body of knowl-
    edge accurately so that physicians can properly prescribe the drug; or, if it
    is to be sold without prescription, so that consumers can properly use the
    drug.

15   The current system of drug investigation in the United States has
    proved very useful and accurate in identifying the common side effects
    associated with new prescription drugs. By the time a new drug is
    approved by the Food and Drug Administration, its side effects are usu-
    ally well described in the package insert for physicians. The investiga-
20 tional process, however, cannot be counted on to detect all adverse effects-
    because of the relatively small number of patients involved in premarket-
    ing studies and the relatively short duration of the studies. Animal toxi-
    cology studies are, of course, done prior to marketing in an attempt to
    identify any potential for toxicity, but negative results do not guarantee
25 the safety of a drug in humans, as evidenced by such well-known exam-
    ples as the birth deformities due to thalidomide.

        This recognition prompted the establishment in many countries of pro-
    grams to which physicians report adverse drug effects. The United States
    and other countries also send reports to an international program oper-
30 ated by the World Health Organization. These programs, however, are
    voluntary reporting programs and are intended to serve a limited goal:
    alerting a government or private agency to adverse drug effects detected
    by physicians in the course of practice. Other approaches must be used to
    confirm suspected drug reactions and to estimate incidence rates. These
35 other approaches include conducting retrospective control studies; for
    example, the studies associating endometrial cancer with estrogen use,
    and systematic monitoring of hospitalized patients to determine the inci-
    dence of acute common side effects, as typified by the Boston Collabora-
    tive Drug Surveillance Program.

40   Thus, the overall drug surveillance system of the United States is com-
    posed of a set of information bases, special studies, and monitoring pro-
    grams, each contributing in its own way to our knowledge about mar-
    keted drugs. The system is decentralized among a number of governmen-
    tal units and is not administered as a coordinated function. Still, it would
45 be inappropriate at this time to attempt to unite all of the disparate ele-
    ments into a comprehensive surveillance program. Instead, the challenge
    is to improve each segment of the system and to take advantage of new
    computer strategies to improve coordination and communication.

1. The author is primarily concerned with discussing

    (A) methods for testing the effects of new drugs on humans
    (B) the importance of having accurate information about the effects of
         drugs
    (C) procedures for determining the long-term effects of new drugs
    (D) attempts to curb the abuse of prescription drugs
    (E) the difference between the therapeutic and nontherapeutic actions of
         drugs

2. The author implies that a drug with adverse side effects

    (A) will not be approved for use by consumers without a doctor's prescrip-
         tion

    (B) must wait for approval until lengthy studies prove the effects are not permanent

    (C) should be used only if its therapeutic value outweighs its adverse effects

    (D) should be withdrawn from the marketplace pending a government investigation

    (E) could be used in foreign countries even though it is not approved for use in the United States

3. Which of the following can be inferred from the passage?

    I. Some adverse drug effects cannot be detected prior to approval because they take a long time to develop.

    II. Drugs with serious adverse side effects are never approved for distribution.

    III. Some adverse drug effects are not discovered during testing because they are very rare.

    (A) I only

    (B) II only

    (C) III only

    (D) I and III only

    (E) II and III only

4. The author introduces the example of thalidomide (line 26) to show that some

    (A) drugs do not have the same actions in humans that they do in animals

    (B) drug-testing procedures are ignored by careless laboratory workers

    (C) drugs have no therapeutic value for humans

    (D) drugs have adverse side effects as well as beneficial actions

    (E) drugs are prescribed by physicians who have not read the manufacturer's recommendations

5. The author of the passage regards current drug investigation procedures as

    (A) important but generally ineffectual

    (B) lackadaisical and generally in need of improvement

    (C) necessary and generally effective

    (D) comprehensive but generally unnecessary

    (E) superfluous but generally harmless

6. It can be inferred that the estrogen study mentioned in line 36

    (A) uncovered long-term side effects of a drug that had already been approved for sale by the Food and Drug Administration

    (B) discovered potential side effects of a drug that was still awaiting approval for sale by the Food and Drug Administration

    (C) revealed possible new applications of a drug that had previously been approved for a different treatment

    (D) is an example of a study that could be more efficiently conducted by a centralized authority than by volunteer reporting

    (E) proved that the use of the drug estrogen was not associated with side effects such as thromboembolism

7. The author is most probably leading up to a discussion of some suggestions about how to

   (A) centralize authority for drug surveillance in the United States
   (B) centralize authority for drug surveillance among international agencies
   (C) coordinate better the sharing of information among the drug surveillance agencies
   (D) eliminate the availability and sale of certain drugs now on the market
   (E) improve drug-testing procedures to detect dangerous effects before drugs are approved

8. The author makes use of which of the following devices in the passage?

   I. Definition of terms
   II. Examples
   III. Analogy

   (A) I only
   (B) II only
   (C) I and II only
   (D) II and III only
   (E) I, II, and III

1. **(B)** This is a main idea question. (B) correctly describes the overall point of the passage. The author starts by stating that all drugs have both good and bad effects, and that correct use of a drug requires balancing the effects. For such a balancing to take place, it is essential to have good information about how the drugs work. Some of this can be obtained prior to approval of the drug, but some information will not become available until after years of use.

   (A) is incorrect, for the different methods for testing drugs are mentioned only as a part of the development just described. The author is not concerned with talking about how drugs are tested but about why it is important that they be tested. (C) is incorrect for the same reason.

   As for (E), this is the starting point for the discussion—not the main point of the discussion. Finally, as for (D), the idea of drug abuse is not part of the passage at all.

2. **(C)** This is an implied idea question. In the first paragraph, the author states that all drugs have effects and that these effects range from the unimportant to the very important. One purpose of drug labeling is to ensure that physicians (and ultimately consumers) are aware of these effects. We can infer, therefore, that drugs with side effects are used—provided the gain is worth the risks. And this is what (C) says.

   (A) seems to be contradicted by the passage. One purpose of labeling, according to the author, is to let consumers of nonprescription drugs know of possible side effects of those drugs. As for (B) and (D), the analysis in the preceding paragraph clearly shows that drugs are approved for use and used even though they have unwanted side effects. Finally, there is nothing in the passage to support the conclusion expressed in (E).

3. **(D)** This is an implied idea question. I can be inferred from the passage. The author does not state this conclusion in so many words, but he says that some effects are not uncovered because of the short duration of the studies. We may therefore infer that some effects do not manifest themselves for a long period. III also is inferable in the same fashion. The author states that the size of the groups studied makes it difficult to uncover some effects, so we may infer that some effects are rare. II, however, is not inferable, as our analysis of question 2 shows.

4. **(A)** This is a logical detail question. The author introduces the example in line 22 where he is discussing animal studies. He says that the fact that a drug shows no dangerous effects in animals does not necessarily mean that it will not adversely affect humans. Then he gives the example. Thus, the example proves that a drug does not necessarily work in humans the same way it does in animals.

5. **(C)** This is an author's attitude question. We have already determined that the author regards drug investigation procedures as necessary, so we can eliminate (D) and (E). And at various points in the passage the author speaks of the current mechanism for gathering information as effective. For example, he states that unwanted side effects are usually described in detail in the pamphlets distributed to physicians. He also mentions that there is an entire discipline devoted to this area, so you can eliminate (A) and (B).

6. **(A)** This is an implied idea question. The key to this question is the word "retrospective." This tells you that the control study mentioned was done after the drug was already in use. (B) is incorrect because although the study uncovered harmful side effects, according to the passage, the drug was already in use. (C) is incorrect because the paragraph in which this study is mentioned deals with methods of reporting adverse drug effects, not new applications for drugs. (D) is incorrect first because the author does not mention the efficiency of the study and second because the author is not in favor of a centralized authority. In fact, in the last paragraph the author says that it would be inappropriate at this time to attempt to unite all of the disparate elements into a comprehensive surveillance program. Finally, (E) is incorrect because although thromboembolism is mentioned in the passage as one of the possible harmful side effects of drugs, it is not mentioned in connection with estrogen. The use of estrogen is mentioned in connection with endometrial cancer.

7. **(C)** This is a further application question. In the last paragraph the author suggests that uniting disparate elements into a comprehensive surveillance program is inappropriate at this time. This eliminates choices (A) and (B). He suggests, however, that improvements are possible in each segment of the system and urges reliance on computers to improve coordination and communication, so (C) is the correct answer. (D) is wrong because although the author might advocate the elimination of the availability of certain drugs, that is not what the passage is leading up to. As for (E), although the author acknowledges that preapproval studies are not infallible, this notion is too narrow in scope to be the next logical topic for discussion.

8. **(C)** The author defines terms in the passage. For example, in the first paragraph he defines "effects" as undesirable actions of a drug. The author also

makes use of examples. He cites thalidomide as an example of a drug that was released for sale because the animal toxicology studies were negative, and yet the drug proved very harmful to humans. The author does not use analogy as a device, so the answer is (C).

ANALYTICAL REASONING

Analytical reasoning problems are just "logical puzzles and games."

EXAMPLE:

There are three musicians, designated by the letters J, K, and L, each of whom plays only one instrument: the piano, the bass, or the sax—though not necessarily in that order. J, whose sister is the sax player, does not play the piano; and L is an only child. Who plays which instrument?

K : sax
J : bass

There are several different logical routes by which to arrive at the correct answer. One way is to reason that L cannot play the sax because L is an only child (the sax player is J's sister). Nor can J be the sax player because it is J's sister who plays the sax. Since the sax player is neither J nor L, we conclude that it is K who plays the sax. If J plays neither the sax (K plays the sax) nor the piano (as we are told), then J must play the bass. Finally, since J plays the bass and K plays the sax, we deduce that L plays the piano. So we now know which musician plays which instrument: J on bass, K on sax, L on piano. Most of us have already encountered such problems in logic books or in the entertainment section of a newspaper or a magazine.

The basic idea of a logical puzzle is fairly intuitive, but the analytical reasoning sets used by the exam are immensely more complicated and therefore more difficult than the example just presented. Problems on the exam may involve six, seven, or even a dozen different individuals. Most students agree that the Analytical Reasoning section is the most difficult part of the exam, and this subjective perception has been confirmed by the test writers.

The difficulty of the section is attributable not so much to the intrinsic difficulty of the logical puzzles or games as to the time pressure created by the 45-minute time limit. Given unlimited time, most students would be able to solve every problem in the Analytical Reasoning section of the test. To be sure, you might encounter a particularly recalcitrant item that, for whatever reason, you could not solve; but generally speaking, the difficulty of the section is created by the time limit and not the problem sets per se.

Expect to experience serious time pressure in this section.

Of course, time pressure is always a factor in every section of a test such as this, but it is more pronounced in this section than in any other section. Very few students, even those who achieve top scores, are able to answer every question in this section. And, if you find that your performance in this section is weak relative to your performance in other sections, this does *not* mean that you are losing ground to other candidates. It is very probable that they are having the same experience—that is, everyone is in the same boat—and since the examination is graded "on the curve," the extraordinary difficulty of the section will not operate to your disadvantage.

Do not interpret a lower proportion of questions answered correctly in Analytical Reasoning as an individual weakness in this section.

Because of the difficulty of this type, you must expect that your performance in Analytical Reasoning will seem to you to be less satisfactory than, say, your performance in Logical Reasoning.

There is no reason for you to settle for a poor performance in this section. Analytical Reasoning, like the other sections on the exam, is susceptible to conscientious preparation. As you do the practice exams in this book, you should gain confidence in your ability to attack the Analytical Reasoning section of your LSAT, and this confidence and familiarity should translate into a higher score on the test. As you will learn, success in this section is largely a matter of learning effective "bookkeeping" methods, that is, techniques that will help you keep track of the information given in the problem set. In our review of this question type, we will first describe the important features of an analytical reasoning set and then we will develop some methods for organizing information.

STRUCTURE OF AN ANALYTICAL REASONING PROBLEM

In this book, you will see a wide variety of problem types, but you will notice that, despite this variety, the initial conditions and questions have some very important characteristics in common.

The initial rules establish the structure by which the logical game will be played.

The initial conditions introduce you to the individuals involved in the puzzle and the logical connections between and among those individuals.

The individuals involved in an analytical reasoning set are usually designated by letters or names, e.g., eight people, J, K, L, M, N, O, P, and Q, are sitting around a table. Sometimes, the individuals in the problem may be designated by some physical characteristic, e.g., six flags are displayed in a horizontal row, two red, two blue, one yellow, and one green. Further, the initial conditions always give some information about the logical relations that join the individuals to one another, e.g., J is sitting next to K, and M is not sitting next to P, or the red flags are hanging next to each other and the yellow flag is not next to the green flag.

Most of the situations described by the initial conditions are common ones with which you should be familiar. For example:

> Six people, J, K, L, M, N, and O, are standing in a single-file line at a movie theater.

> Seven corporations, H, I, J, K, L, M, and N, have offices on four floors in the same building.

> Eight office workers, M, N, O, P, Q, R, S, and T, are deciding in which of three restaurants, X, Y, or Z, they will eat lunch.

> Five people, V, W, X, Y, and Z, are the aunt, the mother, the brother, the sister, and the wife of Mr. X, though it is not clear which person is which relative.

Accept the situation at face value.

One reason for using such situations is that there is less potential for ambiguity, that is, there is much information implicit in a situation such as a single-file line: Each person is a separate person; each letter designates a different individual; one individual is immediately ahead of or behind another individual; and so on. Since the situations are selected for this feature, you should be careful not to "fight" with the setup. It will not do, for example, to argue that J could be standing on L's shoulders or Mr. X might have married his aunt. You can also rest assured that the test writers will add an explicit clarifying note if there is any danger of a legitimate misunderstanding, e.g., each corporation has its own office, etc.

Although you must accept the general situation with a fairly uncritical reading, you must be very careful in reading the particular information given about the individuals.

Pay particular attention to words such as *only, exactly, never, always, must be/can be/cannot be, some, all, no, none, entire, each, every, except, but, unless, if, more/less, before/after, immediately (before, after, etc.) possible/impossible, different/same, at least, at most.*

Also, you should be especially careful not to misinterpret conditions that are asymmetrical, e.g., if P goes on the trip, Q must also go; or S cannot eat at X restaurant unless T also eats there. In both of these examples, the dependency operates in only one direction. In the first, P depends on Q, but not vice versa (Q can go on the trip without P). Similarly, in the second, S depends on T, but not vice versa (S cannot eat at X restaurant without T, but T can eat there without S).

As you practice analytical reasoning problems, you must learn to respect this balance. You must passively accept those elements of the initial conditions which constitute the mere "skeleton" of the puzzle while regarding with critical attention those elements which must be manipulated in order to solve problems.

The situation will be highly "underdetermined" by the initial conditions.

Occasionally, it will be possible to draw some further inference, but rarely will it be possible to determine the entire sequence using just the information in the initial conditions. For example, a problem set might tell you that X must be standing third in line and that Z is two positions behind X. From this, you can deduce that Z is standing fifth in line.

The open-ended nature of analytical reasoning problems bothers many students. Because they are unable to deduce a definite sequence or similar conclusions, they feel that they must have overlooked something in the initial conditions.

RECORD KEEPING

You must develop a "bookkeeping" system. This system will include notational devices and diagramming techniques which you invent for yourself or which you adapt from those we suggest in this book. You should not regard the "bookkeeping" system we use as the only possible system. Rather, you should regard it as a suggested system. Once you understand our system, you can take some parts of it for your own personal system, leaving behind those devices you find cumbersome.

Logical Connective	Symbol
and	&
or	v
not	~
if then	→ or ⊃
same as, next to	=
not same, not next to	≠
greater than, older, before	>
less than, younger, after	<

To show how these devices can be used to summarize information, let us use an example.

A chef is experimenting with eight ingredients to discover new dishes. The ingredients are J, K, L, M, N, O, P, and Q. The ingredients must be used in accordance with the following conditions.

If M is used in a dish, P and Q must also be used in that dish.
If P is used in a dish, then exactly two of the three ingredients, L, M, and N, must also be used in that dish.
L cannot be used in a dish with P.
N can be used in a dish if and only if J is also used in that dish.
K, L, and M cannot all be used in the same dish.

It is absolutely essential to have a system for summarizing this information for ready reference. The information could be summarized as follows:

(1) M ⊃ (P & Q)
(2) P ⊃ (L & M) v (L & N) v (M & N)
(3) L ≠ P
(4) N = J
(5) ~ (K & L & M)

We use the "horseshoe" for the first statement, but we could as well have used the arrow. Notice that we use parentheses as punctuation marks. Had we not set P & Q off in parentheses, the statement M ⊃ P & Q could be misinterpreted to read "If M is used, then P must be used; and Q must be used." The second statement shows us the logical structure of the second condition. If P is used, then either L and M must be used or L and N must be used or M and N must be used. Again, you should observe that we have used parentheses as punctuation marks.

Statement (3) uses the ≠, which has many other uses, to assert that L and P cannot be used together. Similarly, statement (4) uses the = to assert that N and J, if used, must be used together. Of course, the = can have many other meanings. Depending on the context in which the symbol is used, the statement "N = J" could mean any of the following: N and J are the same age; N and J are of the same sex; N and J must ride in the same car; N and J must sit next to one another. The value of the symbol depends on the context in which it appears.

Finally, statement (5) can be read to say that it is not the case that K and L and M are used in the same dish. Of course, our suggestions are just that—suggestions; there are many other ways to summarize the information. Moreover, we will not at this point attempt an exhaustive study of notation. Later, in our explanations we will try different notational devices, explaining them as we introduce them. Remember, however, only adopt those symbols you find convenient and find substitutes for those that do not work for you.

Use the answer choices to create a "feedback loop."

This is a multiple choice examination in which one and only one of the options can be correct. And an option in this section will be correct or incorrect as a matter of logic. (In this respect, this section is similar to a math test.) Thus, if your analysis of a question yields one and only one correct answer, this indicates that you have probably done the problem correctly. If your analysis produces no correct choice, then you have obviously overlooked something. On the other hand, if your analysis produces more than one seemingly correct choice, then you have made an error somewhere.

Some questions provide, by stipulation, information that supplements the initial conditions, e.g., "If the traveler visits Paris on Thursday, then which city will she visit on Friday?"

Additional information provided in a question stem is to be used for that question only.

In fact, different questions may ask you to make contradictory assumptions. The second question in a set may ask you to assume that the traveler visits Rome on Thursday while the third question asks you to assume that she visits Rome on Monday.

Since the problem sets in this section are logical puzzles, the correct answers are determined by logical inference. And the logical status of a statement must fall into one of three categories:

> The statement is logically deducible from the information given.

> The statement is logically inconsistent with (contradicts) the information given.

> The statement is neither logically deducible from the information given nor logically inconsistent with it.

The questions that can be asked fall into one of the following categories:

> Which of the following must be true?

> All of the following must be true EXCEPT:

> Which of the following could be true?

> Which of the following CANNOT be true?

The logical status of each choice dictates whether it is correct or incorrect:

The correct answer to a question asking "Which must be true?" is a statement that is logically deducible from the information given.

The wrong answers to such a question can be statements which are inconsistent with the given information or statements which are not deducible from the information given.

 The correct answer to a question asking "All must be true except" is either a statement that is logically inconsistent with the information given or a statement that is not deducible from the information given.

The wrong answers to this type of question are statements which can be logically deduced from the information given.

 The correct answer to a question asking "Which can be true?" is a statement that is neither deducible from nor inconsistent with the information given.

Finally,

 The correct answer to a question asking "All can be true except" is a statement that is logically inconsistent with the information given.

Although wording may differ from problem set to problem set, every question will fall into one of these four categories. For example, a question that asks:

If the traveler visits Paris on Wednesday, on which day must she visit Rome?

belongs to the first category. It will be possible to deduce from the information given on which day she *must* visit Rome. But a question that asks:

If the traveler visits Paris on Wednesday, then she could visit all of the following cities on Friday EXCEPT:

belongs to the fourth category. The correct answer will generate a logical contradiction with the given information: it will be logically impossible to visit that city on Friday. And a question that asks:

Which of the following is a complete and accurate listing of the cities that the traveler could visit on Thursday?

belongs to the third category. The correct choice will enumerate all of the logical possibilities.

COMMON PROBLEM TYPES

Linear Ordering

The most commonly used type of problem (since Analytical Reasoning was first introduced to the LSAT) has been the linear ordering problem:

> Seven people standing in a line.
> A dozen students in school in grades 1 through 12.
> A musical scale consisting of six notes.

EXAMPLE:

Six people, J, K, L, M, N, and O are sitting in one row of six seats at a concert. The seats all face the stage and are numbered, facing the stage from left to right, 1 through 6, consecutively. Exactly one person is sitting in each seat.

J is not sitting in seat 1 nor in seat 6.
N is not sitting next to L.
N is not sitting next to K.
O is sitting to the immediate left of N.

You would begin your attack by summarizing the initial conditions:

J ≠ (1 or 6)
N ≠ L
N ≠ K
O–N

Are there any further conclusions to be drawn? Yes and no. Yes, it would be possible to determine every possible seating arrangement given these initial conditions, but that obviously would take a lot of time. Therefore, no, there don't appear to be any further obvious conclusions, so we go to the questions.

1. *Which of the following seating arrangements, given in order from seat 1 to seat 6, is acceptable?*

   (A) L, M, K, O, N, J
   (B) L, J, M, O, N, K
   (C) L, N, O, J, M, K
   (D) K, J, L, O, M, N
   (E) M, K, O, N, J, L

Notice that this question provides no additional information, so it must be answerable just on the basis of the initial conditions:

If the question provides no additional information, use the initial conditions to eliminate choices.

The first condition states that J is not seated in seat 1 nor in seat 6. Eliminate (A) because that arrangement is inconsistent with the first of the initial conditions. The second condition requires that N not sit next to L, and on that score we can eliminate (C). According to the third condition, N does not sit next to K, and we eliminate (B). Finally, the fourth condition states that O is seated immediately to N's left, and we can eliminate (D). We have eliminated four of the five choices, so (E) must be the only arrangement that respects all of the initial conditions.

2. *All of the following seating arrangements, given in order from 1 to 6, are acceptable EXCEPT:*

   (A) M, J, L, K, O, N
   (B) K, J, O, N, M, L
   (C) K, O, N, J, M, L
   (D) L, O, N, J, K, M
   (E) K, J, O, N, L, M

This question is the mirror image of the first, but we use the same strategy. Each choice is consistent with the requirement that J not be seated in position 1 or 6. And (A) through (D) respect the second condition that N not sit next to L. In (E), however, N is seated next to L. (E), therefore, must be the choice we are looking for, as it is NOT an acceptable arrangement.

3. *If L is in seat 1 and K is in seat 5, which of the following must be true?*

   (A) J is in seat 2.
   (B) M is in seat 3.
   (C) N is in seat 4.
   (D) O is in seat 4.
   (E) M is in seat 6.

L _ O N J K M

This question provides additional information:

If a question supplies new conditions, begin by determining whether further conclusions can be drawn.

To help us, we'll use a diagram:

1   2   3   4   5   6

The question stem stipulates that L is in seat 1 and K in seat 5:

1   2   3   4   5   6
L   K

Now return to the initial conditions. The first doesn't help us very much, though we can conclude that J is in seat 2, 3, or 4. The second and third conditions by themselves don't operate to place any person on the diagram, but both together tell us that N must be in seat 3:

1   2   3   4   5   6
L   N   K

And since O must be seated to N's left:

```
1    2    3    4    5    6
L    O    N         K
```

And since J cannot sit in seat 6, we have a complete order:

```
1    2    3    4    5    6
L    O    N    J    K    M
```

So the correct answer is (E).

4. If M and O are in seats 2 and 3, respectively, which of the following must be true?

   I. J is in seat 5.
   II. K is in seat 3.
   III. L is in seat 1.

   (A) I only
   (B) II only
   (C) III only
   (D) I and II only
   (E) I and III only

Choice (A) is the correct answer. Begin by processing the initial information:

```
1    2    3    4    5    6
     M    O
```

Since O is seated immediately to N's left:

```
1    2    3    4    5    6
     M    O    N
```

Since neither K nor L can sit next to J, neither can be in seat 5. This means K and L are in seats 1 and 6, though not necessarily respectively:

```
1      2    3    4    5    6
K/L    M    O    N         K/L
```

And, of course, J is in seat 5:

```
1      2    3    4    5    6
K/L    M    O    N    J    K/L
```

Our diagram shows that only statement I is true. Statement II is necessarily false, while statement III might or might not be true.

5. If K and L are separated by exactly three seats, what is the maximum number of different arrangements in which the six people could be seated?

(A) 1
(B) 2
(C) 3
(D) 4
(E) 5

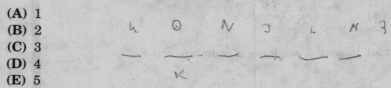

This question really asks "What could be true?" What are the possible arrangements given the additional information?

1	2	3	4	5	6
K				L	
L				K	
	K				L
	L				K

And since N cannot be seated next to either L or K, but O and N must be seated together:

1	2	3	4	5	6
K	O	N		L	
L	O	N		K	
	K	O	N		L
	L	O	N		K

And J cannot sit in seats 1 or 6:

1	2	3	4	5	6
K	O	N	J	L	M
L	O	N	J	K	M
M	K	O	N	J	L
M	L	O	N	J	K

So there are only four possible arrangements given the stipulation that K and L are separated by exactly three seats. The correct answer is (D).

6. If K is in seat 2, which of the following is a complete and accurate listing of the seats which O could occupy?

(A) 1
(B) 3
(C) 3 and 4
(D) 1, 3, and 4
(E) 3, 4, and 5

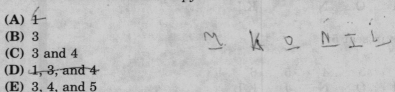

Like the previous question, this question asks about logical possibilities. If K is in seat 2, then there are three possible placements for the O–N pair:

1	2	3	4	5	6
	K	O	N		
	K		O	N	
	K		O		N

Are each of these possible? Yes, as you can prove to yourself by completing the three diagrams. So O could be seated in seat 3, or 4, or 5. So the correct answer is **(E)**.

Distributed Order

In a linear ordering problem, only one individual can occupy a position in the order. In some problem sets, however, a position in the order can accommodate more than one individual.

EXAMPLE:

Six individuals, P, Q, R, S, T, and U, live in a five-story apartment building. Each person lives on one of the floors in the building.
Exactly one of the six lives on the first floor, exactly one of them lives on the fourth floor, and at least two of them live on the second floor.
Of the six people, P lives on the highest floor, and no one lives on the same floor as P.
Q does not live on the first floor or on the second floor.
Neither R nor S lives on the second floor.

When an ordering problem contains distributional restrictions, determine what consequences flow from those restrictions.

The initial conditions establish the following:

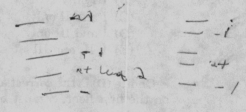

5
4   Exactly one
3
2   At least two, not Q, not R, not S
1   Exactly one, not Q

And, of course, P cannot live on floor two. (P must live on either floor four or floor five.) Since it is a requirement of the distribution that at least two persons live on floor two, we can deduce that T and U (and of the six only T and U) live on floor two:

5
4   Exactly one
3
2   Exactly two: T and U
1   Exactly one, not Q

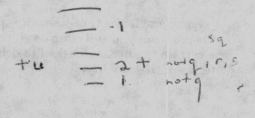

1. *All of the following must be true EXCEPT:*

   (A) Exactly two persons live on floor two.
   (B) At most, one person lives on floor five.
   (C) At least one person lives on floor five.
   (D) At least one person lives on floor three.
   (E) P does not live on floor two.

(C) is the correct answer. Our diagram shows that (A) is necessarily true. And we have already determined that P must be on floor four or five, so (E) is necessarily true. As for (B), this must be true: either P lives on floor five or P lives on floor four (and none of the other five lives above P). As for (D), either P lives on floor five, in which case the distribution of individuals is 1, 2, 1, 1, and 1 (from first to fifth). Or P lives on floor four, in which case the distribution is 1, 2, 2, 1, 0 (from first to fifth). (C), however, is not necessarily true for P could live on the fourth floor.

2. Which of the following could be true?

    (A) Either Q or R lives on the third floor.
    (B) T and U do not live on the second floor.
    (C) T and U live on the third floor.
    (D) T lives on the first floor.
    (E) U lives on the fourth floor.

Our analysis above shows that (A) could be true. The remaining choices must be false since T and U live on the second floor.

3. If P lives on a floor directly above the floor on which R lives, which of the following must be true?

    I. S lives on the first floor.
    II. R and Q live on the same floor.
    III. Q lives on the third floor.

    (A) I only
    (B) III only
    (C) I and II only
    (D) I and III only
    (E) I, II, and III

Choice (D) is the correct answer. If R is directly beneath P, then since Q cannot be on the first floor, S must be on the first floor. This means there are two possible arrangements:

5	4	3	2	1
P	R	Q	T,U	S
-	P	R,Q	T,U	S

Therefore, only statements I and III are necessarily true.

Greater Than/Less Than Problems

Some problem sets rely heavily on the notions of "greater than" and "less than." In the problems you will often be given a list of people, each of whom has more or less of a certain quality, and asked to determine how each one compares to the others in terms of that quality.

EXAMPLE:

The following information is known about a group of five children:

Alice is taller than Bob and heavier than Charles.
Ed is heavier than both Diane and Alice and is shorter than Bob.
Diane is not taller than Bob and is heavier than Charles.
Charles is taller than Diane and heavier than Bob.

Use relational lines to organize clues for a "greater than/less than" set.

Set up two lines, one of which will represent height and the other weight:

Height ---------------------->   Weight ------------------------>

Enter each clue on the diagram. First, Alice is taller than Bob and heavier than Charles:

Height ------------B---A--------->   Weight ------------C---A---------->

Next, Ed is shorter than Bob and heavier than both Diane and Alice:

Height --------E---B---A-------->   Weight ----D?---]
                                        C   A   E ----->

Next, Diane is not taller than Bob and is heavier than Charles:

      ----D?--/   [---D?--]
Height ------E---B---A--->   Weight ------C---A---E----->

Finally, Charles is taller than Diane and heavier than Bob:

               [------C?------
      ----D?--/   [---D?--]
Height ----------E---B---A--->   Weight ----B---C---A---E--->

1. *Which of the following CANNOT be true?*

    (A) Ed is taller than Diane.
    (B) Charles is taller than Alice.
    (C) Bob is taller than Diane.
    (D) Bob weighs more than Diane.
    (E) Ed weighs more than Diane.

Our diagrams show that **(A)** and **(E)** are true and that **(B)** and **(C)** might be true.

2. *Which of the following could be true?*

    I. The tallest child is also the heaviest child.
    II. The shortest child is also the heaviest child.
    III. The lightest child is also the tallest child.

    (A) I only   **(D)** I and III only
    (B) II only   **(E)** I, II, and III
    (C) I and II only

As for statement I, the first diagram shows that the tallest child could be either
Charles or Alice, but neither is the heaviest child. As for statement II, the heaviest
child is Ed, and Ed could be the shortest child. Finally, as for statement III, the
lightest child is Bob, but Bob is not the tallest child. So the correct answer is **(B)**.

Circular Table Problems

In some problem sets, individuals are seated around a circular table.

EXAMPLE:

Eight people, F, G, H, J, K, L, M, and N, are seated in eight equally spaced chairs around a circular table.
K is sitting directly opposite M.
M is sitting immediately to F's left.
G is sitting next to L.
H is sitting opposite J.

For a set based on a circular table, create a seating diagram.

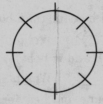

The seats are not distinguishable (that is, there is not a head of the table) so enter the first clue:

K
M

And the second clue:

K
M F

We can't enter the rest of the information without doing a little thinking. H and J are sitting opposite each other, which suggests there are the following possibilities:

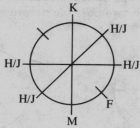

But if either H or J is seated next to F, it isn't possible to place L and G together. Therefore, either H or J is seated next to M:

And finally:

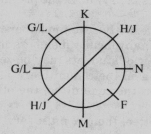

1. *Which of the following must be true?*

   (A) N is seated next to F.
   (B) N is seated next to H.
   (C) N is seated across from G.
   (D) F is seated across from L.
   (E) G is seated across from F.

As the diagram shows, only **(A)** makes a necessarily true statement.

2. *Only one seating arrangement is possible under which of the following conditions?*

   I. G is seated next to J. ✓
   II. H is seated next to N.
   III. Exactly one person is seated between H and L.

   (A) I only
   (B) II only
   (C) I and II only
   (D) I and III only
   (E) I, II, and III

As for statement I, if G is next to J, L is next to K, and H is next to N. So only one order is possible. As for statement II, if H is next to N, then J is next to M. But this doesn't fix the positions of G and L. So II is not part of the correct choice. As for III, this condition is consistent with two possible arrangements:

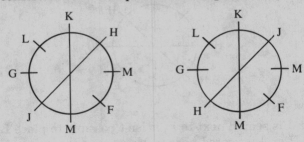

So the correct answer is (A).

Analytical Reasoning: Selection Sets

Selection sets involve choosing a subset of individuals from a larger collection.

EXAMPLE:

From a group of three faculty members, P, S, and R, four administrators, T, U, V, and W, and three students, X, Y, and Z, the president of a college must choose an ad hoc committee.
    The committee will have exactly seven members.
    There must be at least as many faculty members on the committee as there are students, though the number of students may be zero.
    P and Z cannot both serve on the committee.
    If either T or U serves on the committee, the other must also serve on the committee.
    If V serves on the committee, then W must serve on the committee.

With a set like this, you begin by summarizing the information using the notational devices suggested above:

Fac. > or = Stu.
P ≠ Z
T = U
V → W

1. *Which of the following must be true of the committee?*

    (A) It cannot include more students than administrators.
    (B) It cannot include both T and W.
    (C) It cannot include all three faculty members.
    (D) It must include T and U.
    (E) It must include V and W.

(A) is the correct answer. Since P and Z cannot both be on the committee, and since there must be at least as many faculty members on the committee as students, the maximum number of students who could serve on the committe is two. And the maximum number of faculty who could serve is three. This means a minimum of at least two administrators is required. Thus, (A) correctly notes that it is impossible to have more students than administrators on the committee. As for (B) and (C), the committee of seven could include all three faculty and all four administrators with no students. As for (D) and (E), a committee might consist of three faculty members and two students plus either T and U or V and W. Thus, it is not the case that either T and U or V and W must be included.

2. *If the committee is to include exactly two faculty members and exactly two students, which of the following must be true?*
   (A) Z is not included on the committee.
   (B) W is included on the committee.
   (C) X is included on the committee.
   (D) Y is included on the committee.
   (E) S is included on the committee.

The correct answer is (B). If four members of the committee are drawn from faculty and student body, then three must be drawn from the administration. Since T and U cannot be split up, these three must include T and U and either V or W but not both V and W. Since including V requires including W, V cannot be included, therefore W must be included. As for (A), it is possible to include Z by using faculty members S and R (instead of P). As for (C) and (D), either X or Y could serve (with Z) or both X and Y could serve together. Finally, as for (E), any two of the three faculty members could be included on the committee.

3. *If both V and Z are chosen for the committee, then which of the following must be true?*

   I. Neither X nor Y is chosen.
   II. Both S and R are chosen.
   III. T and U are not chosen.

   (A) I only
   (B) I and II only
   (C) I and III only
   (D) II and III only
   (E) I, II, and III

(B) is the correct answer. If V is chosen, then W must also be chosen. And since Z is chosen, we need at least one faculty member. This gives us a total of four people, and we need three more. If we choose another student, this requires another faculty member (for a total of six), but it isn't possible to choose only T or U. Therefore, we cannot include another student. So we must include the other faculty member and T and U. So the committee consists of V, Z, W, S, R, T, and U.

Networks

Some problem sets involve spatial or temporal connections between individuals.

EXAMPLE:

In the subway system of a certain city, passengers can go:
From station P to station Q.
From station Q to station R and from station Q to station S.
From station R to station S and from station R to station T.
From station S to station U and from station S to station P.
From station T to station U and from station T to station R.
From station U to station P and from station U to station S.
A passenger at one station can transfer for another station.

The correct approach to any network problem is to sketch the network.

From station P to station Q.

$$P \longrightarrow Q$$

From station Q to station R and from station Q to station S.

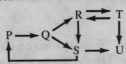

From station R to station S and from station R to station T.

From station S to station U and from station S to station P.

From station T to station U and from station T to station R.

From station U to station P and from station U to station S.

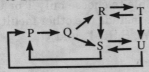

1. *A passenger at station T who wishes to travel to station Q must pass through a minimum of how many other stations before she finally arrives at Q?*

   (A) 1   (D) 4
   (B) 2   (E) 5
   (C) 3

Consult the network diagram. The shortest route is U to P and then on to Q. Therefore, the correct answer is **(B)**.

2. *A passenger at station U who wishes to travel through the system and return to station U before she had passed through any other subway station twice, can choose from how many different routes?*

   (A) 2   (D) 5
   (B) 3   (E) 6
   (C) 4

(C) is the correct answer. Simply trace the possibilities with your finger:

> U to P to Q to S to U
> U to P to Q to R to S to U
> U to P to Q to R to T to U
> U to S to P to Q to R to T to U

Matrix Problems

Sometimes a problem will refer to individuals who have or lack certain characteristics, and some questions may ask which characteristics are in turn shared by which individuals.

EXAMPLE:

Five people, George, Howard, Ingrid, Jean, and Kathy, work in a factory. On an given shift, a person can be assigned to one of five jobs: mechanic, truck driver, packer, weigher, or dispatcher.
George can function as mechanic, packer, or weigher.
Howard can function as either packer or weigher.
Ingrid can function as mechanic, truck driver, or dispatcher.
Jean can function as truck driver or dispatcher.
Kathy can function as truck driver or weigher.
The five workers can fill only these jobs, and only these five workers can fill these jobs.

For a problem set in which individuals do or do not share certain characteristics (and those characteristics are or are not shared by the individuals), use a matrix or table.

	M	TD	P	W	D
G					
H					
I					
J					
K					

George can function as mechanic, packer, or weigher.

	M	TD	P	W	D
G	√		√	√	
H					
I					
J					
K					

Howard can function as either packer or weigher.

	M	TD	P	W	D
G	√		√	√	
H			√	√	
I					
J					
K					

Ingrid can function as mechanic, truck driver, or dispatcher.

	M	TD	P	W	D
G	√		√	√	
H			√	√	
I	√	√			√
J					
K					

Jean can function as truck driver or dispatcher.

	M	TD	P	W	D
G	✓		✓	✓	
H			✓	✓	
I	✓	✓			✓
J		✓			✓
K					

Kathy can function as truck driver or weigher.

	M	TD	P	W	D
G	✓		✓	✓	
H			✓	✓	
I	✓	✓			✓
J		✓			✓
K		✓		✓	

1. *If Jean is NOT assigned to function as dispatcher, which of the other four individuals could be dispatcher?*

   I. George
   II. Howard
   III. Ingrid
   IV. Kathy

   (A) I only   **(D)** I and II only
   (B) III only   **(E)** III and IV only
   (C) IV only

As the table shows, Ingrid is the only person besides Jean who can be assigned as dispatcher. **(B)** is the correct answer.

2. *If George is assigned as mechanic, which of the following must be true?*

   I. Howard is assigned as packer.
   II. Kathy is assigned as weigher.
   III. Ingrid is assigned as truck driver.
   IV. Jean is assigned as dispatcher.

   (A) I and II only   **(D)** I, II, and IV only
   (B) I and III only   **(E)** I, II, III, and IV
   (C) II and IV only

(A) is the correct answer. If George is assigned as mechanic, then he is not available to be packer or weigher. There is only one other person who can be the packer, and that is Howard. So I is true. Then, since Howard is assigned to be the packer, he cannot be the weigher, so Kathy must be the weigher. Ingrid and Jean must be assigned as truck driver and dispatcher, but either can do either job.

Family Relationships

EXAMPLE:
   Barbara, an only child, is married, and she and her husband have two children, Ned and Sally.
   Ned is Paula's nephew by blood and Victor's grandson.
   Victor and his wife had only two children, Frank and his sister, plus four grandchildren, two boys and two girls.
   Wilma is Sally's grandmother.

Use the information to create a family tree.
   Barbara, an only child, is married, and she and her husband have two children, Ned and Sally:

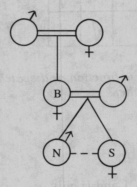

Ned is Paula's nephew by blood and Victor's grandson.

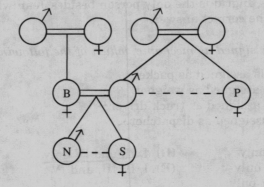

(Since Barbara is an only child, an aunt could be related by blood only by being Ned's father's sister. We don't know, however, whether Victor is Ned's paternal or maternal grandfather.)

Victor and his wife had only two children, Frank and his sister, plus four grand-children, two boys and two girls.

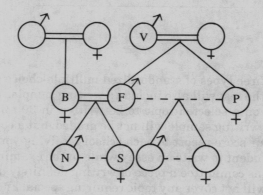

(Since Victor had two children, he could not have been Barbara's father because Barbara is an only child. So in order to be Ned's grandfather, Victor must be Ned's father's father.) It is not possible to enter the last piece of information for it is not clear whether Wilma is Betty's mother or the mother of Frank and Paula.

1. *All of the following must be true EXCEPT:*

   (A) Wilma is Victor's wife.
   (B) Victor is Sally's grandfather.
   (C) Victor is Betty's father-in-law.
   (D) Paula is Betty's sister-in-law.
   (E) Frank is Sally's father.

As we just noted, we cannot definitely place Wilma in the family tree. The diagram, however, confirms that the other statements are true. **(A)** is the correct answer.

2. *Which of the following must be true?*

   I. Ned has exactly two cousins.
   II. Paula has one son and one daughter.
   III. Betty has only one nephew.

   (A) I only
   (B) II only
   (C) I and II only
   (D) I and III only
   (E) I, II, and III

(E) is the correct answer. Since Victor has two grandsons and two granddaughters, Paula must have one son and one daughter. So statement II is true. And since Betty has no siblings and Frank's only sibling is Paula, Frank and Paula's children are Ned's only cousins and Betty's only nieces or nephews. So statements I and III are true as well.

WRITING SAMPLE

In addition to the three types of standardized multiple-choice questions that will appear on the LSAT, the test will also include a writing sample. The writing sample will be a short essay on a selected topic to be written in 30 minutes while in the examining room. The writing sample will not be graded, but a copy of the essay will be forwarded with your score report to each school receiving your LSAT score. The point of requiring a student to write an essay while in the examining room is to give a law school admissions committee a piece of writing definitely done by the student alone. The questions will not cover any topic requiring special knowledge. Paper and pens will be provided at the test center.

The underlying purpose in requiring the essay is to give a law school admissions committee another perspective on a candidate's ability—in this case, to give some idea of how well a student writes. The idea is that this can mitigate to some extent the severity of the artificial, multiple-choice format of the rest of the test. Exactly what role the writing sample is to play in the admissions process is decided by each law school. Many schools use the sample to help choose between otherwise equally qualified candidates. Very few law schools rely heavily upon the writing sample. Most law schools have adopted a middle-of-the-road approach. The writing sample will not figure heavily in the initial screening-out of applications, but it may be used to make decisions in difficult cases. For example, a student with marginal qualifications for a particular law school might be accepted if he or she writes a really good essay, and a student of similar background could be rejected on grounds that the writing sample is just not acceptable. Since no one is assured of a seat at a top law school, applicants to those schools who write a very poor essay will likely suffer.

 The writing sample is *not* as important as the other sections.

It is important to keep in mind that law schools use the LSAT as a screening device (coupled with the grade point average). This means that the LSAT is a threshold requirement that must be met before the writing sample even enters the picture. Moreover, the length of the sample is such that you are not really writing a "term paper." In 30 minutes, no one is going to be able to write the definitive essay on the topic given—and no one is expected to do so. This writing sample is just a check to see if you can write clearly and grammatically; it is not to determine whether you would be a great novelist.

THE TOPICS

Writing sample topics describe a decision that one person or a group of people must make, and you are asked to write an argument for one of the two courses of action.

EXAMPLE:

Margaret Stone will receive her Ph.D. in comparative literature in six months and wants a job teaching on the university level. After several interviews, she received job offers from two institutions, Middleburg College and Central State University. Write an essay arguing that Margaret should choose one of the two job offers. Two considerations should guide your decision:

1.   Martha wants a position that will allow her to maintain a decent standard of living. After eight years as a student, she has virtually no assets and has incurred several thousand dollars in student loans.

2.   Martha wants a position that will allow her to teach higher-level courses in literature rather than the introductory course or courses designed to teach students a foreign language. Additionally, she wants to earn a reputation as a scholar.

MIDDLEBURG COLLEGE is a small, liberal arts college with a student body of approximately 2,000. Although the college has a limited enrollment, its academic reputation is equal to that of many of the nation's best universities. There is no separate Comparative Literature Department at Middleburg. All literature courses are taught in various language departments. Martha would be hired by the French Department and would be expected to teach three courses per semester: one basic French grammar course, one introduction to French literature course, and one upper-level literature course. The starting salary at Middleburg is $23,000 per year. The position is a tenure track position, and Margaret could expect to receive tenure and a raise to $35,000 within three years.

CENTRAL STATE UNIVERSITY is a large public institution with a student body of 35,000. Margaret has been offered a position on the graduate faculty at a salary of $30,000 per year. As a member of the graduate faculty, she would offer courses of her own choosing, subject only to the approval of the Chief Executive Officer of the Department. The Chief Executive Officer is a leading authority on literary criticism, and each year the University sponsors one major and several minor conferences at which scholars from the University and other institutions present papers. The position at Central State is not considered a tenure track position, but Margaret could hope to achieve a permanent appointment in seven or eight years if she earns a substantial academic reputation.

The first thing to note about this topic is that there are good reasons for Margaret to choose either job.

Pick one side or the other—there is no right or wrong answer.

For example, though Margaret receives a better starting salary at Central State, she is more likely to get tenure (and that raise) in a shorter time at Middleburg. And, though Central State is obviously a larger institution where Margaret can teach higher-level courses and associate with leading authorities in the field, the topic specifically states that the academic reputation of Middleburg equals that of many of the nation's best institutions. So there is no right or wrong side. Just pick the one you feel more comfortable with.

WHAT TO SAY

After you have selected the side of the topic you are more comfortable with, construct an outline of your position. Since the entire exercise takes only 30 minutes, you probably cannot write more than four or five *short* paragraphs.

Your essay should be four or five short paragraphs. For example: introduction; first main reason; second main reason; conclusion.

Each paragraph will be only two or three sentences long.

If you think that this is not "grand" enough, remember that this essay is not going to get you into law school. The objective here is to avoid writing something that is totally unacceptable.

Let the statement of criteria be your two major contentions.

The outline above suggests that your essay should be built around two major contentions. Let the statement of the criteria be those major contentions. Find a way of summarizing those two ideas and let those summaries be your main contentions. Using the topic above, you could argue that Margaret is concerned about (1) financial security and (2) professional satisfaction. Thus, your two main contentions would be:

    I.   This job offers Martha with the financial security she wants.
   II.   This job offers Martha the professional satisfaction she seeks.

Then find two or three specific points in the topic to prove each contention.

Let the description of each option provide you with the subpoints needed to support your main points.

Above, we used the general statement of the guiding criteria to construct our main points. Now we will use the specific details provided in the description of each option to find supporting points. For example, if you decide to argue in favor of Central State, your outline might look like this:

    I.   This job offers Martha the financial security she wants.
         A.   The starting salary is a generous $30,000 per year.
         B.   There is the possibility of tenure if she succeeds.
   II.   This job offers Martha the professional satisfaction she seeks.
         A.   She will be able to teach courses she likes.
         B.   She will work with leading figures in her field.
         C.   She will participate in conferences.

(You can also find equally good reasons for selecting the other job.)

Now let's put the substance of our argument together with the formal outline given above. First, we need an introduction. I would recommend an opening paragraph such as:

> Margaret should accept the job offer from Central State for two reasons. First, it will give her the financial security she needs. Second, it will offer her the professional satisfaction that she seeks.

The second paragraph is the development of the first major contention. Begin the paragraph with a restatement of your first main point. Then supply the supporting details:

> First, the position at Central State provides Margaret with the income she needs to maintain a certain standard of living. The starting salary at Central State is a generous $30,000 per year. Additionally, if Margaret is successful, she can expect to receive promotions after a few years, and such promotions usually carry corresponding salary increases.

The third paragraph is the development of the second major contention. Begin this paragraph with a restatement of your second main point. Then supply the supporting details:

> Second, Central State will allow Margaret to achieve her professional goals. In the first place, she will teach higher-level courses and won't be required to teach the introductory courses she might find less interesting. Additionally, she will be able to work with her Chief Executive Officer who is one of the leading authorities in Margaret's field. Finally, the University itself is the center for conferences at which Margaret would meet others in her field and have an opportunity to exchange ideas.

The final paragraph should be a brief summary of the argument—only a sentence or two long:

> Thus, because Central State offers better financial terms and the possibility of professional advancement, Margaret should accept its job offer.

The primary function of this paragraph is just to signal the reader that you have reached the end of your essay.

Now let's put all the paragraphs together. Here is how the essay would read:

> Margaret should accept the job offer from Central State for two reasons. First, it will give her the financial security she needs. Second, it will offer her the professional satisfaction that she seeks.
>
> First, the position at Central State provides Margaret with the income she needs to maintain a certain standard of living. The starting salary at Central State is a generous $30,000 per year. Additionally, if Margaret is successful, she can expect to receive promotions after a few years, and such promotions usually carry corresponding salary increases.
>
> Second, Central State will allow Margaret to achieve her professional goals. In the first place, she will teach higher-level courses and won't be required to teach the introductory courses she might find less interesting. Additionally, she will be able to work with her Chief Executive Officer who is one of the leading authorities in Margaret's field. Finally, the University

itself is the center for conferences at which Margaret would meet others in her field and have an opportunity to exchange ideas.

Thus, because Central State offers better financial terms and the possibility of professional advancement, Margaret should accept its job offer.

If you still doubt that this is sufficient, try copying this essay over in your own hand and see how long it takes you.

HOW TO SAY IT

As we have stressed, this section is going to be used by law school to see whether a student can write English properly. So, as important as finding something to say is the way in which you say it. Obviously, this means composing sentences free of grammatical errors. Beyond that, however, you should strive for conciseness and clarity of expression. We understand that it is difficult to take this general instruction and apply it to a specific exercise: "Right, I agree, write clearly. But how do I do that?" Our best advice here is to do some practice. In the practice exams which follow we have provided four topics. But you can practice on your own by selecting a topic—anything that pops into your mind—and writing a short essay on it. If you feel the need, you can use these questions for additional practice:

> —*It is better to construct classrooms without windows, since the view provided by windows tends to distract students.*

> —*A speaker is more effective if he uses a lectern or podium because he will then make fewer unnecessary and distracting movements.*

> —*It is better to bring household garbage outside as infrequently as possible because it is more efficient to carry fewer large loads than more smaller loads.*

 Make each sentence express a single thought.

Rather than trying to tack on qualifications and exceptions to an already long sentence, break it down:

> Wrong: Although it might be argued that some students will be distracted, but there is no proof of this presented, it is still the case that many students would benefit from the relaxing effect of open scenery, and that could even help them learn.
>
> Better: There is no proof presented that students are distracted by windows. Even assuming some students are distracted, many other students might find the view relaxing. A relaxed student should be a better learner than one who is tense—and learning is the goal of the classroom.

 Think through the entire sentence before you begin to write.

Many errors in writing are the result of an attempt to change structures in mid-sentence. Verb tenses shift; points of view get mixed up; verbs get left out; pronouns get confused; and many other things happen——if the sentence is not already formed when the writing begins. For example:

> Wrong: Even if a student is somewhat distracted, they may be even better able to concentrate when their attention returns to the teacher.

This sentence contains a grammatical error. The pronoun "they," which begins the main clause of the sentence, is plural. But it refers to "student," which is singular. This type of error usually occurs when writers do not have the complete thought or sentence in mind when they begin to write. They lose track of what they have said and shift from the singular to the plural. The best way for you to avoid such errors is to have a good idea of what the completed sentence will say before you begin to write it down.

In addition to "squaring the corners," we offer the following warnings against common errors of grammar and style. The list is not exhaustive, but it does cover some of the most fundamental mistakes.

Watch for subject-verb agreement.

Everyone remembers that a verb must agree with its subject, and by and large we all observe this rule. Where we tend to get into trouble is with sentences with subjects modified by prepositional phrases or other material which comes between the subject and its verb.

> Wrong: This distraction, which occurs in students with more limited attention spans, are easily avoided by arranging desks so that the eyes of a student is directed away from the windows.

Two errors of subject-verb agreement occur here: "distraction . . . are" and "eyes . . . is." In this sentence, a clause including two prepositional phrases comes between the first subject and its verb, and it is therefore likely that one of the two nouns, "students" or "spans," was mistaken for the subject when the writer chose a verb. A prepositional phrase ("of a student") comes between the second subject and its verb, and the writer has mistaken "student" for the subject of the verb and written "is."

Be wary of pronouns.

Many people misuse pronouns. The two most common mistakes in pronoun reference are incorrect number and incorrect case. Sometimes students use a singular pronoun where a plural pronoun is needed and vice versa (incorrect number):

> Wrong: The easiest solution is to have the teacher order each student to keep their eyes directed toward the blackboard.

In this case, the choice of the pronoun "their" is incorrect. The pronoun must refer to "student," which is singular; but "their" is plural. Consider the next example:

Wrong: Under this seating arrangement, all of the people in the classroom, except the class monitor and she, will face the blackboard, not the windows.

In this sentence, the use of the pronoun "she" is incorrect because it is in the wrong case. The pronoun here functions as the object of a preposition ("except"), and it should therefore be in the objective case ("her"). One sure way of avoiding errors in the use of pronouns is to avoid unnecessary pronouns.

Better: Under this seating arrangement, all of the people in the classroom, except the class monitor and the teacher, will. . . .

Avoid the "notorious" dangling modifier.

As a general rule, make sure that your modifiers are close to the words they are intended to modify. Be especially wary of the introductory modifier.

Wrong: While strolling through Central Park, a severe thunderstorm required my companion and me to take shelter in the band shell.

Given the construction of the sentence, it is made to appear that the severe thunderstorm was strolling through the park. When a modifying idea starts a sentence and is set off with a comma, the modifier must be taken to modify the first noun or noun phrase after the comma. A related error to be avoided is the squinting modifier, which is placed so that it may modify either one of two things, producing ambiguity in the sentence.

Wrong: Paul told Mary that he would wed her down by the old mill.

Did Paul tell Mary down by the old mill that he would wed her, or did Paul tell Mary that he would wed her and the wedding would take place down by the old mill?

Avoid the passive voice.

As we have mentioned, it is important to write in straightforward declarative sentences. These sentences are easily used, and they express thoughts clearly. But many students imagine that the more stilted the construction, the better the writing:

Wrong: When the notice was received by me. . . .
Correct: When I received the notice. . . .

Wrong: The cake was baked by the chef to please. . . .
Correct: The chef baked the cake to please. . . .

We do not imply here an absolute prohibition against the passive voice. We only say that a law school admissions committee will be favorably impressed by straightforward and direct composition—even if that writing is a bit dry—but they will not be favorably impressed by needlessly complicated and imprecise sentences.

Avoid slang.

Whatever else you do, do not allow slang to slip into your writing.

> Wrong: Let the kids do their own thing. Its too heavy a trip to always
> have the teacher, the man, laying this guilt business on you. No
> windows would be a head trip. Some of the kids would wind up
> at the shrink's. So just lay off, and let them be themselves.

In conversation we often use expressions that are just not acceptable in formal writing. Can you dig that?

When in doubt, leave it out.

You are in command of the writing sample. Unlike the other sections, in which you are *forced* to choose from among answers, the writing sample allows you to construct and write your own answer. It will be possible, to a certain extent, to "fake it": if you are not sure about the meaning or spelling of a word, find an alternative. There is absolutely no reason to expose yourself to the possibility of error when you could avoid that danger entirely by using another phrase.

Write neatly.

What we have tried to do in this section is reassure you that you will not be caught without anything to say. The questions will be drafted in such a way that you will be able to think of a point or two—and probably more. The important thing is to express yourself clearly in order to impress upon the admissions officers that you can write, a skill every lawyer needs. Finally, although good penmanship is not a prerequisite to being a good lawyer, your writing will be read by some fairly important people. Present yourself in a way of which you can be proud. Some people have naturally beautiful handwriting, others do not. But everyone is capable of legible handwriting. It is only courteous to write clearly, so that the people who have to read your essay can do so easily. So write slowly (without sacrificing coverage), and try to use your best handwriting. Print if necessary.

Do not try to do too much.

After you have practiced a few topics, you will have a pretty good idea of what you can hope to accomplish in the time allotted. The biggest problem for students is not going to be having too little to say, but trying to say too much. Your little essay must be structurally complete. That is, it must have a beginning, a middle, and an end. You do not want to run out of time before you have completed your thought. Far better to write a nicely balanced and self-contained essay on the short side than a longer piece that stops in the middle of the next-to-the-last paragraph. Make sure you can chew what you bite off.

Do not use any legal terminology.

The LSAT is not a test of what you already know about the law, and law school admissions officers are not going to be impressed with your essay just because you flavor it with *henceforth, heretofore mentioned, above cited* or similar terms. Such terms have no place in your essay. Your best bet is to try to write naturally, as though you were speaking to someone sitting across the table (though you should avoid slang expressions you might use in conversation).

Part III
Applying to Law School

THE LAW SCHOOL ADMISSION PROCESS

THE NUMBERS GAME

It is widely claimed that law schools make their admissions decisions entirely on the basis of an applicant's LSAT score and grade point average (GPA). However, this claim, when made without qualification, is demonstrably false. While it is true that every law school relies, to a greater or lesser extent, on the LSAT and the GPA, to our knowledge very few law schools have an admissions process so mechanical that these are the only two factors taken into consideration. To persuade yourself of this, you need only consult the *Pre-Law Handbook,* published by the Association of American Law Schools and the Law School Admissions Council. The *Pre-Law Handbook* is available in many bookstores and can be ordered from Law School Admissions Services, Box 2000, Newtown, Pennsylvania 18940, when you register for the LSAT. It contains much valuable information about the law school admissions process. One of the most important features of the *Pre-Law Handbook* is the descriptive summaries supplied by all law schools accredited by the American Bar Association. In their descriptions submitted to this publication, many of the schools include a breakdown, by LSAT score and GPA, of applications received and applications accepted.

Let us take an example from a recent edition of the *Pre-Law Handbook:*

	LSAT Score (Approximate Percentile Equivalent)			
	33–35 (61–70)	36–37 (71–80)	38–39 (81–90)	40+ (91+)
G.P.A. 4.00 to 3.75	2/51	105/152	94/112	53/59
3.74 to 3.50	0/187	196/368	209/261	85/101
3.49 to 3.25	0/203	77/411	147/316	77/143
3.24 to 3.00	0/164	6/259	11/208	12/85

The number to the right of the slash represents total applications received, and the number to the left of the slash represents the number of applicants accepted.

We will not identify the school that submitted this information, for the name of the particular school is not important. The pattern shown here is representative of most law schools. Further, because the ranges of LSAT scores and percentile rankings do not match as neatly as the chart suggests, we were forced to make some minor adjustments in the brackets used in the table. These adjustments, however, though they distort slightly the picture for this particular law school, do not affect the overall validity of the point we are trying to make.

The information supplied in the table seems to support the claim that admissions decisions are based solely on LSAT score and GPA, but a closer look will reveal that the claim is actually disproved by the numbers shown there. First, it must be admitted that the table does show that this law school places considerable weight on the LSAT and the GPA: The ratio of acceptances to applications is highest in the upper right-hand corner of the table (where the LSAT scores and GPAs are highest) and declines as we move toward the lower left-hand corner of the chart (where LSAT scores and GPAs are lowest).

The explanation for this is probably that the law school sets some absolute minimum LSAT and GPA below which it will not accept an application. Typically, a law school will use some mathematical formula to combine an applicant's LSAT score and GPA into an index which gives an admissions committee a rough idea of the competitiveness of an application. One way of accomplishing this is to multiply an applicant's GPA by 10 and add that product to the LSAT score. For example, an applicant with a GPA of 3.5 and an LSAT score of 33 would have an index of $(3.5 \times 10) + 33 = 68$. Notice that this formula gives approximately equal weight to the GPA and the LSAT score. If the index of an application is too low, the applicant is rejected.

This is not to say, of course, that every law school uses such a formula, but enough law schools use some such device that we would not be wrong in taking this as the paradigm for an admissions decision. We can then understand particular admissions processes in the way that they vary from this paradigm. Some schools have a highly mechanical decision-making process, e.g., if the index falls below a minimum, the application is rejected, and if the index exceeds a certain minimum, the application is accepted. Some schools have a highly flexible admissions process in which they attempt to deemphasize seemingly objective factors such as the LSAT score in favor of more subjective factors such as applicant motivation.

The general rule, then, is that you should not apply to a school unless you have some chance of being accepted. If you have a GPA of 3.25 and an LSAT score of 34, it would simply be a waste of money to apply to the school we have been discussing. On the other hand, if you have a GPA of 3.75 and an LSAT score of 38, you would have a fairly good chance of acceptance at this school. The information provided in the *Pre-Law Handbook* will guide you in making your decisions about to which schools you should submit applications.

To a certain extent, then, the LSAT and the GPA are determinative of an application's disposition; but the table also shows that these measures are not the only factors being taken into account. The law school in question received 261 applications with LSAT scores of 38 or 39 and GPAs between 3.50 and 3.74. It accepted 209 of them, which means it rejected 52 of them. It also received 411 applications with LSAT scores of 36 or 37 and GPAs in the range of 3.25 to 3.49. It accepted 77 of them. In other words, this law school rejected 52 seemingly better qualified applicants in favor of 77 seemingly less well-qualified applicants. This proves that the LSAT score and the GPA are not the only factors being considered by law schools.

OTHER FACTORS

What, then, are the other factors that are taken into account by admissions committees? If you consult a law school's catalog, you will find reference to ''nonacademic activities, work experience, level of maturity, and other personal qualifications''; ''work experience and extracurricular or community activity''; ''demonstrated excellence in a particular activity, such as musical accomplishments, literary ability reflected in published works, or achievement in intercollegiate athletics''; and ''circumstances which indicate an educational disadvantage.'' In other words, an admissions committee will usually consider anything in your background which indicates that you will be able to complete the law school curriculum and become a successful attorney. We might summarize these factors under the general headings of **ability, motivation, and additional dimension.**

Put yourself in the position of a law school admissions officer, and you will be able to appreciate why these additional factors are important. As for the first two, it should be obvious that both ability and motivation are prerequisites for successful completion of the law school course of study. Raw ability without direction does not make a good student; that ability must be harnessed and directed toward a goal. Conversely, desire without ability is vain hope. The LSAT is regarded by most law school admissions officers as one measure, if highly imperfect, of "intellectual horsepower" or ability. The GPA demonstrates something about a student's ability and that student's motivation. But these are only two measures of ability and motivation——and they are not entirely accurate. So law school admissions officers look for further guidance.

There is also the third dimension. Most law schools receive many more applications than they can possibly accept. Many receive two times, three times, or even ten times as many applications as they have seats available for an entering class. Yet most of the applicants are reasonably well qualified; that is, most of the applicants, if given the chance, could probably complete the law school curriculum. In a way, law school admissions officers are in the happy position (from their perspective) of being able to "shop" for applicants. Their task is not so much one of selecting minimally well-qualified applicants as it is of selecting from among reasonably well-qualified applicants. For this reason, all other things being equal, the interesting applicants——that is, those with some unusual features in their backgrounds——will be accepted.

A word of caution is in order here. We are not suggesting that some unique feature in your background is going to allow you to overcome an otherwise unsatisfactory LSAT score or GPA. We have already demonstrated that an unacceptable LSAT score or GPA may constitute an insuperable barrier. What we are saying here is that you must design your application so that it conveys the message that you have the three characteristics just mentioned.

PERSUADING THE ADMISSION COMMITTEE

You will have very little control over much of the application. Most of the questions asked must be answered with short answers, e.g., *Did you work while in school? What is your address?* etc. In answering these questions, you will want to make certain that you include anything that is relevant and makes you appear in a better light. Aside from these short-answer questions, one open-ended question is usually included in an application form: *Why do you want to go to law school?* The exact wording of this question varies from school to school, but the implication for you is the same. You can take this as an invitation to add anything about yourself you did not get into your answers to the standard questions of the application.

Some questions will provide you with greater flexibility than others, but, for the purpose of discussion, let us assume that you are answering a question which is completely open-ended: *Add anything you think might aid the committee in making its decision.* In addressing yourself to this question, you should remember the three factors the admissions committee will regard as important, and you should marshall arguments to support your contention that you possess these characteristics. In fact, you may find it useful to organize your response to this question along the lines of: (1) I do have the ability; (2) I do have the motivation; and (3) I possess an added dimension. Then you present the important features of your background within this scheme.

Of course, each of us has unique points which we want to include in our answer to such a question, and this makes it impossible to offer a formula that is applicable to every case. Here are two outlines, however, which indicate how the question might be answered.

Outline 1

    I. I have the ability.
        A. My academic performance was outstanding.
            i. I graduated with honors.
           ii. I took a graduate-level course while still an undergraduate.
          iii. I took a double major.

B. My extracurricular participation shows ability.
    i. I was a member of the Student Council.
    ii. I was a member of the debating team.
II. I have the motivation.
    A. I worked for a lawyer, so I know what lawyers do.
    B. I want to practice criminal law.
III. There is something special about my background.
    A. I am a member of a church choir.
    B. I am fluent in French.

Outline 2

I. 'I have the ability.
    A. My employment experience indicates I have ability.
        i. I am presently an assistant manager in my company.
        ii. I have responsibility for a $500,000 budget.
    B. My academic performance was good.
        i. My GPA would have been higher except I worked my way through school.
        ii. I took a graduate degree.
II. I have the motivation.
    A. My job brings me into contact with lawyers, and I understand what they do.
    B. With a law degree, I could bring my special business experience into play.
III. There is something unusual about my background.
    A. I spent two years in the Peace Corps.
    B. I play the piano.

So much variation is possible that we could devote an entire volume to this topic alone. These outlines are merely intended to suggest what you might include in your response to such a question and to suggest a way of organizing your response. The most important thing to keep in mind is that you must prove you have ability and motivation; then you can try to demonstrate that extra dimension.

Not all applications explicitly allow such leeway. Some applications will include a question like the following: *In 250 words, please explain why you want to go to law school.* With such a question you are more limited. You will want to abide by the word limitation, but you may feel that there is more you want to say. In that case, you should write a response to the question, abiding by the word limitation; then you can attach a fuller justification of your application as an "extra." The overall idea is to comply with the instructions contained in the application but to supply the admissions committee with material that will favorably affect your chances of acceptance.

LETTERS OF RECOMMENDATION

We say often, and have written elsewhere, that "letters of recommendation" is a misnomer. These letters should rather be regarded as letters of "evaluation." This is in keeping with remarks made earlier: The task of the application is to persuade the admissions committee that you have the ability and the motivation. Your letters of recommendation/evaluation are included to support your argument. They are not character references.

Many students fail to appreciate this distinction, so they seek out letters from famous people. Now, it cannot be denied that a letter of support from a Supreme Court Justice would be valuable, but you must understand that what makes a letter of evaluation valuable is the following: The letter writer knows you and so has some basis for the evaluation. Unless the letter writer has some basis for making his or her remarks, then that letter is likely to be discounted by the admissions committee. A letter from a Senator that begins "I do not really know the candidate, but . . ." is obviously not going to help your cause very much.

The rule on letters of recommendation/evaluation, then, is to solicit them from professors or employers who are familiar with your work. These are the people who are in a position to make meaningful recommendations regarding your strengths and weaknesses. A title or position is, of course, an added benefit, but you should seek letters not on the basis of title but on the basis of personal knowledge of your accomplishments.

CONCLUDING ADVICE

There is, of course, much more to be said on the subject of law school admissions, but the topic of this book is preparation for the LSAT, not law school admissions in general. We recommend, therefore, that you consult other sources. You should obtain a copy of the *Pre-Law Handbook*. Additionally, there are several interesting books available in the bookstore on law school admissions. We recommend that you consult *How to Get Into Law School,* by Rennard Strickland (Hawthorne Books), and *Inside the Law Schools,* by Sally Goldfarb (E.P. Dutton). Finally, every law school makes available to you, free of charge, a copy of its catalog, where you will find much valuable information on the particular law school that interests you.

Our parting word of advice is to complete the application carefully. This application represents you—both figuratively and literally. Since most law schools do not arrange personal interviews, the application you prepare must represent you literally. This is your only contact with the school. Beyond that, the application will also represent you figuratively. Since the law school will not actually see you, *the written application is you,* so far as the admissions committee is concerned. Just as you would dress for an interview in neat attire and would pay careful attention to your conduct, so must you also prepare the application with great care. It must be neatly typed and carefully edited. Remember, this application is your alter ego.

Part IV

Four Full-Length Practice Examinations

Use a No. 2 pencil only. Be sure each mark is dark and completely fills the intended oval. Completely erase any errors or stray marks.

□ A R C O □

Start with number 1 for each new section. If a section has fewer than 50 questions, leave the extra answer spaces blank.

SECTION 1	SECTION 2	SECTION 3	SECTION 4
1 Ⓐ Ⓑ Ⓒ Ⓓ Ⓔ	1 Ⓐ Ⓑ Ⓒ Ⓓ Ⓔ	1 Ⓐ Ⓑ Ⓒ Ⓓ Ⓔ	1 Ⓐ Ⓑ Ⓒ Ⓓ Ⓔ
2 Ⓐ Ⓑ Ⓒ Ⓓ Ⓔ	2 Ⓐ Ⓑ Ⓒ Ⓓ Ⓔ	2 Ⓐ Ⓑ Ⓒ Ⓓ Ⓔ	2 Ⓐ Ⓑ Ⓒ Ⓓ Ⓔ
3 Ⓐ Ⓑ Ⓒ Ⓓ Ⓔ	3 Ⓐ Ⓑ Ⓒ Ⓓ Ⓔ	3 Ⓐ Ⓑ Ⓒ Ⓓ Ⓔ	3 Ⓐ Ⓑ Ⓒ Ⓓ Ⓔ
4 Ⓐ Ⓑ Ⓒ Ⓓ Ⓔ	4 Ⓐ Ⓑ Ⓒ Ⓓ Ⓔ	4 Ⓐ Ⓑ Ⓒ Ⓓ Ⓔ	4 Ⓐ Ⓑ Ⓒ Ⓓ Ⓔ
5 Ⓐ Ⓑ Ⓒ Ⓓ Ⓔ	5 Ⓐ Ⓑ Ⓒ Ⓓ Ⓔ	5 Ⓐ Ⓑ Ⓒ Ⓓ Ⓔ	5 Ⓐ Ⓑ Ⓒ Ⓓ Ⓔ
6 Ⓐ Ⓑ Ⓒ Ⓓ Ⓔ	6 Ⓐ Ⓑ Ⓒ Ⓓ Ⓔ	6 Ⓐ Ⓑ Ⓒ Ⓓ Ⓔ	6 Ⓐ Ⓑ Ⓒ Ⓓ Ⓔ
7 Ⓐ Ⓑ Ⓒ Ⓓ Ⓔ	7 Ⓐ Ⓑ Ⓒ Ⓓ Ⓔ	7 Ⓐ Ⓑ Ⓒ Ⓓ Ⓔ	7 Ⓐ Ⓑ Ⓒ Ⓓ Ⓔ
8 Ⓐ Ⓑ Ⓒ Ⓓ Ⓔ	8 Ⓐ Ⓑ Ⓒ Ⓓ Ⓔ	8 Ⓐ Ⓑ Ⓒ Ⓓ Ⓔ	8 Ⓐ Ⓑ Ⓒ Ⓓ Ⓔ
9 Ⓐ Ⓑ Ⓒ Ⓓ Ⓔ	9 Ⓐ Ⓑ Ⓒ Ⓓ Ⓔ	9 Ⓐ Ⓑ Ⓒ Ⓓ Ⓔ	9 Ⓐ Ⓑ Ⓒ Ⓓ Ⓔ
10 Ⓐ Ⓑ Ⓒ Ⓓ Ⓔ	10 Ⓐ Ⓑ Ⓒ Ⓓ Ⓔ	10 Ⓐ Ⓑ Ⓒ Ⓓ Ⓔ	10 Ⓐ Ⓑ Ⓒ Ⓓ Ⓔ
11 Ⓐ Ⓑ Ⓒ Ⓓ Ⓔ	11 Ⓐ Ⓑ Ⓒ Ⓓ Ⓔ	11 Ⓐ Ⓑ Ⓒ Ⓓ Ⓔ	11 Ⓐ Ⓑ Ⓒ Ⓓ Ⓔ
12 Ⓐ Ⓑ Ⓒ Ⓓ Ⓔ	12 Ⓐ Ⓑ Ⓒ Ⓓ Ⓔ	12 Ⓐ Ⓑ Ⓒ Ⓓ Ⓔ	12 Ⓐ Ⓑ Ⓒ Ⓓ Ⓔ
13 Ⓐ Ⓑ Ⓒ Ⓓ Ⓔ	13 Ⓐ Ⓑ Ⓒ Ⓓ Ⓔ	13 Ⓐ Ⓑ Ⓒ Ⓓ Ⓔ	13 Ⓐ Ⓑ Ⓒ Ⓓ Ⓔ
14 Ⓐ Ⓑ Ⓒ Ⓓ Ⓔ	14 Ⓐ Ⓑ Ⓒ Ⓓ Ⓔ	14 Ⓐ Ⓑ Ⓒ Ⓓ Ⓔ	14 Ⓐ Ⓑ Ⓒ Ⓓ Ⓔ
15 Ⓐ Ⓑ Ⓒ Ⓓ Ⓔ	15 Ⓐ Ⓑ Ⓒ Ⓓ Ⓔ	15 Ⓐ Ⓑ Ⓒ Ⓓ Ⓔ	15 Ⓐ Ⓑ Ⓒ Ⓓ Ⓔ
16 Ⓐ Ⓑ Ⓒ Ⓓ Ⓔ	16 Ⓐ Ⓑ Ⓒ Ⓓ Ⓔ	16 Ⓐ Ⓑ Ⓒ Ⓓ Ⓔ	16 Ⓐ Ⓑ Ⓒ Ⓓ Ⓔ
17 Ⓐ Ⓑ Ⓒ Ⓓ Ⓔ	17 Ⓐ Ⓑ Ⓒ Ⓓ Ⓔ	17 Ⓐ Ⓑ Ⓒ Ⓓ Ⓔ	17 Ⓐ Ⓑ Ⓒ Ⓓ Ⓔ
18 Ⓐ Ⓑ Ⓒ Ⓓ Ⓔ	18 Ⓐ Ⓑ Ⓒ Ⓓ Ⓔ	18 Ⓐ Ⓑ Ⓒ Ⓓ Ⓔ	18 Ⓐ Ⓑ Ⓒ Ⓓ Ⓔ
19 Ⓐ Ⓑ Ⓒ Ⓓ Ⓔ	19 Ⓐ Ⓑ Ⓒ Ⓓ Ⓔ	19 Ⓐ Ⓑ Ⓒ Ⓓ Ⓔ	19 Ⓐ Ⓑ Ⓒ Ⓓ Ⓔ
20 Ⓐ Ⓑ Ⓒ Ⓓ Ⓔ	20 Ⓐ Ⓑ Ⓒ Ⓓ Ⓔ	20 Ⓐ Ⓑ Ⓒ Ⓓ Ⓔ	20 Ⓐ Ⓑ Ⓒ Ⓓ Ⓔ
21 Ⓐ Ⓑ Ⓒ Ⓓ Ⓔ	21 Ⓐ Ⓑ Ⓒ Ⓓ Ⓔ	21 Ⓐ Ⓑ Ⓒ Ⓓ Ⓔ	21 Ⓐ Ⓑ Ⓒ Ⓓ Ⓔ
22 Ⓐ Ⓑ Ⓒ Ⓓ Ⓔ	22 Ⓐ Ⓑ Ⓒ Ⓓ Ⓔ	22 Ⓐ Ⓑ Ⓒ Ⓓ Ⓔ	22 Ⓐ Ⓑ Ⓒ Ⓓ Ⓔ
23 Ⓐ Ⓑ Ⓒ Ⓓ Ⓔ	23 Ⓐ Ⓑ Ⓒ Ⓓ Ⓔ	23 Ⓐ Ⓑ Ⓒ Ⓓ Ⓔ	23 Ⓐ Ⓑ Ⓒ Ⓓ Ⓔ
24 Ⓐ Ⓑ Ⓒ Ⓓ Ⓔ	24 Ⓐ Ⓑ Ⓒ Ⓓ Ⓔ	24 Ⓐ Ⓑ Ⓒ Ⓓ Ⓔ	24 Ⓐ Ⓑ Ⓒ Ⓓ Ⓔ
25 Ⓐ Ⓑ Ⓒ Ⓓ Ⓔ	25 Ⓐ Ⓑ Ⓒ Ⓓ Ⓔ	25 Ⓐ Ⓑ Ⓒ Ⓓ Ⓔ	25 Ⓐ Ⓑ Ⓒ Ⓓ Ⓔ
26 Ⓐ Ⓑ Ⓒ Ⓓ Ⓔ	26 Ⓐ Ⓑ Ⓒ Ⓓ Ⓔ	26 Ⓐ Ⓑ Ⓒ Ⓓ Ⓔ	26 Ⓐ Ⓑ Ⓒ Ⓓ Ⓔ
27 Ⓐ Ⓑ Ⓒ Ⓓ Ⓔ	27 Ⓐ Ⓑ Ⓒ Ⓓ Ⓔ	27 Ⓐ Ⓑ Ⓒ Ⓓ Ⓔ	27 Ⓐ Ⓑ Ⓒ Ⓓ Ⓔ
28 Ⓐ Ⓑ Ⓒ Ⓓ Ⓔ	28 Ⓐ Ⓑ Ⓒ Ⓓ Ⓔ	28 Ⓐ Ⓑ Ⓒ Ⓓ Ⓔ	28 Ⓐ Ⓑ Ⓒ Ⓓ Ⓔ
29 Ⓐ Ⓑ Ⓒ Ⓓ Ⓔ	29 Ⓐ Ⓑ Ⓒ Ⓓ Ⓔ	29 Ⓐ Ⓑ Ⓒ Ⓓ Ⓔ	29 Ⓐ Ⓑ Ⓒ Ⓓ Ⓔ
30 Ⓐ Ⓑ Ⓒ Ⓓ Ⓔ	30 Ⓐ Ⓑ Ⓒ Ⓓ Ⓔ	30 Ⓐ Ⓑ Ⓒ Ⓓ Ⓔ	30 Ⓐ Ⓑ Ⓒ Ⓓ Ⓔ
31 Ⓐ Ⓑ Ⓒ Ⓓ Ⓔ	31 Ⓐ Ⓑ Ⓒ Ⓓ Ⓔ	31 Ⓐ Ⓑ Ⓒ Ⓓ Ⓔ	31 Ⓐ Ⓑ Ⓒ Ⓓ Ⓔ
32 Ⓐ Ⓑ Ⓒ Ⓓ Ⓔ	32 Ⓐ Ⓑ Ⓒ Ⓓ Ⓔ	32 Ⓐ Ⓑ Ⓒ Ⓓ Ⓔ	32 Ⓐ Ⓑ Ⓒ Ⓓ Ⓔ
33 Ⓐ Ⓑ Ⓒ Ⓓ Ⓔ	33 Ⓐ Ⓑ Ⓒ Ⓓ Ⓔ	33 Ⓐ Ⓑ Ⓒ Ⓓ Ⓔ	33 Ⓐ Ⓑ Ⓒ Ⓓ Ⓔ
34 Ⓐ Ⓑ Ⓒ Ⓓ Ⓔ	34 Ⓐ Ⓑ Ⓒ Ⓓ Ⓔ	34 Ⓐ Ⓑ Ⓒ Ⓓ Ⓔ	34 Ⓐ Ⓑ Ⓒ Ⓓ Ⓔ
35 Ⓐ Ⓑ Ⓒ Ⓓ Ⓔ	35 Ⓐ Ⓑ Ⓒ Ⓓ Ⓔ	35 Ⓐ Ⓑ Ⓒ Ⓓ Ⓔ	35 Ⓐ Ⓑ Ⓒ Ⓓ Ⓔ
36 Ⓐ Ⓑ Ⓒ Ⓓ Ⓔ	36 Ⓐ Ⓑ Ⓒ Ⓓ Ⓔ	36 Ⓐ Ⓑ Ⓒ Ⓓ Ⓔ	36 Ⓐ Ⓑ Ⓒ Ⓓ Ⓔ
37 Ⓐ Ⓑ Ⓒ Ⓓ Ⓔ	37 Ⓐ Ⓑ Ⓒ Ⓓ Ⓔ	37 Ⓐ Ⓑ Ⓒ Ⓓ Ⓔ	37 Ⓐ Ⓑ Ⓒ Ⓓ Ⓔ
38 Ⓐ Ⓑ Ⓒ Ⓓ Ⓔ	38 Ⓐ Ⓑ Ⓒ Ⓓ Ⓔ	38 Ⓐ Ⓑ Ⓒ Ⓓ Ⓔ	38 Ⓐ Ⓑ Ⓒ Ⓓ Ⓔ
39 Ⓐ Ⓑ Ⓒ Ⓓ Ⓔ	39 Ⓐ Ⓑ Ⓒ Ⓓ Ⓔ	39 Ⓐ Ⓑ Ⓒ Ⓓ Ⓔ	39 Ⓐ Ⓑ Ⓒ Ⓓ Ⓔ
40 Ⓐ Ⓑ Ⓒ Ⓓ Ⓔ	40 Ⓐ Ⓑ Ⓒ Ⓓ Ⓔ	40 Ⓐ Ⓑ Ⓒ Ⓓ Ⓔ	40 Ⓐ Ⓑ Ⓒ Ⓓ Ⓔ
41 Ⓐ Ⓑ Ⓒ Ⓓ Ⓔ	41 Ⓐ Ⓑ Ⓒ Ⓓ Ⓔ	41 Ⓐ Ⓑ Ⓒ Ⓓ Ⓔ	41 Ⓐ Ⓑ Ⓒ Ⓓ Ⓔ
42 Ⓐ Ⓑ Ⓒ Ⓓ Ⓔ	42 Ⓐ Ⓑ Ⓒ Ⓓ Ⓔ	42 Ⓐ Ⓑ Ⓒ Ⓓ Ⓔ	42 Ⓐ Ⓑ Ⓒ Ⓓ Ⓔ
43 Ⓐ Ⓑ Ⓒ Ⓓ Ⓔ	43 Ⓐ Ⓑ Ⓒ Ⓓ Ⓔ	43 Ⓐ Ⓑ Ⓒ Ⓓ Ⓔ	43 Ⓐ Ⓑ Ⓒ Ⓓ Ⓔ
44 Ⓐ Ⓑ Ⓒ Ⓓ Ⓔ	44 Ⓐ Ⓑ Ⓒ Ⓓ Ⓔ	44 Ⓐ Ⓑ Ⓒ Ⓓ Ⓔ	44 Ⓐ Ⓑ Ⓒ Ⓓ Ⓔ
45 Ⓐ Ⓑ Ⓒ Ⓓ Ⓔ	45 Ⓐ Ⓑ Ⓒ Ⓓ Ⓔ	45 Ⓐ Ⓑ Ⓒ Ⓓ Ⓔ	45 Ⓐ Ⓑ Ⓒ Ⓓ Ⓔ
46 Ⓐ Ⓑ Ⓒ Ⓓ Ⓔ	46 Ⓐ Ⓑ Ⓒ Ⓓ Ⓔ	46 Ⓐ Ⓑ Ⓒ Ⓓ Ⓔ	46 Ⓐ Ⓑ Ⓒ Ⓓ Ⓔ
47 Ⓐ Ⓑ Ⓒ Ⓓ Ⓔ	47 Ⓐ Ⓑ Ⓒ Ⓓ Ⓔ	47 Ⓐ Ⓑ Ⓒ Ⓓ Ⓔ	47 Ⓐ Ⓑ Ⓒ Ⓓ Ⓔ
48 Ⓐ Ⓑ Ⓒ Ⓓ Ⓔ	48 Ⓐ Ⓑ Ⓒ Ⓓ Ⓔ	48 Ⓐ Ⓑ Ⓒ Ⓓ Ⓔ	48 Ⓐ Ⓑ Ⓒ Ⓓ Ⓔ
49 Ⓐ Ⓑ Ⓒ Ⓓ Ⓔ	49 Ⓐ Ⓑ Ⓒ Ⓓ Ⓔ	49 Ⓐ Ⓑ Ⓒ Ⓓ Ⓔ	49 Ⓐ Ⓑ Ⓒ Ⓓ Ⓔ
50 Ⓐ Ⓑ Ⓒ Ⓓ Ⓔ	50 Ⓐ Ⓑ Ⓒ Ⓓ Ⓔ	50 Ⓐ Ⓑ Ⓒ Ⓓ Ⓔ	50 Ⓐ Ⓑ Ⓒ Ⓓ Ⓔ

EXAMINATION FORECAST

Section Number	Type	Minutes	Questions
	Writing Sample	30	—
I	Analytical Reasoning	45	30
II	Logical Reasoning	45	35
III	Analytical Reasoning	45	30
IV	Reading Comprehension	45	35

Writing Sample

Time: 30 Minutes

Joyce Peterson, a French major, is graduating from college at the end of the spring term. Beginning in the fall, she will start teaching French at a high school in the South. She wants to spend her summer studying in France. Write an essay in favor of one of two summer programs, one offered by the American Institute in Paris, the other by the University of Reims. Two considerations should guide your thinking:

1. Joyce wants to improve her French accent and learn the kind of informal speech used by ordinary French people. She also wants to become as familiar as possible with the routine of French life.

2. Joyce wants to visit some of the typical attractions in France, but she also wants to avoid spending too much money on her summer studies.

The AMERICAN INSTITUTE IN PARIS is an extension of an American University which offers French language and culture study programs in Paris. It offers a six-week program in the modern French language. Students from over twenty different countries will be enrolled in the program. Students attend classes five hours each day, five days a week; and all classes are taught by native speakers. The cost of the six-week program is $500, but that sum does not include room and board.

The UNIVERSITY OF REIMS is a public institution located in the small town of Reims, about 60 minutes by train from Paris, in the heart of the champagne-producing region. The University offers a four-week program in French and French literature. The classes are all taught by the faculty at the University. Additionally, University students attending summer school conduct small group tutorials. Students spend an average of six hours a day in formal classes and another two hours each day in their small group tutorials. Saturdays and Sundays are free days. The fee for the program is $1,400 which includes double occupancy housing in University dormitories and two meals a day in the University cafeteria.

PRACTICE EXAMINATION 1

SECTION I

Time—45 Minutes
35 Questions

Directions: In this section, the questions ask you to analyze and evaluate the reasoning in short paragraphs or passages. For some questions, all of the answer choices may conceivably be answers to the question asked. You should select the *best* answer to the question, that is, an answer which does not require you to make assumptions which violate commonsense standards by being implausible, redundant, irrelevant or inconsistent. After choosing the best answer, blacken the corresponding space on the answer sheet.

1. There are no lower bus fares from Washington, D.C. to New York City than those of Flash Bus Line.

   Which of the following is logically inconsistent with the above advertising claim?

   I. Long Lines Airways has a Washington, D.C. to New York City fare which is only one-half that charged by Flash.
   II. Rapid Transit Bus Company charges the same fare for a trip from Washington, D.C. to New York City as Flash charges.
   III. Cherokee Bus Corporation has a lower fare from New York City to Boston than does Flash.

   (A) I only
   (B) II only
   (C) I and II only
   (D) I, II, and III
   (E) None of the statements is inconsistent.

Questions 2 and 3

   Roberts is accused of a crime, and Edwards is the prosecution's key witness.

   I. Roberts can be convicted on the basis of Edwards' testimony against him.

   II. Edwards' testimony would show that Edwards himself participated in Roberts' wrongdoing.
   III. The crime of which Roberts is accused can only be committed by a person acting alone.
   IV. If the jury learns that Edwards himself committed some wrong, they will refuse to believe any part of his testimony.

2. If propositions I, II, and III are assumed to be true and IV false, which of the following best describes the outcome of the trial?
   (A) Both Edwards and Roberts will be convicted of the crime of which Roberts is accused.
   (B) Both Edwards and Roberts will be convicted of some crime other than the one with which Roberts is already charged.
   (C) Roberts will be convicted while Edwards will not be convicted.
   (D) Roberts will not be convicted.
   (E) Roberts will testify against Edwards.

3. If all four propositions are taken as a group, it can be pointed out that the scenario they describe is
   (A) a typical situation for a prosecutor
   (B) impossible because the propositions are logically inconsistent
   (C) unfair to Edwards, who may have to incriminate himself
   (D) unfair to Roberts, who may be convicted of the crime
   (E) one which Roberts' attorney has created

Questions 4 and 5

   There is a curious, though nonetheless obvious, contradiction in the suggestion that one person ought

105

to give up his life to save the life of the one other person who is not a more valuable member of the community. It is true that we glorify the sacrifice of the individual who throws herself in front of the attacker's bullets saving the life of her lover at the cost of her own. But here is the ____ (4) ____: Her life is as important as his. Nothing is gained in the transaction; not from the community's viewpoint, for one life was exchanged for another equally as important; not from the heroine's viewpoint, for she is ____ (5) ____; and not from the rescued lover's perspective, for he would willingly have exchanged places.

4. (A) beauty of human love
   (B) tragedy of life
   (C) inevitability of death
   (D) defining characteristic of human existence
   (E) paradox of self-sacrifice

5. (A) dying
   (B) in love
   (C) dead
   (D) a heroine
   (E) a faithful companion

6. It is a well-documented fact that for all teenaged couples who marry, the marriages of those who do not have children in the first year of their marriage survive more than twice as long as the marriages of those teenaged couples in which the wife does give birth within the first 12 months of marriage. Therefore, many divorces could be avoided if teenagers who marry were encouraged to seek counseling on birth control as soon after marriage as possible.

   The evidence regarding teenaged marriages supports the author's conclusion only if
   (A) in those couples to which a child was born within the first 12 months, there is not a significant number in which the wife was pregnant at the time of marriage
   (B) the children born during the first year of marriage to those divorcing couples lived with the teenaged couple
   (C) the child born into such a marriage did not die at birth
   (D) society actually has an interest in determining whether or not people should be divorced if there are not children involved
   (E) encouraging people to stay married when they do not plan to have any children is a good idea

7. CLARENCE: Mary is one of the most important executives at the Trendy Cola Company.
   PETER: How can that be? I know for a fact that Mary drinks only Hobart Cola.

   Peter's statement implies that
   (A) Hobart Cola is a subsidiary of Trendy Cola
   (B) Mary is an unimportant employee of Hobart Cola
   (C) all cola drinks taste pretty much alike
   (D) an executive uses only that company's products
   (E) Hobart is a better-tasting cola than Trendy

8. ERIKA: Participation in intramural competitive sports teaches students the importance of teamwork, for no one wants to let his teammates down.
   NICHOL: That is not correct. The real reason students play hard is that such programs place a premium on winning and no one wants to be a member of a losing team.

   Which of the following comments can most reasonably be made about the exchange between Erika and Nichol?
   (A) If fewer and fewer schools are sponsoring intramural sports programs now than a decade ago, Erika's position is undermined.
   (B) If high schools and universities provide financial assistance for the purchase of sports equipment, Nichol's assertion about the importance of winning is weakened.
   (C) If teamwork is essential to success in intramural competitive sports, Erika's position and Nichol's position are not necessarily incompatible.
   (D) Since the argument is one about motivation, it should be possible to resolve the issue by taking a survey of deans at schools which have intramural sports programs.
   (E) Since the question raised is about hidden psychological states, it is impossible to answer it.

9. Clark must have known that his sister Janet and not the governess pulled the trigger, but he silently stood by while the jury convicted the governess. Any person of clear conscience would have felt terrible for not having come forward with the information about his sister, and Clark lived with

that information until his death 30 years later. Since he was an extremely happy man, however, I conclude that he must have helped Janet commit the crime.

Which of the following assumptions must underlie the author's conclusion of the last sentence?
(A) Loyalty to members of one's family is conducive to contentment.
(B) Servants are not to be treated with the same respect as members of the peerage.
(C) Clark never had a bad conscience over his silence because he was also guilty of the crime.
(D) It is better to be virtuous than happy.
(E) It is actually better to be content in life than to behave morally towards one's fellow humans.

10. Current motion pictures give children a distorted view of the world. Animated features depict animals as loyal friends, compassionate creatures, and tender souls, while "spaghetti Westerns" portray men and women as deceitful and treacherous, cruel and wanton, hard and uncaring. Thus, children are taught to value animals more highly than other human beings.

Which of the following, if true, would weaken the author's conclusion?

 I. Children are not allowed to watch "spaghetti Westerns."
 II. The producers of animated features do not want children to regard animals as higher than human beings.
 III. Ancient fables, such as *Androcles and the Lion,* tell stories of the cooperation between humans and animals, and they usually end with a moral about human virtue.

(A) I only
(B) II only
(C) I and II only
(D) III only
(E) I, II, and III

11. There is something irrational about our system of laws. The criminal law punishes a person more severely for having successfully committed a crime than it does a person who fails in his attempt to commit the same crime—even though the same evil intention is present in both cases. But under the civil law a person who attempts to defraud his victim but is unsucessful is not required to pay damages.

Which of the following, if true, would most weaken the author's argument?
(A) Most persons who are imprisoned for crimes will commit another crime if they are ever released from prison.
(B) A person is morally culpable for his evil thoughts as well as for his evil deeds.
(C) There are more criminal laws on the books than there are civil laws on the books.
(D) A criminal trial is considerably more costly to the state than a civil trial.
(E) The goal of the criminal law is to punish the criminal, but the goal of the civil law is to compensate the victim.

12. In his most recent speech, my opponent, Governor Smith, accused me of having distorted the facts, misrepresenting his own position, suppressing information, and deliberately lying to the people.

Which of the following possible responses by this speaker would be LEAST relevant to his dispute with Governor Smith?
(A) Governor Smith would not have begun to smear me if he did not sense that his own campaign was in serious trouble.
(B) Governor Smith apparently misunderstood my characterization of his position, so I will attempt to state more clearly my understanding of it.
(C) At the time I made those remarks, certain key facts were not available, but new information uncovered by my staff does support the position I took at that time.
(D) I can only wish Governor Smith had specified those points he considered to be lies so that I could have responded to them now.
(E) With regard to the allegedly distorted facts, the source of my information is a Department of Transportation publication entitled "Safe Driving."

13. Politicians are primarily concerned with their own survival; artists are concerned with revealing truth. Of course, the difference in their reactions is readily predictable. For example, while the governmental leaders wrote laws to ensure the truimph of industrialization in Western Europe, artists painted, wrote about, and composed music in response to the horrible conditions created by the Industrial Revolution. Only later did political leaders come to see what the artists had immediately perceived, and then only through a glass darkly. Experience teaches us that _____.

Which of the following represents the most logical continuation of the passage?
(A) artistic vision perceives in advance of political practice
(B) artists are utopian by nature while governmental leaders are practical
(C) throughout history political leaders have not been very responsive to the needs of their people
(D) the world would be a much better place to live if only artists would become kings
(E) history is the best judge of the progress of civilization

14. A parent must be constant and even-handed in the imposition of burdens and punishments and the distribution of liberties and rewards. In good times, a parent who too quickly bestows rewards creates an expectation of future rewards which he may be unable to fulfill during bad times. In bad times, a parent who waits too long to impose the punishment gives the impression that his response was forced, and the child may interpret this as ―――――――.

Which of the following represents the most logical continuation of the passage?
(A) a signal from his parent that the parent is no longer interested in the child's welfare
(B) a sign of weakness in the parent which he can exploit
(C) indicating a willingness on the part of the parent to bargain away liberties in exchange for the child's assuming some new responsibilities
(D) an open invitation to retaliate
(E) a symbol of his becoming an adult

15. As dietitian for this 300-person school I am concerned about the sudden shortage of beef. It seems that we will have to begin to serve fish as our main source of protein. Even though beef costs more per pound than fish, I expect that the price I pay for protein will rise if I continue to serve the same amount of protein using fish as I did with beef.

The speaker makes which of the following assumptions?
(A) Fish is more expensive per pound than beef.
(B) Students will soon be paying more for their meals.
(C) Cattle ranchers make greater profits than fishermen.

(D) Per measure of protein, fish is more expensive than beef.
(E) Cattle are more costly to raise than fish.

Questions 16 and 17

New Weight Loss Salons invites all of you who are dissatisfied with your present build to join our Exercise for Lunch Bunch. Instead of putting on even more weight by eating lunch, you actually cut down on your daily caloric intake by exercising rather than eating. Every single one of us has the potential to be slim and fit, so take the initiative and begin losing excess pounds today. Don't eat! Exercise! You'll lose weight and feel stronger, happier, and more attractive.

16. Which of the following, if true, would weaken the logic of the argument made by the advertisement?

I. Most people will experience increased desire for food as a result of the exercise and will lose little weight as a result of enrolling in the program.
II. Nutritionists agree that skipping lunch is not a healthy practice.
III. In our society, obesity is regarded as unattractive.
IV. A person who is too thin is probably not in good health.

(A) I only
(B) I and II only
(C) II and III only
(D) III and IV only
(E) I, II, and III

17. A person hearing this advertisement countered, "I know some people who are not overweight and are still unhappy and unattractive." The author of the advertisement could logically and consistently reply to this objection by pointing out that he never claimed that
(A) being overweight is always caused by unhappiness
(B) being overweight is the only cause of unhappiness and unattractiveness
(C) unhappiness and unattractiveness can cause someone to be overweight
(D) unhappiness necessarily leads to being overweight
(E) unhappiness and unattractiveness are always found together

18. Since all swans which I have encountered have been white, it follows that the swans I will see when I visit the Bronx Zoo will also be white.

Which of the following most closely parallels the reasoning of the preceding argument?
(A) Some birds are incapable of flight; therefore, swans are probably incapable of flight.
(B) Every ballet I have attended has failed to interest me; so a theatrical production which fails to interest me must be a ballet.
(C) Since all cases of severe depression I have encountered were susceptible to treatment by chlorpromazine, there must be something in the chlorpromazine which adjusts the patient's brain chemistry.
(D) Because every society has a word for *justice*, the concept of fair play must be inherent in the biological makeup of the human species.
(E) Since no medicine I have tried for my allergy has ever helped, this new product will probably not work either.

Questions 19–21

The blanks in the following paragraph mark deletions from the text. For each question, select the phrase which most appropriately completes the text.

Libertarians argue that laws making suicide a criminal act are both foolish and an unwarranted intrusion on individual conscience. With regard to the first, they point out that there is no penalty which the law can assess which inflicts greater injury than the crime itself. As for the second, they argue that it is no business of the state to prevent suicide, for whether it is right for a person to inflict fatal injury on himself as opposed to others is a matter between him and his God— one in which the state, by the terms of the Constitution, may not interfere. Such arguments, however, seem to me to be ill-conceived. In the first place, the libertarian makes the mistaken assumption that deterrence is the only goal of the law. I maintain that the laws we have proscribing suicide are ——(19)——.

By making it a crime to take any life—even one's own—we make a public announcement of our shared conviction that each person is unique and valuable. In the second place, while it must be conceded that the doctrine of the separation of church and state is a useful one, it need not be admitted that suicide is a crime ——(20)——. And here we need not have recourse to the possi-

bility that a potential suicide might, if given the opportunity, repent of his decision. Suicide inflicts a cost upon us all: the emotional cost on those close to the suicide; an economic cost in the form of the loss of production of a mature and trained member of the society which falls on us all; and a cost to humanity at large for the loss of a member of our human community. The difficulty with the libertarian position is that it is an oversimplification. It assesses the evil of ——(21)——.

19. (A) drafted to make it more difficult to commit suicide
(B) passed by legislators in response to pressures by religious lobbying groups
(C) written in an effort to protect our democratic liberties, not undermine them
(D) important because they educate all to the value of human life
(E) outdated because they belong to a time when church and state were not so clearly divided

20. (A) which does not necessarily lead to more serious crimes
(B) without victim
(C) as well as a sin
(D) which cannot be prevented
(E) without motive

21. (A) crimes only in economic terms
(B) suicide only from the perspective of the person taking his life
(C) laws by weighing them against the evil of the liberty lost by their enforcement
(D) the mingling of church and state without sufficient regard to the constitutional protections
(E) suicide in monetary units without proper regard to the importance of life

22. All high-powered racing engines have stochastic fuel injection. Stochastic fuel injection is not a feature which is normally included in the engines of production-line vehicles.
Passenger sedans are production-line vehicles.

Which of the following conclusions can be drawn from these statements?
(A) Passenger sedans do not usually have stochastic fuel injection.
(B) Stochastic fuel injection is found only in high-powered racing cars.

(C) Car manufacturers do not include stochastic fuel injection in passenger cars because they fear accidents.

(D) Purchasers of passenger cars do not normally purchase stochastic fuel injection because it is expensive.

(E) Some passenger sedans are high-powered racing vehicles.

23. During New York City's fiscal crisis of the late 1970's, governmental leaders debated whether to offer federal assistance to New York City. One economist who opposed the suggestion asked, "Are we supposed to help out New York City every time it gets into financial problems?"

The economist's question can be criticized because it

(A) uses ambiguous terms

(B) assumes everyone else agrees New York City should be helped

(C) appeals to emotions rather than using logic

(D) relies upon second-hand reports rather than first-hand accounts

(E) completely ignores the issue at hand

24. Some philosophers have argued that there exist certain human or natural rights which belong to all human beings by virtue of their humanity. But a review of the laws of different societies shows that the rights accorded a person vary from society to society and even within a society over time. Since there is no right that is universally protected, there are no natural rights.

A defender of the theory that natural rights do exist might respond to this objection by arguing that

(A) some human beings do not have any natural rights

(B) some human rights are natural while others derive from a source such as a constitution

(C) people in one society may have natural rights which people in another society lack

(D) all societies have some institution which protects the rights of an individual in that society

(E) natural rights may exist even though they are not protected by some societies

Questions 25 and 26

The single greatest weakness of American parties is their inability to achieve cohesion in the legislature. Although there is some measure of party unity, it is not uncommon for the majority party to be unable to implement important legislation. The unity is strongest during election campaigns; after the primary elections, the losing candidates all promise their support to the party nominee. By the time the Congress convenes, the unity has dissipated. This phenomenon is attributable to the fragmented nature of party politics. The national committees are no more than feudal lords who receive nominal fealty from their vassals. A congressman builds his own power upon a local base. Consequently, a congressman is likely to be responsive to local special interest groups. Evidence of this is seen in the differences in voting patterns between the upper and lower houses. In the Senate, where terms are longer, there is more party unity.

25. Which of the following, if true, would most strengthen the author's argument?

(A) On 30 key issues, 18 of the 67 majority party members in the Senate voted against the party leaders.

(B) On 30 key issues, 70 of the 305 majority party members in the House voted against the party leaders.

(C) On 30 key issues, over half the members of the minority party in both houses voted with the majority party against the leaders of the minority party.

(D) Of 30 key legislative proposals introduced by the president, only eight passed both houses.

(E) Of 30 key legislative proposals introduced by a president whose party controlled a majority in both houses, only four passed both houses.

26. Which of the following, if true, would most weaken the author's argument?

(A) Congressmen receive funds from the national party committee.

(B) Senators vote against the party leaders only two-thirds as often as House members.

(C) The primary duty of an officeholder is to be responsive to his local constituency rather than party leaders.

(D) There is more unity among minority party members than among majority party members.

(E) Much legislation is passed each session despite party disunity.

27. MME. CHARPENTIER: Research has demonstrated that the United States, which has the most extensive health care industry in the world, has only

the 17th lowest infant mortality rate in the world. This forces me to conclude that medical technology causes babies to die.

M. ADAMANTE: That is ludicrous. We know that medical care is not equally available to all. Infant mortality is more likely a function of low income than of medical technology.

M. Adamante attacks Mme. Charpentier's reasoning in which way?
(A) by questioning the validity of her supporting data
(B) by offering an alternative explanation of the data
(C) by suggesting that her argument is circular
(D) by defining an intermediate cause
(E) by implying that her data leads to the opposite conclusion

28. When this proposal to reduce welfare benefits is brought up for debate, we are sure to hear claims by the liberal Congressmen that the bill will be detrimental to poor people. These politicians fail to understand, however, that budget reductions are accompanied by tax cuts—so everyone will have more money to spend, not less.

Which of the following, if true, would undermine the author's position?

I. Poor people tend to vote for liberal Congressmen who promise to raise welfare benefits.
II. Poor people pay little or no taxes so that a tax cut would be of little advantage to them.
III. Any tax advantage which the poor will receive will be more than offset by cuts in the government services they now receive.

(A) I only
(B) III only
(C) II and III only
(D) II only
(E) I, II, and III

29. Many people ask, "How effective is Painaway?" So to find out we have been checking the medicine cabinets of the apartments in this typical building. As it turns out, eight out of ten contain a bottle of Painaway. Doesn't it stand to reason that you, too, should have the most effective pain-reliever on the market?

The appeal of this advertisement would be most weakened by which of the following pieces of evidence?

(A) Painaway distributed complimentary bottles of medicine to most apartments in the building two days before the advertisement was made.
(B) The actor who made the advertisement takes a pain-reliever manufactured by a competitor of Painaway.
(C) Most people want a fast, effective pain-reliever.
(D) Many people take the advice of their neighborhood druggists about pain-relievers.
(E) A government survey shows that many people take a pain-reliever before it is really needed.

Questions 30 and 31

An artist must suffer for his art say these successful entrepreneurs who attempt to pass themselves off as artists. They auction off to the highest bidder, usually a fool in his own right, the most mediocre of drawings; and then, from their well-laid tables, they have the unmitigated gall to imply that they themselves——(30)——.

30. Choose the answer which best completes the paragraph.
(A) are connoisseurs of art
(B) suffer deprivation for the sake of their work
(C) are artists
(D) know art better than the art critics do
(E) do not enjoy a good meal

31. Which of the following must underlie the author's position?

I. One must actually suffer to do great art.
II. Financial deprivation is the only suffering an artist undergoes.
III. Art critics have little real expertise and are consequently easily deceived.

(A) I only
(B) II only
(C) I and II only
(D) II and III only
(E) I, II, and III

Questions 32 and 33

Stock market analysts always attribute a sudden drop in the market to some domestic or international political crisis. I maintain, however, that these declines are attributable to the phases of the moon, which also cause periodic political upheavals and increases in tension in world affairs.

32. Which of the following best describes the author's method of questioning the claim of market analysts?
    (A) He presents a counter-example.
    (B) He presents statistical evidence.
    (C) He suggests an alternative causal linkage.
    (D) He appeals to generally accepted beliefs.
    (E) He demonstrates that market analysts' reports are unreliable.

33. It can be inferred that the author is critical of the stock analysts because he
    (A) believes that they have oversimplified the connection between political crisis and fluctuations of the market
    (B) knows that the stock market generally shows more gains than losses
    (C) suspects that stock analysts have a vested interest in the stock market, and are therefore likely to distort their explanations
    (D) anticipates making large profits in the market himself
    (E) is worried that if the connection between political events and stock market prices becomes well-known, unscrupulous investors will take advantage of the information

34. This piece of pottery must surely date from the late Minoan period. The dress of the female figures, particularly the bare and emphasized breasts, and the activities of the people depicted, note especially the importance of the bull, are both highly suggestive of this period. These factors, when coupled with the black, semi-gloss glaze which results from firing the pot in a sealed kiln at a low temperature, make the conclusion a virtual certainty.

Which of the following is a basic assumption made by the author of this explanation?
(A) Black, semi-gloss glazed pottery was made only during the late Minoan period.
(B) The bull is an animal which was important to most ancient cultures.
(C) Throughout the long history of the Minoan people, their artisans decorated pottery with semi-nude women and bulls.
(D) By analyzing the style and materials of any work of art, an expert can pinpoint the date of its creation.
(E) There are key characteristics of works of art which can be shown to be typical of a particular period.

35. Most radicals who argue for violent revolution and complete overthrow of our existing society have no clear idea what will emerge from the destruction. They just assert that things are so bad now that any change would have to be a change for the better. But surely this is mistaken, for things might actually turn out to be worse.

The most effective point which can be raised against this argument is that the author says nothing about
(A) the manner in which the radicals might foment their revolution
(B) the specific results of the revolution which would be changes for the worse
(C) the economic arguments the radicals use to persuade people to join in their cause
(D) the fact that most people are really satisfied with the present system so that the chance of total revolution is very small
(E) the loss of life and property which is likely to accompany total destruction of a society

STOP

IF YOU FINISH BEFORE TIME IS CALLED, CHECK YOUR WORK ON THIS SECTION ONLY. DO NOT WORK ON ANY OTHER SECTION IN THE TEST.

SECTION II

Time—45 Minutes
30 Questions

Directions: Each group of questions is based on a set of propositions or conditions. Drawing a rough picture or diagram may help in answering some of the questions. Choose the best answer for each question and blacken the corresponding space on your answer sheet.

Questions 1–6

A railway system consists of six stations, G, H, I, J, K, and L. Trains run only according to following conditions:

From G to H
From H to G and from H to I
From I to J
From J to H and from J to K
From L to G; from L to K, and from L to I
From K to J

It is possible to transfer at a station for another train.

1. How is it possible to get from H to J?
   (A) a direct train from H to J
   (B) a train to G and transfer for a train to J
   (C) a train to L and transfer for a train to J
   (D) a train to I and transfer for a train to J
   (E) It is impossible to reach J from H.

2. Which of the following stations CANNOT be reached by a train from any of the other stations?
   (A) G
   (B) H
   (C) I
   (D) K
   (E) L

3. From which of the following stations is it possible to reach I with exactly one transfer?
   I. G
   II. H
   III. J
   IV. K

   (A) I only
   (B) I and III only
   (C) I, II, and IV only
   (D) I, III, and IV only
   (E) I, II, III, and IV

4. What is the greatest number of stations that can be visited without visiting any station more than once?
   (A) 2
   (B) 3
   (C) 4
   (D) 5
   (E) 6

5. Which of the following trips requires the greatest number of transfers?
   (A) G to I
   (B) H to K
   (C) L to H
   (D) L to I
   (E) L to K

6. If station I is closed, which of the following trips is impossible?
   (A) G to J
   (B) J to K
   (C) L to K
   (D) L to J
   (E) L to G

Questions 7–12

A travel agent is arranging tours which visit various cities: L, M, N, O, P, Q, R, S, T. Each tour must be arranged in accordance with the following restrictions:

If M is included in a tour, both Q and R must also be included.
P can be included in a tour only if O is also included.
If Q is included in a tour, M must be included along with N or T or both.
P and Q cannot both be included in a tour.
A tour cannot include O, R, and T.
A tour cannot include N, S, and R.
A tour cannot include L and R.

7. If M is included in a tour, what is the minimum number of other cities which must be included in the tour?
   (A) 2
   (B) 3

(C) 4
(D) 5
(E) 6

8. Which of the following cities cannot be included in a tour which includes P?
   (A) M
   (B) N
   (C) O
   (D) S
   (E) R

9. Which of the following is an acceptable group of cities for a tour?
   (A) M, N, O, P
   (B) M, N, Q, R
   (C) M, N, Q, S
   (D) L, M, Q, R
   (E) N, S, R, T

10. Which one city would have to be deleted from the group M, Q, O, R, T to form an acceptable tour?
    (A) M
    (B) Q
    (C) O
    (D) R
    (E) T

11. Which of the following could be made into an acceptable tour by adding exactly one more city?
    (A) L, O, R
    (B) M, P, Q
    (C) M, Q, R
    (D) N, S, R
    (E) R, T, P

12. Exactly how many of the cities could be used for a tour consisting of only one city?
    (A) 2
    (B) 3
    (C) 4
    (D) 5
    (E) 6

Questions 13–18

A child is stringing 11 different colored beads on a string.

Of the 11, four are yellow, three are red, two are blue, and two are green.
The red beads are adjacent to one another.

The blue beads are adjacent to one another.
The green beads are not adjacent to one another.
A red bead is at one end of the string and a green bead is at the other end.

13. If the sixth and seventh beads are blue and the tenth bead is red, which of the following must be true?
    (A) The second bead is green.
    (B) The fifth bead is yellow.
    (C) The eighth bead is green.
    (D) A green bead is next to a yellow bead.
    (E) A blue bead is next to a green bead.

14. If the four yellow beads are next to each other, and if the tenth bead is yellow, which of the following beads must be blue?
    (A) the fourth
    (B) the fifth
    (C) the sixth
    (D) the seventh
    (E) the eighth

15. If each blue bead is next to a green bead, and if the four yellow beads are next to each other, then which of the following beads must be yellow?

    I.   the fourth
    II. the fifth
    III. the sixth
    IV. the seventh

    (A) I and II only
    (B) II and III only
    (C) III and IV only
    (D) I, II, and III
    (E) II, III, and IV

16. If the fifth and sixth beads are blue and the ninth bead is red, which of the following must be true?
    (A) One of the green beads is next to a blue bead.
    (B) One of the red beads is next to a green bead.
    (C) Each yellow bead is next to at least one other yellow bead.
    (D) The second bead is yellow.
    (E) The eighth bead is yellow.

17. If the fifth, eighth, ninth, and tenth beads are yellow, which of the following must be true?

    I. The fourth bead is green.
    II. The sixth bead is blue.

III. Each green bead is next to at least one yellow bead.

(A) I only
(B) II only
(C) I and II only
(D) I and III only
(E) I, II, and III

18. If one green bead is next to a red bead and the other green bead is next to a blue bead, which of the following must be true?
(A) The second bead is blue.
(B) The fourth bead is green
(C) The fourth bead is yellow.
(D) The seventh bead is yellow.
(E) The eighth bead is green.

Questions 19–24

The Executive Officer of a college English department is hiring adjunct-faculty for her evening courses. She must offer exactly eight courses during the academic year, four in the fall semester and four in the spring semester. The candidates are: J, K, L, M, N and O. Each person, if hired, must teach the following:

J must teach one course on Marlowe and one course on Joyce.
K must teach one course on Shakespeare and one course on Keats.
L must teach one course on Marlowe and one course on Chaucer.
M must teach one course on Shakespeare, one course on Marlowe, and one course on Keats.
N must teach one course on Joyce, one course on Keats, and one course on Chaucer.
O must teach one course on Shakespeare, one course on Marlowe, and one course on Joyce.

Only one course on an author can be offered in a single semester.

19. Which of the following combinations of teachers can be hired?
(A) J, K, and N
(B) K, M, and N
(C) K, M, and O
(D) L, M, and O
(E) L, N, and O

20. If L and N are hired, and if N is assigned to teach only in the spring semester, which of the following could be true?

(A) Neither M nor O will be hired.
(B) L will teach only in the spring semester.
(C) L will teach only in the fall semester.
(D) Courses on Keats and Joyce will be offered in the fall semester.
(E) Courses on Shakespeare and Marlowe will be offered in the spring semester.

21. If M and N are hired, and if M will teach only one of the two semesters and N the other, which of the following must be true?
(A) J is hired.
(B) K is hired.
(C) L is hired.
(D) A course on Shakespeare will be offered in the fall semester.
(E) A course on Marlowe will be offered in the spring semester.

22. If K and N are hired, which of the following must be true?

I. A course on Shakespeare is offered both semesters.
II. A course on Marlowe is offered both semesters.
III. A course on Joyce is offered both semesters.

(A) I only
(B) III only
(C) I and II only
(D) I and III only
(E) I, II, and III

23. If L is hired and will teach both her courses in the fall semester, which of the following must be true?
(A) M and N are hired.
(B) M and O are hired.
(C) N and O are hired.
(D) A course on Joyce will be offered in the spring semester.
(E) A course on Chaucer will be offered in the spring semester.

24. If K, N, and O are hired, and if N will teach all three of her courses in the fall semester, all of the following must be true EXCEPT:
(A) A course on Keats will be taught in the spring semester.
(B) A course on Marlowe will be taught in the spring semester.
(C) Courses on Keats and Joyce will be taught in both semesters.

(D) A course on Marlowe and a course on Shakespeare will be taught in the spring semester.

(E) A course on Shakespeare and a course on Chaucer will be taught in the spring semester.

Questions 25–30

Five boys—J, K, L, M, and N—and five girls—V, W, X, Y, and Z—will march in a graduation procession. The procession will consist of five rows of two children each, one behind the other. The order of the procession is governed by the following conditions:

Each row must consist of exactly one boy and one girl.

W must march somewhere ahead of X, and Y must march somewhere ahead of Z.

J must march somewhere ahead of both K and L.

L must march somewhere ahead of both K and M.

N cannot march in the same row as V.

25. Which of the following is a possible order for the procession?

	First	Second	Third	Fourth	Fifth
(A)	J,W	L,Y	M,X	K,Z	N,V
(B)	J,V	L,X	K,Y	N,W	M,Z
(C)	K,W	N,X	J,Y	L,Z	M,V
(D)	N,Y	J,V	L,W	M,X	K,Z
(E)	N,W	J,V	K,Y	L,Z	M,X

26. All of the following are acceptable orders for the procession EXCEPT:

	First	Second	Third	Fourth	Fifth
(A)	J,W	L,X	M,Y	K,V	N,Z
(B)	J,Y	L,Z	M,V	N,W	K,X
(C)	J,V	N,Z	K,Y	L,W	M,X
(D)	N,W	J,X	L,Y	K,Z	M,V
(E)	N,Y	J,W	L,Z	K,X	M,V

27. Which of the following must be true of the procession?
(A) J must march ahead of M.
(B) J must march ahead of N.
(C) K must march ahead of M.
(D) W must march ahead of Y.
(E) X must march ahead of Z.

28. If L marches in the second row and V marches in the fourth row, then which of the following is a complete and accurate list of the rows in which N could march?
(A) first
(B) first, third
(C) third, fourth
(D) third, fifth
(E) third, fourth, fifth

29. If N marches two rows ahead of L and Z, which of the following must be true?
(A) J marches in the second row.
(B) W marches in the first row.
(C) W marches with N.
(D) Y marches with J.
(E) Z marches with M.

30. If L and Z march in the row immediately ahead of N, then which of the following must be true?
(A) J marches with V.
(B) J marches with W.
(C) N marches with W.
(D) N marches with X.
(E) M marches with V.

STOP

END OF SECTION. IF YOU HAVE ANY TIME LEFT, GO OVER YOUR WORK IN THIS SECTION ONLY. DO NOT WORK IN ANY OTHER SECTION OF THE TEST.

SECTION III

Time—45 Minutes
35 Questions

Directions: Below each of the following passages, you will find questions or incomplete statements about the passage. Each statement or question is followed by five lettered words or expressions. Select the word or expression that most satisfactorily completes each statement, or answers each question in accordance with the meaning of the passage. After you have chosen the best answer, blacken the corresponding space on the answer sheet.

War has escaped the battlefield and now can, with modern guidance systems on missiles, touch virtually every square yard of the earth's surface. It no longer involves only the military profession, but engulfs also
5 entire civilian populations. Nuclear weapons have made major war unthinkable. We are forced, however, to think about the unthinkable because a thermonuclear war could come by accident or miscalculation. We must accept the paradox of maintaining a capacity
10 to fight such a war so that we will never have to do so.
War has also lost most of its utility in achieving the traditional goals of conflict. Control of territory carries with it the obligation to provide subject
15 peoples certain administrative, health, education, and other social services; such obligations far outweigh the benefits of control. If the ruled population is ethnically or racially different from the rulers, tensions and chronic unrest often exist which further reduce the
20 benefits and increase the costs of domination. Large populations no longer necessarily enhance state power and, in the absence of high levels of economic development, can impose severe burdens on food supply, jobs, and the broad range of services expected of mod-
25 ern governments. The noneconomic security reasons for the control of territory have been progressively undermined by the advances of modern technology. The benefits of forcing another nation to surrender its wealth are vastly outweighed by the benefits of per-
30 suading that nation to produce and exchange goods and services. In brief, imperialism no longer pays.
Making war has been one of the most persistent of human activities in the 80 centuries since men and women settled in cities and became thereby "civi-
35 lized," but the modernization of the past 80 years has fundamentally changed the role and function of war. In pre-modernized societies, successful warfare

brought significant material rewards, the most obvious of which were the stored wealth of the defeated.
40 Equally important was human labor——control over people as slaves or levies for the victor's army——and the productive capacity of agricultural lands and mines. Successful warfare also produced psychic benefits. The removal or destruction of a threat brought a
45 sense of security, and power gained over others created pride and national self-esteem.
Warfare was also the most complex, broad-scale and demanding activity of pre-modernized people. The challenges of leading men into battle, organizing,
50 moving and supporting armies, attracted the talents of the most vigorous, enterprising, intelligent and imaginative men in the society. "Warrior" and "statesman" were usually synonymous, and the military was one of the few professions in which an able, ambitious
55 boy of humble origin could rise to the top. In the broader cultural context, war was accepted in the pre-modernized society as a part of the human condition, a mechanism of change, and an unavoidable, even noble, aspect of life. The excitement and drama of war
60 made it a vital part of literature and legends.

1. The primary purpose of the passage is to
   (A) theorize about the role of the warrior-statesman in pre-modernized society
   (B) explain the effects of war on both modernized and pre-modernized societies
   (C) contrast the value of war in a modernized society with its value in pre-modernized society
   (D) discuss the political and economic circumstances which lead to war in pre-modernized societies
   (E) examine the influence of the development of nuclear weapons on the possibility of war

2. According to the passage, leaders of pre-modernized society considered war to be
   (A) a valid tool of national policy
   (B) an immoral act of aggression
   (C) economically wasteful and socially unfeasible
   (D) restricted in scope to military participants
   (E) necessary to spur development of unoccupied lands

3. The author most likely places the word "civilized" in quotation marks (lines 34–35) in order to
   (A) show dissatisfaction at not having found a better word
   (B) acknowledge that the word was borrowed from another source
   (C) express irony that war should be a part of civilization
   (D) impress upon the reader the tragedy of war
   (E) raise a question about the value of war in modernized society

4. The author mentions all of the following as possible reasons for going to war in a pre-modernized society EXCEPT
   (A) possibility of material gain
   (B) promoting deserving young men to higher positions
   (C) potential for increasing the security of the nation
   (D) desire to capture productive farming lands
   (E) need for workers to fill certain jobs

5. The author is primarily concerned with discussing how
   (A) political decisions are reached
   (B) economic and social conditions have changed
   (C) technology for making war has improved
   (D) armed conflict has changed
   (E) war lost its value as a policy tool

6. Which of the following best describes the tone of the passage?
   (A) outraged and indignant
   (B) scientific and detached
   (C) humorous and wry
   (D) fearful and alarmed
   (E) concerned and optimistic

7. With which of the following statements about a successfully completed program of nuclear disarmament would the author most likely agree?
   (A) Without nuclear weapons, war in modernized society would have the same value it had in pre-modernized society.
   (B) In the absence of the danger of nuclear war, national leaders could use powerful conventional weapons to make great gains from war.
   (C) Eliminating nuclear weapons is likely to in-

crease the danger of an all-out, world-wide military engagement.
   (D) Even without the danger of a nuclear disaster, the costs of winning a war have made armed conflict on a large scale virtually obsolete.
   (E) War is caused by aggressive instincts, so if nuclear weapons were no longer available, national leaders would use conventional weapons to reach the same end.

Although it is now possible to bring most high blood pressure under control, the causes of essential hypertension remain elusive. Understanding how hypertension begins is at least partly a problem of under-
5 standing when in life it begins; and this may be very early—perhaps within the first few months. Since the beginning of the century, physicians have been aware that hypertension may run in families, but before the 1970's, studies of the familial aggregation of blood
10 pressure treated only populations 15 years of age or older. Few studies were attempted in younger persons because of a prevailing notion that blood pressures in this age group were difficult to measure or unreliable and because essential hypertension was widely re-
15 garded as a disease of adults.
In 1971, a study of 700 children, ages two to fourteen, used a special blood pressure recorder which minimizes observer error and allows for standardization of blood pressure readings. Before then, it had
20 been well established that the blood pressure of adults aggregates familially, that is, the similarities between the blood pressure of an individual and his siblings are generally too great to be explained by chance. The 1971 study showed that familial clustering was mea-
25 surable in children as well, suggesting that factors responsible for essential hypertension are acquired in childhood. Additional epidemiological studies demonstrated a clear tendency for the children to retain the same blood pressure patterns, relative to their peers,
30 four years later. Thus a child with blood pressure higher or lower than the norm would tend to remain higher or lower with increasing age.
Meanwhile, other investigators uncovered a complex of physiologic roles—including blood pres-
35 sure—for a vasoactive system called the kallikrein-kinin system. Kallikreins are enzymes in the kidney and blood plasma which act on precursors called kininogens to produce vasoactive peptides called kinins. Several different kinins are produced, at least
40 three of which are powerful blood vessel dilators. Apparently, the kallikrein-kinin system normally tends to offset the elevations in arterial pressure which

result from the secretion of salt-conserving hormones
such as aldosterone on the one hand and from activa-
45 tion of the sympathetic nervous system (which tends
to constrict blood vessels) on the other hand.

It is also known that urinary kallikrein excretion is
abnormally low in subjects with essential hypertension. Levels of urinary kallikrein in children are
50 inversely related to the diastolic blood pressures of
both children and their mothers. Children with the
lowest kallikrein levels are found in the families with
the highest blood pressures. In addition, black children tend to show somewhat lower urinary kallikrein
55 levels than white children, and blacks are more likely
to have high blood pressure. There is a great deal to be
learned about the biochemistry and physiologic roles
of the kallikrein-kinin system. But there is the possibility that essential hypertension will prove to have
60 biochemical precursors.

8. The author is primarily concerned with
   (A) questioning the assumption behind certain
       experiments involving children under the
       age of 15
   (B) describing new scientific findings about high
       blood pressure and suggesting some implica-
       tions
   (C) describing two different methods for study-
       ing the causes of high blood pressure
   (D) revealing a discrepancy between the findings
       of epidemiological studies and laboratory
       studies on essential hypertension
   (E) arguing that high blood pressure may be
       influenced by familial factors

9. Which of the following are factors mentioned by
   the author which discouraged studies of essential
   hypertension in children?

   I. the belief that children generally did not suf-
      fer from essential hypertension
   II. the belief that it was difficult or impossible
       to measure accurately blood pressure in chil-
       dren
   III. the belief that blood pressure in adults aggre-
        gates familially

   (A) I only
   (B) II only
   (C) III only
   (D) I and II only
   (E) I, II, and III

10. The argument in the passage leads most naturally
    to which of the following conclusions?

(A) A low output of urinary kallikrein is a likely
    cause of high blood pressure in children.
(B) The kallikrein-kinin system plays an impor-
    tant role in the regulation of blood pres-
    sure
(C) Essential hypertension may have biochemi-
    cal precursors which may be useful predic-
    tors even in children.
(D) The failure of the body to produce sufficient
    amounts of kinins is the cause of essential
    hypertension.
(E) It is now possible to predict high blood pres-
    sure by using familial aggregations and uri-
    nary kallikrein measurement.

11. The author refers to the somewhat lower urinary
    kallikrein levels in black children (lines 53–55)
    in order to
    (A) support the thesis that kallikrein levels are
        inversely related to blood pressure
    (B) highlight the special health problems in-
        volved in treating populations with high con-
        centrations of black children
    (C) offer a causal explanation for the difference
        in urinary kallikrein levels between black
        and white children
    (D) suggest that further study needs to be done
        on the problem of high blood pressure
        among black adults
    (E) prove that hypertension can be treated if
        those persons likely to have high blood pres-
        sure can be found

12. The author suggests that the kallikrein-kinin sys-
    tem may affect blood pressure in which of the
    following ways?

    I. by directly opposing the tendency of the
       sympathetic nervous system to constrict
       blood vessels
    II. by producing kinins which tend to dilate
        blood vessels
    III. by suppressing the production of hormones
         such as aldosterone

    (A) I only
    (B) II only
    (C) I and III only
    (D) II and III only
    (E) I, II, and III

13. The evidence that a child with blood pressure
    higher or lower than the norm would tend to

remain so with increasing age (lines 30–32) is introduced by the author in order to

(A) suggest that essential hypertension may have biochemical causes

(B) show that high blood pressure can be detected in children under the age of 15

(C) provide evidence that factors affecting blood pressure are already present in children

(D) propose that screening of children for high blood pressure should be increased

(E) refute arguments that blood pressure in children cannot be measured reliably

14. The author presents his argument primarily by

(A) contrasting two methods of doing scientific research

(B) providing experimental evidence against a conclusion

(C) presenting new scientific findings for a conclusion

(D) analyzing a new theory and showing its defects

(E) criticizing scientific research on blood pressure done before 1971

Many critics of the current welfare system argue that existing welfare regulations foster family instability. They maintain that those regulations, which exclude most poor husband-and-wife families from Aid to Families with Dependent Children assistance grants, contribute to the problem of family dissolution. Thus, they conclude that expanding the set of families eligible for family assistance plans or guaranteed income measures would result in a marked strengthening of the low-income family structure.

If all poor families could receive welfare, would the incidence of instability change markedly? The answer to this question depends on the relative importance of three categories of potential welfare recipients. The first is the "cheater"——the husband who is reported to have abandoned his family, but in fact disappears only when the social caseworker is in the neighborhood. The second consists of a loving husband and devoted father who, sensing his own inadequacy as a provider, leaves so that his wife and children may enjoy the relative benefit provided by public assistance. There is very little evidence that these categories are significant.

The third category is the unhappily married couple, who remain together out of a sense of economic responsibility for their children, because of the high costs of separation, or because of the consumption benefits of marriage. This group is large. The formation, maintenance, and dissolution of the family is in large part a function of the relative balance between the benefits and costs of marriage as seen by the individual members of the marriage. The major benefit generated by the creation of a family is the expansion of the set of consumption possibilities. The benefits from such a partnership depend largely on the relative dissimilarity of the resources or basic endowments each partner brings to the marriage. Persons with similar productive capacities have less economic "cement" holding their marriage together. Since the family performs certain functions society regards as vital, a complex network of social and legal buttresses has evolved to reinforce marriage. Much of the variation in marital stability across income classes can be explained by the variation in costs of dissolution imposed by society, e.g., division of property, alimony, child support, and the social stigma attached to divorce.

Marital stability is related to the costs of achieving an acceptable agreement on family consumption and production and to the prevailing social price of instability in the marriage partners' social-economic group. Expected AFDC income exerts pressures on family instability by reducing the cost of dissolution. To the extent that welfare is a form of government-subsidized alimony payments, it reduces the institutional costs of separation and guarantees a minimal standard of living for wife and children. So welfare opportunities are a significant determinant of family instability in poor neighborhoods, but this is not the result of AFDC regulations that exclude most intact families from coverage. Rather, welfare-related instability occurs because public assistance lowers both the benefits of marriage and the costs of its disruption by providing a system of government-subsidized alimony payments.

15. The author is primarily concerned with

(A) interpreting the results of a survey

(B) discussing the role of the father in low-income families

(C) analyzing the causes of a phenomenon

(D) recommending reforms to the welfare system

(E) changing public attitudes toward welfare recipients

16. Which of the following would provide the most logical continuation of the final paragraph?

(A) Paradoxically, any liberalization of AFDC eligibility restrictions is likely to intensify rather than mitigate pressures on family stability.

(B) Actually, concern for the individual recipients should not be allowed to override considerations of sound fiscal policy.

(C) In reality, there is virtually no evidence that AFDC payments have any relationship at all to problems of family instability in low-income marriages.

(D) In the final analysis, it appears that government welfare payments, to the extent that the cost of marriage is lowered, encourage the formation of low-income families.

(E) Ultimately, the problem of low-income family instability can be eliminated by reducing welfare benefits to the point where the cost of dissolution equals the cost of staying married.

17. All of the following are mentioned by the author as factors tending to perpetuate a marriage EXCEPT
(A) the stigma attached to divorce
(B) the social class of the partners
(C) the cost of alimony and child support
(D) the loss of property upon divorce
(E) the greater consumption possibilities of married people

18. Which of the following best summarizes the main idea of the passage?
(A) Welfare restrictions limiting the eligibility of families for benefits do not contribute to low-income family instability.
(B) Contrary to popular opinion, the most significant category of welfare recipients is not the ''cheating'' father.
(C) The incidence of family dissolution among low-income families is directly related to the inability of families with fathers to get welfare benefits.
(D) Very little of the divorce rate among low-income families can be attributed to fathers deserting their families so that they can qualify for welfare.
(E) Government welfare payments are at present excessively high and must be reduced in order to slow the growing divorce rate among low-income families.

19. The tone of the passage can best be described as
(A) confident and optimistic
(B) scientific and detached
(C) discouraged and alarmed
(D) polite and sensitive
(E) calloused and indifferent

20. With which of the following statements about marriage would the author most likely agree?
(A) Marriage is an institution which is largely shaped by powerful but impersonal economic and social forces.
(B) Marriage has a greater value to persons in higher income brackets than to persons in lower income brackets.
(C) Society has no legitimate interest in encouraging people to remain married to one another.
(D) Marriage as an institution is no longer economically viable and will gradually give way to other forms of social organization.
(E) The rising divorce rate across all income brackets indicates that people are more self-centered and less concerned about others than before.

21. The passage would most likely be found in a
(A) pamphlet on civil rights
(B) basic economics text
(C) book on the history of welfare
(D) religious tract on the importance of marriage
(E) scholarly journal devoted to public policy questions

An assumption that underlies most discussions of electric facility siting is that the initial selection of a site is the responsibility of the utility concerned—subject to governmental review and approval only after the site has been chosen. This assumption must be changed so that site selection becomes a joint responsibility of the utilities and the appropriate governmental authorities from the outset. Siting decisions would be made in accordance with either of two strategies. The metropolitan strategy takes the existing distribution of population and supporting facilities as given. An attempt is then made to choose between dispersed or concentrated siting and to locate generating facilities in accordance with some economic principle. For example, the economic objectives of least-cost construction and rapid start-up may be achieved, in part, by a metropolitan strategy which takes advantage of existing elements of social and physical infrastructure in the big cities. Under the frontier strategy, the energy park may be taken as an independent variable, subject to manipulation by policy-makers as a means of achieving desired demographic or social goals, e.g., rural-town-city mix. Thus, population distribution is taken as a goal of national social policy, not as a given of a national energy policy. In the frontier strategy, the option of dispersed siting is irrelevant from the standpoint of community impact because there is no pre-existing community of any size.

Traditionally, the resource-endowment of a location—and especially its situation relative to the primary industry of the hinterland—has had a special importance in American history. In the early agricultural period, the most valued natural endowment was arable land with good climate and available water. America's oldest cities were mercantile outposts of such agricultural areas. Deepwater ports developed to serve the agricultural hinterlands, which produced staple commodities in demand on the world market. From the 1840's onward, the juxtaposition of coal, iron ore, and markets afforded the impetus for manufacturing growth in the northeastern United States. The American manufacturing heartland developed westwards to encompass Lake Superior iron ores, the Pennsylvania coalfields, and the Northeast's financial, entrepreneurial, and manufacturing roles. Subsequent metropolitan growth has been organized around this national core.

Against the theory of urban development, it is essential to bear in mind the unprecedented dimensions of an energy park. The existing electric power plant at Four Corners in the southwest United States—the only human artifact visible to orbiting astronauts—generates only 4 thousand megawatts electric. The smallest energy parks will concentrate five times the thermal energy represented by the Four Corners plant. An energy park, then, would seem every bit as formidable as the natural harbor conditions or coal deposits which underwrote the growth of the great cities of the past—with a crucial difference. The founders of past settlements could not choose the geographic locations of their natural advantages.

The frontier strategy implements the principle of man-made opportunity; and this helps explain why some environmentalists perceive the energy park idea as a threat to nature. But the problems of modern society, with or without energy parks, require ever more comprehensive planning. And energy parks are a means of advancing American social history rather than merely responding to power needs in an unplanned, ad hoc manner.

22. Which of the following statements best describes the main point of the passage?
   (A) Government regulatory authorities should participate in electric facility site selection to further social goals.
   (B) Energy parks will have a significant influence on the demographic features of the American population.
   (C) Urban growth in the United States was largely the result of economic forces rather than conscientious planning.

(D) Under the frontier siting strategy for energy parks, siting decisions are influenced by the natural features of the land.
(E) America needs larger power-production facilities in urban and rural areas to meet the increased demand for energy.

23. All of the following are mentioned in the passage as characteristics of energy parks EXCEPT
   (A) energy parks will be built upon previously undeveloped sites
   (B) energy parks will be built in areas remote from major population centers
   (C) energy parks will produce considerably more thermal energy than existing facilities
   (D) energy parks will be built at sites that are near fuel sources such as coal
   (E) energy parks may have considerable effects on population distribution

24. According to the passage, which of the following are characteristics of past siting decisions for electric facilities?
   I. Government authority exercised only a review function.
   II. Decisions were made without regard to the effect the facility would have on people.
   III. Sites selected by utilities were often opposed by environmentalist groups.

   (A) I only
   (B) II only
   (C) I and II only
   (D) I and III only
   (E) I, II, and III

25. Which of the following, if true, would most seriously WEAKEN the author's position?
   (A) The first settlements in America were established in order to provide trading posts with Native Americans.
   (B) The cost of constructing an electric power plant in an urban area is not significantly greater than that for a rural area.
   (C) An energy park will be so large that it will be impossible to predict the demographic consequences of its construction.
   (D) Cities in European countries grew up in response to political pressures during the feudal period rather than economic pressures.
   (E) The United States is presently in a period of population migration which will change the rural-town-city mix.

26. With which one of the following statements would the author most likely agree?
    (A) Decisions about the locations for power plants should be left to the utilities.
    (B) Government leaders in the nineteenth century were irresponsible in not supervising urban growth more closely.
    (C) Natural features of a region such as cultivatable land and water supply are no longer important to urban growth.
    (D) Modern society is so complex that governments must take greater responsibility for decisions such as power plant siting.
    (E) The Four Corners plant should not have been built because of its mammoth size.

27. According to the passage, the most important difference between the natural advantages of early cities and the features of an energy park is
    (A) the features of an energy park will be located where the builders choose
    (B) natural advantages are no longer as important as they once were
    (C) natural features cannot be observed from outer space but energy parks can
    (D) early cities grew up close to agricultural areas while energy parks will be located in mountains
    (E) policy planners have learned to minimize the effects of energy parks on nature

28. The author's attitude toward energy parks can best be described as
    (A) cautious uncertainty
    (B) circumspect skepticism
    (C) studied indifference
    (D) qualified endorsement
    (E) unrestrained enthusiasm

There is extraordinary exposure in the United States to the risks of injury and death from motor vehicle accidents. More than 80 percent of all households own passenger cars or light trucks and each of these is driven an average of more than 11,000 miles each year. Almost one-half of fatally injured drivers have a blood alcohol concentration (BAC) of 0.1 percent or higher. For the average adult, over five ounces of 80 proof spirits would have to be consumed over a short period of time to attain these levels. A third of drivers who have been drinking, but fewer than 4 percent of all drivers, demonstrate these levels. Although less than 1 percent of drivers with BAC's of 0.1 percent or more are involved in fatal crashes, the probability of their involvement is 27 times higher than for those without alcohol in their blood.

There are a number of different approaches to reducing injuries in which intoxication plays a role. Based on the observation that excessive consumption correlates with the total alcohol consumption of a country's population, it has been suggested that higher taxes on alcohol would reduce both. While the heaviest drinkers would be taxed the most, anyone who drinks at all would be penalized by this approach.

To make drinking and driving a criminal offense is an approach directed only at intoxicated drivers. In some states, the law empowers police to request breath tests of drivers cited for any traffic offense and elevated BAC can be the basis for arrest. The National Highway Traffic Safety Administration estimates, however, that even with increased arrests, there are about 700 violations for every arrest. At this level there is little evidence that laws serve as deterrents to drinking while intoxicated. In Britain, motor vehicle fatalities fell 25 percent immediately following implementation of the Road Safety Act in 1967. As Britishers increasingly recognized that they could drink and not be stopped, the effectiveness declined, although in the ensuing three years the fatality rate seldom reached that observed in the seven years prior to the Act.

Whether penalties for driving with a high BAC or excessive taxation on consumption of alcoholic beverages will deter the excessive drinker responsible for most fatalities is unclear. In part, the answer depends on the extent to which those with high BAC's involved in crashes are capable of controlling their intake in response to economic or penal threat. Therapeutic programs which range from individual and group counseling and psychotherapy to chemotherapy constitute another approach, but they have not diminished the proportion of accidents in which alcohol was a factor. In the few controlled trials that have been reported there is little evidence that rehabilitation programs for those repeatedly arrested for drunken behavior have reduced either the recidivism or crash rates. Thus far, there is no firm evidence that Alcohol Safety Action Project supported programs, in which rehabilitation measures are requested by the court, have decreased recidivism or crash involvement for clients exposed to them, although knowledge and attitudes have improved. One thing is clear, however; unless we deal with automobile and highway safety and reduce accidents in which alcoholic intoxication plays a role, many will continue to die.

29. The author is primarily concerned with
    (A) interpreting the results of surveys on traffic fatalities
    (B) reviewing the effectiveness of attempts to curb drunk driving

(C) suggesting reasons for the prevalence of drunk driving in the United States

(D) analyzing the causes of the large number of annual traffic fatalities

(E) making an international comparison of experience with drunk driving

30. It can be inferred that the 1967 Road Safety Act in Britain
    (A) changed an existing law to lower the BAC level defining driving while intoxicated
    (B) made it illegal to drive while intoxicated
    (C) increased drunk driving arrests
    (D) placed a tax on the sale of alcoholic drinks
    (E) required drivers convicted under the law to undergo rehabilitation therapy

31. The author implies that a BAC of 0.1 percent
    (A) is unreasonably high as a definition of intoxication for purposes of driving
    (B) penalizes moderate drinkers but allows heavy drinkers to consume without limit
    (C) will effectively deter over 90 percent of the people who might drink and drive
    (D) is well below the BAC of most drivers who are involved in fatal collisions
    (E) proves a driver has consumed five ounces of 80 proof spirits over a short time

32. With which of the following statements about making driving while intoxicated a criminal offense versus increasing taxes on alcohol consumption would the author most likely agree?
    (A) Making driving while intoxicated a criminal offense is preferable to increased taxes on alcohol because the former is aimed only at those who abuse alcohol by driving while intoxicated.
    (B) Increased taxation on alcohol consumption is likely to be more effective in reducing traffic fatalities because taxation covers all consumers and not just those who drive.
    (C) Increased taxation on alcohol will constitute less of an interference with personal liberty because of the necessity of blood alcohol tests to determine BAC's in drivers suspected of intoxication.
    (D) Since neither increased taxation nor enforcement of criminal laws against drunk drivers is likely to have any significant impact, neither measure is warranted.

(E) Because arrests of intoxicated drivers have proved to be expensive and administratively cumbersome, increased taxation on alcohol is the most promising means of reducing traffic fatalities.

33. The author cites the British example in order to
    (A) show that the problem of drunk driving is worse in Britain than in the U.S.
    (B) prove that stricter enforcement of laws against intoxicated drivers would reduce traffic deaths
    (C) prove that a slight increase in the number of arrests of intoxicated drivers will not deter drunk driving
    (D) suggest that taxation of alcohol consumption may be more effective than criminal laws
    (E) demonstrate the need to lower BAC levels in states that have laws against drunk driving

34. Which of the following, if true, most WEAKENS the author's statement that the effectiveness of proposals to stop the intoxicated driver depends, in part, on the extent to which the high-BAC driver can control his intake?
    (A) Even if the heavy drinker cannot control his intake, criminal laws against driving while intoxicated can deter him from driving while intoxicated.
    (B) Rehabilitation programs aimed at drivers convicted of driving while intoxicated have not significantly reduced traffic fatalities.
    (C) Many traffic fatalities are caused by factors unrelated to the excessive consumption of alcohol of the driver.
    (D) Even though severe penalties may not deter the intoxicated driver, these laws will punish him for the harm he causes if he drives while intoxicated.
    (E) Some sort of therapy may be effective in helping the problem drinker to control his intake of alcohol, thereby keeping him off the road.

35. The author's closing remarks can best be described as
    (A) ironic
    (B) indifferent
    (C) admonitory
    (D) indecisive
    (E) indignant

STOP

IF YOU FINISH BEFORE TIME IS CALLED, CHECK YOUR WORK ON THIS SECTION ONLY. DO NOT WORK ON ANY OTHER SECTION IN THE TEST.

SECTION IV

Time——45 Minutes
30 Questions

Directions: Each group of questions is based on a set of propositions or conditions. Drawing a rough picture or diagram may help in answering some of the questions. Choose the best answer for each question and blacken the corresponding space on your answer sheet.

Questions 1–6

Six contestants, F, G, H, I, J, and K, are to be ranked first (highest) through sixth (lowest), though not necessarily in that order, at the start of a singles Ping-Pong challenge tournament.

F is ranked above G.
J is ranked above both H and I.
K is ranked two places above H.
F is ranked either third or fourth.

During the tournament, a player may challenge only the player ranked immediately above him or the player ranked two places above him.

1. Which of the following is a possible initial ranking from highest to lowest?
   (A) J, H, K, F, I, G
   (B) K, I, H, J, F, G
   (C) K, G, H, F, J, I
   (D) J, K, F, H, I, G
   (E) J, K, H, F, I, G

2. If K is initially ranked first, which of the following must also be true of the initial ranking?
   (A) J is ranked second.
   (B) H is ranked second.
   (C) F is ranked third.
   (D) G is ranked fifth.
   (E) I is ranked sixth.

3. If F is initially ranked third, which of the following must also be true of the initial ranking?
   (A) J is ranked first.
   (B) K is ranked second.
   (C) G is ranked fourth.
   (D) I is ranked fourth.
   (E) I is ranked sixth.

4. If K is initially ranked third, and if K makes the first challenge, which of the following contes-

tants could K play in the first match?
   I. F
   II. H
   III. I
   IV. J

   (A) I and II only
   (B) I and III only
   (C) II and IV only
   (D) III and IV only
   (E) I, II, and IV

5. If the first challenge of the tournament is made by F against H, all of the following must be true of the initial ranking EXCEPT
   (A) K is ranked first.
   (B) J is ranked second.
   (C) H is ranked third.
   (D) F is ranked fourth.
   (E) I is ranked fifth.

6. If J makes the first challenge of the tournament against K, then which of the following must be true of the initial rankings?
   (A) K is ranked first.
   (B) J is ranked third.
   (C) F is ranked third.
   (D) H is ranked fourth.
   (E) G is ranked fifth.

Questions 7–10

The supervisor of a commuter airline is scheduling pilots to fly the round trip from City X to City Y. The trip takes only two hours, and the airline has one round-trip flight in the morning and one round-trip flight in the afternoon, each day, Monday through Friday. Pilots must be scheduled in accordance with the following rules:

Only W, X, and Y can fly the morning flight.
Only V, X, and Z can fly the afternoon flight.
No pilot may fly twice on the same day.
No pilot may fly on two consecutive days.
X must fly the Wednesday morning flight.
Z must fly the Tuesday afternoon flight.

7. Which of the following must be true?
   (A) W flies the Monday morning flight.
   (B) X flies the Monday afternoon flight.
   (C) Y flies the Tuesday morning flight.
   (D) W flies the Thursday morning flight.
   (E) Z flies the Thursday afternoon flight.

8. If X flies on Friday morning, which of the following must be true?
   (A) X does not fly on Monday afternoon.
   (B) V flies on Friday afternoon.
   (C) W flies Thursday morning.
   (D) Y flies Thursday morning.
   (E) Neither W nor Y flies Thursday morning.

9. If X flies only one morning flight during the week, which of the following must be true?
   (A) W flies exactly two days during the week.
   (B) X flies exactly three days during the week.
   (C) Y flies only one day during the week.
   (D) Z flies Monday afternoon and Friday afternoon.
   (E) X flies more times during the week than V.

10. If W is not scheduled to fly at all during the week, all of the following must be true EXCEPT
   (A) X flies on Monday morning.
   (B) V flies on Monday afternoon.
   (C) Y flies on Thursday morning.
   (D) Z flies on Friday afternoon.
   (E) X flies on Friday morning.

Questions 11–15

A restaurant offers three daily specials each day of the week. The daily specials are selected from a list of dishes: P, Q, R, S, T, and U. The daily specials for the menu are selected in accordance with the following restrictions:

On any day that S is on the menu, Q must also be on the menu.

If R is on the menu one day, it cannot be included on the menu the following day.

U can be on the menu only on a day following a day on which T is on the menu.

Only one of the three specials from a given day can be offered the following day.

11. Which of the following could be the list of daily specials offered two days in a row?
   (A) S, R, and T; R, P, and Q
   (B) Q, S, and R; Q, S, and T

(C) P, Q, and S; S, R, and T
(D) Q, S, and P; T, U, and Q
(E) S, Q, and R; Q, T, and P

12. If P and S are on the menu one day, which of the following must be true of the menu the following day?
   I. U is on the menu.
   II. S is on the menu.
   III. T is on the menu.
   IV. R is on the menu.

   (A) I and II only
   (B) I and III only
   (C) III and IV only
   (D) I, II, and III
   (E) II, III, and IV

13. If P, R, and Q are on the menu one day and P, T, and R are on the menu two days later, which daily specials must have appeared on the menu for the intervening day?
   (A) P, R, and T
   (B) P, S, and T
   (C) Q, S, and T
   (D) Q, S, and U
   (E) S, T, and U

14. If on a certain day neither Q nor T is on the menu, how many different combinations of daily specials are possible for that day?
   (A) 1
   (B) 2
   (C) 3
   (D) 4
   (E) 5

15. If Q, R, and S are on the menu one day, which specials must be offered the following day?
   (A) P, Q, and T
   (B) P, R, and T
   (C) P, R, and U
   (D) R, S, and Q
   (E) T, S, and U

Questions 16–20

The personnel director of a company is scheduling interviews for eight people—J, K, L, M, N, O, P, and Q. Each person will have one interview, and all interviews are to be held on Monday through Friday of the same week.

At least one person will be interviewed each day.

More than one interview will be scheduled on exactly two of the days.

O is the only person who will be interviewed on Wednesday.

M and N must be scheduled for interviews exactly three days after Q.

P must be interviewed later in the week than K.

16. Which of the following CANNOT be true?
    (A) O's interview is later in the week than K's interview.
    (B) L's interview is later in the week than J's interview.
    (C) K's interview is later in the week than N's interview.
    (D) L's interview is on the same day as N's interview.
    (E) J's interview is on the same day as K's interview.

17. Which of the following must be true?
    (A) A third interview is scheduled on the same day with M and N.
    (B) Exactly three interviews will be held on one of the days.
    (C) Exactly one person will be interviewed on Monday.
    (D) Exactly two persons will be interviewed on Friday.
    (E) Q will have the only interview on Tuesday.

18. If Q and J are the only persons interviewed on Tuesday, which of the following must be true?
    (A) K's is the only interview on one of the days.
    (B) L's is the only interview on one of the days.
    (C) P's is the only interview on one of the days.
    (D) P's interview is earlier in the week than N's interview.
    (E) L's interview is earlier in the week than O's interview.

19. If M, N, and K are interviewed on the same day, which of the following must be true?
    (A) J is interviewed on Monday.
    (B) Q is interviewed on Monday.
    (C) L is interviewed on Tuesday.
    (D) J and L are interviewed on the same day.
    (E) J and Q are interviewed on the same day.

20. If L is interviewed later in the week than P, which of the following CANNOT be true?
    (A) P is the only person interviewed on one of the days.
    (B) K is the only person interviewed on one of the days.
    (C) L and Q are interviewed on the same day.
    (D) L and J are interviewed on the same day.
    (E) M and P are interviewed on the same day.

Questions 21–24

A university acting class is presenting a series of five skits using six performers, M, N, O, P, Q, and R. Each performer must perform in exactly three of the skits.

Only O and P will perform in the first skit.

R and three others will perform in the second skit.

Only N will perform in the third skit.

More people will perform in the fourth skit than in the fifth skit.

21. Which of the following must be true?
    (A) N and Q perform in the second skit.
    (B) N and R perform in the fifth skit.
    (C) Q does not perform in the fifth skit.
    (D) Exactly four people perform in the fourth skit.
    (E) Exactly five people perform in the fifth skit.

22. For which of the following pairs of performers is it true that if one appears in a skit, the other must also appear?
    (A) M and N
    (B) M and R
    (C) P and O
    (D) P and R
    (E) Q and O

23. Which of the following CANNOT be true?
    (A) Neither O nor P appears in the second skit.
    (B) Neither O nor P appears in the fifth skit.
    (C) N and Q appear in the second skit.
    (D) N appears in the second skit.
    (E) O, P, and Q appear in the fifth skit.

24. If N does not appear in the fifth skit, all of the following must be true EXCEPT:
    (A) P appears in the second skit.
    (B) N appears in the second skit.

(C) O appears in the fifth skit.
(D) P appears in the fifth skit.
(E) Q appears in the fifth skit.

Questions 25–30

In a certain military organization, there are six ranks—M, N, O, P, Q, and R. Within the organization, a superior officer can give a direct order only to persons whose rank is immediately below his rank, or two ranks below his rank.

N is a higher rank than M.
Both Q and O are higher ranks than P.
O is two ranks above R.
M is either the second or third highest rank in the organization.

25. Which of the following could be the order of the ranks in the military organization, from lowest to highest?
(A) P, R, M, O, Q, N
(B) P, Q, R, M, N, O
(C) Q, P, R, M, O, N
(D) R, P, O, M, Q, N
(E) R, Q, O, P, M, N

26. If R is the lowest rank in the organization, which of the following must be true?
(A) Q is the highest rank.
(B) N is the highest rank.
(C) M is the second highest rank.
(D) P is the fifth highest rank.
(E) Q is the fifth highest rank.

27. If M is the third highest rank, then how many different orderings of the ranks are possible?
(A) 1

(B) 2
(C) 3
(D) 4
(E) 5

28. If R is the fourth highest rank in the organization, then which of the following must be true?

I. Q is the fifth highest rank.
II. M is the third highest rank.
III. N is the highest rank.

(A) I only
(B) II only
(C) I and II only
(D) II and III only
(E) I, II, and III

29. If Q is the third highest rank in the organization, then an officer of rank M could give direct orders to officers of which ranks?

I. R
II. P
III. Q

(A) II only
(B) III only
(C) I and II only
(D) I and III only
(E) II and III only

30. If M is the second highest rank, then which of the following must be a valid order?
(A) M to P
(B) M to R
(C) Q to O
(D) Q to P
(E) P to R

STOP

END OF SECTION. IF YOU HAVE ANY TIME LEFT, GO OVER YOUR WORK IN THIS SECTION ONLY. DO NOT WORK IN ANY OTHER SECTION OF THE TEST.

PRACTICE EXAMINATION 1
ANSWER KEY

SECTION I

1.	E	8.	C	15.	D	22.	A	29.	A
2.	D	9.	C	16.	B	23.	E	30.	B
3.	B	10.	A	17.	B	24.	E	31.	B
4.	E	11.	E	18.	E	25.	E	32.	C
5.	C	12.	A	19.	D	26.	C	33.	A
6.	A	13.	A	20.	B	27.	B	34.	E
7.	D	14.	B	21.	B	28.	D	35.	B

SECTION II

1.	D	7.	B	13.	D	19.	E	25.	D
2.	E	8.	A	14.	B	20.	C	26.	C
3.	B	9.	B	15.	E	21.	E	27.	A
4.	E	10.	C	16.	D	22.	D	28.	D
5.	B	11.	C	17.	E	23.	E	29.	A
6.	A	12.	E	18.	D	24.	E	30.	C

SECTION III

1.	C	8.	B	15.	C	22.	A	29.	B
2.	A	9.	D	16.	A	23.	D	30.	B
3.	C	10.	C	17.	B	24.	C	31.	A
4.	B	11.	A	18.	A	25.	C	32.	A
5.	E	12.	B	19.	B	26.	D	33.	C
6.	B	13.	C	20.	A	27.	A	34.	A
7.	D	14.	C	21.	E	28.	E	35.	C

SECTION IV

1.	D	7.	E	13.	C	19.	B	25.	D
2.	A	8.	B	14.	A	20.	C	26.	D
3.	A	9.	A	15.	A	21.	E	27.	C
4.	D	10.	D	16.	C	22.	B	28.	E
5.	E	11.	E	17.	B	23.	B	29.	B
6.	A	12.	C	18.	A	24.	A	30.	D

EXPLANATORY ANSWERS

SECTION I

1. **(E)** This question is primarily a matter of careful reading. The phrase "no lower bus fares" must not be read to mean that Flash uniquely has the lowest fare; it means only that no one else has a fare lower than that of Flash. It is conceivable that several companies share the lowest fare. So II is not inconsistent with the claim made in the advertisement. III is not inconsistent since it mentions the New York City to Boston route, and it is the Washington, D.C. to New York City route which is the subject of the ad's claim. Finally, I is not inconsistent since it speaks of an *air* fare and the ad's language carefully restricts the claim to *bus* fares.

2. **(D)** We take the first three propositions together and ignore the fourth since we are to assume it is false. Roberts cannot be convicted without Edwards' testimony (I), but that testimony will show that Edwards participated in the crime (II). But if Edwards participated in the crime, Roberts cannot be convicted of it because he is accused of a crime which can be committed only by a person acting alone (III). Either Edwards will testify or Edwards will not testify—that is a tautology (logically true). If Edwards testifies, according to our reasoning, Roberts cannot be convicted. If Edwards does not testify, Roberts cannot be convicted (I). Either way, Roberts will not be convicted. (E) cannot be correct since we have no way of knowing, as a matter of logic, whether Edwards will or will not testify. We know only that *if* he does, certain consequences will follow, and *if* he does not, other consequences will follow. (A) can be disregarded since the crime is one which only a solo actor can commit (III). (C) is incorrect because we have proven that, regardless of Edwards' course of action, Roberts cannot be convicted. Finally, (B) is a logical *possibility*, which is not precluded by the given information, but we cannot logically deduce it from the information given.

3. **(B)** Examine carefully the connection between II and IV. Suppose Edwards testifies. His testimony will show he, too, has committed some wrong (II); but when the jury learns this, they will not believe any part of that testimony (IV), which means that they will not believe Edwards committed the wrong——a contradiction, Since II and IV cannot both be true at the same time, the scenario they describe is an impossible one——like saying a circle is a square. The remaining answers are all distractions. There is nothing in the information to suggest that the situation was created by Roberts' attorney, so (E) is incorrect. (C) and (D) are value judgments which cannot be inferred from the information given and so are wrong——even if the situation is *difficult* for them, what reason is there for concluding that it is unfair? In any event, the situation is not even difficult for Roberts, who will be acquitted (see our analysis of the preceding question). (A) is wrong, and remember that the LSAT does not presuppose you have any information about the law or its workings.

4. **(E)** In the very first sentence, the author remarks that this is "curious" and a "contradiction," so the only correct answer choice will be one which follows up on this idea as (E) does when it speaks of *paradox*. Nothing which precedes the blank suggests that the author is speaking of "beauty" or "tragedy," so (A) and (B) can be disregarded. As for (C), the passage does speak about death, but not of death's inevitability; rather it dwells on death under certain circumstances which may not be inevitable. As for (D), while death may characterize human existence, the kind of death mentioned——self-sacrifice——is not indicated to be an inherent part of all human life.

5. **(C)** The author is explaining why the sacrifice is meaningless. From three different perspectives, he shows that it can have no value. The community does not win, because both lives were equally important. The lover who is saved does not

profit, and that is shown by the fact that he would be perfectly willing to do the transaction the other way. If he has no preference (or even prefers the alternative outcome, his death), it cannot be said that he benefited from the exchange of lives. Finally, the need to prove that the action has no value to the heroine: He says she does not benefit, because she is not in a position to enjoy or savor, or whatever, her heroism. The reason for that is that she is *dead* (C), not dying (A), for dying would leave open the possibility that her sacrifice would bring her joy in her last minutes, and then the author's contention that the transaction has *no* value would be weakened. (D) is wrong, for it is specifically stated that she is a heroine, so it is an inappropriate *completion* of the sentence. (B) and (E) may both be true, but they do not explain why the action has no value to anyone.

6. **(A)** The main point of the passage is that pregnancy and a child put strain on a young marriage, and so such marriages would have a higher survival rate without the strain of children. It would seem, then, that encouraging such couples not to have children would help them stay married; but that will be possible only if they have not already committed themselves, so to speak, to having a child. If the wife is already pregnant at the time of marriage, the commitment has already been made so the advice is too late. (B) and (C) are wrong for similar reasons. It is not only the continued presence of the child in the marriage which causes the stress, but the very pregnancy and birth. So (B) and (C) do not address themselves to the *birth* of the child, and that is the factor to which the author attributes the dissolution of the marriage. (D) is wide of the mark. Whether society does or does not have such an interest, the author has shown us a causal linkage, that is, a mere fact of the matter. He states: If this, then fewer divorces. He may or may not believe there should be fewer divorces. (E) is wrong for this reason also and for the further reason that it says "do not *plan*" to have children. The author's concern is with children during the early part of the marriage. He does not suggest that couples should never have children.

7. **(D)** Peter's surprise is over the fact that an important executive of a company would use a competitor's product, hence (D). (B) is wrong because Peter's surprise is not that Mary is unimportant; rather he knows Mary is important, and that is the reason for surprise. (E) is irrelevant to the exchange, for Peter imagines that regardless of taste, Mary ought to consume the product she is responsible in part for producing. The same reasoning can be applied to (C). Finally, (A) is a distraction. It has legal overtones, but it is important to always keep in mind that this section, like all sections of the LSAT, tests reasoning and reading abilities——not knowledge of business or law.

8. **(C)** The dispute here is over the motivation to compete seriously in intramural sports. Erika claims it is a sense of responsibility to one's fellows; Nichol argues it is a desire to win. But the two may actually support one another. In what way could one possibly let his fellows down? If the sport was not competitive, it would seem there would be no opportunity to disappoint them. So the desire to win contributes to the desire to be an effective member of the team. Nothing in the exchange presupposes anything about the structure of such programs beyond the fact that they are competitive, that is, that they have winners and losers. How many such programs exist, how they are funded, and similar questions are irrelevant, so both (A) and (B) are incorrect. (D) is close to being correct, but it calls for a survey of *deans*. The dean is probably not in a position to describe the motivation of the *participants*. Had (D) specified participants, it too would have been a correct answer. Of course, only one answer can be correct on the LSAT. Finally, (E) must be wrong for the reason cited in explaining (D); it should be possible to find out about the motivation.

9. **(C)** Clark was unhappy if he had a clear conscience but knew, or Clark was happy if he knew but had an unclear conscience. It is not the case that Clark was unhappy, so he must have been happy. Since he knew, however, his happiness must stem from an unclear conscience. (A), (D), and (E) are incorrect because they make irrelevant value judgments. As was just shown, the author's point can be analyzed as a purely logical one. (B) is just distraction, playing on the connection between "governess" and "servant," which, of course, are not the same thing.

10. **(A)** The author's point depends upon the *assumption* that children see both animated features and "spaghetti Westerns." Obviously, if that assumption is untrue, he cannot claim that his conclusion follows. It may be true that children

get a distorted picture of the world from other causes, but the author has not claimed that. He claims only that it comes from their seeing animated features and ''spaghetti Westerns.'' Presumably the two different treatments cause the inversion of values. The intention of the producers in making the films is irrelevant since an action may have an effect not intended by the actor. Hence, II would not touch the author's point. Further, that there are other sources of information which present a proper view of the world does not prove that the problem cited by the author does not produce an inverted view of the world. So III would not weaken his point.

11. **(E)** The point of the passage is that there is a seeming contradiction in our body of laws. Sometimes a person pays for his attempted misdeeds, and other times he does not pay for them. If there could be found a good reason for this difference, then the contradiction could be explained away. This is just what (E) does. It points out that the law treats the situations differently because it has different goals: Sometimes we drive fast because we are in a hurry; other times we drive slowly because we want to enjoy the scenery. (B) would not weaken the argument for it only intensifies the contradiction. (D) makes an attempt to reconcile the seemingly conflicting positions by hinting at a possible goal of one action which is not a goal of the other. But, if anything, it intensifies the contradiction because one might infer that we should not try persons for attempted crimes because criminal trials are expensive, yet we should allow compensation for attempted frauds because civil trials are less expensive. (C) and (A) are just distractions. Whether there are more of one kind of law than another on the books has nothing to do with the seeming contradiction. And whether persons are more likely to commit a second crime after they are released from prison does not speak to the issue of whether an unsuccessful attempt to commit a crime should be a crime in the first place.

12. **(A)** The question stem asks us to focus on the ''dispute'' between the two opponents. What will be relevant to it will be those items which affect the merits of the issues, or perhaps those which affect the credibility of the parties. (C) and (E) both mention items—facts and their source— which would be relevant to the substantive issues. (B) and (D) are legitimate attempts to clarify the issues and so are relevant. (A) is not relevant to the issues nor is it relevant to the credi-

bility (e.g., where did the facts come from) of the debaters. (A) is the least relevant because it is an *ad hominem* attack of the illegitimate sort.

13. **(A)** The point of the passage is that artists see things as they really are, while politicians see things as they want them to be. (B) is wrong, for if anything, it is the politicians who see things through rose-colored glasses, while the artists see the truth of a stark reality. (C) can be overruled, for the passage implies that political leaders are responsive to the needs of people—it is just that they are a little late. Moreover, the point of the passage is to draw a contrast between artists and politicians; and even if the conclusion expressed in (C) is arguably correct, it is not as good an answer choice as (A), which *completes* the comparison. (D) has no ground in the passage. Be careful not to move from an analysis of facts— artists saw the problems earlier than the politicians did—to a conclusion of value or policy: therefore we should turn out the politicians. The author may very well believe that as sad as these circumstances are, nothing can be done about them, e.g., things are bad enough with the politicians in charge, but they would be much worse with artists running things. (E) also finds no ground in the passage.

14. **(B)** The argument for consistency is that it avoids the danger that actions will be misinterpreted. If a parent is overly generous, a child will think the parent will always be generous, even when generosity is inappropriate. By the same token, if a parent does not draw the line until he is pushed to do so, the child will believe that he *forced* the parent's response. A parent, so goes the argument, should play it safe and leave himself a cushion. (D) makes an attempt to capture this thought but overstates the case. The author implies only that this may show weakness, not that the child will necessarily exploit that weakness and certainly not that the child will exploit it violently. And if the author had intended that thought, he surely would not have used the word ''retaliate'' which implies a *quid pro quo*. Both (A) and (E) have no basis in the passage, and neither is relevant to the idea of rewards and punishments. (C) does treat the general idea of the passage, but it confuses the idea of weakness with the more specific notion of willingness to bargain.

15. **(D)** The key phrase in this paragraph is ''beef costs more per pound than fish.'' A careful read-

ing would show that (A) is in direct contradiction to the explicit wording of the passage. (B) cannot be inferred since the dietitian merely says, ''I pay.'' Perhaps he intends to keep the price of a meal stable by cutting back in other areas. In any event, this is another example of not going beyond a mere factual analysis to generate policy recommendations (see #13) unless the question stem specifically invites such an extension, e.g., which of the following courses of action would the author recommend? (C) makes an unwarranted inference. From the fact that beef is more costly one would not want to conclude that it is more profitable. (E) is wrong for this reason also. (D) is correct because it focuses upon the ''per measure of protein'' which explains why a fish meal will cost the dietitian more than a beef meal, even though fish is less expensive per pound.

16. **(B)** I would undermine the advertisement considerably. Since the point of the ad is that you will lose weight, any unforeseen effects which would make it impossible to lose weight would defeat the purposes of the program. II is less obvious, but it does weaken the ad somewhat. Although the ad does not specifically say you will be healthier for having enrolled in the program, surely the advantages of the program are less significant if you have to pay an additional, hidden cost, i.e., health. III, if anything, supports the advertisement. IV is irrelevant since the ad does not claim you will become too thin.

17. **(B)** This question is like one of those simple conversation questions: ''X: All bats are mammals. Y: Not true, whales are mammals too.'' In this little exchange, Y misunderstands X to have said that ''all mammals are bats.'' In the question, the objection must be based on a misunderstanding. The objector must think that the ad has claimed that the only cause of unhappiness, etc., is being overweight, otherwise he would not have offered his counter-example. (A) is wrong because the ad never takes a stand on the *causes* of overweight conditions——only on a possible cure. This reasoning invalidates (C) and (D) as well. (E) makes a similar error, but about effects, not about causes. The ad does not say everyone who is unhappy is unattractive, or vice versa.

18. **(E)** The sample argument is a straightforward generalization: All observed S are P. X is an S. Therefore, X is P. Only (E) replicates this form. The reasoning in (A) is: ''Some S are P. All M

are S. (All swans are birds, which is suppressed assumption.) Therefore, all M are P.'' That is like saying: ''Some children are not well behaved. All little girls are children. Therefore, all little girls are not well behaved.'' (B), too, contains a suppressed premise. Its structure is: ''All S are P. All S are M. (All ballets are theatrical productions, which is suppressed.) Therefore, all M are P.'' That is like saying ''All little girls are children. All little girls are human. Therefore, all humans are little girls.'' (C) is not a generalization at all. It takes a generalization and attempts to explain it by uncovering a causal linkage. (D) is simply a *non sequitur*. It moves from the universality of the *concept* of justice to the conclusion that justice is a *physical* trait of man.

19. **(D)** The author is attempting to argue that laws against suicide are legitimate. He argues against a simplistic libertarian position which says suicide hurts only the victim. The goal of the law, he argues, is not just to protect the victim from himself. A society passes such a law because it wants to underscore the importance of human life. Reading beyond the blank in the second paragraph makes clear the author's views on the value of human life. (A) flies in the face of the explicit language of the passage. The author does not defend the law as being a deterrent to suicide. (B) might be something the author believes, but it is not something he develops in the passage. He is not concerned here with explaining how the laws came to be on the books; he is concerned only with defending them. If anything, (B) would be more appropriate in the context of an argument against such laws. (C) also is something the author may believe, but his defense of the suicide law is not that it protects liberties——only that it serves a function and does not interfere with constitutional liberties any more than laws that prohibit doing violence to others. (E) is wrong for the same reasons that (B) is wrong. It seems to belong more in the context of an argument against suicide laws.

20. **(B)** With the comments in #19 in mind, it is clear that (B) must be correct. The author wants to make the point that suicide is not a victimless crime; it affects a great many people——even, he claims, some who were never personally acquainted with the suicide. Again, reading the whole passage is helpful. (A) is a joke——obviously suicide does not lead to more serious crimes. That is like saying the death penalty is designed to rehabilitate the criminal. (C) simply focuses on the superficial content of the sentence:

One, it's talking about church and state, so (C), which mentions sin, must be correct. (D) is wrong because the author is not concerned to defend the laws as deterrents to suicide, as we discussed in #19. Finally, (E) is irrelevant to the point that the entire community is affected by the death of any one of its members.

21. **(B)** This third question, too, can be answered once the comments of #19 are understood. The key word here is "oversimplification." The libertarian oversimplifies matters by imagining that the only function of the law is to protect a person from himself. This is oversimplified because it overlooks the fact that such laws also serve the functions of (1) underscoring the value of life, and (2) protecting the community as a whole from the loss of any of its members. (A) is incorrect because the libertarian does not make this error but the related one of evaluating the function of the law only from the perspective of the suicide. (C) is wrong, for the author apparently shares with the libertarian the assumption that a law must not illegitimately interfere with individual liberty. His whole defense of the laws against suicide is that they have a legitimate function. (D) is wrong for the same reasons that (C) of #20 is wrong. Finally, (E) is very much like (A).

22. **(A)** (C) and (D) are wrong because they extrapolate without sufficient information. These are very much like answers (C) and (E) in #15. (E) contradicts the last given statement and so cannot be a conclusion of it. That would be like trying to infer "all men are mortal" from the premise that "no men are mortal." (B) commits an error by moving from "all S are P" to "all P are S." Just because all racing engines have SFI does not mean that all SFIs are in racing engines. Some may be found in tractors and heavy-duty machinery.

23. **(E)** This is a very sticky question, but it is similar to ones which have been on the LSAT. The key here is to keep in mind that you are to pick the BEST answer, and sometimes you will not be very satisfied with any of them. Here (E) is correct by default of the others. (A) has some merit. After all, the economist really isn't very careful in his statement of his claim. He says "here we go again" when there is no evidence that we have ever been there before. But there is no particular term he uses which we could call ambiguous. (B) is wrong because, although the economist as-

sumes some people take that position (otherwise, against whom would he be arguing), he does not imply that he alone thinks differently. (C) is like (A), a possible answer, but this interpretation requires additional information. You would have to have said to yourself. "Oh, I see that he is against it. He is probably saying this in an exasperated tone and in the context of a diatribe." If there were such additional information, you would be right, and (C) would be a good answer. But there isn't. (E) does not require this additional speculation and so is truer to the given information. (D) would also require speculation. (E) is not perfect, just BEST by comparison.

24. **(E)** The argument assumes that a right cannot exist unless it is recognized by the positive law of a society. Against this assumption, it can be argued that a right may exist even though there is no mechanism for protecting or enforcing it. That this is at least plausible has been illustrated by our own history, e.g., minority groups have often been denied rights. These rights, however, existed all the while——they were just not protected by the government. (A) is incorrect, for the proponent of the theory of natural rights cannot deny that some human beings do not have them. That would contradict the very definition of natural right on which he bases his claim. (B) is incorrect because it is not responsive to the argument. Even if (B) is true, the attacker of natural rights still has his argument that there are no universally recognized rights, so there are no universal (natural) rights at all. (C), like (A), is inconsistent with the very idea of a "natural" right. (D) is incorrect because it does not respond to the attacker's claim that no one right is protected universally. Consistency or universality within one society does not amount to consistency or universality across all societies.

25. **(E)** The author is arguing that political parties in America are weak because there is no party unity. Because of this lack of unity, the party is unable to pass legislation. (E) would strengthen this contention. (E) provides an example of a government dominated by a single party (control of the presidency and both houses), yet the party is unable to pass its own legislation. (A) provides little, if any, support for the argument. If there are only 18 defectors out of a total of 67 party members, that does not show tremendous fragmentation. (B) is even weaker by the same analysis: 70 defectors out of a total of 305 party members. (C)

is weak because it focuses on the minority party. (D) strengthens the argument less clearly than (E) because there are many possible explanations for the failure, e.g., a different party controlled the legislature.

26. **(C)** Here we are looking for the argument that will undermine the position taken by the paragraph. Remember that the ultimate conclusion of the paragraph is that this disunity is a weakness and that this prevents legislation from being passed. One very good way of attacking this argument is to attack the value judgment upon which the conclusion is based: Is it good to pass the legislation? The author assumes that it would be better to pass the legislation. We could argue, as in (C), that members of the Congress should not pass legislation simply because it is proposed by the party leadership. Rather, the members should represent the views of their constituents. Then, if the legislation fails, it must be the people who did not want it. In that case, it is better not to pass the legislation. (A) does not undermine the argument. That members receive funding proves nothing about unity after elections. As for (B), this seems to strengthen rather than weaken the argument. The author's thesis argues that there is greater unity in the Senate than in the House. (D) would undermine the argument only if we had some additional information to make it relevant. Finally, (E) does not weaken the argument greatly. That some legislation is passed is not a denial of the argument that more should be passed.

27. **(B)** The basic move by M. Adamante is to offer a competing explanation for the phenomenon. That is, he seems to agree that the U.S. has the 17th lowest infant mortality rate, but he attributes this to distributional factors rather than to medical technology itself. (D) is the second most attractive answer. But Adamante does not introduce any intervening variables, e.g., technology allows more pregnancies that would otherwise abort to go to term, which in turn means that weaker infants are born, and so more die. (A) is incorrect since Adamante seems to accept the validity of the data and to contest the explanation. (E) is incorrect for the same reason. Finally, (C) is incorrect since Adamante does not suggest that the first speaker has made a logical error—only a factual one.

28. **(D)** The author is arguing that the budget cuts will not ultimately be detrimental to the poor since the adverse effects will be more than offset by beneficial ones. II and III attack both elements of this reasoning. II points out that there will be no beneficial effects to offset the harmful ones, and III notes that the harmful effects will be so harmful that they will outweigh any beneficial ones that might result. I, however, is not relevant to the author's point. The author is arguing a point of economics. How the Congressmen get themselves elected has no bearing on that point.

29. **(A)** The author reasons from the premise "there are bottles of this product in the apartments" to the conclusion "therefore, these people believe the product is effective." The ad obviously wants the hearer to infer that the residents of the apartments decided themselves to purchase the product because they believed it to be effective. (A) directly attacks this linkage. If it were true that the company gave away bottles of the product, this would sever that link. (B) does weaken the ad, but only marginally. To be sure, we might say to ourselves, "Well, a person who touts a product and does not use it himself is not fully to be trusted." But (B) does not aim at the very structure of the argument as (A) does. (C) can hardly weaken the argument, since it appears to be a premise on which the argument itself is built. (C), therefore, actually strengthens the appeal of the advertisement. It also does not link to Painaway's effectiveness. (D) seems to be irrelevant to the *appeal* of the ad. The ad is designed to *change* the hearer's mind, so the fact that he does not now accept the conclusion of the ad is not an argument against the ability of the ad to accomplish its stated objective. Finally, (E) is irrelevant to the purpose of the ad for reasons very similar to those cited for (D).

30. **(B)** The author is accusing the artists of being inconsistent. He claims they give lip service to the idea that an artist must suffer, but that they then live in material comfort—so they do not themselves suffer. Only (B) completes the paragraph in a way so that this inconsistency comes out. (A) and (D) can be dismissed because the author is concerned with those whom he attacks as *artists,* not as connoisseurs or purchasers of art, nor as critics of art. (C) is inadequate for it does not reveal the inconsistency. The author apparently allows that these people are, after a fashion, artists; what he objects to is their claiming that it is necessary to suffer while they do not

themselves suffer. (E) is the second best answer, but it fails, too. The difficulty with (E) is that the author's point is that there is a contradiction between the actions and the words of those he accuses: They claim to suffer but they do not. But the claimed suffering goes beyond matters of eating and has to do with deprivation generally.

31. **(B)** II is an assumption of the author because the inconsistency of which he accuses others would disappear if, though they were not poor, they nonetheless endured great suffering, e.g., emotional pain or poor health. I is not an assumption of the author. He is trying to prove that he has uncovered a contradiction in another's words and actions: It is the others who insist suffering is necessary. The author himself never says one way or the other whether he considers that suffering is necessary to produce art—only that these others claim it is, and then eat well. Finally, III incorrectly construes the author's reference to purchasers of art. He never mentions the role of the critic.

32. **(C)** Take careful note of the exact position the author ascribes to the analysts: They *always* attribute a sudden drop to a crisis. The author then attacks this simple causal explanation by explaining that, though a crisis is followed by a market drop, the reason is not that the crisis causes the drop but that both are the effects of some common cause, the changing of the moon. Of course, the argument seems implausible, but our task is not to grade the argument, only to describe its structure. (A) is not a proper characterization of that structure since the author never provides a specific example. (B), too, is inapplicable since no statistics are produced. (D) can be rejected since the author is attacking generally accepted beliefs rather than appealing to them to support his position. Finally, though the author concedes the reliability of the reports in question, he wants to draw a different conclusion from the data, (E).

33. **(A)** Given the implausibility of the author's alternative explanation, he is probably speaking tongue-in-cheek, that is, he is ridiculing the analysts for *always* attributing a drop in the market to a political crisis. But whether you took the argument in this way or as a serious attempt to explain the fluctuations of the stock market, (A) will be the correct answer. (E) surely goes beyond the mere factual description at which the author is aiming, as does (D) as well. The author is con-

cerned with the *causes* of fluctuations; nothing suggests that he or anyone else is in a position to exploit those fluctuations. (C) finds no support in the paragraph for nothing suggests that he wishes to attack the credibility of the source rather than the argument itself. Finally, (B) is inappropriate to the main point of the passage. Whether the market ultimately evens itself out has nothing to do with the causes of the fluctuations.

34. **(E)** The assumption necessary to the author's reasoning is the fairly abstract or minimal one that there is a connection between the characteristics of a work of art and the period during which it was produced. If there were no such connection, that is, if there were not styles of art which lasted for some time but only randomly produced works unrelated to one another by medium, content, or detail, the argument would fail. Every other answer, however, attributes too much to the author. (D) for example states that the expert can *pinpoint* the date of the work, but this goes far beyond the author's attempt to date generally the piece of pottery he is examining. (C) says more than the author does. He mentions that the details of semi-nude women and bulls are characteristic of the *late* Minoan period, not that they generally characterize the entire history of that people. (B) also goes far beyond the details offered. The author connects the bull with a period of *Minoan* civilization—not ancient civilizations in general. Finally, (A) fails because, while the author apparently believes that Minoan pottery of this period was made in a certain way, he does not claim that all such pottery came from this period. He uses a group of characteristics in combination to date the pottery: It is the combination which is unique to the period, not each individual characteristic taken in isolation.

35. **(B)** The weakness in the argument is that it makes an assertion without any supporting argumentation. The author states that things might turn out to be worse, but he never mentions any specific way in which the result might be considered less desirable than what presently exists. As for (A), the author might have chosen to attack the radicals in this way, but that he did not adopt a particular line of attack available to him is not nearly so severe a criticism as the expressed by (B)—that the line of attack he did adopt is defective, or at least incomplete. The same reasoning applies to both (C) and (E). It is true the author might have taken the attack proposed by (C), but that he chose not to is not nearly so serious a

weakness as that pointed out by (B). (E) comes perhaps the closest to expressing what (B) says more explicitly. (E) hints at the specific consequences which might occur, but it is restricted to the *transition* period. It is not really detailing the bad results which might finally come out of a revolution, only the disadvantages of undertaking the change. Finally, (D) describes existing conditions, but it does not treat the question whether there *should* be a revolution; and, in any event, to defend against the question whether there *should* be a revolution by arguing there *will not be* one would itself be weak, had the author used the argument.

SECTION II

Questions 1–6

This is a fairly simple "connective" set. A "connective" set is a problem set in which one event is somehow connected with another event, e.g., X causes Y, or Y leads to Z. The connection can be expressed by an arrow. We begin with the first condition:

$$G \longrightarrow H$$

Adding the second condition:

$$G \rightleftarrows H \longrightarrow I$$

And the third:

$$G \rightleftarrows H \longrightarrow I \longrightarrow J$$

And the fourth:

$$G \rightleftarrows H \longrightarrow I \longrightarrow J \longrightarrow K$$

And the fifth:

$$L \longrightarrow G \rightleftarrows H \longrightarrow I \longrightarrow J \longrightarrow K$$

And the sixth:

$$L \longrightarrow G \rightleftarrows H \longrightarrow I \longrightarrow J \rightleftarrows K$$

Of course, there is no necessity that the stations be oriented in exactly this way on the page, so long as the relative connections are specified. An equivalent diagram is:

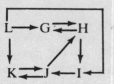

Once the diagram is drawn, answering the questions is merely a matter of using the picture.

1. **(D)** The diagram shows that it is possible to get from H to J only via I. (A) is incorrect since the direct connection between J and H runs only from J to H, not vice versa. As for (B), while it is possible to get from H to G, there is no connecting train between G and J. (C) is incorrect because there is no train from H to L. Finally, (E) is incorrect for there is a route from H to J, via I.

2. **(E)** Notice that there are no arrows in the diagram which point toward L. This means that it is possible only to leave L. It is not possible to arrive at L. As for (A), one can arrive at G from L or H. (B) is incorrect since one can arrive at H from either G or J. (C) is incorrect since there is a connection between H and I and between L and I. Finally, (D) is incorrect since K can be reached from either L or J.

3. **(B)** Consulting the diagram, we see that I can be reached from either H or L. H, however, can be reached from either G or J. Thus one can go from G and J via H and reach I with only one transfer. So the correct answer must be I and III only, (B). As for II, there is only a direct connection between H and I, so a transfer is not possible. And as for IV, the trip from K to I goes via J and H, so two transfers are required.

4. **(E)** All six stations can be visited, without revisiting any station, if we begin at L. The trip then proceeds: L to G to H to I to J to K.

5. **(B)** To get to K from H, we must go via I and J, and that is a total of two transfers. As for (A), the trip from G to I is accomplished by transferring only at H. As for (C), the trip from L to H is accomplished by going via G, again requiring only one transfer. As for (D), though the trip

from L to I would require two transfers if the L, G, H, I route is selected, note that the trip can be made directly from L to I without *any* transfers. (E) is incorrect because a direct route is available from L to K.

6. **(A)** If I is closed, the only transfer point from H to J is closed, and that means that it is not possible to get from G to J. (B) is incorrect since there is a direct link between J and K. (C) is incorrect since there is a direct link between L and K. (D) is incorrect since the L to K to J route remains unimpaired. (E) is incorrect since there is a direct link from L to G.

Questions 7–12

This is a "selection" set, that is, we must select cities for the tours according to the restrictions set forth in the problem set. There are many different ways of summarizing the information, and each of us has his or her own idiosyncratic system of notational devices. There are, however, some fairly standard symbols used by logicians, and we will employ them here. We summarize the information in the following way:

1. $M \rightarrow (Q \ \& \ R)$
2. $P \rightarrow O$
3. $Q \rightarrow (M \ \& \ N) \ v \ (M \ \& \ T) \ v \ (M \ \& \ N \ \& \ T)$
4. $P \neq Q$
5. $\sim (O \ \& \ R \ \& \ T)$
6. $\sim (N \ \& \ S \ \& \ R)$
7. $L \neq R$

Some clarifying remarks about this system are in order. We are using the capital-letter designation of each city to make the statement that the city will be included on the tour, e.g., "M" means "M will be included on the tour." The $\rightarrow$ stands for "if. . . , then. . . ."; the "&" stands for "and"; the "v" stands for "or"; the $\sim$ stands for "not." We use parentheses as punctuation devices to avoid possible confusion. So the first condition is to be read, "If M, then both Q and R," that is, "If M is included on the trip, then both Q and R must be included on the trip." Notice that the parentheses were necessary, for the statement

$$M \rightarrow Q \ \& \ R$$

might be misinterpreted to mean "If M is included on the tour, then Q must also be included. In addition, R must be included on the trip." That would be punctuated with parentheses as:

$$(M \rightarrow Q) \ \& \ R$$

As for the second condition, we note simply that if P is included, O must also be included.

As for the third condition, some students will find it easier to write this condition out rather than use the notational system. That is fine.

Statement 3 is to be read, "If Q, then M and N, or M and T, or all three," which is, of course, equivalent to the statement included in the initial conditions of the problem.

The fourth condition is similar to the second in that we use a non-standard symbol, "$\neq$". The same information could be written as $\sim(P \ \& \ Q)$ or $P \rightarrow \sim Q$. This last notation is equivalent to $Q \rightarrow \sim P$, for logically $P \rightarrow \sim Q$ is the same as $Q \rightarrow \sim P$.

The fifth and sixth conditions are to be read, respectively, "It is not the case that O and R and T are included" and "It is not the case that N and S and R are included." And finally, condition seven is summarized using the "$\neq$", which we have already discussed.

We now have the information ready for easy reference, and we turn to the individual questions.

7. **(B)** If M is included on the trip, we know that we must also include Q and R. And if Q is included on the trip, we must include N or T (or both, but we are looking for the minimum number of other cities). No other cities need be included. So, including M requires both Q and R plus one of the pair N and T. So a total of three *additional* cities are needed.

8. **(A)** By condition 4, Q cannot be included with P. Unfortunately, that is not an available answer choice, so we will have to dig a little deeper. If Q cannot be included on the tour, then we conclude that M cannot be included, for condition 1 requires that Q be included on any tour on which M is a stop.

9. **(B)** This question requires only that we check each of the choices against the summary of conditions. (A) is not acceptable because we have M without Q. (C) is not acceptable because we have M without R. (D) is not acceptable because we have L with R (in violation of condition 7) and because we have Q without either N or T. (E) is not acceptable because we have N, S, and R together, in violation of condition 6. The group in (B), however, meets all of the requirements for an acceptable tour.

10. **(C)** By deleting O, we have the tour M, Q, R, and T. This satisfies condition 1, since Q and R are included with M. And this satisfies condi-

tion 3 since we have M and T. No other condition is violated, so the group M, Q, R, T is acceptable. (A) is incorrect, for eliminating M leaves Q in the group (without M), in violation of condition 3. Similarly, eliminating Q leaves M on the tour without Q, violating condition 1. (D) is incorrect because it also violates condition 1. (E) is incorrect for this would leave Q on the tour without the (M & N) or (M & T) combination required by condition 3.

11. **(C)** To make the group M, Q, R into an acceptable tour, we need only to add N or T. This will finally satisfy both conditions 1 and 3 without violating any other requirement. (A) is incorrect, for adding another city will not remedy the violation of condition 7 (L ≠ R). (B) is incorrect, because satisfying the conditions requires the addition of O (condition 2), R (condition 1), and either N or T (condition 3). (D) is incorrect since the addition of another city will not correct the violation of condition 6. Finally, (E) is incorrect because the addition of O to satisfy condition 2 would then violate condition 5 (O, R, and T on the same tour).

12. **(E)** Here we must test each lettered city. M cannot constitute a tour in and of itself, for condition 1 requires that Q and R be included on any tour that includes M. P, by condition 2, cannot constitute a tour of a single city. Finally, by condition 3, Q's inclusion requires more cities. The remaining cities, L, N, O, R, S and T, however, can be used as single-city tours.

Questions 13–18

This set is a linear ordering set. At first glance, the set appears to be very complex, involving as it does the positioning of 11 items. But a closer examination shows the questions are not that difficult, since the particular restrictions considerably simplify the problem. For example, we know that a red bead is on one end, and we know further that all three red beads are together. So there are only two possible arrangements for the red beads:

```
1  2  3  4  5  6  7  8  9  10  11
R  R  R
         or

                        R  R  R
```

In fact, each additional condition on the placement of the beads tends to simplify matters for us because it eliminates possible arrangements.

With a linear ordering set, we begin by summarizing the information:

Color	Number	
Blue	2	B = B
Red	3	G ≠ G
Green	2	R = R = R
Yellow	4	G or R = ends
	11	

We have made a note of the number of beads of each color, and we have summarized the particular conditions: Blue is next to blue (B = B); green is not next to green (G ≠ G); red is always next to red (R = R = R); and green or red is on each end (G or R = ends). Now we turn to the questions.

13. **(D)** From the given information and our own deductions based on the restrictions that all red be together and that one end be red and the other green, we set up the following diagram:

```
1  2  3  4  5  6  7  8  9  10  11
               B  B           R
G              B  B     R  R  R
```

This leaves the four yellow beads and the one remaining green bead to be positioned. The only restriction on the placement of these five beads is that the green bead may not be next to the other green bead, that is, the remaining green bead cannot be in position 2. This eliminates (C), since the green bead might be in position 8, though it could also be in positions 3, 4, and 5. This also eliminates (B), since position 5 might be filled by a green bead. (A) is clearly incorrect since that is the one remaining position which cannot be occupied by the other green bead. (E) is incorrect since the green bead could be placed in position 3 or 4, separated from the blue beads by one or more yellow beads. We do know, however, that at least one green bead, the one in position 1, will be next to a yellow bead, for a yellow bead is needed to separate the green beads. Of course, the other green bead may also be next to a yellow bead, but that is not necessary. In any event, the fact that the green bead must be separated from the other green bead is sufficient to show the correctness of (D).

14. **(B)** The question stem stipulates

```
1 2 3 4 5 6 7 8 9 10 11
                Y    Y = Y = Y = Y
```
and we fill in YYYY

since the last position cannot be yellow. This then allows us to deduce

```
1  2  3  4  5  6  7  8  9  10 11
               Y  Y  Y  Y  G
```

since the three red beads are together and one of them must be on the end of the string. Then, since the two blue beads must be together, we know that only two different arrangements are possible:

```
1  2  3  4  5  6  7  8  9  10 11
R  R  R  G  B  B  Y  Y  Y  Y  G
```

or: R R R B B G Y Y Y Y G

Under either arrangement, the fifth bead must be blue.

15. **(E)** The question stem stipulates that each blue bead be next to a green bead. Because the blue beads are next to each other, this means the blue and green beads are arranged as a bloc: GBBG. According to the stipulation in the question stem, the four yellow beads are also arranged as a bloc: YYYY. And we know from the initial presentation of restrictions that the three red beads are a bloc: RRR. The only open question is which end of the string is green and which is red. So there are only two possible arrangements:

```
1  2  3  4  5  6  7  8  9  10 11
G  B  B  G  Y  Y  Y  Y  R  R  R
```

OR: R R R Y Y Y Y G B B G

Under either arrangement, positions 5, 6, and 7 are occupied by yellow beads.

16. **(D)** The question stem stipulates

```
1  2  3  4  5  6  7  8  9  10 11
            B  B        R
```

and, given the restriction on the reds and the further restriction on the end beads, we can deduce

```
1  2  3  4  5  6  7  8  9  10 11
G           B  B        R  R  R
```

The only restriction which remains to be observed is the separation of the green beads. This means that the remaining one can occupy positions 3, 4, 7, or 8—though not 2. What is established, however, is that 2 must be yellow, not green.

17. **(E)** The question stem stipulates

```
1  2  3  4  5  6  7  8  9  10 11
            Y        Y  Y  Y
```

and we deduce

```
1  2  3  4  5  6  7  8  9  10 11
R  R  R     Y        Y  Y  Y  G
```

on the basis of the restrictions regarding the placement of the red beads and the colors of the end beads. Further, there is only one open pair left for the blue beads, 6 and 7, which means bead 4 will be green:

```
1  2  3  4  5  6  7  8  9  10 11
R  R  R  G  Y  B  B  Y  Y  Y  G
```

So all three statements are true.

18. **(D)** Since we do not know on which end to place the red beads (nor the green bead), we have the possibility

```
1  2  3  4  5  6  7  8  9  10 11
R  R  R  G                 B  G
```

and its mirror image

```
1  2  3  4  5  6  7  8  9  10 11
G  B                 G  R  R  R
```

We know also that the two blue beads are together, and this means the yellow beads must form a bloc:

```
1 2 3 4 5 6 7 8 9 10 11
R R R G Y Y Y Y B B  G
```

or: G B B Y Y Y Y G R R R

In either case, the seventh bead must be yellow.

Questions 19–24

The key to this set is organizing the information in such a way that it is usable. We recommend a table:

	Marlowe	Joyce	Shakespeare	Keats	Chaucer
J	YES	YES			
K			YES	YES	
L	YES				YES
M	YES		YES	YES	
N		YES		YES	YES
O	YES	YES	YES		

If you study the table, you will see that only one teacher can be chosen from the group J, K, and L. Two teachers must be chosen from the group M, N, and O. The reason for this is that the only distribution that will give the Executive Officer exactly eight assignments is to have three courses taught by each of two faculty members and two courses by a third, 3 + 3 + 2 = 8. This is an important insight which should have occurred to you.

Further study would also show that there is a limited number of permissible combinations. Theoretically, there are nine possibilities:

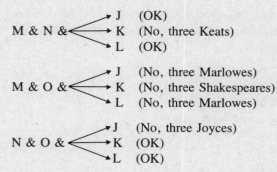

M & N &
→ J (OK)
→ K (No, three Keats)
→ L (OK)

M & O &
→ J (No, three Marlowes)
→ K (No, three Shakespeares)
→ L (No, three Marlowes)

N & O &
→ J (No, three Joyces)
→ K (OK)
→ L (OK)

To see this without careful study, however, requires not only powerful insight but considerable luck as well. In any event, it is not necessary to perceive this to answer the questions, for the questions will guide you to the conclusion that some groupings are not permissible.

Having done this preliminary work, we can use our chart of possibilities in explaining the answers to the individual questions.

19. **(E)** (A) is incorrect because it generates a total of only seven courses. (B), (C), and (D) are shown to be incorrect by our chart. (E) is the only acceptable combination listed.

20. **(C)** Using the information provided in the question stem, we know:

Spring
Joyce
Keats   } (by N)
Chaucer

and that L will teach Marlowe and Chaucer. Then our chart informs us that there are two teachers who can teach with L and N, O or M. Thus, the additional courses will be Marlowe, Joyce, and Shakespeare (by O) or Marlowe, Keats, and Shakespeare (by M). We know, therefore, that both Marlowe and Shakespeare will be offered during the year since both O and M offer those courses. This means Marlowe must be offered in

both the fall and the spring, and further that L will teach Chaucer in the fall.

Fall	Spring	
Marlowe (by ?)	Joyce	
Chaucer (by L)	Keats	} (by N)
Shakes. (by ?)	Chaucer	
Joyce or Keats (by ?)	Marlowe (by ?)	

From this we can see that (C) is correct. It is possible that L will teach Marlowe in the fall, so L *could* teach only in the fall semester. (A) is incorrect as shown by our chart—either M or O must be hired with L and N. (B) is incorrect since the question stipulates that N will teach only in the spring and that accounts for three of the four courses that semester. (D) is incorrect since either Joyce or Keats, though not both, will be offered in the fall. Finally, (E) is incorrect since Shakespeare can be offered only in the fall.

21. **(E)** Our chart shows that if M and N are hired, either J or L can be hired. (A) and (C), therefore, are possibly, though not necessarily, true. Hence, they are both incorrect answers. (B) must also be incorrect as shown by the chart. Hiring M and N, and separating their courses by semester, we have

Semester—M	Semester—N
Marlowe	Joyce
Shakes.	Keats
Keats	Chaucer

The remaining two courses will be Marlowe and Joyce (by J) or Marlowe and Chaucer (by L). Since both J and L teach Marlowe, that will give a total of two Marlowe courses, so one of them must be offered in the spring. (D) is possibly true, provided that M teaches that course in the fall, but (D) is not necessarily true.

22. **(D)** If K and N are hired, O must also be hired. This gives us a course mix of Shakespeare and Keats, (by K); Joyce, Keats, and Chaucer (by N); and Marlowe, Joyce, and Shakespeare (by O). We have two courses on Shakespeare, two on Keats, and two on Joyce. So those three courses must be offered both semesters, proving that I and III are correct statements. II, however, is false, since there is only one offering of Marlowe.

23. **(E)** If L is hired to teach only in the fall, this means Marlowe and Chaucer will be offered then. With L, it is possible to hire either M and N or N and O. We must hire N, and this means

Joyce, Keats, and Chaucer will be taught. Since both L and N offer Chaucer, N must teach Chaucer in the spring. As for (D), this is possible but is necessarily true only if O, rather than M, is hired. Since that is not a logically necessary choice, (D) is merely possible.

24. **(E)** For this question we are told which teachers will be hired. So the course mix will be

Fall
Joyce
Keats   (by N)
Chaucer

with courses on Marlowe, Joyce, and Shakespeare (by O) and on Shakespeare and Keats (by K). Observing the restriction that the same courses may not be offered in a single semester, we have

Fall	Spring
Joyce	Joyce (by O)
Keats (by N)	Shakes. (by ?)
Chaucer	Marlowe (by O)
Shakes. (by ?)	Keats (by K)

We can see that (A), (B), (C), and (D) are all logically necessary. (E) is our exception since Chaucer is taught only in the fall.

Questions 25-30

This is a fancy ordering set. Begin by summarizing the initial conditions:

W < X
Y < Z
J < K
J < L
L < K
L < M
N ≠ V

There is one further conclusion you can draw: J < M. Now we go to the questions.

25. **(D)** Since this item provides no further information, use the initial conditions to eliminate answer choices. Using the second condition, we eliminate (B). Using the third condition, we eliminate (C). Using the fourth condition, we eliminate (E). And using the final condition, we eliminate (A).

26. **(C)** Again, we have a question which supplies no additional information. Just test each choice until

you find one that violates one of the conditions. In choice (C), Z follows Y, in violation of the second condition.

27. **(A)** This question provides no additional information, so there must be some further conclusion deducible from the initial conditions. As we learned in our overview, since J comes before L and L before M, J must come before M. The other choices describe orders that are possible, but not necessary.

28. **(D)** This question does provide additional information, so enter the new information on a diagram:

```
       1   2   3   4   5
Boy        L
Girl           V
```
J comes before L:
```
       1   2   3   4   5
Boy    J   L
Girl               V
```

The initial conditions also require that K and M follow L, but that does not fix their positions. And the initial conditions state that N cannot march in the same row as V. This is as far as we can go. N could be in row 3 or row 5.

29. **(A)** You'll need to enter the new information on a diagram. You know that N, L, and Z create a formation like this:

$$N - (L\&Z)$$

But in which rows should you place them? First, given this small formation, you know that the only possibilities are 1 and 3, 2 and 4, and 3 and 5. Now look at the initial conditions to determine whether they preclude any of these possibilities. Since L comes before both K and M, L cannot come any later that the third row, and this fixes the order of our small formation:

```
        1   2   3   4   5
Boys    N       L
Girls           Z
```
And since J comes ahead of L:
```
        1   2   3   4   5
Boys    N   J   L
Girls           Z
```

But we cannot fix the order of M and K. What about the girls? Z must come after Y, so Y is in either the first or second row. X might be in either the first or second row. And V might be in the second row.

It doesn't appear that we can draw any further conclusions, so we go to the answer choices. Our diagram shows that (A) is necessarily true, while the other choices are only possibly true.

30. **(C)** Again we have additional information that creates a small formation: (L&Z), N, but where should we put this formation? L must be ahead of both K and M and behind J, so L must be in the second row:

```
      1  2  3  4  5
Boys  J  L  N
Girls    Z
```

And the second initial condition requires that Y come before Z:

```
      1  2  3  4  5
Boys  J  L  N
Girls Y  Z
```

Finally, W comes before X, so W and X are either in rows three and four, three and five, or four and five, respectively. But V cannot be in row three. Therefore, V and X are in rows four and five, though not necessarily in that order, and W is in row three:

```
      1  2  3  4  5
Boys  J  L  N
Girls Y  Z  W
```

The diagram shows that only (C) is necessarily true.

SECTION III

1. **(C)** This is a main idea question, and the task is to find a choice which expresses the main thesis of the passage without being too narrow and without being overly broad and going beyond the scope of the argument. (A) is too narrow, since this is but a minor feature of the discussion. (E) can be eliminated on the same grounds, since the possibility of nuclear destruction is but one important difference between war in a modernized society and war in a pre-modernized society. (B) is an attractive choice, but it is not the main thesis of the passage. The author does indeed discuss some of the effects of war on both modernized and pre-modernized societies, but this discussion is subordinate to a larger goal: to show that because of changing circumstance (effects are different), the value of war has changed. (D) is incorrect because it misses this main point, and it is incorrect for the further reason that the author discusses more than just pre-modernized societies.

2. **(A)** The second paragraph describes the attitude of pre-modernized society toward war: accepted, even noble, necessary. Coupled with the goals of war in pre-modernized societies, described in the first paragraph, we can infer that leaders of pre-modernized society regarded war as a valid policy tool. On this ground we select (A), eliminating (B) and (C). As for (D), although this can be inferred to have been a feature of war in pre-modernized society, (D) is not responsive to the question: What did the leaders think of war, that is, what was their attitude? (E) can be eliminated on the same ground and on the further ground that "necessity" for war was not that described in (E).

3. **(C)** The author is discussing war, a seemingly uncivilized activity. Yet, the author argues that war, at least in pre-modernized times, was the necessary result of certain economic and social forces. His use of the term "civilized" is ironic. Under other circumstances, the explanations offered by (A) and (B) might be plausible, but there is nothing in this text to support either of those. (D), too, might under other circumstances be a reason for placing the word in quotation marks, but it does not appear that this author is attempting to affect the reader's emotions; the passage is too detached and scientific for that. Finally, (E) does articulate one of the author's objectives, but this is not the reason for putting the one word in quotations. The explanation for that is something more specific than an overall idea of the passage.

4. **(B)** This is an explicit idea question, and (A), (C), (D), and (E) are all mentioned at various points in the passage as reasons for going to war. (B), too, is mentioned, but it is mentioned as a feature of the military establishment in pre-modernized society—not as a reason for going to war.

5. **(E)** This is another main idea question, and (B), (C), and (D) can be eliminated as too narrow. It is true the author mentions that economic and social conditions, technology, and armed conflict have all changed, but this is not the ultimate point to be

proved. The author's main point is that *because* of such changes, the value of war has changed. (A) is only tangentially related to the text. Though we may learn a bit about how decisions are made, in part, this is not the main burden of the argument.

6. **(B)** We have already mentioned that the tone of the passage is neutral—scientific and detached. As for the remaining choices, (A) and (D) can be eliminated as overstatements. To be sure, the author seems to deplore the destruction which might result from a nuclear war, but that concern does not rise to the status of outrage, indignation, fear, or alarm. (E) is a closer call. While it is true that the author expresses concern about the ability of modernized society to survive war, and while there is arguably a hint of optimism or hope, it cannot be said that these are the *defining* features of the passage. A better description of the prevailing tone is offered by (B). As for (C), the one ironic reference ("civilized") does not make the entire passage humorous.

7. **(D)** This is an application question, and we must take the information from the passage and apply it to a new situation. The author offers two reasons for the conclusion that war is no longer a viable policy tool: (1) the danger of world-wide destruction and (2) the costs after victory outweigh the benefits to be won. We can conclude that even in the absence of nuclear weapons, war will still lack its traditional value, as argued by the author in the fourth paragraph. Thus, we can eliminate (A) and (B) on the grounds that they are contradicted by the author's thinking. (E) can be eliminated for the same reason and because no such "instincts" are discussed in the text. A close look at (C) shows that it is not in agreement with the author's view, since the author believes that though nuclear weapons deter nuclear war, war is obsolete for other reasons as well.

8. **(B)** This is a main idea question. As correctly described by (B), the author explains the results of some studies and suggests some implications of these findings for detecting high blood pressure. (E) is incorrect since it is but a minor aspect of the passage. Although the author does note that there is such a correlation, he is not primarily concerned to prove the existence of such a relationship. (C) can be eliminated because the main point is not to describe the epidemiological and clinical studies from a methodological point of view. Rather, the author is concerned with the findings of these studies. (D) can be eliminated on similar grounds, for the author indicates that the two methods of study both point to the existence of a familial connection. (A) can be eliminated since the author does not criticize but rather relies on these experiments.

9. **(D)** This is an explicit idea question. We find both statement I and statement II mentioned at the end of the first paragraph as factors discouraging studies of blood pressure in children. As for III, though this belief is mentioned in the passage, it is not mentioned as a factor discouraging research on children. If anything, this belief suggested that such research might be valuable, but the research was never undertaken for the reasons just mentioned.

10. **(C)** This is a question which asks us to make a further application of the arguments given in the passage, and the greatest danger may be the temptation to overstate the case. This is the difficulty with answer (E). The author qualifies his remarks in the closing sentences. It may be "possible"; it is never asserted that it is now possible to do this. (D) also overstates the case. The author states that these chemical deficiencies are associated with high blood pressure, not that such deficiencies *cause* high blood pressure. And to the extent that one wants to argue that such deficiencies *contribute* to high blood pressure (based on paragraph three), that is not sufficient to support the causal statement expressed in (D). As for (A), the author notes that the low output of urinary kallikrein is associated with high blood pressure, that is, it may be another symptom of whatever physiological disorder causes high blood pressure; but that means it is an effect of the underlying cause and not the cause itself. Finally, (B) can be eliminated because it is not a further conclusion of the passage. To the extent that (B) reiterates what is stated already [and note that (B) states the kallikrein-kinin system is important in determining blood pressure, not that the system *causes* high blood pressure], it is not appropriate as a further statement based on arguments presented. (C) is, however, a natural extension of the argument. Remember, the author begins by noting that it is important to determine when high blood pressure begins, and he suggests that it may begin as early as infancy.

11. **(A)** This is a logical detail question. In essence

the question stipulates that the author does introduce such evidence and then asks for what reason. In the final paragraph the author is discussing the connection between low urinary kallikrein excretion and high blood pressure. By noting that black children often show this and noting further that blacks often have high blood pressure, he hopes to provide further evidence for the connection. As for (B), though this may be an incidental effect of the reference, it cannot be said that this is the logical function of the argument in the overall development of the passage. (C) is incorrect since the author is not asserting a causal connection but only a correlation. (D) is incorrect for a reason similar to that which eliminates (B). Though this might be a further application for the point, it is not the reason the author incorporates the data into the argument of this passage. Finally, (E) is one of the main themes of the passage, but it does not explain why the author introduced the particular point at the particular juncture in the argument.

12. **(B)** This is an explicit detail question. In the third paragraph, the author discusses the operation of the kallikrein-kinin system. There he mentions that it produces chemicals which operate to dilate blood vessels, so II is part of the correct answer. I and III, however, are not part of the correct answer. The author does not state that the kallikrein-kinin system interferes directly with either the sympathetic nervous system or the production of aldosterone—only that it *offsets* the effects of those actions.

13. **(C)** This is a logical detail question: Why does the author introduce this information? In the second paragraph, the author is describing new research, done on children, which suggests that the factors related to high blood pressure are already detectable in children. (A) is incorrect since the author has not yet begun to discuss the biochemical research; he is only discussing epidemiological surveys. (B) is incorrect since it is not a correct response to the question. The author does state that such research is actually possible, but he does not cite the results of the study in order to prove the study was possible. Rather, he cites the results to prove the further conclusion outlined in answer (C). (D) is incorrect for it is not a response to the question. To be sure, one might use the results of the study cited to support the recommendation articulated in (D), but that is not the author's motivation for introducing them

in his argument. As for (E), this fails for the same reason that (B) fails.

14. **(C)** This is a logical structure question. The author develops his argument primarily by describing findings and supporting a conclusion. As for (A), though the author does mention two types of research, epidemiological studies and clinical studies, he does not contrast these. (B) is incorrect since his main purpose is to support a conclusion, and whatever refutation is offered in the passage (e.g., against the position that blood pressure in children cannot be measured accurately) is offered in the service of a greater point. (E) must fail for a similar reason. And (D) fails for this reason as well: The author is supporting a position, not refuting it.

15. **(C)** This is a main idea question. The main point of the passage is that those who believe AFDC restrictions contribute to family dissolution are in error. It is not the restrictions on aid but the aid itself, according to the author, which contributes to low-income family dissolution. So the primary purpose of the passage is to analyze the causes of a phenomenon. (A) is incorrect, for any such results are mentioned only obliquely and are only incidental to the main development. (B) describes something which is integral to, but is not the main point of, the argument. As for (D), the author himself offers no such recommendation. While an argument for reform might use the argument in the passage for such recommendations, we cannot attribute any proposal for reform to the author. Finally, (E) describes what may be a result of the argument, but changing the attitude of the public, as opposed to engaging in scholarly debate, does not appear to be the objective of the text.

16. **(A)** As we noted above, the author argues that it is not restrictions on aid which create pressures on low-income families; it is the aid itself. We can apply this reasoning to answer this question. The analysis in the text can be used to predict that an increase in the availability of aid would tend to increase pressures on the family unit. Thus, reducing restrictions, because it would result in an increase in aid availability, would actually tend to create more pressure for divorce. This would have the exact opposite effect predicted by those who call for welfare reforms such as eliminating restrictions. (A) is nice also because of the word "paradoxically" which opens the state-

ment, for the result would be paradoxical from the standpoint of the reformer. (C) and (D) can be eliminated because they are contradicted by the analysis given in the passage. (B) is eliminated because the author never addresses questions of fiscal policy. Finally, (E) goes too far in two respects. First, it overstates the author's case. The author does not suggest that the only factor operating in the dissolution of low-income families is welfare; therefore, he would not likely suggest that the problem could be entirely controlled by manipulating benefit levels. Further, it is not clear that the author advocates any particular policy. The scholarly tone of the article suggests that the author may or may not believe public policy on welfare should take into account the problem of divorce.

17. **(B)** This is an explicit idea question. In discussing the costs of divorce in the third paragraph (costs meaning both economic and social costs), the author mentions (B), (C), and (D) as encouraging people to stay married. Earlier in that same paragraph, he mentions consumption possibilities as a factor tending to hold a marriage together. (B) is never mentioned in this respect. Although the author is primarily interested in low-income family stability, he never states that social or economic class is a factor in perpetuating a marriage. And to the extent that one mounts an argument to the effect that the pressures described in paragraph three (costs of divorce and greater consumption possibilities) would naturally tend to operate more powerfully for lower-income families, he is applying that reasoning to a new situation. So that argument, since it is new, cannot be a factor mentioned by the author in this passage, and cannot, therefore, be an answer to the question asked.

18. **(A)** This is obviously a main idea question, and we have already analyzed the main point of the passage. It is nicely stated by (A). (B) is not the main idea but only an incidental feature of the argument. (C) is incorrect since this is in direct contradiction to the main point of the passage. (D) fails for the same reason that (B) fails. Finally, (E) is incorrect because there is no warrant in the passage to support the conclusion that the author himself would make such a recommendation. The author argues his point in a very scholarly and neutral fashion. Given that, we cannot attribute any attitude to him about the wisdom of welfare policy.

19. **(B)** As we have just noted, the scholarly treatment of the passage is best described as scientific and detached. As for (A), though the author may be confident in his presentation, there is no hint of optimism. (C) can be eliminated for a similar reason; there is no hint of alarm or discouragement. As for (D), to the extent that it can be argued that the author's treatment is scholarly, and therefore polite and sensitive, (B) is a better description of the overall tone. The defining elements of a scholarly treatment are those set forth in (B). Those elements suggested by (D) would be merely incidental to and parasitic upon the main features of scientific neutrality and detachment. Finally, though the author's treatment is detached, it would be wrong to say that the author is callous and indifferent——any more than we would want to say that a doctor who analyzes the causes of a disease in clinical terms is therefore callous and indifferent.

20. **(A)** With an application question of this sort, we must be careful not to overstate the strength of the author's case. This is the reason (D) is incorrect. Though the author points out that there are economic pressures on families which tend to encourage divorce, it would go beyond that analysis to attribute to the author the statement in (D). (E), too, overstates the case. Though the author prefers to analyze family stability primarily in economic terms, the text will not support the judgment that people are getting more self-centered. If anything, a rising divorce rate would be analyzed by the author in broad social and economic terms, rather than in personal terms as suggested by (E). (B) is incorrect because it takes us too far beyond the analysis given in paragraph three. While it is conceivable that further analysis would generate the conclusion in (B), (A) is much closer to the actual text. This is not to say that (B) is necessarily a false statement; rather, this is to accept the structure of the question: Would the author *most likely* agree? Finally, (C) attributes to the author a value judgment which has no support in the text.

21. **(E)** This, too, is an application question and, as was just pointed out, we are looking for the most likely source. It is not impossible that the passage was taken from a basic economics text or a book on the history of welfare. It could, conceivably, be one of several readings included in such books, but on balance it seems more likely, given the scholarly tone and the particular subject, that

(E) is the correct answer. It seems unlikely that this would have appeared in (A) or (D).

22. **(A)** Here we have a main idea question. The structure of the passage is first to explain that previous siting decisions have been made by regulatory agencies with only a review function exercised by government. The author then explains that in the past the most important features affecting the demographic characteristics of the population were natural ones. Then he argues that, given the effect siting decisions will have in the future, the government ought to take an active role in making those decisions, and that the government ought to take social considerations into account in making such decisions. Given this brief synopsis of the argument, we can see that (A) neatly restates this thesis. Further, we can see that (B) constitutes only a part, not the entirety, of the argument. (C), too, forms only one subpart of the whole analysis. (D) can be eliminated since the author believes that future siting decisions need not be governed by only natural features. Finally, (E) may very well be true, but it surely is not the main point of the argument presented.

23. **(D)** This is an explicit idea question. (A) is mentioned in the final sentence of the first paragraph along with (B). (E) is a theme which runs generally through that paragraph, and (C) is specifically mentioned in the third paragraph. Nowhere does the author suggest that proximity to fuel sources needs to be taken into the siting decision.

24. **(C)** Again we have an explicit idea question. In the opening remarks, the author specifically supports statement I. Then, this remark, taken in conjunction with the point made at the end of the first paragraph, tells us that II also is a characteristic of past siting decisions. As for III, the passage states in the final paragraph that environmentalists may oppose the construction of energy parks, but this is in opposition to future siting decisions—not to past siting decisions.

25. **(C)** This is a logical structure question. The author's analysis and recommendation depend on the assumption that it will be possible to predict the demographic consequences of an energy park. Without this assumption, the recommendation that the government use electric facility siting decisions to effect social goals loses much of

its persuasiveness. As for (A) and (D), the historical explanation is in large part expository only, that is, background information which is not, strictly speaking, essential to the argument supporting the recommendation. To the extent, then, that either (A) or (D) does weaken the historical analysis, and that is doubtful, the damage to the overall argument would not be great. As for (B) and (E), these are both irrelevant, and the proof is that whether (B) and (E) are true or false does not affect the argument.

26. **(D)** The correct answer to this application question is clearly supported by the concluding remarks of the passage. (A) is contradicted by these remarks and must be incorrect. (B) goes beyond the scope of the passage. We cannot attribute such a critical judgment (". . . . were irresponsible") to the author. In fact, the passage at least implies that decisions during the nineteenth century were made in a natural (no pun intended) way. (C) overstates the case. Though the author believes that siting decisions for power plants need not depend on natural features, there is no support in the text for such a broad conclusion as that given in (C). Finally, as for (E), there is no evidence that the author would make such a judgment.

27. **(A)** This is an explicit idea question the answer to which is found at the end of the third paragraph. The most important feature of an energy park is that the place in which the massive effects will be manifested can be chosen. So, unlike the harbor, a natural feature located without regard to human desires, the energy park can be located where it will serve goals other than the production of energy. As for (B), even to the extent that (B) makes an accurate statement, the statement is not responsive to the question. This is not an important difference between the natural advantages of an early city and the man-made features of the energy park. A similar argument invalidates (D). As for (C), this is obviously irrelevant to the question asked. Finally, (E) is incorrect for two reasons. First, such a conclusion is not supported by the passage. Second, it is not a response to the question asked.

28. **(E)** There can be little doubt that the author is an advocate of energy parks. What criticism he notes in passing in the final paragraph, he simply dismisses. Thus, we can conclude that his attitude is one of wholehearted support, as indicated

by answer (E). We can eliminate (D) because the author in no way qualifies his recommendation. (A), (B), and (C) can be eliminated because of the author's positive attitude.

29. **(B)** This is a main idea question. The author begins by stating that a large number of auto traffic fatalities can be attributed to drivers who are intoxicated. He then reviews two approaches to controlling this problem, taxation and drunk driving laws. Neither is very successful. The author finally notes that therapy may be useful, though the extent of its value has not yet been proved. (B) fairly well describes this development. (A) can be eliminated since any conclusions drawn by the author from studies on drunk driving are used for the larger objective described in (B). (C) is incorrect since, aside from suggesting possible ways to reduce the extent of the problem, the author never treats the causes of drunk driving. (D) is incorrect for the same reason. Finally, (E) is incorrect, because the comparison between the U.S. and Britain is only a small part of the passage.

30. **(B)** This is an inference question. In the third paragraph, the author discusses the effect of drunk driving laws. He states that after the implementation of the Road Safety Act in Britain, motor vehicle fatalities fell considerably. On this basis, we infer that the RSA was a law aimed at drunk driving. We can eliminate (D) and (E) on this ground. (C) can be eliminated as not warranted on the basis of this information. It is not clear whether the number of arrests increased. Equally consistent with the passage is the conclusion that the number of arrests dropped because people were no longer driving while intoxicated. (C) is incorrect for a further reason, the justification for (B). (B) and (A) are fairly close since both describe the RSA as a law aimed at drunk driving. But the last sentence of the third paragraph calls for (B) over (A). As people learned that they would not get caught for drunk driving, the law became less effective. This suggests that the RSA made drunk driving illegal, not that it lowered the BAC required for conviction. This makes sense of the sentence ". . . they could drink and not be stopped." If (A) were correct, this sentence would have to read, ". . . they could drink the same amount and not be convicted."

31. **(A)** This is an inference question. In the first paragraph, the author states that for a person to attain a BAC of 0.1 percent, he would need to drink over five ounces of 80 proof spirits over a *short period of time*. The author is trying to impress on us that that is a considerable quantity of alcohol for most people to drink. (A) explains why the author makes this comment. (B) is incorrect and confuses the first paragraph with the second paragraph. (C) is incorrect since the point of the example is that the BAC is so high most people will not exceed it. This is not to say, however, that people will not drink and drive because of laws establishing maximum BAC levels. Rather, they can continue to drink and drive because the law allows them a considerable margin in the level of BAC. (D) is a misreading of that first paragraph. Of all the very drunk drivers (BAC in excess of 0.1), only 1 percent are involved in accidents. But this does not say that most drivers involved in fatal collisions have BAC levels in excess of 0.1 percent, and that is what (D) says. As for (E), the author never states that the only way to attain a BAC of 0.1 percent is to drink five ounces of 80 proof spirits in a short time—there may be other ways of becoming intoxicated.

32. **(A)** This is an application question. In the second paragraph, the author states that increased taxation on alcohol would tax the heaviest drinkers most, but he notes that this would also penalize the moderate and light drinker. In other words, the remedy is not sufficiently focused on the problem. Then, in the third paragraph, the author notes that drunk driving laws are aimed at the specific problem drivers. We can infer from this discussion that the author would likely advocate drunk driving laws over taxation for the reasons just given. This reasoning is presented in answer (A). (B) is incorrect for the reasons just given and for the further reason that the passage never suggests that taxation is likely to be more effective in solving the problem. The author never really evaluates the effectiveness of taxation in reducing drunk driving. (C) is incorrect for the reason given in support of (A) and for the further reason that the author never raises the issue of personal liberty in conjunction with the BAC test. (D) can be eliminated because the author does not discount the effectiveness of anti-drunk driving measures entirely. Even the British example gives some support to the conclusion that such laws have an effect. (E) is incorrect for the author never mentions the expense or administrative feasibility of BAC tests.

33. **(C)** This is a question about the logical structure of the passage. In paragraph 3, the author notes that stricter enforcement of laws against drunk driving may result in a few more arrests; but a few more arrests is not likely to have much impact on the problem because the number of arrests is small compared to those who do not get caught. As a consequence, people will continue to drink and drive. The author supports this with the British experience. Once people realize that the chances of being caught are relatively small, they will drink and drive. This is the conclusion of answer (C). (A) is incorrect since the passage does not support the conclusion that the problem is any worse or any better in one country or the other. (B) is incorrect since this is the conclusion the author is arguing against. (D) is wrong because the author is not discussing the effectiveness of taxation in paragraph 3. (E) is a statement the author would likely accept, but that is not the reason for introducing the British example. So answer (E) is true but non-responsive.

34. **(A)** This is an application question which asks us to examine the logical structure of the argument. In the fourth paragraph, the author argues that the effectiveness of deterrents to drunk driving will depend upon the ability of the drinker to control his consumption. But drunk driving has two aspects: drunk and driving. The author assumes that drunk driving is a function of drinking only. Otherwise, he would not suggest that control on consumption is *necessary* as opposed to *helpful*. (A) attacks this assumption by pointing out that it is possible to drink to excess without driving. It is possible that stiff penalties could be effective deterrents to drunk driving if not to drinking to excess. (B) is incorrect because the author himself makes this point, so this choice does not weaken the argument. (C) is incorrect since the author is concerned only with the problem of fatalities caused by drunk driving. It is hardly an attack on his argument to contend that he has not solved all of the world's ills. Then (D) can be eliminated since the author is concerned to eliminate fatalities caused by drunk driving. He takes no position on whether the drunk driver ought to be punished, only that he ought to be deterred from driving while intoxicated. (E) is not a strong attack on the argument since the author does leave open the question of the value of therapy in combating drunk driving.

35. **(C)** This is a tone question which focuses on the final sentence of the paragraph. There the author states again that the problem is a serious one and that we must find a solution. Since he admonishes us to look for a solution, (C) is an excellent description. (A) can be eliminated since there is no irony in the passage. (B) can be eliminated since the author is concerned to find a solution. (E), however, overstates the case. Concern is not indignation. Finally, (D) may seem plausible. The author does leave us with a project. But to acknowledge that a problem exists and that a clear solution has not yet been found is not to be indecisive. The author is decisive in his assessment of the problem.

SECTION IV

Questions 1–6

This problem set is a linear ordering set with the additional complication of the challenge provision. You would probably want to summarize the information:

F > G (F above G)
J > (H & I) (J above both H and I)
K = H + 2 (K is two above H)
F = 3 or 4 (F is 3rd or 4th)

1. **(D)** For this question, we need only check each of the choices against the conditions. (A) can be eliminated since K is not ranked two places above H. (B) can be eliminated since J is not ranked above H and I, and for the further reason that F is out of place. (C) is not acceptable since G is ranked above F. (E) is incorrect since K and H are together, not separated by another person. Only (D) meets all of the requirements for the initial ranking.

2. **(A)** For this question we are given additional information. On the assumption that K is ranked first, we know that H must be ranked third, which in turn places F fourth. Since J must be ranked above H, J must be ranked second. No further conclusion can be definitely drawn about the positions of G and I, so our order is

1	2	3	4	5	6
K	J	H	F	G/I	

At this juncture, we check our deductions against the answer choices. (B) and (C) are contradicted by the diagram. (D) and (E) are possible—not necessary. (A), however, makes a statement which is confirmed by the diagram.

3. **(A)** For this question we assume that F is ranked third. On that assumption, there are only two positions available for K: 2 (with H in 4) and 4 (with H in 6).

```
1  2  3  4  5  6      1  2  3  4  5  6
   K  F  H                F  K     H
```

As for the first possibility, G must be in position 5 with I in 6, or vice versa, for J must be above H, and that means J must be in first position. As for the second possibility, G must be in position 5, which forces J and I to occupy positions 1 and 2, respectively:

```
1  2  3  4  5  6      1  2  3  4  5  6
J  K  F  H  I/G       J  I  F  K  G  H
```

So there are a total of three possible arrangements. We are looking, however, for a statement which is necessarily true. That is (A), since J is ranked first in all three possibilities. (B) is incorrect since it is only possible, not necessary, that K be second. (C) is incorrect for it makes a false statement. (D) is incorrect for the same reason. Finally, (E) makes a statement which could be true, but is not necessarily true.

4. **(D)** For this question we assume that K is ranked third. This means F is fourth, H is fifth, and G must be sixth. Finally, since J must be above I, J is first, with I second.

```
1  2  3  4  5  6
J  I  K  F  H  G
```

K can challenge only the players one or two ranks above him, and those players are J and I.

5. **(E)** If F is able to issue a challenge to H, this can only be because F is ranked fourth with H third. It is not possible for F to be in the third position with H in the first or second. With H and F in third and fourth, respectively, we are able to deduce the following:

```
1  2  3  4  5  6
K  J  H  F  G/I
```

K must be in the first position since that is two

positions above H, who is in third. Since J must be above H, this means J must be second. Now we check our answer choices. (A), (B), (C), and (D) are all necessarily true as shown by the diagram. While (E) is possible, but is not necessary, so (E) is the exception and therefore our correct answer.

6. **(A)** We assume that J challenges K, so K must be ranked above J. But J can be ranked no lower than second, so K must be first with H in third and F in fourth:

```
1  2  3  4  5  6
K  J  H  F  G/I
```

Checking the answer choices, we see that (A) is necessarily true, while (B), (C), and (D) are necessarily false and (E) only possibly true.

Questions 7–10

Although this problem set involves a temporal ordering, we render that ordering spatially:

```
              M   Tu  Wed  Th   F
W,Y  A.M.               X
X
V,Z  P.M.          Z   (V) (Z)
```

With X flying on Wednesday morning, X cannot fly Tuesday or Thursday morning, nor on Wednesday or Thursday afternoon. Further, with Z flying on Tuesday, Z is not available for Wednesday afternoon. This means V must fly Wednesday afternoon and Z Thursday afternoon.

7. **(E)** We were able to draw only two further conclusions from the initial conditions: V flies Wednesday afternoon and Z flies Thursday afternoon. (A), (B), (C), and (D) are all possibly true; only (E) is necessarily true.

8. **(B)** We begin by processing the additional information. Since X is flying Friday morning, X cannot fly either Thursday morning or Friday afternoon. This means that either W or Y will fly on Thursday morning and that V will fly on Friday afternoon.

```
        M   Tu  Wed  Th   F
A.M.              X        X
P.M.         Z    V   Z    V
```

The diagram shows that (A), (C), and (D) are possibly true and that (E) is necessarily false. Only (B) is necessarily true.

9. **(A)** We assume that X flies only one morning flight. This does not allow us to draw any specific conclusion about a particular flight, so we are forced to look to the answer choices; that is, we must test each choice and arrive at the correct answer by the process of elimination. (A) is correct. W and Y must cover Monday, Tuesday, Thursday, and Friday. And since a pilot cannot fly on consecutive days, W must do either Monday or Tuesday and either Thursday or Friday. (B) is incorrect since V could do both Monday and Friday afternoons, and then X would make only the one flight each week. (C) is incorrect as shown by our analysis of (A)——Y also must fly two days each week. (D) is incorrect for Z cannot fly either Monday or Friday. (E) is possibly, though not necessarily, true. We do not know whether Monday and Friday afternoons will go to X or V.

10. **(D)** We begin by processing the additional information:

	Mon	Tu	Wed	Th	Fri
A.M.	X	Y	X	Y	X
P.M.	V	Z	V	Z	V

If W does not fly at all during the week, then Y must fly on Tuesday and Thursday. This means that X must fly on Monday morning and Friday morning. Further, we must assign V to Monday and Friday afternoons. The diagram shows that (A), (B), (C), and (E) are all necessarily true and that (D) is necessarily false.

Questions 11–15

This is a selection set, and we begin by summarizing the restrictions on our selections:

S → Q (S requires Q)
R → ~R (Not two consecutive days)
T ← U (U can only follow T)
Only one carryover

11. **(E)** For a question such as this, which does not supply any additional information, we simply check each answer choice against the restrictions we have summarized. (A) is not acceptable because R is used on two consecutive days and, further, because S appears the first day without Q. (B) can be eliminated because two selections carry over from day 1 to day 2 (S and Q). (C) can

be eliminated because S appears on day 2 unaccompanied by Q. (D) can be eliminated because U appears on day 2, but T did not appear on day 1. Only (E) is consistent with all of the restrictions.

12. **(C)** If P and S are on the menu, then Q is also on the menu for that day. As for the next day, U cannot be used since T was not offered the day before. Further, S cannot be used since S requires Q and we cannot carry over both S and Q. This leaves us with R and T to be offered along with one dish from the first day (either P or Q). So III and IV are necessarily offered the second day.

13. **(C)** We know that neither R nor U can be offered on the intervening day. R cannot be used on two consecutive days, and U must follow T. So we must use S and T. With S offered, we must also offer Q. So the three specials for the intervening day are S, Q, and T.

14. **(A)** If neither Q nor T is on the menu, this leaves us with P, R, S, and U. But S cannot be used without Q, so this leaves only P, R, and U. Hence, there is only one possible combination of specials, given the assumption that Q and T are not offered.

15. **(A)** On the assumption that Q, R, and S are offered on one day, R cannot be offered the following day. Nor can U be offered since T did not appear on the preceding day. This means that both P and T will have to be included since only one of the original three can be carried over. S cannot be carried over because that would also require the carrying over of Q. Q, however, can appear without S (Q is not "dependent" on S). So the second day, the specials must be P, Q, and T.

Questions 16–20

Here we have an ordering set, but the ordering is not strictly linear. That is, rather than having a single file of items (e.g., books on a shelf), several people here could occupy the same position simultaneously, e.g., three people interviewed on Thursday. We begin by summarizing the information:

M Tu Wed Th F
            O
(M & N) =Q + 3 (M and N interviewed 3
   days after Q)
P later than K

It does not appear possible to draw any definite conclusions about which individual will be interviewed on which day (other than O). But there are some general conclusions which are available. First, we know that Q must be interviewed on either Monday or Tuesday, with M and N coming on Thursday or Friday, respectively, for those are the only ways of observing the restriction that M and N be interviewed exactly three days after Q. Second, we can also deduce that on one day three persons will be interviewed, on one day two persons will be interviewed, and on the remaining three days only one person will be interviewed. Given that Wednesday is used for only one interview and that only two days have more than one interview, a 1–1–1–2–3 arrangement (though not necessarily in that order) is the only possible distribution.

16. **(C)** This problem does not supply us with additional information, so we must find the correct choice using only the initial conditions. You will observe that the answer choices all make relative statements, e.g., O's interview is later in the week than K's interview, and not specific statements, e.g., K is enterviewed on Thursday. The incorrect answers can all be shown to be possible by constructing examples:

M	Tu	Wed	Th	F
Q	K	O	M	P
	J		N	
			L	

This, of course, is not the only possible schedule, but the diagram shows that (A), (B), (D), and (E) are possible. (C), however, is not possible. At the latest, K could be interviewed on Thursday, since K must be followed by P. At the earliest, M and N could be interviewed on Thursday, since they are interviewed on the third day following Q's interview. So it is impossible to interview K on a day *later* in the week than that set aside for N.

17. **(B)** Again, we have a question which does not supply us with any more information. Our analysis regarding the distribution of interviews proves that (B) is necessarily true. As for the incorrect answers, using our diagram from the preceding explanation, we can prove that they are not necessarily true. As for (A), L can be interviewed on Tuesday with K and J, which proves that the M-N day need not be the day with three interviews. As for (C), we can change the diagram to have K and J on Monday and Q on Tuesday. As for (D) and (E), the diagram already proves these statements are not necessarily true.

18. **(A)** Here we have additional information:

Mon	Tu	Wed	Th	Fri
	Q			M
	J			N

We know that M and N must be scheduled for Friday, and we know further that a third person must be scheduled for Friday in order to meet the 1–1–1–2–3 distributional requirement. Beyond that, no further conclusions are evident, and we must turn for guidance to the choices. (A) is the correct answer since P must follow K. This means that K cannot be interviewed on Friday, and we know that K cannot be interviewed on Tuesday. This means that K must be interviewed on either Monday or Thursday, days reserved for only one interview. (B), (C), (D), and (E) are all possible, but not necessarily true.

19. **(B)** Since P must follow K, and since M and N can be interviewed only on Thursday or Friday, the stipulation that K is interviewed with M and N forces us to schedule M and N for Thursday. This requires that we schedule Q for Monday. The remaining statements are all possible, but none of them is necessarily true.

20. **(C)** If L is interviewed later in the week than P, then Thursday is the earliest available date for L (P must follow K). However, the latest date by which Q can be interviewed is Tuesday. So L and Q cannot be scheduled for the same day.

Questions 21-24

For this set we will use an information matrix:

	M	N	O	P	Q	R
1						
2						
3						
4						
5						

This allows us to keep track of which performers are used in which skits. We enter the information:

	M	N	O	P	Q	R
1	NO	NO	YES	YES	NO	NO
2						YES
3	NO	YES	NO	NO	NO	NO
4						
5						

Is there anything more to be learned? Yes. If each of the 6 performers is to appear 3 times, we need a total of 6 × 3, or 18, appearances. Thus far, we have 2 for the first performance, 4 for the second, and 1 for the third, for a total of 7. We need 11 more appearances. Skits 4 and 5 have spaces for 12 performers (6 for each performance), but we are told that fewer people are used in the fifth than in the fourth skit. So skit 5 can use a maximum of 5 people, and 4 can use a maximum of 6 people. But that is exactly the number we need, 11. So all 6 performers must appear in skit 4, and 5 out of 6 in skit 5. Thus, the distribution is 2, 4, 1, 6, and 5, for a total of 18. Now, we can enter further information on our matrix:

	M	N	O	P	Q	R	
1	NO	NO	YES	YES	NO	NO	2
2						YES	4
3	NO	YES	NO	NO	NO	NO	1
4	YES	YES	YES	YES	YES	YES	6
5							5
						Total	18

But we also know that each performer must appear three times, so we deduce:

	M	N	O	P	Q	R	
1	NO	NO	YES	YES	NO	NO	2
2	YES				YES	YES	4
3	NO	YES	NO	NO	NO	NO	1
4	YES	YES	YES	YES	YES	YES	6
5	YES				YES	YES	5
	3	3	3	3	3	3	18

Totals

For example, if M does not appear in skits 1 and 3, we know M must appear in 2, 4, and 5.

21. **(E)** We were able to deduce this by reflecting on the overall distributional requirements. Our chart shows that (A) and (B) are possibly, though not necessarily, true. (C) and (D) are shown to be false by our chart.

22. **(B)** The chart confirms that (B) is the correct answer, for M and R both appear in skits 2, 4, and 5. (C) is perhaps, though not necessarily, true, as shown by the chart. (A), (D), and (E) are shown by the chart to be false.

23. **(B)** Since we need a total of five performers in the fifth skit (two in addition to M, Q, and R), at least one member of the pair, P and O, must be used. As for (A), it is possible that N will be used and therefore neither P nor O. As for (C) and (D), the same reasoning shows that they are possible. Finally, (E) is possible if N appears in the second skit rather than in the fifth.

24. **(A)** For this question, we add the additional information to our matrix:

	M	N	O	P	Q	R	
1	NO	NO	YES	YES	NO	NO	2
2	YES	(YES)	(NO)	(NO)	YES	YES	4
3	NO	YES	NO	NO	NO	NO	1
4	YES	YES	YES	YES	YES	YES	6
5	YES	(NO)	(YES)	(YES)	YES	YES	5
	3	3	3	3			18

Questions 25–30

This is an ordinary ordering set. Begin by summarizing the initial conditions:

N > M
(Q & O) > P
O = R + 2
M = 2nd or 3rd

25. **(D)** This question stem supplies no additional information, so use the initial conditions to eliminate choices. Using the second condition, you can eliminate (C) and (E). Using the third condition, you can eliminate (B). And using the final condition, you can eliminate (A).

26. **(D)** This question stem stipulates that R is the lowest rank in the organization:

```
6   5   4   3   2   1
R
```

What else can be concluded? Look at the initial conditions to find one that connects another rank with R, and that is the third condition:

```
6   5   4   3   2   1
R           O
```

Now look for a condition that connects O with another rank, and that is the second:

```
6   5   4   3   2   1
R   P   O
```

There are no further obvious conclusions to be drawn, so go to the choices. As the diagram shows, (A), (B), and (C) are possibly, though not necessarily true, while (E) is necessarily false. (D), however, is necessarily true.

27. **(C)** Remember that a question that asks for the maximum number of possible orders is really asking you to find the number of "could be" solutions. Begin by entering the new information on the diagram:

```
6   5   4   3   2   1
            M
```

Given that M is in position 3, R and O must be in 6 and 4 or 4 and 2, respectively:

```
6   5   4   3   2   1
R       O   M
        R   M   O
```

On the first assumption, P must be the fifth rank, and Q and N are either first or second, though not necessarily in that order:

```
6   5   4   3    2     1
R   P   O   M   Q/N   Q/N
```

On the second assumption, N must be the first rank, Q the fifth, and P the sixth:

```
6   5   4   3   2   1
P   Q   R   M   O   N
```

So there are exactly three possible orderings.

28. **(E)** Start with the additional information:

```
6   5   4   3   2   1
        R
```

And R is connected to another individual by that third initial condition:

```
6   5   4   3   2   1
        R       O
```

And M is restricted to either the third or second position:

```
6   5   4   3   2   1
        R   M   O
```

Which means that N must be the highest rank, Q the fifth, and P the lowest:

```
6   5   4   3   2   1
P   Q   R   M   O   N
```

29. **(B)** If Q is the third rank, then M must be the second rank:

```
6   5   4   3   2   1
            Q   M
```

And R and O must be the sixth and fourth ranks, respectively:

```
6   5   4   3   2   1
R       O   Q   M
```

And finally:

```
6   5   4   3   2   1
R   P   O   Q   M   N
```

Therefore, an M could give orders either to a Q or an O.

30. **(D)** If M is the second highest rank, then N must be the highest:

```
6   5   4   3   2   1
                M   N
```

And there are only two places to put R and O:

```
6   5   4   3   2   1
R       O       M   N
    R       O   M   N
```

And complete the possibilities:

```
6   5   4   3   2   1
```

```
R   P   O   Q   M   N
P   R   Q   O   M   N
```

An officer can give a direct order to an officer of either of the two ranks immediately below him. Under both possibilities, an officer of rank Q can issue a valid order to an officer of rank P. As for the other choices, (A) and (B) cannot be valid orders. As for (C) and (E), these may or may not be valid orders.

Use a No. 2 pencil only. Be sure each mark is dark and completely fills the intended oval. Completely erase any errors or stray marks.

☐ A R C O ☐

Start with number 1 for each new section. If a section has fewer than 50 questions, leave the extra answer spaces blank.

SECTION 1		SECTION 2		SECTION 3		SECTION 4	
1	(A) (B) (C) (D) (E)	1	(A) (B) (C) (D) (E)	1	(A) (B) (C) (D) (E)	1	(A) (B) (C) (D) (E)
2	(A) (B) (C) (D) (E)	2	(A) (B) (C) (D) (E)	2	(A) (B) (C) (D) (E)	2	(A) (B) (C) (D) (E)
3	(A) (B) (C) (D) (E)	3	(A) (B) (C) (D) (E)	3	(A) (B) (C) (D) (E)	3	(A) (B) (C) (D) (E)
4	(A) (B) (C) (D) (E)	4	(A) (B) (C) (D) (E)	4	(A) (B) (C) (D) (E)	4	(A) (B) (C) (D) (E)
5	(A) (B) (C) (D) (E)	5	(A) (B) (C) (D) (E)	5	(A) (B) (C) (D) (E)	5	(A) (B) (C) (D) (E)
6	(A) (B) (C) (D) (E)	6	(A) (B) (C) (D) (E)	6	(A) (B) (C) (D) (E)	6	(A) (B) (C) (D) (E)
7	(A) (B) (C) (D) (E)	7	(A) (B) (C) (D) (E)	7	(A) (B) (C) (D) (E)	7	(A) (B) (C) (D) (E)
8	(A) (B) (C) (D) (E)	8	(A) (B) (C) (D) (E)	8	(A) (B) (C) (D) (E)	8	(A) (B) (C) (D) (E)
9	(A) (B) (C) (D) (E)	9	(A) (B) (C) (D) (E)	9	(A) (B) (C) (D) (E)	9	(A) (B) (C) (D) (E)
10	(A) (B) (C) (D) (E)	10	(A) (B) (C) (D) (E)	10	(A) (B) (C) (D) (E)	10	(A) (B) (C) (D) (E)
11	(A) (B) (C) (D) (E)	11	(A) (B) (C) (D) (E)	11	(A) (B) (C) (D) (E)	11	(A) (B) (C) (D) (E)
12	(A) (B) (C) (D) (E)	12	(A) (B) (C) (D) (E)	12	(A) (B) (C) (D) (E)	12	(A) (B) (C) (D) (E)
13	(A) (B) (C) (D) (E)	13	(A) (B) (C) (D) (E)	13	(A) (B) (C) (D) (E)	13	(A) (B) (C) (D) (E)
14	(A) (B) (C) (D) (E)	14	(A) (B) (C) (D) (E)	14	(A) (B) (C) (D) (E)	14	(A) (B) (C) (D) (E)
15	(A) (B) (C) (D) (E)	15	(A) (B) (C) (D) (E)	15	(A) (B) (C) (D) (E)	15	(A) (B) (C) (D) (E)
16	(A) (B) (C) (D) (E)	16	(A) (B) (C) (D) (E)	16	(A) (B) (C) (D) (E)	16	(A) (B) (C) (D) (E)
17	(A) (B) (C) (D) (E)	17	(A) (B) (C) (D) (E)	17	(A) (B) (C) (D) (E)	17	(A) (B) (C) (D) (E)
18	(A) (B) (C) (D) (E)	18	(A) (B) (C) (D) (E)	18	(A) (B) (C) (D) (E)	18	(A) (B) (C) (D) (E)
19	(A) (B) (C) (D) (E)	19	(A) (B) (C) (D) (E)	19	(A) (B) (C) (D) (E)	19	(A) (B) (C) (D) (E)
20	(A) (B) (C) (D) (E)	20	(A) (B) (C) (D) (E)	20	(A) (B) (C) (D) (E)	20	(A) (B) (C) (D) (E)
21	(A) (B) (C) (D) (E)	21	(A) (B) (C) (D) (E)	21	(A) (B) (C) (D) (E)	21	(A) (B) (C) (D) (E)
22	(A) (B) (C) (D) (E)	22	(A) (B) (C) (D) (E)	22	(A) (B) (C) (D) (E)	22	(A) (B) (C) (D) (E)
23	(A) (B) (C) (D) (E)	23	(A) (B) (C) (D) (E)	23	(A) (B) (C) (D) (E)	23	(A) (B) (C) (D) (E)
24	(A) (B) (C) (D) (E)	24	(A) (B) (C) (D) (E)	24	(A) (B) (C) (D) (E)	24	(A) (B) (C) (D) (E)
25	(A) (B) (C) (D) (E)	25	(A) (B) (C) (D) (E)	25	(A) (B) (C) (D) (E)	25	(A) (B) (C) (D) (E)
26	(A) (B) (C) (D) (E)	26	(A) (B) (C) (D) (E)	26	(A) (B) (C) (D) (E)	26	(A) (B) (C) (D) (E)
27	(A) (B) (C) (D) (E)	27	(A) (B) (C) (D) (E)	27	(A) (B) (C) (D) (E)	27	(A) (B) (C) (D) (E)
28	(A) (B) (C) (D) (E)	28	(A) (B) (C) (D) (E)	28	(A) (B) (C) (D) (E)	28	(A) (B) (C) (D) (E)
29	(A) (B) (C) (D) (E)	29	(A) (B) (C) (D) (E)	29	(A) (B) (C) (D) (E)	29	(A) (B) (C) (D) (E)
30	(A) (B) (C) (D) (E)	30	(A) (B) (C) (D) (E)	30	(A) (B) (C) (D) (E)	30	(A) (B) (C) (D) (E)
31	(A) (B) (C) (D) (E)	31	(A) (B) (C) (D) (E)	31	(A) (B) (C) (D) (E)	31	(A) (B) (C) (D) (E)
32	(A) (B) (C) (D) (E)	32	(A) (B) (C) (D) (E)	32	(A) (B) (C) (D) (E)	32	(A) (B) (C) (D) (E)
33	(A) (B) (C) (D) (E)	33	(A) (B) (C) (D) (E)	33	(A) (B) (C) (D) (E)	33	(A) (B) (C) (D) (E)
34	(A) (B) (C) (D) (E)	34	(A) (B) (C) (D) (E)	34	(A) (B) (C) (D) (E)	34	(A) (B) (C) (D) (E)
35	(A) (B) (C) (D) (E)	35	(A) (B) (C) (D) (E)	35	(A) (B) (C) (D) (E)	35	(A) (B) (C) (D) (E)
36	(A) (B) (C) (D) (E)	36	(A) (B) (C) (D) (E)	36	(A) (B) (C) (D) (E)	36	(A) (B) (C) (D) (E)
37	(A) (B) (C) (D) (E)	37	(A) (B) (C) (D) (E)	37	(A) (B) (C) (D) (E)	37	(A) (B) (C) (D) (E)
38	(A) (B) (C) (D) (E)	38	(A) (B) (C) (D) (E)	38	(A) (B) (C) (D) (E)	38	(A) (B) (C) (D) (E)
39	(A) (B) (C) (D) (E)	39	(A) (B) (C) (D) (E)	39	(A) (B) (C) (D) (E)	39	(A) (B) (C) (D) (E)
40	(A) (B) (C) (D) (E)	40	(A) (B) (C) (D) (E)	40	(A) (B) (C) (D) (E)	40	(A) (B) (C) (D) (E)
41	(A) (B) (C) (D) (E)	41	(A) (B) (C) (D) (E)	41	(A) (B) (C) (D) (E)	41	(A) (B) (C) (D) (E)
42	(A) (B) (C) (D) (E)	42	(A) (B) (C) (D) (E)	42	(A) (B) (C) (D) (E)	42	(A) (B) (C) (D) (E)
43	(A) (B) (C) (D) (E)	43	(A) (B) (C) (D) (E)	43	(A) (B) (C) (D) (E)	43	(A) (B) (C) (D) (E)
44	(A) (B) (C) (D) (E)	44	(A) (B) (C) (D) (E)	44	(A) (B) (C) (D) (E)	44	(A) (B) (C) (D) (E)
45	(A) (B) (C) (D) (E)	45	(A) (B) (C) (D) (E)	45	(A) (B) (C) (D) (E)	45	(A) (B) (C) (D) (E)
46	(A) (B) (C) (D) (E)	46	(A) (B) (C) (D) (E)	46	(A) (B) (C) (D) (E)	46	(A) (B) (C) (D) (E)
47	(A) (B) (C) (D) (E)	47	(A) (B) (C) (D) (E)	47	(A) (B) (C) (D) (E)	47	(A) (B) (C) (D) (E)
48	(A) (B) (C) (D) (E)	48	(A) (B) (C) (D) (E)	48	(A) (B) (C) (D) (E)	48	(A) (B) (C) (D) (E)
49	(A) (B) (C) (D) (E)	49	(A) (B) (C) (D) (E)	49	(A) (B) (C) (D) (E)	49	(A) (B) (C) (D) (E)
50	(A) (B) (C) (D) (E)	50	(A) (B) (C) (D) (E)	50	(A) (B) (C) (D) (E)	50	(A) (B) (C) (D) (E)

EXAMINATION FORECAST

Section Number	Type	Minutes	Questions
	Writing Sample	30	—
I	Analytical Reasoning	45	30
II	Logical Reasoning	45	35
III	Analytical Reasoning	45	30
IV	Reading Comprehension	45	35

Writing Sample

Time: 30 Minutes

Joyce Peterson, a French major, is graduating from college at the end of the spring term. Beginning in the fall, she will start teaching French at a high school in the South. She wants to spend her summer studying in France. Write an essay in favor of one of two summer programs, one offered by the American Institute in Paris, the other by the University of Reims. Two considerations should guide your thinking:

1. Joyce wants to improve her French accent and learn the kind of informal speech used by ordinary French people. She also wants to become as familiar as possible with the routine of French life.

2. Joyce wants to visit some of the typical attractions in France, but she also wants to avoid spending too much money on her summer studies.

The AMERICAN INSTITUTE IN PARIS is an extension of an American University which offers French language and culture study programs in Paris. It offers a six-week program in the modern French language. Students from over twenty different countries will be enrolled in the program. Students attend classes five hours each day, five days a week; and all classes are taught by native speakers. The cost of the six-week program is $500, but that sum does not include room and board.

The UNIVERSITY OF REIMS is a public institution located in the small town of Reims, about 60 minutes by train from Paris, in the heart of the champagne-producing region. The University offers a four-week program in French and French literature. The classes are all taught by the faculty at the University. Additionally, University students attending summer school conduct small group tutorials. Students spend an average of six hours a day in formal classes and another two hours each day in their small group tutorials. Saturdays and Sundays are free days. The fee for the program is $1,400 which includes double occupancy housing in University dormitories and two meals a day in the University cafeteria.

PRACTICE EXAMINATION 2

SECTION I

Time——45 Minutes
30 Questions

Directions: Each group of questions is based on a set of propositions or conditions. Drawing a rough picture or diagram may help in answering some of the questions. Choose the best answer for each question and blacken the corresponding space on your answer sheet.

Questions 1–6

A genealogist has determined that M, N, P, Q, R, S, and T are the father, the mother, the aunt, the brother, the sister, the wife, and the daughter of X, but she has been unable to determine which person has which status. She does know:

P and Q are the same sex.
M and N are not of the same sex.
S was born before M.
Q is not the mother of X.

1. How many of the seven people——M, N, P, Q, R, S, and T——are female?
   (A) 3
   (B) 4
   (C) 5
   (D) 6
   (E) 7

2. Which of the following must be true?
   (A) M is a female.
   (B) N is a female.
   (C) P is a female.
   (D) Q is a male.
   (E) S is a male.

3. If T is the daughter of X, which of the following must be true?
   (A) M and P are of the same sex.
   (B) M and Q are of the same sex.

(C) P is not of the same sex as N.
(D) R is not of the same sex as S.
(E) S is not of the same sex as T.

4. If M and Q are sisters, all of the following must be true EXCEPT
   (A) N is a male.
   (B) M is X's mother.
   (C) Q is X's aunt.
   (D) T is X's daughter.
   (E) S is not X's brother.

5. If S is N's grandfather, then which of the following must be true?
   (A) R is N's aunt.
   (B) X is P's son.
   (C) M is X's brother.
   (D) Q is S's husband.
   (E) P is N's aunt.

6. If M is X's wife, all of the following could be true EXCEPT
   (A) S is X's daughter.
   (B) P is X's sister.
   (C) Q is X's sister.
   (D) R is X's father.
   (E) N is X's brother.

Questions 7–12

Seven persons, J, K, L, M, N, O, and P, participate in a series of swimming races in which the following are always true of the results:

K finishes ahead of L.
N finishes directly behind M.
Either J finishes first and O last, or O finishes first and J last.

There are no ties in any race, and everyone finishes each race.

7. If exactly two swimmers finish between J and L, which of the following must be true?
    (A) J finishes first.
    (B) O finishes first.
    (C) K finishes second.
    (D) M finishes fifth.
    (E) N finishes fourth.

8. Which of the following CANNOT be true?
    (A) K finishes third.
    (B) K finishes sixth.
    (C) M finishes second.
    (D) N finishes fourth.
    (E) P finishes third.

9. If O and K finish so that one is directly behind the other, which of the following must be true?

    I. K finishes second.
    II. L finishes sixth.
    III. J finishes seventh.

    (A) I only
    (B) I and II only
    (C) I and III only
    (D) II and III only
    (E) I, II, and III

10. If K finishes fourth, which of the following must be true?
    (A) J finishes first.
    (B) N finishes third.
    (C) P finishes third.
    (D) P finishes fifth.
    (E) L finishes fifth.

11. If J finishes first, and if L finishes ahead of N, in how many different orders is it possible for the other swimmers to finish?
    (A) 2
    (B) 3
    (C) 4
    (D) 5
    (E) 6

12. Which of the following additional conditions makes it certain that P finishes sixth?
    (A) J finishes first.
    (B) K finishes second.
    (C) M finishes second.
    (D) N finishes third.
    (E) L finishes fifth.

Questions 13–18

A group of six players, P, Q, R, S, T, and U, are participating in a challenge tournament. All matches played are challenge matches and are governed by the following rules:

A player may challenge another player if and only if that player is ranked either one or two places above her.

If a player successfully challenges the player ranked immediately above her, the two players exchange ranks.

If a player successfully challenges the player two ranks above her, she moves up two ranks, and both the loser of the match and the player ranked below the loser move down one rank.

If a player is unsuccessful in her challenge, she and the player immediately below her exchange ranks, unless the unsuccessful challenger was already ranked last, in which case the rankings remain unchanged.

The initial rankings from the highest (first) to the lowest (sixth) are P, Q, R, S, T, U.

Only one match is played at a time.

13. Which of the following is possible as the first match of the tournament?
    (A) P challenges Q.
    (B) Q challenges R.
    (C) R challenges P.
    (D) S challenges P.
    (E) T challenges Q.

14. If S reaches first place after the first two matches of the tournament, which of the following must be ranked fourth at that point in play?
    (A) P
    (B) Q
    (C) R
    (D) T
    (E) U

15. All of the following are possible rankings, from highest to lowest, after exactly two matches EXCEPT
    (A) P, R, Q, T, S, U
    (B) P, R, Q, S, U, T
    (C) R, P, Q, U, S, T
    (D) Q, P, S, R, T, U
    (E) Q, P, S, R, U, T

16. If exactly two matches have been played, what is the maximum number of players whose initial ranks could have been changed?

(A) 2
(B) 3
(C) 4
(D) 5
(E) 6

17. If after a certain number of matches the players are ranked from highest to lowest in the order R, Q, P, U, S, T, what is the minimum number of matches which could have been played?
(A) 2
(B) 3
(C) 4
(D) 5
(E) 6

18. If after the initial two matches two players have improved their rankings and four players have each dropped in rank, which of the following could be the third match of the tournament?
(A) R challenges P.
(B) R challenges Q.
(C) Q challenges U.
(D) U challenges P.
(E) T challenges Q.

Questions 19–24

A farmer has three fields, 1, 2, and 3, and is deciding which crops to plant. The crops are F, G, H, I, and J.

F will grow only in fields 1 and 3, but in order for F to grow it must be fertilized with X.
G will grow in fields 1, 2, and 3, but in order for G to grow, fertilizer X must not be used.
H will grow in fields 1, 2, and 3, but in order for H to grow in field 3, it must be fertilized with Y.
I will grow only in fields 2 and 3, but in order for I to grow in field 2 it must be sprayed with pesticide Z, and in order for I to grow in field 3, it must not be sprayed with Z.
J will grow only in field 2, but in order for J to grow, H must not be planted in the same field.

All crops are planted and harvested at the same time. More than one crop may be planted in a field.

19. It is possible to grow which of the following pairs of crops together in field 1?

I. F and G
II. G and H
III. F and H
IV. H and J

(A) I and II only
(B) I and III only
(C) II and III only
(D) I, II, and III only
(E) II, III, and IV only

20. It is possible for which of the following groups of crops to grow together in field 2?
(A) F, G, and H
(B) F, H, and I
(C) G, H, and J
(D) G, I, and J
(E) H, I, and J

21. Which of the following is a complete and accurate listing of all crops that will grow alone in field 2 if the only pesticide or fertilizer used is Y?
(A) F
(B) F and H
(C) G and H
(D) G, H, and J
(E) G, H, I, and J

22. Which of the following pairs of crops will grow together in field 3 if no other crops are planted in the field and no fertilizers or pesticides are applied?
(A) F and H
(B) F and I
(C) G and H
(D) G and I
(E) H and J

23. What is the maximum number of different crops that can be planted together in field 3?
(A) 1
(B) 2
(C) 3
(D) 4
(E) 5

24. Which of the following is a complete and accurate list of the crops that will grow alone in field 2 if X is the only pesticide or fertilizer applied?
(A) H, J
(B) I, G
(C) I, H
(D) I, J
(E) J, G

Questions 25–30

A tourist visiting the capital of a foreign country plans to visit eight attractions—J, K, L, M, N, O, P, and Q—in one week. She will visit two attractions on each of the days, Monday, Tuesday, and Thursday, and one attraction each on Wednesday and Friday.

She must visit J on Wednesday.

She must visit K before she visits either N or L.

She must visit P before she visits M.

She cannot visit L on Friday.

25. Which of the following CANNOT be true?
    (A) She visits K on Tuesday.
    (B) She visits K on Thursday.
    (C) She visits M on Thursday.
    (D) She visits M on Friday.
    (E) She visits Q on Friday.

26. Which of the following is a complete and accurate list of the day(s) on which she could visit both K and P?
    (A) Monday
    (B) Tuesday
    (C) Monday, Tuesday
    (D) Monday, Thursday
    (E) Monday, Tuesday, Thursday

27. If she visits L the day after she visits O, which of the following must be true?
    (A) She visits K on Monday.
    (B) She visits P on Monday.
    (C) She visits N on Tuesday.
    (D) She visits M on Thursday.
    (E) She visits Q on Friday.

28. If she visits O and Q on Tuesday, then which of the following must be true?
    (A) She visits K and P on Monday.
    (B) She visits L and N on Thursday.
    (C) She visits L and M on Thursday.
    (D) She visits M and N on Thursday.
    (E) She visits M and K on Thursday.

29. If she visits P on Thursday, which of the following must be true?
    (A) She visits K on Monday.
    (B) She visits N on Tuesday.
    (C) She visits L on Tuesday.
    (D) She visits N on Thursday.
    (E) She visits L on Thursday.

30. Which of the following could be true?
    (A) She visits K two days before P.
    (B) She visits K the day after M.
    (C) She visits L the day after M.
    (D) She visits L the day after N.
    (E) She visits N the day after L.

STOP

SECTION II

Time——45 Minutes
35 Questions

Directions: In this section, the questions ask you to analyze and evaluate the reasoning in short paragraphs or passages. For some questions, all of the answer choices may conceivably be answers to the question asked. You should select the *best* answer to the question, that is, an answer which does not require you to make assumptions which violate commonsense standards by being implausible, redundant, irrelevant or inconsistent. After choosing the best answer, blacken the corresponding space on the answer sheet.

1. Children in the first three grades who attend private schools spend time each day working with a computerized reading program. Public schools have very few such programs. Tests prove, however, that public-school children are much weaker in reading skills when compared to their private-school counterparts. We conclude, therefore, that public-school children can be good readers only if they participate in a computerized reading program.

   The author's initial statements logically support his conclusion only if which of the following is also true?
   (A) All children can learn to be good readers if they are taught by a computerized reading program.
   (B) All children can learn to read at the same rate if they participate in a computerized reading program.
   (C) Better reading skills produce better students.
   (D) Computerized reading programs are the critical factor in the better reading skills of private-school students.
   (E) Public-school children can be taught better math skills.

2. Is your company going to continue to discriminate against women in its hiring and promotion policies?

   The above question might be considered unfair for which of the following reasons?

   I. Its construction seeks a "yes" or "no" answer where both might be inappropriate.
   II. It is internally inconsistent.
   III. It contains a hidden presupposition which the responder might wish to contest.

(A) I only
(B) II only
(C) I and II only
(D) I and III only
(E) I, II, and III

Questions 3 and 4

Ms. Evangeline Rose argued that money and time invested in acquiring a professional degree are totally wasted. As evidence supporting her argument, she offered the case of a man who, at considerable expense of money and time, completed his law degree and then married and lived as a house-husband, taking care of their children and working part time at a day care center so his wife could pursue her career.

3. Ms. Rose makes the unsupported assumption that
   (A) an education in the law is useful only in pursuing law-related activities
   (B) what was not acceptable 25 years ago may very well be acceptable today
   (C) wealth is more important than learning
   (D) professional success is a function of the quality of one's education
   (E) only the study of law can be considered professional study

4. The logical reasoning of Ms. Rose's argument is closely parallelled by which of the following?
   (A) A juvenile delinquent who insists that his behavior should be attributable to the fact that his parents did not love him.
   (B) A senator who votes large sums of money for military equipment, but who votes against programs designed to help the poor.
   (C) A conscientious objector who bases his draft resistance on the premise that there can be no moral wars.
   (D) When a policeman is found guilty of murdering his wife, an opponent of police brutality who says, "That's what these people mean by law and order."
   (E) A high school senior who decides that rather than going to college he will enroll in a vocational training program to learn to be an electrician.

5. A cryptographer has intercepted an enemy message that is in code. He knows that the code is a simple substitution of numbers for letters. Which of the following would be the least helpful in breaking the code?
   (A) knowing the frequency with which the vowels of the language are used
   (B) knowing the frequency with which two vowels appear together in the language
   (C) knowing the frequency with which odd numbers appear relative to even numbers in the message
   (D) knowing the conjugation of the verb *to be* in the language on which the code is based
   (E) knowing every word in the language that begins with the letter *R*

6. One way of reducing commuting time for those who work in the cities is to increase the speed at which traffic moves in the heart of the city. This can be accomplished by raising the tolls on the tunnels and bridges connecting the city with other communities. This will discourage auto traffic into the city and will encourage people to use public transportation instead.

   Which of the following, if true, would LEAST weaken the argument above?
   (A) Nearly all of the traffic in the center of the city is commercial traffic which will continue despite toll increases.
   (B) Some people now driving alone into the city would choose to car-pool with each other rather than use public transportation.
   (C) Any temporary improvement in traffic flow would be lost because the improvement itself would attract more cars.
   (D) The numbers of commuters who would be deterred by the toll increases would be insignificant.
   (E) The public transportation system is not able to handle any significant increase in the number of commuters using the system.

7. An independent medical research team recently did a survey at a mountain retreat founded to help heavy smokers quit or cut down on their cigarette smoking. Eighty percent of those persons smoking three packs a day or more were able to cut down to one pack a day after they began to take End-Smoke with its patented desire suppressant. Try End-Smoke to help you cut down significantly on your smoking.

   Which of the following could be offered as valid criticism of the above advertisement?

   I. Heavy smokers may be physically as well as psychologically addicted to tobacco.
   II. A medicine that is effective for very heavy smokers may not be effective for the population of smokers generally.
   III. A survey conducted at a mountain retreat to aid smokers may yield different results than one would expect under other circumstances.

   (A) I only
   (B) II only
   (C) III only
   (D) II and III only
   (E) I, II, and III

8. JOKEY: Horses are the most noble of all animals. They are both loyal and brave. I knew of a farm horse which died of a broken heart shortly after its owner died.

   VETERINARIAN: You're wrong. Dogs can be just as loyal and brave. I had a dog who would wait every day on the front steps for me to come home, and if I did not arrive until midnight, he would still be there.

   All of the following are true of the claims of the jockey and the veterinarian EXCEPT:
   (A) both claims assume that loyalty and bravery are characteristics which are desirable in animals.
   (B) both claims assume that the two most loyal animals are the horse and the dog.
   (C) both claims assume that human qualities can be attributed to animals.
   (D) both claims are supported by only a single example of animal behavior.
   (E) neither claim is supported by evidence other than the opinions and observations of the speakers.

9. Rousseau assumed that human beings in the state of nature are characterized by a feeling of sympathy toward their fellow humans and other living creatures. In order to explain the existence of social ills, such as the exploitation of man by man, Rousseau maintained that our natural feelings are crushed under the weight of unsympathetic social institutions.

Rousseau's argument described above would be most strengthened if it could be explained how
(A) creatures naturally characterized by feelings of sympathy for all living creatures could create unsympathetic social institutions
(B) we can restructure our social institutions so that they will foster our natural sympathies for one another
(C) modern reformers might lead the way to a life which is not inconsistent with the ideals of the state of nature
(D) non-exploitative conduct could arise in conditions of the state of nature
(E) a return to the state of nature from modern society might be accomplished

10. Every element on the periodic chart is radioactive, though the most stable elements have half-lives which are thousands and thousands of years long. When an atom decays, it splits into two or more smaller atoms. Even considering the fusion taking place inside of stars, there is only a negligible tendency for smaller atoms to transmute into larger ones. Thus, the ratio of lighter to heavier atoms in the universe is increasing at a measurable rate.

Which of the following sentences provides the most logical continuation of this paragraph?
(A) Without radioactive decay of atoms, there could be no solar combustion and no life as we know it.
(B) Therefore, it is imperative that scientists begin developing ways to reverse the trend and restore the proper balance between the lighter and the heavier elements.
(C) Consequently, it is possible to use a shifting ratio of light to heavy atoms to calculate the age of the universe.
(D) Therefore, there are now more light elements in the universe than heavy ones.
(E) As a result, the fusion taking place inside stars has to produce enough atoms of the heavy elements to offset the radioactive decay of large atoms elsewhere in the universe.

Questions 11 and 12

SPEAKER: The great majority of people in the United States have access to the best medical care available anywhere in the world.

OBJECTOR: There are thousands of poor in this country who cannot afford to pay to see a doctor.

11. Which of the following is true of the objector's comment?
(A) It uses emotionally charged words.
(B) It constitutes a hasty generalization on few examples.
(C) It is not necessarily inconsistent with the speaker's remarks.
(D) It cites statistical evidence which tends to confirm the speaker's points.
(E) It overlooks the distinction the speaker draws between a cause and its effect.

12. A possible objection to the speaker's comments would be to point to the existence of
(A) a country which has more medical assistants than the United States
(B) a nation where medical care is provided free of charge by the government
(C) a country in which the people are given better medical care than Americans
(D) government hearings in the United States on the problems poor people have getting medical care
(E) a country which has a higher hospital bed per person ratio than the United States

13. We must do something about the rising cost of our state prisons. It now costs an average of $132 per day to maintain a prisoner in a double-occupancy cell in a state prison. Yet, in the most expensive cities, one can find rooms in the finest hotels which rent for less than $125 per night.

The argument above might be criticized in all of the following ways EXCEPT
(A) it introduces an inappropriate analogy
(B) it relies on an unwarranted appeal to authority
(C) it fails to take account of costs which prisons have but hotels do not have
(D) it misuses numerical data
(E) it draws a faulty comparison

Questions 14–16

The blanks in the following paragraph indicate deletions from the text. For questions 14 and 15, select the completion that is most appropriate.

I often hear smokers insisting that they have a *right* to smoke whenever and wherever they choose, as though there are no conceivable circumstances in which the law might not legitimately prohibit smoking. This contention is obviously indefensible. Implicit in the development of the concept of a right is the notion that one person's freedom of action is circumscribed by the___(14)___. It requires nothing more than common sense to realize that there are situations in which smoking presents a clear and present danger: in a crowded theater, around flammable materials, during take-off in an airplane. No one would seriously deny that the potential harm of smoking in such circumstances more than outweighs the satisfaction a smoker would derive from smoking. Yet, this balancing is not unique to situations of potential catastrophe. It applies equally as well to situations where the potential injury is small, though in most cases, as for example a person's table manners, the injury of the offended person is so slight we automatically strike the balance in favor of the person acting. But once it is recognized that a balance of freedoms must be struck, it follows that a smoker has a *right* to smoke only when and where___(15)___.

14. (A) Constitution of our nation
    (B) laws passed by Congress and interpreted by the Supreme Court
    (C) interest of any other person to not be injured or inconvenienced by that action
    (D) rights of other persons not to smoke
    (E) rights of non-smoking persons not to have to be subjected to the noxious fumes of tobacco smoking

15. (A) the government chooses to allow him to smoke.
    (B) he finally decides to light up
    (C) his interest in smoking outweighs the interests of other persons in his not smoking
    (D) he can ensure that no other persons will be even slightly inconvenienced by his smoking
    (E) there are signs which explicitly state that smoking is allowed in that area

16. The author's strategy in questioning the claim that smokers have a right to smoke is to
    (A) cite facts which are not generally known
    (B) clarify and fully define a key concept
    (C) entertain arguments on a hypothetical case
    (D) uncover a logical inconsistency
    (E) probe the reliability of an empirical generalization

17. Some judges are members of the bar. No member of the bar is a convicted felon. Therefore, some judges are not convicted felons.

    Which of the following is logically most similar to the argument developed above?

    (A) Anyone who jogs in the heat will be sick. I do not jog in the heat, and will therefore likely never be sick.
    (B) People who want to avoid jury duty will not register to vote. A person may not vote until he is 18. Therefore, persons under 18 are not called for jury duty.
    (C) All businesses file a tax return, but many businesses do not make enough money to pay taxes. Therefore, some businesses do not make a profit.
    (D) All men are excluded from the women's dormitory, but some men are polite. Therefore, some polite men are not allowed in the women's dormitory.
    (E) The Grand Canyon is large. The Grand Canyon is in Arizona. Therefore, Arizona is large.

Questions 18 and 19

A study published by the Department of Education shows that children in the central cities lag far behind students in the suburbs and the rural areas in reading skills. The report blames this differential on the overcrowding in the classrooms of city schools. I maintain, however, that the real reason that city children are poorer readers than non-city children is that they do not get enough fresh air and sunshine.

18. Which of the following best describes the form of the above argument?
    (A) It attacks the credibility of the Department of Education.
    (B) It indicts the methodology of the study of the Department of Education.
    (C) It attempts to show that central city students read as well as non-city students.
    (D) It offers an alternative explanation for the differential.
    (E) It argues from analogy.

19. Which of the following would LEAST strengthen the author's point in the preceding argument?
    (A) medical research which shows a correlation between air pollution and learning disabilities
    (B) a report by educational experts demonstrating there is no relationship between the number of students in a classroom and a student's ability to read
    (C) a notice released by the Department of Education retracting that part of their report which mentions overcrowding as the reason for the differential

(D) the results of a federal program which indicates that city students show significant improvement in reading skills when they spend the summer in the country

(E) a proposal by the federal government to fund emergency programs to hire more teachers for central city schools in an attempt to reduce overcrowding in the classrooms

20. Some judges have allowed hospitals to disconnect life-support equipment of patients who have no prospects for recovery. But I say that is murder. Either we put a stop to this practice now, or we will soon have programs of euthanasia for the old and infirm as well as others who might be considered a burden. Rather than disconnecting life-support equipment, we should let nature take its course.

Which of the following are valid objections to the above argument?

  I. It is internally inconsistent.
  II. It employs emotionally charged terms.
  III. It presents a false dilemma.

(A) I only
(B) II only
(C) III only
(D) II and III only
(E) I, II, and III

21. If Paul comes to the party, Quentin leaves the party. If Quentin leaves the party, either Robert or Steve asks Alice to dance. If Alice is asked to dance by either Robert or Steve and Quentin leaves the party, Alice accepts. If Alice is asked to dance by either Robert or Steve and Quentin does not leave the party, Alice does not accept.

If Quentin does not leave the party, which of the following statements can be logically deduced from the information given?
(A) Robert asks Alice to dance.
(B) Steve asks Alice to dance.
(C) Alice refuses to dance with either Robert or Steve.
(D) Paul does not come to the party.
(E) Alice leaves the party.

22. All students have submitted applications for admission. Some of the applications for admissions have not been acted upon. Therefore, some more students will be accepted.

The logic of which of the following is most similar to that of the argument above?

(A) Some of the barrels have not yet been loaded on the truck, but all of the apples have been put into barrels. So, some more apples will be loaded onto the truck.

(B) All students who received passing marks were women. X received a passing mark. Therefore, X is a woman.

(C) Some chemicals will react with glass bottles, but not with plastic bottles. Therefore, those chemicals should be kept in plastic bottles and not glass ones.

(D) All advertising must be approved by the Council before it is aired. This television spot for a new cola has not yet been approved by the Council. Therefore, it is not to be aired until the Council makes its decision.

(E) There are six blue marbles and three red marbles in this jar. Therefore, if I blindly pick out seven marbles, there should be two red marbles left to pick.

23. New Evergreen Gum has twice as much flavor for your money as Spring Mint Gum, and we can prove it. You see, a stick of Evergreen Gum is twice as large as a stick of Spring Mint Gum, and the more gum, the more flavor.

Which of the following, if true, would undermine the persuasive appeal of the above advertisement?

  I. A package of Spring Mint Gum contains twice as many sticks as a package of Evergreen Gum at the same price.
  II. Spring Mint Gum has more concentrated flavor than Evergreen Gum.
  III. Although a stick of Evergreen Gum is twice as large in volume as a stick of Spring Mint Gum, it weighs only 50% as much.

(A) I only
(B) II only
(C) I and II only
(D) II and III only
(E) I, II, and III

24. Judging from the tenor of the following statements and the apparent authoritativeness of their sources, which is the most reasonable and trustworthy?

(A) FILM CRITIC: Beethoven is really very much overrated as a composer. His music is not really that good; it's just very well known.

(B) SPOKESMAN FOR A MANUFACTURER: The jury's verdict against us for $2 million is ridiculous, and we are sure that the Appeals Court will agree with us.

(C) SENIOR CABINET OFFICER: Our administration plans to cut inefficiency, and we have already begun to discuss plans which we calculate will save the federal government nearly $50 billion a year in waste.

(D) FRENCH WINE EXPERT: The best buy in wines in America today is the California chablis which is comparable to the French chablis and is available at half the cost.

(E) UNION LEADER: We plan to stay out on strike until management meets each and every one of the demands we have submitted.

25. That it is impossible to foretell the future is easily demonstrated. For if a man should foresee himself being injured by a mill wheel on the next day, he would cancel his trip to the mill and remain at home in bed. Since he would not be injured the next day by the mill wheel, it cannot in any way be said that he foretold the future.

Which of the following best explains the weakness in this argument?

(A) The author fails to explain how one could actually change the future.

(B) The author uses the word *future* in two different ways.

(C) The author does not explain how anyone could foresee the future.

(D) The argument is internally inconsistent.

(E) The argument is circular.

26. PUBLIC ANNOUNCEMENT: When you enroll with Future Careers Business Institute (FCBI), you will have access to our placement counseling service. Last year, 92% of our graduates who asked us to help them find jobs found them. So go FCBI for your future!

Which of the following would be appropriate questions to ask in order to determine the value of the preceding claim?

   I. How many of your graduates asked FCBI for assistance?

  II. How many people graduated from FCBI last year?

 III. Did those people who asked for jobs find ones in the areas for which they were trained?

 IV. Was FCBI responsible for finding the jobs or did graduates find them independently?

(A) I and II only

(B) I, II, and III only

(C) I, II, and IV only

(D) III and IV only

(E) I, II, III, and IV

Questions 27 and 28

Having just completed Introductory Logic 9, I feel competent to instruct others in the intricacies of this wonderful discipline. Logic is concerned with correct reasoning in the form of syllogisms. A syllogism consists of three statements, of which two are premises, and the third is the conclusion. Here is an example:

MAJOR PREMISE: The American buffalo is disappearing.

MINOR PREMISE: This animal is an American buffalo.

CONCLUSION: Therefore, this animal is disappearing.

Once one has been indoctrinated into the mysteries of this arcane science, there is no statement he may not assert with complete confidence.

27. The reasoning of the author's example is most similar to that contained in which of the following arguments?

(A) Any endangered species must be protected; this species is endangered; therefore, it should be protected.

(B) All whales are mammals; this animal is a whale; therefore, this animal is a mammal.

(C) Engaging in sexual intercourse with a person to whom one is not married is a sin; and since pre-marital intercourse is, by definition, without the institution of marriage, it is, therefore, a sin.

(D) There are 60 seconds in a minute; there are 60 minutes in an hour; therefore, there are 3600 seconds in an hour.

(E) Wealthy people pay most of the taxes; this man is wealthy; therefore, this man pays most of the taxes.

28. The main purpose of the author's argument is to

(A) provide instruction in logic

(B) supply a definition

(C) cast doubt on the value of formal logic

(D) present an argument for the protection of the American buffalo

(E) show the precise relationship between the premises and conclusion of his example

Questions 29 and 30

On a recent trip to the Mediterranean, I made the acquaintance of a young man who warned me against trusting Cretans. ''Everything they say is a lie,'' he told me, ''and I should know because I come from Crete myself.'' I thanked the fellow for his advice but told him in light of what he had said I had no intention of believing it.

29. Which of the following best describes the author's behavior?
    (A) It was unwarranted because the young man was merely trying to be helpful to a stranger.
    (B) It was paradoxical for in discounting the advice he implicitly relied on it.
    (C) It was understandable inasmuch as the young man, by his own admission, could not possibly be telling the truth.
    (D) It was high-handed and just the sort of thing that gives American tourists a bad name.
    (E) It was overly cautious for not everyone in a foreign country will try to take advantage of a tourist.

30. Which of the following is most nearly analogous to the warning issued by the young man?
    (A) an admission by a witness under cross-examination that he has lied
    (B) a sign put up by the Chamber of Commerce of a large city alerting visitors to the danger of pickpockets
    (C) the command of a military leader to his marching troops to do an about-face
    (D) a sentence written in chalk on a blackboard which says, ''This sentence is false.''
    (E) the advice of a veteran worker to a newly hired person: ''You don't actually have to work hard so long as you look like you're working hard.''

31. Doctors, in seeking a cure for *aphroditis melancholias,* are guided by their research into the causes of *metaeritocas polymanias* because the symptoms of the two diseases occur in populations of similar ages, manifesting symptoms in both cases of high fever, swollen glands, and lack of appetite. Moreover, the incubation period for both diseases is virtually identical. So these medical researchers are convinced that the virus re-sponsible for *aphroditis melancholias* is very similar to that responsible for *metaeritocas polymanias.*

The conclusion of the author rests on the presupposition that
(A) *metaeritocas polymanias* is a more serious public health hazard than *aphroditis melancholias*
(B) for every disease, modern medical science will eventually find a cure
(C) saving human life is the single most important goal of modern technology
(D) *aphroditis melancholias* is a disease which occurs only in human beings
(E) diseases with similar symptoms will have similar causes

32. I. Whenever some of the runners are leading off and all of the infielders are playing in, all of the batters attempt to bunt.
    II. Some of the runners are leading off but some of the batters are not attempting to bunt.

Which of the following conclusions can be deduced from the two statements above?
(A) Some of the runners are not leading off.
(B) Some of the batters are attempting to bunt.
(C) None of the infielders is playing in.
(D) All of the infielders are playing in.
(E) Some of the infielders are not playing in.

Questions 33 and 34

The federal bankruptcy laws illustrate the folly of do-good protectionism at its most extreme. At the debtor's own request, the judge will list all of his debts, take what money the debtor has, which will be very little, and divide that small amount among his creditors. Then the judge declares that those debts are thereby satisfied, and the debtor is free from those creditors. Why, a person could take his credit card and buy a car, a stereo, and a new wardrobe and then declare himself bankrupt! In effect, he will have conned his creditors into giving him all those things for nothing.

33. Which of the following adages best describes the author's attitude about a bankrupt debtor?
    (A) ''A penny saved is a penny earned.''
    (B) ''You've made your bed, now lie in it.''
    (C) ''Absolute power corrupts absolutely.''
    (D) ''He that governs least governs best.''
    (E) ''Millions for defense, but not one cent for tribute.''

34. Which of the following does the author imply?
    (A) A judge will not use all of a debtor's assets, including personal possessions, to pay his creditors.
    (B) Most persons who own credit cards are financially irresponsible.
    (C) A bankrupt debtor ought to be imprisoned until he is able to raise the money to pay all of his debts.
    (D) Most personal bankruptcy proceedings are initiated at the request of the creditors.
    (E) Borrowing money is immoral.

35. Either you punish a child severely when he is bad or he will grow up to be a criminal. Your child has just been bad. Therefore, you should punish him severely.

All EXCEPT which of the following would be appropriate objection to the argument?
    (A) What do you consider to be a severe punishment?
    (B) What do you mean by the term "bad"?
    (C) Isn't your "either-or" premise an oversimplification?
    (D) Don't your first and second premises contradict one another?
    (E) In what way has this child been bad?

STOP

IF YOU FINISH BEFORE TIME IS CALLED, CHECK YOUR WORK ON THIS SECTION ONLY. DO NOT WORK ON ANY OTHER SECTION IN THE TEST.

SECTION III

Time——45 Minutes
30 Questions

Directions: Each group of questions is based on a set of propositions or conditions. Drawing a rough picture or diagram may help in answering some of the questions. Choose the best answer for each question and blacken the corresponding space on your answer sheet.

Questions 1-6

Six persons, J, K, L, M, N, and O, run a series of races with the following results.

O never finishes first or last
L never finishes immediately behind either J or K.
L always finishes immediately ahead of M.

1. Which of the following, given in order from first to last, is an acceptable finishing sequence of the runners?
   (A) J, L, M, O, N, K
   (B) L, O, J, K, M, N
   (C) L, M, J, K, N, O
   (D) L, M, J, K, O, N
   (E) N, K, L, M, O, J

2. If, in an acceptable finishing sequence, J and K finish first and fifth respectively, which of the following must be true?
   (A) L finishes second.
   (B) O finishes third.
   (C) M finishes third.
   (D) N finishes third.
   (E) N finishes sixth.

3. If, in an acceptable finishing sequence, L finishes second, which of the following must be true?
   I. O must finish fourth.
   II. N must finish fifth.
   III. Either J or K must finish sixth.

   (A) I only
   (B) II only
   (C) III only
   (D) I and III only
   (E) I, II, and III

4. All of the following finishing sequences, given in order from 1 to 6, are acceptable EXCEPT

   (A) J, N, L, M, O, K
   (B) J, N, O, L, M, K
   (C) L, M, J, K, O, N
   (D) N, J, L, M, O, K
   (E) N, K, O, L, M, J

5. Only one acceptable finishing sequence is possible under which of the following conditions?
   I. Whenever J and K finish second and third, respectively.
   II. Whenever J and K finish third and fourth, respectively.
   III. Whenever J and K finish fourth and fifth, respectively.

   (A) I only
   (B) II only
   (C) III only
   (D) I and II only
   (E) I, II, and III

6. If, in an acceptable finishing sequence, exactly three runners finish between J and K, which of the following CANNOT be true?
   (A) O does not finish fourth.
   (B) Either J, K, or N finishes first.
   (C) L finishes either third or fourth.
   (D) If O finishes second, either J or K finishes last.
   (E) If O finishes third, either J or K finishes last.

Questions 7-12

Nine people, J, K, L, M, N, O, P, Q, and R, have rented a small hotel for a weekend. The hotel has five floors, numbered consecutively 1 (bottom) to 5 (top). The top floor has only one room while floors 1 through 4 each have two rooms. Each person will occupy one and only one room for the weekend.

Q and R will occupy the rooms on the third floor.
P will stay on a lower floor than M.
K will stay on a lower floor than either N or L.
J and L will occupy rooms on the same floor.

7. Which of the following CANNOT be true?
   (A) J stays on the first floor.
   (B) K stays on the first floor.
   (C) O stays on the second floor.
   (D) M stays on the fourth floor.
   (E) N stays on the fifth floor.

8. If M occupies a room on the second floor, which of the following must be true?
   (A) J stays on the fifth floor.
   (B) N stays on the fifth floor.
   (C) J stays on the fourth floor.
   (D) K stays on the second floor.
   (E) O stays on the first floor.

9. Which of the following is a complete and accurate list of the persons who could stay on the first floor?
   (A) K, O
   (B) M, N
   (C) M, O
   (D) K, M, O
   (E) K, O, P

10. If M occupies a room on the fourth floor, which of the following must be true?

    I. N stays on the fifth floor.
    II. O stays on the second floor.
    III. K stays on the first floor.

    (A) I only
    (B) III only
    (C) I and III only
    (D) II and III only
    (E) I, II, and III

11. If K and M stay in rooms on the same floor, which of the following is a complete and accurate list of the floors on which they could stay?
    (A) 1
    (B) 2
    (C) 4
    (D) 1 and 4
    (E) 2 and 4

12. Which of the following, if true, provides sufficient additional information to determine on which floor each person will stay?
    (A) P stays on the first floor.
    (B) M stays on the second floor.
    (C) K stays on the second floor.
    (D) M stays on the fourth floor.
    (E) N stays on the fifth floor.

Questions 13–18

The planning committee of an academic conference is planning a series of panels using eight professors, M, N, Q, R, S, T, U, and V. Each panel must be put together in accordance with the following conditions:

N, T, and U cannot all appear on the same panel.

M, N, and R cannot all appear on the same panel.

Q and V cannot appear on the same panel.

If V appears on a panel, at least two professors of the trio M, S, and U must also appear on the panel.

Neither R nor Q can appear on a panel unless the other also appears on the panel.

If S appears on a panel, both N and V must also appear on that panel.

13. Which of the following CANNOT appear on a panel with R?
    (A) M
    (B) N
    (C) Q
    (D) S
    (E) T

14. Exactly how many of the professors can appear on a panel alone?
    (A) 1
    (B) 2
    (C) 3
    (D) 4
    (E) 5

15. If S appears on a panel, that panel must consist of at least how many professors?
    (A) 3
    (B) 4
    (C) 5
    (D) 6
    (E) 7

16. Which of the following is an acceptable group of professors for a panel?
    (A) M, N, Q, R
    (B) M, Q, R, T
    (C) M, R, T, U
    (D) M, S, U, V
    (E) N, R, T, U

17. Which of the following groups of professors can form an acceptable panel by doing nothing more than adding one more professor to the group?
    (A) M, R, T
    (B) N, Q, M
    (C) Q, R, S
    (D) Q, R, V
    (E) V, R, N

18. Of the group N, S, T, U, V, which professor will have to be removed to form an acceptable panel?
    (A) N
    (B) S
    (C) T
    (D) U
    (E) V

Questions 19–25

On a certain railway route, five trains each day operate between City X and City Y: the Meteor, the Comet, the Flash, the Streak, and the Rocket. Each train consists of exactly five cars, and each car is either a deluxe-class car or a coach car.

On the Meteor, only the first, second, and fifth cars are coach.
On the Comet, only the second and third cars are coach.
On the Flash, only the second car is coach.
On the Streak, only the third and fourth cars are coach.
On the Rocket, all cars are coach.

19. On a typical day, which of the following must be true of the railway's trains operating between City X and City Y?
    (A) More deluxe cars than coach cars are used as first cars.
    (B) More deluxe cars than coach cars are used as second cars.
    (C) Every train uses a deluxe car for the fifth car.
    (D) More deluxe cars are used than coach cars.
    (E) More deluxe cars are used on the Rocket and the Streak combined than on the Flash and the Comet combined.

20. Which of the following cars cannot both be deluxe cars on the same train?
    (A) first and second

(B) first and third
(C) second and third
(D) third and fourth
(E) fourth and fifth

21. To determine which train is the Streak, correct information on whether a car is deluxe or coach is needed for which car or cars?
    (A) first
    (B) second
    (C) third
    (D) first and fifth
    (E) third and fifth

22. If a train has a coach car as the second car, then that train could be any train EXCEPT the
    (A) Meteor
    (B) Comet
    (C) Flash
    (D) Streak
    (E) Rocket

23. If a train has deluxe cars as the first and third cars of the train, that train must be the
    (A) Meteor
    (B) Comet
    (C) Flash
    (D) Streak
    (E) Rocket

24. If only one of the third, fourth, and fifth cars of a train is a deluxe car, then that train must be the
    (A) Meteor
    (B) Comet
    (C) Flash
    (D) Streak
    (E) Rocket

25. Which of the following must be true?

    I. If the second car of the Meteor were changed to a deluxe car, then the Meteor would have the same configuration of cars as the Flash.

    II. If the fourth car of the Comet were changed to a coach car, then the Comet would have the same configuration of cars as the Streak.

    III. If every coach car on the Meteor were changed to a deluxe car and every deluxe car to a coach car, then the Meteor would have the same configuration as the Streak.

(A) I only
(B) III only
(C) I and II only
(D) II and III only
(E) I, II, and III

Questions 26–30

A certain civic organization has four standing committees, the Finance Committee, the Operations Committee, the Membership Committee, and the Service Committee.

At least one member of the Finance Committee is also a member of the Operations Committee and the Service Committee.

At least one member of the Operations Committee is also a member of the Finance Committee and the Membership Committee.

At least one member of the Membership Committee is also a member of the Operations Committee and the Service Committee.

26. Which of the following statements must be true?

   I. At least one person is a member of all four committees.
   II. At least one person is a member of the Service Committee, the Finance Committee, and the Membership Committee.
   III. At least one person is a member of the Membership Committee, the Finance Committee, and the Operations Committee.

   (A) III only
   (B) I and II only
   (C) I and III only
   (D) II and III only
   (E) I, II and III

27. Which of the following statements must be false?

   I. No member of the Operations Committee is also a member of the other three committees.
   II. No member of the Service Committee is also a member of both the Finance Committee and the Membership Committee.
   III. No member of the Finance Committee is

also a member of both the Operations Committee and the Service Committee.

(A) I only
(B) II only
(C) III only
(D) I and III only
(E) I, II, and III

28. If Jack is the only member of the Finance Committee who is also a member of the Operations Committee, which of the following statements must be true?

   I. Jack is also a member of the Service Committee.
   II. Jack is also a member of the Membership Committee.
   III. Jack is not a member of the Service Committee.

   (A) I only
   (B) II only
   (C) III only
   (D) I and II only
   (E) II and III only

29. If exactly one person is a member of all four committees, then which of the following must be true?

   I. Only one person is a member of the Finance Committee, the Operations Committee, and the Service Committee.
   II. Only one person is a member of the Finance Committee, the Operations Committee, and the Membership Committee.
   III. Only one person is a member of the Membership Committee, the Operations Committee, and the Service Committee.

   (A) I and II only
   (B) I and III only
   (C) II and III only
   (D) I, II, and III
   (E) None of the statements is necessarily true.

30. If Ellen is the only member of the Membership Committee who is not also a member of the Service Committee, then which of the following must be true?

   I. Ellen is not a member of the Operations Committee.

II. Ellen is a member of the Finance Committee.

III. Every member of the Membership Committee but Ellen is also on the Operations Committee.

(A) II only
(B) I and II only
(C) I and III only
(D) II and III only
(E) None of the statements is necessarily true.

STOP

IF YOU FINISH BEFORE TIME IS CALLED, CHECK YOUR WORK ON THIS SECTION ONLY. DO NOT WORK ON ANY OTHER SECTION IN THE TEST.

SECTION IV

Time—45 Minutes
35 Questions

Directions. Below each of the following passages, you will find questions or incomplete statements about the passage. Each statement or question is followed by lettered words or expressions. Select the word or expression that most satisfactorily completes each statement, or answers each question in accordance with the meaning of the passage. After you have chosen the best answer, blacken the corresponding space on the answer sheet.

Like our political society, the university is under severe attack today and perhaps for the same reason; namely, that we have accomplished much of what we have set out to do in this generation, that we have done so imperfectly, and while we have been doing so, we have said a lot of things that simply are not true. For example, we have earnestly declared that full equality of opportunity in universities exists for everyone, regardless of economic circumstance, race or religion. This has never been true. When it was least true the assertion was not attacked. Now that it is nearly true, not only the assertion but the university itself is locked in mortal combat with the seekers of perfection.

In another sense the university has failed. It has stored great quantities of knowledge; it teaches more people; and despite its failures, it teaches them better. It is in the application of this knowledge that the failure has come. Of the great branches of knowledge—the sciences, the social sciences and humanities—the sciences are applied, sometimes almost as soon as they are learned. Strenuous and occasionally successful efforts are made to apply the social sciences, but almost never are the humanities well applied. We do not use philosophy in defining our conduct. We do not use literature as a source of real and vicarious experience to save us the trouble of living every life again in our own.

The great tasks of the university in the next generation are to search the past to form the future, to begin an earnest search for a new and relevant set of values, and to learn to use the knowledge we have for the questions that come before us. The university should use one-fourth of a student's time in his undergraduate years and organize it into courses which might be called history, and literature and philosophy, and anything else appropriate and organize these around primary problems. The difference between a primary problem and a secondary or even tertiary problem is that primary problems tend to be around for a long time, whereas the less important ones get solved.

One primary problem is that of interfering with what some call human destiny and others call biological development, which is partly the result of genetic circumstance and partly the result of accidental environmental conditions. It is anticipated that the next generation, and perhaps this one, will be able to interfere chemically with the actual development of an individual and perhaps biologically by interfering with his genes. Obviously, there are benefits both to individuals and to society from eliminating, or at least improving, mentally and physically deformed persons. On the other hand, there could be very serious consequences if this knowledge were used with premeditation to produce superior and subordinate classes, each genetically prepared to carry out a predetermined mission. This can be done, but what happens to free will and the rights of the individual? Here we have a primary problem which will still exist when we are all dead.

Of course, the traditional faculty members would say, "But the students won't learn enough to go to graduate school." And certainly they would not learn everything we are in the habit of making them learn, but they would learn some other things. Surely, in the other three-quarters of their time, they would learn what they usually do, and they might even learn to think about it by carrying new habits into their more conventional courses. The advantages would be overwhelmingly greater than the disadvantages. After all, the purpose of education is not only to impart knowledge, but to teach students to use the knowledge which they either have or will find, to teach them to ask and seek answers for important questions.

1. The author suggests that the university's greatest shortcoming is its failure to
   (A) attempt to provide equal opportunity for all
   (B) offer courses in philosophy and the humanities
   (C) prepare students adequately for professional studies
   (D) help students see the relevance of the humanities to real problems
   (E) require students to include in their curricula liberal arts courses

2. It can be inferred that the author presupposes that the reader will regard a course in literature as a course
   (A) with little or no practical value
   (B) of interest only to academic scholars
   (C) required by most universities for graduation
   (D) uniquely relevant to today's primary problems
   (E) used to teach students good writing skills

3. Which of the following questions does the author answer in the passage?
   (A) What are some of the secondary problems faced by the past generation?
   (B) How can we improve the performance of our political society?
   (C) Has any particular educational institution tried the proposal introduced by the author?
   (D) What is a possible objection to the proposal offered in the passage?
   (E) Why is the university of today a better imparter of knowledge than the university of the past?

4. Which of the following questions would the author most likely consider a primary question?
   (A) Should Congress increase the level of Social Security benefits?
   (B) Is it appropriate for the state to use capital punishment?
   (C) Who is the best candidate for president in the next presidential election?
   (D) At what month can the fetus be considered medically viable outside the mother's womb?
   (E) What measures should be taken to solve the problem of world hunger?

5. With which of the following statements about the use of scientific techniques to change an individual's genetic makeup would the author LEAST likely agree?
   (A) Society has no right to use such techniques without the informed consent of the individual.
   (B) Such techniques can have a positive benefit for the individual in some cases.
   (C) Use of such techniques may be appropriate even though society, but not the individual, benefits.
   (D) The question of the use of such techniques

must be placed in a philosophical as well as a scientific context.
   (E) The answers to questions about the use of such techniques will have important implications for the structure of our society.

6. The primary purpose of the passage is to
   (A) discuss a problem and propose a solution
   (B) analyze a system and defend it
   (C) present both sides of an issue and allow the reader to draw a conclusion
   (D) outline a new idea and criticize it
   (E) raise several questions and provide answers to them

7. The development discussed in the passage is primarily a problem of
   (A) political philosophy
   (B) educational philosophy
   (C) scientific philosophy
   (D) practical science
   (E) practical politics

Helplessness and passivity are central themes in describing human depression. Laboratory experiments with animals have uncovered a phenomenon designated "learned helplessness." Dogs given ines-
5 capable shock initially show intense emotionality, but later become passive in the same situation. When the situation is changed from inescapable to escapable shock, the dogs fail to escape even though escape is possible. Neurochemical changes resulting from
10 learned helplessness are similar to those found in separation loss, changes which produce an avoidance-escape deficit in laboratory animals.

Is the avoidance deficit caused by prior exposure to inescapable shock, learned helplessness, or simply a
15 stress-induced noradrenergic deficiency leading to a deficit in motor activation? Avoidance-escape deficit can be produced in rats by stress alone, i.e., by a brief swim in cold water. But a deficit produced by exposure to extremely traumatic events must be produced
20 by a very different mechanism than the deficit produced by exposure to the less traumatic uncontrollable aversive events in the learned-helplessness experiments. A nonaversive parallel to the learned helplessness induced by uncontrollable shock, e.g., induced
25 by uncontrollable food delivery, produces similar results. Moreover, studies have shown the importance of prior experience in learned helplessness. Dogs can be "immunized" against learned helplessness by prior experience with controllable shock. Rats also
30 show a "mastery effect" after extended experience with escapable shock. They work far longer trying to

escape from inescapable shock than do rats lacking this prior mastery experience. Conversely, weanling rats given inescapable shock fail to escape shock as
35 adults. These adult rats are also poor at nonaversive discrimination learning.

Certain similarities have been noted between conditions produced in animals by the learned-helplessness procedure and by the experimental neurosis paradigm.
40 In the latter, animals are first trained on a discrimination task and are then tested with discriminative stimuli of increasing similarity. Eventually, as the discrimination becomes very difficult, animals fail to respond and begin displaying abnormal behaviors,
45 first agitation, then lethargy.

It has been suggested that both learned helplessness and experimental neurosis involve inhibition of motivation centers and pathways by limbic forebrain inhibitory centers, especially in the septal area. The main
50 function of this inhibition is compensatory, providing relief from anxiety or distress. In rats subjected to the learned-helplessness and experimental-neurosis paradigms, stimulation of the septum produces behavioral arrest, lack of behavioral initiation and lethargy,
55 while rats with septal lesions do not show learned helplessness. How analogous the model of learned helplessness and the paradigm of stress-induced neurosis are to human depression is not entirely clear. Inescapable noise or unsolvable problems have been
60 shown to result in conditions in humans similar to those induced in laboratory animals, but an adequate model of human depression must also be able to account for the cognitive complexity of human depression.

8. The primary purpose of the passage is to
   (A) propose a cure for depression in human beings
   (B) discuss research possibly relevant to depression in human beings
   (C) criticize the result of experiments which induce depression in laboratory animals
   (D) raise some questions about the propriety of using laboratory animals for research
   (E) suggest some ways in which depression in animals differs from depression in humans

9. The author raises the question at the beginning of the second paragraph in order to
   (A) prove that learned helplessness is caused by neurochemical changes
   (B) demonstrate that learned helplessness is also caused by nonaversive discrimination learning
   (C) suggest that further research is needed to

determine the exact causes of learned helplessness
   (D) refute a possible objection based on an alternative explanation of the cause of learned helplessness
   (E) express doubts about the structure of the experiments which created learned helplessness in dogs

10. It can be inferred from the passage that rats with septal lesions (lines 52–56) do not show learned helplessness because
   (A) such rats were immunized against learned helplessness by prior training
   (B) the lesions blocked communication between the limbic forebrain inhibitory centers and motivation centers
   (C) the lesions prevented the rats from understanding the inescapability of the helplessness situation
   (D) a lack of stimulation of the septal area does not necessarily result in excited behavior
   (E) lethargy and other behavior associated with learned helplessness can be induced by the neurosis paradigm

11. It can be inferred that the most important difference between experiments inducing learned helplessness by inescapable shock and the nonaversive parallel mentioned at line 23 is the nonaversive parallel
   (A) did not use pain as a stimulus to be avoided
   (B) failed to induce learned helplessness in subject animals
   (C) reduced the extent of learned helplessness
   (D) caused a more traumatic reaction in the animals
   (E) used only rats rather than dogs as subjects

12. The author cites the "mastery effect" (line 30) primarily in order to
   (A) prove that the avoidance deficit caused by exposure to inescapable shock is not caused by shock per se but by the inescapability of the shock
   (B) cast doubt on the validity of models of animal depression when applied to depression in human beings
   (C) explain the neurochemical changes in the brain which cause learned helplessness
   (D) suggest that the experimental neurosis paradigm and learned-helplessness procedure produce similar behavior in animals

(E) argue that learned helplessness is simply a stress-induced noradrenergic deficiency

13. Which of the following would be the most logical continuation of the passage?
    (A) an explanation of the connection between the septum and the motivation centers of the brains of rats
    (B) an examination of techniques used to cure animals of learned helplessness
    (C) a review of experiments designed to create stress-induced noradrenergic deficiencies in humans
    (D) a proposal for an experiment to produce learned helplessness and experimental neurosis in humans
    (E) an elaboration of the differences between human depression and similar animal behavior

14. In developing her argument, the author relies on conclusions based on all of the following EXCEPT
    (A) studies of humans exposed to inescapable noise
    (B) experiments exposing animals to inescapable shock
    (C) experiments exposing animals to escapable shock
    (D) reports on neurochemical changes in experimental subjects
    (E) programs to cure human beings of learned helplessness

Under existing law, a new drug may be labeled, promoted and advertised only for those conditions in which safety and effectiveness have been demonstrated and which the Food and Drug Administration
5 (FDA) has approved, or so-called "approved uses." Other uses have come to be called "unapproved uses," and cannot be legally promoted. In a real sense, the term "unapproved" is a misnomer because it includes in one phrase two categories of marketed
10 drugs which are very different. It is common for new research and new insights to identify valid new uses for drugs already on the market. This is an important method of discovery in the field of therapeutics, and there are numerous examples of medical progress
15 resulting from the serendipitous observations and therapeutic innovations of physicians. Before such advances can result in new indications for inclusion in drug labeling, however, the available data must meet the legal standard of substantial evidence derived from
20 adequate and well-controlled clinical trials. Such evi-

dence may require time to develop, and, without initiative on the part of the drug firm, it may not occur at all for certain uses. However, because medical literature on new uses exists, and these are uses medically
25 beneficial, physicians often use these drugs for such purposes prior to FDA review or changes in labeling. This is referred to as "unlabeled uses" of drugs.

A different problem arises when a particular use for a drug has been examined scientifically and has been
30 found to be ineffective or unsafe, and yet physicians who either are uninformed or who refuse to accept the available scientific evidence continue their use. Such use may have been reviewed by FDA and rejected, or, in some cases, the use may actually be warned against
35 in the labeling. This subset of uses may be properly termed "disapproved uses."

Government policy should minimize the extent of unlabeled uses. If such uses are valid—and many are—it is important that scientifically sound evidence
40 supporting them be generated and that the regulatory system accommodate them into drug labeling. Continuing rapid advances in medical care and the complexity of drug usage, however, makes it impossible for government to keep drug labeling up to date for
45 every conceivable situation. Thus, when a particular use of this type appears, it is also important, and in the interest of good medical care, that no stigma be attached to such use by practitioners while the formal evidence is assembled between the time of discovery
50 and the time the new use is included in the labeling. In the case of disapproved uses, however, it is proper policy to warn against these in the package insert. Whether use of a drug for these purposes by the uninformed or intransigent physician constitutes a viola-
55 tion of the current Federal Food, Drug and Cosmetic Act is a matter of debate that involves a number of technical and legal issues. Regardless of that, the inclusion of disapproved uses in the form of contraindications, warnings, and other precautionary state-
60 ments in package inserts is an important practical deterrent to improper use. Except for clearly disapproved uses, however, it is in the best interests of patient care that physicians not be constrained by regulatory statutes from exercising their best judgment in
65 prescribing a drug for both its approved uses and any unlabeled uses it may have.

15. The author is primarily concerned to
    (A) refute a theory
    (B) draw a distinction
    (C) discredit an opponent
    (D) describe a new development
    (E) condemn an error

16. According to the passage, an unlabeled use of a drug is any use which
    (A) has been reviewed by the FDA and specifically rejected
    (B) is medically beneficial despite the fact that such use is prohibited by law
    (C) has medical value but has not yet been approved by FDA for inclusion as a labeled use
    (D) is authorized by the label approved by the FDA on the basis of scientific studies
    (E) is made in experiments designed to determine whether a drug is medically beneficial

17. It can be inferred from the passage that the intransigent physician (line 54)
    (A) continues to prescribe a drug even though he or she knows it is not in the best interest of the patient
    (B) refuses to use a drug for an unlabeled purpose out of fear that he or she may be stigmatized by its use
    (C) persists in using a drug for disapproved uses because he or she rejects the evidence of its ineffectiveness or dangers
    (D) experiments with new uses for tested drugs in an attempt to find medically beneficial uses for the drugs
    (E) is violating the Federal Food, Drug and Cosmetic Act in using drugs for disapproved uses

18. All of the following are mentioned in the passage as reasons for allowing unlabeled uses of drugs EXCEPT
    (A) the increased cost to the patient of buying an FDA-approved drug
    (B) the medical benefits which can accrue to the patient through unlabeled use
    (C) the time lag between initial discovery of a medical use and FDA approval of that use
    (D) the possibility that a medically beneficial use may never be clinically documented
    (E) the availability of publications to inform physicians of the existence of such uses

19. With which of the following statements about the distinction between approved and unlabeled uses would the author most likely agree?
    (A) Public policy statements have not adequately distinguished between uses already approved by the FDA and medically beneficial uses which have not yet been approved.
    (B) The distinction between approved and unlabeled uses has been obscured because government regulatory agencies approve only those uses which have been clinically tested.
    (C) Practicing physicians are in a better position than the FDA to distinguish between approved and unlabeled uses because they are involved in patient treatment on a regular basis.
    (D) The distinction between approved and unlabeled uses should be discarded so that the patient can receive the full benefits of any drug use.
    (E) The practice of unlabeled uses of drugs exists because of the time lag between the discovery of a beneficial use and the production of data needed for FDA approval.

20. The author regards the practice of using drugs for medically valid purposes before FDA approval as
    (A) a necessary compromise
    (B) a dangerous policy
    (C) an illegal activity
    (D) an unqualified success
    (E) a short-term phenomenon

21. Which of the following statements best summarizes the point of the passage?
    (A) Patients have been exposed to needless medical risk because the FDA has not adequately regulated unlabeled uses as well as disapproved uses.
    (B) Physicians who engage in the practice of unlabeled use make valuable contributions to medical science and should be protected from legal repercussions of such activity.
    (C) Pharmaceutical firms develop and test new drugs which initially have little or no medical value but later are found to have value in unlabeled uses.
    (D) Doctors prescribe drugs for disapproved purposes primarily because they fail to read manufacturers' labels or because they disagree with the clinical data about the value of drugs.
    (E) The government should distinguish between unlabeled use and disapproved use of a drug, allowing the practice of unlabeled use and condemning disapproved use.

The existence of both racial and sexual discrimination in employment is well documented, and policy makers and responsible employers are particularly sensitive to the plight of the black female employee on

5 the theory that she is doubly the victim of discrimination. That there exist differences in income between whites and blacks is clear, but it is not so clear that these differences are solely the result of racial discrimination in employment. The two groups differ in
10 productivity, so basic economics dictates that their incomes will differ.

To obtain a true measure of the effect of racial discrimination in employment it is necessary to adjust the gross black/white income ratio for these productivity
15 factors. White women in urban areas have a higher educational level than black women and can be expected to receive larger incomes. Moreover, state distribution of residence is important because blacks are overrepresented in the South, where wage rates are
20 typically lower than elsewhere and where racial differentials in income are greater. Also, blacks are overrepresented in large cities, and incomes of blacks would be greater if blacks were distributed among cities of different sizes in the same manner as whites.
25 After standardization for the productivity factors, the income of black urban women is estimated to be between 108 and 125 percent of the income of white women. This indicates that productivity factors more than account for the actual white/black income differ-
30 ential for women. Despite their greater education, white women's *actual* median income is only 2 to 5 percent higher than that of black women in the North. Unlike the situation of men, the evidence indicates that the money income of black urban women was as
35 great as, or greater than, that of whites of similar productivity in the North, and probably in the United States as a whole. For men, however, the adjusted black/white income ratio is approximately 80 percent.
40 At least two possible hypotheses may explain why the adjustment for productivity more than accounts for the observed income differential for women, whereas a differential persists for men. First, there may be more discrimination against black men than against
45 black women. The different occupational structures for men and women give some indication why this could be the case, and institutionalized considerations—for example, the effect of unionization in cut-
50 ting competition—may also contribute. Second, the data are consistent with the hypothesis that the intensity of discrimination against women differs little between whites and blacks. Therefore, racial discrimi-
55 nation adds little to effects of existing sex discrimination.

These findings suggest that a black woman does not necessarily suffer relatively more discrimination in the labor market than does a white woman. Rather, for
60 women, the effects of sexual discrimination are so pervasive that the effects of racial discrimination are negligible. Of course, this is not to say that the more

generalized racial discrimination of which black women, like men, are victims does not disadvantage
65 black women in their search for work. After all, one important productivity factor is level of education, and the difference between white and black women on this scale is largely the result of racial discrimination.

22. The primary purpose of the passage is to
(A) explain the reasons for the existence of income differentials between men and women
(B) show that racial discrimination against black women in employment is less important than sexual discrimination
(C) explore the ways in which productivity factors such as level of education influence the earning power of black workers
(D) sketch a history of racial and sexual discrimination against black and female workers in the labor market
(E) offer some suggestions as to how public officials and private employers can act to solve the problem of discrimination against black women

23. According to the passage, the gross black/white income ratio is not an accurate measure of discrimination in employment because the gross ratio
(A) fails to include large numbers of black workers who live in the large cities and in the South
(B) must be adjusted to reflect the longer number of hours and greater number of days worked by black employees
(C) represents a subjective interpretation by the statistician of the importance of factors such as educational achievement
(D) is not designed to take account of the effects of the long history of racial discrimination
(E) includes income differences attributable to real economic factors and not to discrimination

24. Which of the following best describes the relationship between the income level for black women and that for black men?
(A) In general, black men earn less money than black women.
(B) On the average, black women in the South earn less money than black men in large Northern cities.
(C) Productivity factors have a greater dollar value in the case of black women.

(D) Black men have a higher income level than black women because black men have a higher level of education.

(E) The difference between income levels for black and white women is less than that for black and white men.

25. Which of the following best describes the logical relationship between the two hypotheses presented in lines 40–56?
    (A) The two hypotheses may both be true since each phenomenon could contribute to the observed differential.
    (B) The two hypotheses are contradictory, and if one is proved to be correct, the other is proved incorrect.
    (C) The two hypotheses are dependent on each other, and empirical disconfirmation of the one is disconfirmation of the other.
    (D) The two hypotheses are logically connected so that proof of the first entails the truth of the second.
    (E) The two hypotheses are logically connected so that it is impossible to prove either one to be true without also proving the other to be true.

26. Which of the following best describes the tone of the passage?
    (A) confident and overbearing
    (B) ill-tempered and brash
    (C) objective and critical
    (D) tentative and inconclusive
    (E) hopeful and optimistic

27. If the second hypothesis mentioned by the author (lines 50–56) is correct, a general lessening of discrimination against women should lead to a(n)
    (A) higher white/black income ratio for women
    (B) lower white/black income ratio for women
    (C) lower female/male income ratio
    (D) increase in the productivity of women
    (E) increase in the level of education of women

28. The author's attitude toward racial and sexual discrimination in employment can best be described as one of
    (A) apology
    (B) concern
    (C) indifference
    (D) indignation
    (E) anxiety

At the present time, 98 percent of the world energy consumption comes from stored sources, such as fossil fuels or nuclear fuel. Only hydroelectric and wood energy represent completely renewable sources on
5 ordinary time scales. Discovery of large additional fossil fuel reserves, solution of the nuclear safety and waste disposal problems, or the development of controlled thermonuclear fusion will provide only a short-term solution to the world's energy crisis. Within
10 about 100 years, the thermal pollution resulting from our increased energy consumption will make solar energy a necessity at any cost.

Man's energy consumption is currently about one part in ten thousand that of the energy we receive from
15 the sun. However, it is growing at a 5 percent rate, of which about 2 percent represents a population growth and 3 percent a per capita energy increase. If this growth continues, within 100 years our energy consumption will be about 1 percent of the absorbed solar
20 energy, enough to increase the average temperature of the earth by about one degree centigrade if stored energy continues to be our predominant source. This will be the point at which there will be significant effects in our climate, including the melting of the
25 polar ice caps, a phenomenon which will raise the level of the oceans and flood parts of our major cities. There is positive feedback associated with this process, since the polar ice cap contributes to the partial reflectivity of the energy arriving from the sun: As the
30 ice caps begin to melt, the reflectivity will decrease, thus heating the earth still further.

It is often stated that the growth rate will decline or that energy conservation measures will preclude any long-range problem. Instead, this only postpones the
35 problem by a few years. Conservation by a factor of two together with a maintenance of the 5 percent growth rate delays the problem by only 14 years. Reduction of the growth rate to 4 percent postpones the problem by only 25 years; in addition, the inequi-
40 ties in standards of living throughout the world will provide pressure toward an increase in growth rate, particularly if cheap energy is available. The problem of a changing climate will not be evident until perhaps ten years before it becomes critical due to the nature of
45 an exponential growth rate together with the normal annual weather variations. This may be too short a period to circumvent the problem by converting to other energy sources, so advance planning is a necessity.

50　　The only practical means of avoiding the problem of thermal pollution appears to be the use of solar energy. (Schemes to "air-condition" the earth do not appear to be feasible before the twenty-second century.) Using the solar energy before it is dissipated to

55 heat does not increase the earth's energy balance. The cost of solar energy is extremely favorable now; particularly when compared to the cost of relocating many of our major cities.

29. The author is primarily concerned with
    (A) describing a phenomenon and explaining its causes
    (B) outlining a position and supporting it with statistics
    (C) isolating an ambiguity and clarifying it by definition
    (D) presenting a problem and advocating a solution for it
    (E) citing a counter-argument and refuting it

30. According to the passage, all of the following are factors which will tend to increase thermal pollution EXCEPT
    (A) the earth's increasing population
    (B) melting of the polar ice caps
    (C) increase in per capita energy consumption
    (D) pressure to redress standard of living inequities by increasing energy consumption
    (E) expected anomalies in weather patterns

31. The positive feedback mentioned in line 27 means that the melting of the polar ice caps will
    (A) reduce per capita energy consumption
    (B) accelerate the transition to solar energy
    (C) intensify the effects of thermal pollution
    (D) necessitate a shift to alternative energy sources
    (E) result in the inundations of major cities

32. The author mentions the possibility of energy conservation (lines 32–34) in order to
    (A) preempt and refute a possible objection to his position
    (B) support directly the central thesis of the passage
    (C) minimize the significance of a contradiction in the passage

(D) prove that such measures are ineffective and counterproductive
(E) supply the reader with additional background information

33. It can be inferred that the "air-conditioning" of the earth (lines 53–55) refers to proposals to
    (A) distribute frigid air from the polar ice caps to coastal cities as the temperature increases due to thermal pollution
    (B) dissipate the surplus of the release of stored solar energy over absorbed solar energy into space
    (C) conserve completely renewable energy sources by requiring that industry replace these resources
    (D) avoid further thermal pollution by converting to solar energy as opposed to conventional and nuclear sources
    (E) utilize hydroelectric and wood energy to replace non-conventional energy sources such as nuclear energy

34. The tone of the passage is best described as one of
    (A) unmitigated outrage
    (B) cautious optimism
    (C) reckless abandon
    (D) smug self-assurance
    (E) pronounced alarm

35. Which of the following would be the most logical topic for the author to address in a succeeding paragraph?
    (A) the problems of nuclear safety and waste disposal
    (B) a history of the development of solar energy
    (C) the availability and cost of solar energy technology
    (D) the practical effects of flooding of coastal cities
    (E) the feasibility of geothermal energy

STOP

IF YOU FINISH BEFORE TIME IS CALLED, CHECK YOUR WORK ON THIS SECTION ONLY. DO NOT WORK ON ANY OTHER SECTION IN THE TEST.

PRACTICE EXAMINATION 2
ANSWER KEY

SECTION I

1.	C	7.	D	13.	C	19.	C	25.	B
2.	C	8.	B	14.	C	20.	D	26.	C
3.	D	9.	C	15.	E	21.	D	27.	A
4.	D	10.	B	16.	E	22.	D	28.	A
5.	C	11.	C	17.	B	23.	C	29.	A
6.	A	12.	E	18.	D	24.	A	30.	E

SECTION II

1.	D	8.	B	15.	C	22.	A	29.	B
2.	D	9.	A	16.	B	23.	E	30.	D
3.	A	10.	C	17.	D	24.	D	31.	E
4.	D	11.	C	18.	D	25.	B	32.	E
5.	C	12.	C	19.	E	26.	E	33.	B
6.	B	13.	B	20.	E	27.	E	34.	A
7.	D	14.	C	21.	D	28.	C	35.	D

SECTION III

1.	D	7.	A	13.	D	19.	A	25.	B
2.	E	8.	C	14.	D	20.	C	26.	A
3.	C	9.	E	15.	B	21.	B	27.	C
4.	D	10.	B	16.	B	22.	D	28.	D
5.	E	11.	B	17.	A	23.	C	29.	E
6.	D	12.	C	18.	C	24.	D	30.	E

SECTION IV

1.	D	8.	B	15.	B	22.	B	29.	D
2.	A	9.	D	16.	C	23.	E	30.	E
3.	D	10.	B	17.	C	24.	E	31.	C
4.	B	11.	A	18.	A	25.	A	32.	A
5.	A	12.	A	19.	E	26.	C	33.	B
6.	A	13.	E	20.	A	27.	A	34.	B
7.	B	14.	E	21.	E	28.	B	35.	C

EXPLANATORY
ANSWERS

SECTION I

Questions 1–6

This set is based upon family relationships. At the outset we note that of the seven people related to X, two are males (father, brother) and five are females (mother, aunt, sister, wife, and daughter). And we summarize the additional information:

P = Q (same sex)
M ≠ N (not same sex)
S > M (born before)
Q ≠ mother (Q is not X's mother.)

There is a further deduction to be drawn. There are only two male relatives. Of the four individuals, P, Q, M, and N, three are of the same sex and one is of the opposite sex. Since there are only two males in the scheme, this means that the three of the same sex are female. So P, Q, and either M or N are females; either M or N is male.

1. **(C)** The answer to this question is evident from the analysis above.

2. **(C)** This question is also answerable on the basis of our previous analysis. As for (A) and (B), though we know that of M and N one is male and the other is female, we have no information to justify a judgment as to who is the female. Nor is there any information to support the conclusions in (D) and (E).

3. **(D)** We have established that P and Q are females, and that either M or N is female. So M or N is male, and of the remaining three relatives, S, R, and T, one is male as well. If T is the daughter of X, this establishes that she is female and, further, that either R or S is the remaining male. (A), (B) and (C) are incorrect since the additional stipulation of this question does not add anything to the analysis of sexual distribution above. (E) is incorrect since it asserts that S is the male, but there is nothing to support that conclusion. (D), however, is necessarily true. Of the pair R and S, one must be male and the other female, so they are not of the same sex.

4. **(D)** In the scheme of relations, there is only one possible pair of sisters: the mother and the aunt. It will not do to argue that X might have married his sister, especially when an ordinary sister relationship is available. In any event, if M and Q represent the mother and the aunt, since Q is not the mother, M must be X's mother, so (B) and (C) are both true. Further, since M must be female, N must be male, and (A) is true. Then, since M is X's mother, and since S was born before M, S could not be X's brother and (E) is true. As for (D), M, Q, and N (a male) are eliminated as daughters, but this still leaves several possibilities.

5. **(C)** There is only one available grandfather-grandchild relationship: S must be X's father and N his daughter. If N is female, then M is male and must be X's brother. So (C) is necessarily true. As for the remaining choices, (A) is possible though not necessary. (B) is also possible since P might be X's mother. (D) is not possible since Q is female. Finally, (E) is possible since P is a female and might be X's sister and so N's aunt.

6. **(A)** Since M was born after S, if M is the mother of X's daughter, S cannot be the daughter. (Again, it will not do to argue about stepdaughters, for that is clearly outside the bounds of the problem.) The remaining choices, however, are possible. As for (B) and (C), no restriction is placed on P and Q. And as for (D), R is not further defined. As for (E), we do know that N is male if M is female, and N could therefore be X's brother.

Questions 7–12

This set is a fairly straightforward linear ordering set: Individuals are arranged in a single file from 1 to 7. We summarize the information for easy reference:

K > L (L behind K)

M → N (N directly behind M)

J/O = 1/7 (J and O are first and last or vice versa.)

7. **(D)** We know that J finishes first or last, though we do not know which, so (A) and (B) are incorrect. The fourth position is the middle position of the seven. Regardless of whether J finishes first or last, if L is in position 4, L and J are separated by two swimmers. So M and N are 5 and 6. (E) is not possible; (C) is only possible.

8. **(B)** We are given no additional information, so the question must be solvable by some general conclusions based on the initial information. We are looking for the one statement that cannot, under any circumstances, be true. Since K finishes ahead of L, and since L cannot be in last place, L can finish at worst sixth, and K can finish at worst fifth. That the remaining statements are possible can be proved by examples.

9. **(C)** If O and K are to finish one after the other, it must be because O finishes first and K second. Since L finishes after K, K and O cannot finish one after the other if O is seventh. So statement I is true. Further, if O is first, J must be seventh, and statement III is true. As for II, knowing that K is second does not fix the position of L.

10. **(B)** If K is fourth, there is only one pair of adjacent finishing positions available for the M-N pairing: second and third. So M finishes second and N third. As for L, we know that L finishes after K, but it is not clear whether it is L or P who finishes in fifth versus sixth position, nor is it established who finishes first and who finishes last.

11. **(C)** If L finishes ahead of N we know that K finishes somewhere ahead of M. So we have the bloc K . . . M-N . . . L. And it is stipulated that J finishes first, so O finishes last. We have the order: J, K, L, M-N, O. The only unresolved issue is where P goes. There are four possibilities:

P(?)   P(?)   P(?)   P(?)

J   K   L   M–N   O

12. **(E)** We must test each condition. As for (A), knowing the first and last finishers tells us nothing about the order between 2 and 6. As for (B), this establishes nothing about positions 3 through 6. As for (C), this establishes only that N is third and leaves open positions 4, 5, and 6. (D) does tell us that M finishes second, but that is all. (E), however, allows us to infer that M and N finish before L (they must be together); and we know that K finishes before L. This leaves only position 6 for P.

Questions 13–18

For this set no diagram is needed since the relationships are inherent in the system of arithmetic, that is, five is one more than six, etc. You may find it useful to make a marginal note or two, e.g., "challenge +1 or +2."

13. **(C)** The setup for this group of questions is fairly long, but once the rules of the game are understood, this question is easy. (A) and (B) are incorrect, for a challenge must issue from a player of lower rank. (D) and (E) are incorrect, for a challenge can be issued only to a player at most two ranks superior.

14. **(C)** Since S begins in fourth position, S can reach first in two plays by issuing and winning two challenges. This can be done in two ways. S can first challenge Q and then P, or S can first challenge R and then P. Either way, R must be in fourth position.

15. **(E)** This arrangement could come about only after a minimum of *three* matches: P versus Q, S versus R, and U versus T, with the challenger prevailing in each case. The other rankings are possible after only two matches:
    (A) R versus Q and T versus S
    (B) R versus Q and U versus T
    (C) R versus P and U versus S
    (D) Q versus P and S versus R

16. **(E)** If U challenges and defeats S, the bottom half of the ranking changes from STU to UST; and if R challenges and defeats P, the top half of the ranking changes from PQR to RPQ. So in just two matches, all 6 players could be displaced from their initial rank.

17. **(B)** For P to be moved down to third place, at least two matches must have been played (Q challenging and defeating P and then R challenging and defeating Q, or R challenging and defeating P with Q in turn challenging and defeating P). The UST ordering of the bottom half of the ranking could be obtained in one match, with U challenging and defeating S.

18. **(D)** For one player to improve and two to drop in a single match, a player must have challenged and defeated a player two ranks superior. For such challenges to have the stipulated results, it must have been player 3 challenging and defeating player 1, and player 6 challenging and defeating player 4. So the rankings at the end of two matches will be RPQUST. The third match could pit U against P.

Questions 19–24

The primary task here is to organize the information. And for that we will use a matrix:

	F	G	H	I	J
1	YES(X)	YES(~X)	YES	NO	NO
2	NO	YES(~X)	YES	YES(Z)	YES(~H)
3	YES(X)	YES(~X)	YES(Y)	YES(~Z)	NO

Once the information has been organized, the questions are readily answerable.

19. **(C)** With regard to statement I, F and G cannot grow together since F requires the presence of X and G requires the absence of X. H can grow with or without X, so G and H can grow together, and F and H can grow together. So II and III are possible. IV, however, is not possible since J does not grow in field 1 at all.

20. **(D)** Since F does not grow at all in field 2, (A) and (B) can be eliminated. Then, since J will not grow with H, both (C) and (E) can be eliminated. Combination G, I, and J, however, is consistent with all conditions.

21. **(D)** Notice that this question asks for a list of all crops which could grow *alone*. F cannot, since F simply does not grow in field 2. G grows in field 2 so long as X is not applied to the field, so G is part of the correct answer. I will not grow since it

requires Z. Finally, J will grow since the question stipulates the crops will grow alone. So the correct answer consists of G, H, and J.

22. **(D)** Neither F nor H will grow in field 3 unless certain fertilizers or pesticides are added, so we can eliminate choices (A), (B), and (C). (E) can be eliminated on the further ground that J simply does not grow in field 3.

23. **(C)** J does not grow in field 3, so that reduces the number of possible crops to four. But F and G cannot grow together, which further reduces the number to three. So the maximum number of crops which can be planted together is three—F, H, and I or G, H, and I.

24. **(A)** Consulting the chart, we see that F does not grow there at all. G will not grow in the presence of X, and I will only grow in the presence of Z. So only H and J will grow under the stipulated conditions.

Questions 25–30

This is another ordering set. Begin by summarizing the information.

K < (N & L)   Wed = J,   Fri = 1,
Mon = 2,   Th = 2,   P < M
Tue = 2,

25. **(B)** Since this is the first item in this group, it likely won't require a lot of work. Therefore, look through the answer choices to find one that violates a single initial condition. The correct answer is (B). The tourist cannot visit K on Thursday for then it would be impossible to visit both N and L later in the week (to wit, on Friday).

26. **(C)** Test each day:

M	Tu	W	Th	Fri
KP	MN	J	QL	O
OQ	KP	J	ML	N

But she cannot visit both K and P on Thursday, for then it would be impossible to visit M, N, and L later in the week.

27. **(A)** The question stem sets up the spacing O L, but where can this pair be put? Since J is the only attraction scheduled for Wednesday, the only possibilities are Monday and Tuesday or Thurs-

day and Friday. But L cannot be scheduled for Friday, so:

M	Tu	W	Th	F
O	L	J		

And this means that K must be scheduled for Monday:

M	Tu	W	Th	F
OK	L	J		

The schedule for the other attractions is not fixed.

28. **(A)** Enter the new information on a diagram:

M	Tu	W	Th	F
	OQ	J		

The most powerful initial condition is the first, for it controls the placement of three individuals. Since K must come before N and L, and since only one attraction can be scheduled for Friday, K cannot be scheduled for either Thursday or Friday:

M	Tu	W	Th	F
K	OQ	J		

L must be scheduled for Thursday and N for Thursday or Friday:

M	Tu	W	Th	F
K	OQ	J	L(N?)	(N?)

And P must come before M:

M	Tu	W	Th	F
KP	OQ	J	L(M/N)	(M/N)

29. **(A)** Enter the new information on a diagram:

M	Tu	W	Th	F
	J	P		

So M must be scheduled for Friday:

M	Tu	W	Th	F
	J	P		M

And that most powerful condition requires that K be scheduled for Monday:

M	Tu	W	Th	F
K	J	P		M

Although we can't draw any further conclusions, we have done enough work to find the correct answer. Only (A) is necessarily true, while the other choices are only possibly true.

30. **(E)** With a question like this you must test each choice to determine which constitute a possible arrangement. It is possible for the tourist to visit N the day after L:

M	Tu	W	Th	F
KP	OQ	J	ML	N

If you try to construct an order using the other answer choices, you will find that you run into a contradiction between those answer choices and the initial conditions.

SECTION II

1. **(D)** The author's recommendation that public schools should have computerized reading programs depends upon the correctness of his explanation of the present deficiency in reading skills in the public schools. His contrast with private-school students shows that he thinks the deficiency can be attributed to the lack of such a program in the public schools. So, one of the author's assumptions, and that is what the question stem is asking about, is that the differential in reading skills is a result of the availability of a computerized program in the private-school system and the lack thereof in the public-school system. (E) is, of course, irrelevant to the question of *reading* skills. (C) tries to force the author to assume a greater burden than he has undertaken. He claims that the reading skills of public-school children could be improved by a computerized reading program. He is not concerned to argue the merits of having good reading skills. (A) and (B) are wrong for the same reason. The author's claim must be interpreted to mean "of children who are able to learn, all would benefit from a computerized reading program." When the author claims that "public-school children can be good readers," he is not implying that all children can learn to be good readers nor that all can learn to read equally well.

2. **(D)** The question contains a hidden assumption: that the person questioned agrees that his company has, in the past, discriminated. So I is applicable, since the speaker may wish to answer neither "yes" nor "no." He may wish to object to the question: "But I do not admit that our company has ever discriminated, so your question is unfair." III is just another way of describing the

difficulty we have just outlined. II is not applicable to the question. Since a simple question never actually makes a statement, it would seem impossible for it to contradict itself. A contradiction occurs only between statements or assertions.

3. **(A)** There are two weaknesses in Ms. Rose's argument. One will be treated in the explanation of the following question——she reaches a very general conclusion on the basis of one example. We are concerned for the moment with the second weakness. Even if Rose had been able to cite numerous examples like the case she mentions, her argument would be weak because it overlooks the possibility that an education may be valuable even if it is not used to make a living. Importantly, Rose may be correct in her criticism of the man she mentions——we need make no judgment about that——but the assumption is nonetheless *unsupported* in that she gives no arguments to support it. (B) plays on the superficial detail of the paragraph——the inversion of customary role models. But that is not relevant to the structure of the argument; the form could have been as easily shown using a woman with a law degree who decided to become a sailor, or a child who studied ballet but later decided to become a doctor. (D) also is totally beside the point. Rose never commits herself to so specific a conclusion. She simply says professional education is a waste; she never claims success is related to quality of education. (E) is wrong because Rose is making a general claim about professional education——the man with the law degree was used merely to illustrate her point. (C) is perhaps the second-best answer, but it is still not nearly as good as (A). The author's objection is that the man she mentions did not use his law degree in a law-related field. She never suggests that such a degree should be used to make money. She might not have objected to his behavior if he had used the degree to work in a public interest capacity.

4. **(D)** As we noted at the beginning of our discussion of question 3, there is another weakness in Rose's argument: She takes a single example and from it draws a very general conclusion. (D) exemplifies this weakness. Here, too, we have a person who rests his claim on a single example, and obviously this makes the claim very weak. (E) mentions education, but here education is a detail of the argument. The form of the argument——a foolish generalization——is not restricted to education. (A), (B), and (C) are all wrong because they do not reflect the form of the argument, a generalization on a single example.

5. **(C)** To break the code, the cryptographer needs information about the language which the code conceals. (A), (B), (D), and (E) all provide such information. (C), however, says nothing about the underlying language. The code could even use all even or all odd numbers for the symbol substitutions without affecting the information to be encoded.

6. **(B)** The question is one which tests the validity or strength of a causal inference. Often such arguments can be attacked by finding intervening causal linkages, that is, variables which might interfere with the predicted result. (A) cites such a variable. If the traffic problem is created by commercial traffic which will not be reduced by toll increases, then the proposed increases will not solve the problem. (C), too, is such a variable. It suggests that the proposal is essentially self-defeating. (D) undermines the claim by arguing that the deterrent effect of a price increase is simply not significant, so the proposal will have little, if any, effect. (E) attacks the argument on a different ground. The ultimate objective of the plan is to reduce commuting time. Even assuming a drop in auto traffic because some commuters use public transportation, no advantage is gained if the public transportation system cannot handle the increase in traffic. (B), however, does very little to the argument. In fact, it could be argued that (B) is one of the predicted results of the plan: a drop in the number of autos because commuters begin to car-pool.

7. **(D)** The ad is weak for two reasons. First, although it is addressed to smokers in general, the evidence it cites is restricted to heavy (three-packs-a-day) smokers. Second, the success achieved by the product was restricted to a highly specific and unusual location——the mountain retreat of a clinic with a population trying hard to quit smoking. Thus, II will undermine the appeal of the advertisement because it cites the first of the weaknesses. III also will tell against the ad since it mentions the second of these weaknesses. I, however, is irrelevant to the ad's appeal since the cause of a smoker's addiction plays no role in the claim of this ad to assist smokers in quitting or cutting down.

8. **(B)** Notice that there is much common ground between the jockey and the veterinarian. The question stem asks you to uncover the areas on which they are in agreement, by asking which of the answer choices in NOT a shared assumption. Note that the exception can be an area neither has as well as an area only one has. Examine the dialogue. Both apparently assume that human emotions can be attributed to animals since they talk about them being loyal and brave (C), and both take those characteristics as being noble—that is, admirable (A). Neither speaker offers scientific evidence; each rests content with an anecdote (E) and (D). As for (B), though each speaker defends his choice for the first (*most* loyal), neither speaker takes a position on the second most loyal animal. For example, the jockey might believe that horses are the most loyal animals and that goldfish are the second most loyal animals.

9. **(A)** Although we do not want to argue theology, perhaps a point taken from that discipline will make this question more accessible: "If God is only good, from where does evil come?" Rousseau, at least as far as his argument is characterized here, faced a similar problem. If man is by his very nature sympathetic, what is the source of his non-sympathetic social institutions? (A) poses this critical question. The remaining choices each commit the same fundamental error. Rousseau *describes* a situation. The paragraph never suggests that he proposed a *solution*. Perhaps Rousseau considered the problem of modern society irremediable.

10. **(C)** The last sentence of the paragraph is very important. It tells us that the proportion of light atoms in the universe is increasing (because heavy ones decay into light ones, but the reverse process does not occur) and that this trend can be measured. By extrapolation back into time on the basis of present trends, scientists can find out when it all began. (B) and (E) are incorrect for the same reason. The author describes a physical phenomenon occurring on a grand scale. He never hints that it will be possible for man to reverse it (B). Further, (E) is in direct contradiction with information given in the paragraph: The ratio is not stable because the stars do not produce enough heavy atoms to offset the decay. (D) cannot be inferred from the passage. Although the *ratio* of light to heavy atoms is increasing, we should not conclude that the ratio is greater than 1:1. And, in any event, this would not be nearly

so logical a conclusion to the passage as (C). Finally, (A) is a distraction. It picks up on a minor detail in the passage and inflates that into a conclusion. Moreover, the passage clearly states that the process which keeps the stars going is fusion, not decay.

11. **(C)** It is important to pay careful attention to the ways in which a speaker qualifies his claims. In this case, the speaker has said only that the *great majority* of people can get medical care—he does not claim that *all* can. Thus, built into the claim is the implicit concession that some people may not have access to medical care. Thus, the objector's response fails to score against the speaker. The speaker could just respond, "Yes, I realize that and that is the reason why I qualified my remarks." (A) is incorrect for the only word in the objector's statement which is the least bit emotional is "poor," and it seems rather free from emotional overtones here. It would have been a different case had the objector claimed, "There are thousands of poor and starving people who have no place to live. . . ." (D) is wrong for two reasons. First, the evidence is really not statistical; it is only numerical. Second, and more important, the evidence, if anything, cuts against the speaker's claim—not that it does any damage given the speaker's qualifications on his claim; but it surely does not strengthen the speaker's claim. Finally, inasmuch as the speaker does not offer a cause-effect explanation, (E) must be wrong.

12. **(C)** There are really two parts to the speaker's claim. First, he maintains that the majority of Americans can get access to the medical care in this country; and, second, that the care they have access to is the best in the world. As for the second, good medical care is a function of many variables: number and location of facilities, availability of doctors, quality of education, etc. (A) and (E) may both be consistent with the speaker's claim. Even though we have fewer assistants (A) than some other country, we have more doctors, and that more than makes up for the fewer assistants. Or, perhaps, we have such good preventive medicine that people do not need to go into the hospital as frequently as the citizens of other nations, (E). (B) is wrong for a similar reason. Although it suggests there is a country in which people have greater access to the available care, it does not come to grips with the second element of the speaker's claim: that the care we get is the

best. (C), however, does meet both because it cites the existence of a country in which people are *given* (that is the first element) *better* (the second element) care. (D) hardly tells against the speaker's claim since he has implicitly conceded that some people do not have access to the care.

13. **(B)** The chief failing of the argument is that it draws a false analogy. Since prisons are required to feed and maintain as well as house prisoners (not to mention the necessity for security), the analogy to a hotel room is weak at best. (C) focuses on this specific shortcoming. Remember, in evaluating the strength of an argument from analogy it is important to look for dissimilarities which might make the analogy inappropriate. Thus, (A) and (E) are also good criticisms of the argument. They voice the general objection of which (C) is the specification. (D) is also a specific objection—the argument compares two numbers which are not at all similar. So the numerical comparison is a false one. (B) is not a way in which the argument can be criticized, for the author never cites any authority.

14. **(C)** Note the word *right* is italicized in the first sentence of the paragraph. The author is saying that this idea of a right can be only understood as the outcome of a balancing of demands. The smoker has an interest in smoking; the non-smoker has an interest in being free from smoke; so the question of which one actually has a *right* to have his *interest* protected depends upon which of those interests is considered to be more important. In some cases the balance is easily struck; in other cases it is difficult; but in all cases, the weighing, implicitly or explicitly, occurs. (C) captures the essence of this thought. In the case of smoking, the interests of both parties must be taken into account. (A) is a distraction. It is true the passage treats "rights," and it is also true that our Constitution protects our rights; but the connection suggested by (A) is a spurious one. It fails to address itself to the logic of the author's argument. The same objections can be leveled against (B). The wording of (D) makes it wrong. The passage is concerned with the demands of the nonsmoker *to be free from* the smoke of others, not with whether he himself chooses to smoke. (E) is premature. At this juncture the author is laying the foundation for his argument. He is speaking about rights in general. He reaches his conclusion with regard to smoking only at the end

of the paragraph. (See discussion of the following question.) (E) is wrong also because it mentions the "rights" of non-smoking persons. The whole question the author is addressing is whether the non-smoking person has a *right* as opposed to an interest or a mere claim.

15. **(C)** Here is where the author makes his general discussion of the balancing of interests to determine rights specifically applicable to the question of smoking. A smoker will have a *right* to smoke when and where his interests outweigh the interests of those who object, and (C) provides a pretty clear statement of this conclusion. (A) overstates the author's case. While it may be true that ultimately it will be some branch of the government which strikes the balance of interests, the phrase "chooses to allow" does not do justice to the author's concept of the balancing. The government is not simply choosing; it is weighing. Of course, since the balance may or may not be struck in favor of the smoker, (B) is incorrect. (E) confuses the problem of enforcement with the process of balancing. The passage leads to the conclusion that the balance must be struck. How that decision is later enforced is a practical matter the author is not concerned to discuss in this passage. Finally, (D), like (A), overstates the case. The smoker has an interest in being allowed to smoke, just as much as the non-smoker has an interest in being free from the smoke. A balance must be struck by giving proper weight to both. The author never suggests that the interest of the smokers can be completely overridden. Thus, for example, a smoker may have a more powerful interest in smoking than a non-smoker has in his being free from smoke, if the non-smoker can—with some small inconvenience—protect himself from the smoke.

16. **(B)** The whole passage is to clear up a misunderstanding about the concept of a *right*. The author explains that the term is misused since most people fail to realize that the right is not absolute, but is qualified by the interests and claims of other persons. While it is true that this is not generally known, (A) is incorrect because the author's *strategy* in argument is to clarify that term, not merely to bring up facts to support a contention that is already well defined. (C) also fails to describe his strategy. It is true that the author mentions hypothetical cases, but that is a detail, not his principal strategy. As for (D), though the author argues that smokers who claim an unqual-

ified right to smoke are wrong, he does not argue that they have fallen into contradiction. Finally, although the author argues that the general claim of smokers is ill-founded, the general claim he attacks (smokers have a right to smoke) is not an induction based on *empirical* evidence. A person who makes such a claim is not generalizing on observed instances (All swans I have seen are white. . . .); he is making a conceptual claim.

17. **(D)** Let us use our technique of substituting capital letters for categories. The sample argument can be rendered:

Some J are B. (Some Judges are Bar members)
No B are F. (No Bar members are Felons)
Therefore, Some J are not F. (Some Judges are not Felons)

This is a perfectly valid (logical) argument. (D) shares its form and validity:

Some M are P. (Some Men are Polite)
No M are D. (No Men are Dorm-allowed)
Therefore, Some P are not D. (Some Polite Men are not Dorm-allowed)

(E) has the invalid argument form:

G is L.
G is A.
Therefore, A is L.

(B) and (C) are both set up using more than three categories; therefore, they cannot possibly have the structure of the sample argument which uses only three categories:

(B)—people, people who want to avoid jury duty, people who do not register to vote, persons under 18
(C)—business, entities filing tax returns, business making enough money to pay taxes, business making a profit.

Finally, (A) does not parallel the sample argument since it contains the qualification "likely."

18. **(D)** The author's argument is admittedly not a very persuasive one, but the question stem does not ask us to comment on its relative strength. Rather, we are asked to identify the form of argumentation. Here the author suggests an alternative explanation, albeit a somewhat outlandish one. Thus, (D) is correct, (E) is incorrect because the claim about fresh air and the country is intro-

duced as a causal explanation, not an analogy to the city. (C) is wrong for the author accepts the differential described by the report; he just tries to explain the existence of the differential in another way. By the same token we can reject both (A) and (B) since the author takes the report's conclusion as his starting point. Although he attacks the explanation provided by the *report* published by the Department of Education, he does not attack the *credibility* of the *department* itself. Further, though he disagrees with the *conclusion* drawn by the report, he does not attack the way in which the *study* itself was *conducted*. Rather, he disagrees with the interpretation of the data gathered.

19. **(E)** The question stem asks us to find the one item which will not strengthen the author's argument. That is (E). Remember, the author's argument is an attempt (to be sure, a weak one) to develop an alternative causal explanation. (A) would provide some evidence that the author's claim—which at first glance seems a bit farfetched—actually has some empirical foundation. While (B) does not add any strength to the author's own explanation of the phenomenon being studied, it does strengthen the author's overall position by undermining the explanation given in the report. (C) strengthens the author's position for the same reason that (B) does: It weakens the position he is attacking. (D) strengthens the argument in the same way that (A) does, by providing some empirical support for the otherwise seemingly far-fetched explanation.

20. **(E)** Perhaps the most obvious weakness in the argument is that it oversimplifies matters. It is like the domino theory arguments adduced to support the war in Vietnam: Either we fight Communism now or it will take us over. The author argues, in effect: Either we put a stop to this now, or there will be no stopping it. Like the proponents of the domino theory, he ignores the many intermediate positions one might take. III is one way of describing this shortcoming: The dilemma posed by the author is a false one because it overlooks positions between the two extremes. II is also a weakness of the argument: "Cold-blooded murder" is obviously a phrase calculated to excite negative feelings. Finally, the whole argument is also internally inconsistent. The conclusion is that we should allow nature to take its course. How? By prolonging life with artificial means.

21. **(D)** We can summarize the information, using capital letters to represent each statement:

If P, then Q.
If Q, then R or S.
If R or S, and if Q, then A.
If R or S and if not-Q, then not-A.

where P represents "Paul comes to the party," Q represents "Quentin leaves the party," R represents "Robert asks Alice to dance," S represents "Steve asks Alice to dance," (and conversely R represents "Alice is asked by Robert to dance" and S represents "Alice is asked by Steve to dance"), and A represents Alice accepts. If we have not-Q, then we can deduce not-P from the first statement; thus, we have (D). (A), (B) and (C) are incorrect since there is no necessity that Robert or Steve ask Alice to dance. (E) is incorrect since this statement is different from our other statements and must be assigned a different letter, perhaps X. Notice that "Alice will accept . . . " tells us nothing about whether Alice leaves the party.

22. **(A)** The question stem has the form:

All S are AP. (All Students are APplicants)
Some AP are AC (Some APplicants are ACcepted)
Some *more* S are AC. (Some more Students are ACcepted)

Notice that (A) preserves very nicely the parallel in the conclusion because it uses the word "more." Thus, the error made in the stem argument (that some *more* students will be *accepted*) is preserved in (A): *more* apples will be *loaded*. (B) has a valid argument form (All S are W; X is an S; therefore, X is a W), so it is not parallel to the sample argument. (C) is not similar for at least two reasons. First, its conclusion is a recommendation ("should"), not a factual claim. Second, (C) uses one premise, not two premises as the sample argument does. (D) would have been parallel to the sample argument only if the sample had the conclusion "some more applications must be acted upon." Finally, (E) contains an argument which is fallacious, but the fallacy is not similar to that of the question stem.

23. **(E)** The advertisement employs the term "more" in an ambiguous manner. In the context, one might expect the phrase "more flavor" to mean "more highly concentrated flavor," that is, "more flavor per unit weight." What the ad actu-

ally says, however, is that the sticks of Evergreen are *larger,* so if they are larger, there must be more *total* flavor. All three propositions, if they are true (as we are asked to assume they are), are good attacks on the ad. First, in I, it is possible to beat the ad at its own game. If flavor is just a matter of chewing enough sticks, then Spring Mint is as good a deal because, flavor unit for flavor unit, it is no more expensive than Evergreen. Second, II would also undermine the ad by focusing on the ambiguity we have just discussed. Finally, III also uncovers another potential ambiguity. If the ad is comparing volume rather than weight, Spring Mint may be a better value. After all, who wants to buy a lot of air?

24. **(D)** Again, we remind ourselves that we are looking for the most reliable statement. Even the most reliable, however, will not necessarily be perfectly reliable. Here (D) is fairly trustworthy. We note that the speaker is an expert and so is qualified to speak about wines. In (A), the speaker is making a judgment about something on which he is not qualified to speak. Also, in (D) there is no hint of self-interest—if anything, the speaker is admitting against a possible self-interest that American chablis is a better buy than French chablis. By comparison, (B) and (C), which smack of a self-serving bias, are not so trustworthy. Finally, (E) sounds like a statement made for dramatic effect and so is not to be taken at face value.

25. **(B)** The weakness in the argument is the fallacy of ambiguity. It uses the term "future" in two different ways. In the first instance, it uses the word "future" to mean that which is fixed and definite, that which must occur. But then comes the shift. The author subtly changes his usage so that "future" denotes events which might, though not necessarily will, come to pass. As for (A), the author gives a good example of how one might very well be able to change the future. As for (C), the author is concerned to refute the idea of foreseeing future events, so it is not surprising that he does not attempt to explain the mechanism by which such foresight is achieved. (D) and (E) are incorrect because the fallacy is that of ambiguity, not of internal inconsistency (self-contradiction) nor circular reasoning (begging the question).

26. **(E)** This advertisement is simply rife with ambiguity. The wording obviously seeks to create the

impression that FCBI found jobs for its many graduates and generally does a lot of good for them. But first we should ask how many graduates FCBI had—one, two, three, a dozen, or a hundred. If it had only 12 or so, finding them jobs might have been easy; but if many people enroll at FCBI, they may not have the same success. Further, we might want to know how many people graduated compared with how many enrolled. Do people finish the program, or does FCBI just take their money and then force them out of the program? So II is certainly something we need to know in order to assess the validity of the claim. Now, how many of those who graduated came in looking for help in finding a job? Maybe most people had jobs waiting for them (only a few needed help), in which case the job placement assistance of FCBI is not so impressive. Or, perhaps the graduates were so disgusted they did not even seek assistance. So I is relevant. III is also important. Perhaps FCBI found them jobs sweeping streets—not in business. The ad does not say what jobs FCBI helped its people find. Finally, maybe the ad is truthful—FCBI graduates found jobs—but maybe they did it on their own. So IV also is a question worth asking.

27. **(E)** The sample syllogism uses its terms in an ambiguous way. In the first premise the category "American buffalo" is used to refer to the group as a whole, but in the second premise it is used to denote a particular member of that group. In the first premise, "disappearing" refers to extinction of a group, but in the second premise "disappearing" apparently means fading from view. (E) is fraught with similar ambiguities. The argument there moves from wealthy people as a group to a particular wealthy person, an illegitimate shifting of terminology. (A) is a distraction. It mentions subject matter similar to that of the question stem, but our task is to parallel the *form* of the argument, not to find an argument on a similar topic. (A), incidentally, is an unambiguous and valid argument. So, too, is (B), and a moment's reflection will reveal that it is very similar to (A). (C) is not similar to (A) and (B), but then again it is not parallel to the question stem. (C) contains circular reasoning—the very thing to be proved had to be assumed in the first place—but while circular reasoning is incorrect reasoning, it does not parallel the error committed by the question stem: ambiguity. (D) is clearly a correct argument so it cannot be parallel to the question stem which contains a fallacious argument.

28. **(C)** The tone of the paragraph is tongue-in-cheek. The author uses phrases such as "mysteries of this arcane science" and "wonderful discipline," but then gives a silly example of the utility of logic. Obviously, he means to be ironic. The real point he wants to make is that formal logic has little utility and that it may even lead one to make foolish errors. (A) cannot be correct because the example is clearly not an illustration of correct reasoning. (B) can be rejected since the author does not attempt to define the term "logic"; he only gives an example of its use. (D) is a distraction. The author's particular illustration does mention the American buffalo, but he could as easily have taken another species of animal or any other group term which would lend itself to the ambiguous treatment of his syllogism. (E) is incorrect since the author never examines the relationship between the premises and the conclusion. He gives the example and lets it speak for itself.

29. **(B)** The author's behavior is paradoxical because he is going along with the young man's paradoxical statement. He concludes the young man is lying because the young man told him so, but that depends on believing what the young man told him is true. So he accepts the content of the young man's statement in order to reject the statement. Once it is seen that there is a logical twist to this problem, the other answer choices can easily be rejected. (A), of course, overlooks the paradoxical nature of the tourist's behavior. The stranger may have been trying to be helpful, but what is curious about the tourist's behavior is not that he rejected the stranger's offer of advice, *but* that he relied on that very advice at the moment he rejected it! (C) also overlooks the paradox. It is true the tourist rejects the advice, but his rejection is not *understandable;* if anything it is self-contradictory, and therefore completely incomprehensible. (D) is the poorest possible choice since it makes a value judgment totally unrelated to the point of the passage. Finally, (E) would have been correct only if the tourist were possibly being victimized.

30. **(D)** As we explained in the previous question, the tourist's behavior is self-contradictory. The sentence mentioned in (D) is also self-contradictory. For if the sentence is taken to be true, what it asserts must be the case, so the sentence turns out to be false. On the other hand, if the sentence is taken to be false, then what it says is correct, so the sentence must be true. In other words, the

sentence is true only if it is false, and false only if it is true: a paradox. (A) is not paradoxical. The witness *later* admits that he lied in the first instance. Thus, though his later testimony contradicts his earlier testimony, the statements taken as a group are not paradoxical, since he is not claiming that the first and the second are true *at the same time*. (B) and (C) do not have even the flavor of paradox. They are just straightforward statements. Do not be deceived by the fact that (C) refers to an about-face. To change directions, or even one's testimony, is not self-contradictory——see (A). Finally (E) is a straightforward, self-consistent statement. Although the worker is advised to dissemble, he does not claim that he is both telling the truth and presenting a false image at the same time.

31. **(E)** The author cites a series of similarities between the two diseases, and then in his last sentence he writes, "So. . . ," indicating that his conclusion that the causes of the two diseases are similar rests upon the other similarities he has listed. Answer (E) correctly describes the basis of the argument. (A) is incorrect, for nothing in the passage indicates that either disease is a public health hazard, much less that one disease is a greater hazard than the other. (B) is unwarranted, for the author states only that the scientists are looking for a cure for *aphroditis melancholias*. He does not state that they will be successful; and even if there is a hint of that in the argument, we surely would not want to conclude on that basis that scientists will eventually find a cure for *every* disease. (C), like (A), is unrelated to the conclusion the author seeks to establish. All he wants to maintain is that similarities in the symptoms suggest that scientists should look for similarities in the causes of these diseases. He offers no opinion of the ultimate goal of modern technology, nor does he need to do so. His argument is complete without any such addition. (D) is probably the second best answer, but it is still completely wrong. The author's argument based on the assumption that similarity of effect depends upon similarity of cause would neither gain nor lose persuasive force if (D) were true. After all, many diseases occur in both man and other animals, but at least (D) has the merit——which (A), (B), and (C) all lack——of trying to say something about the connection between the causes and effects of disease.

32. **(E)** This item tests logical deduction. Statement I establishes that all batters bunt whenever two

conditions are met: Some runners lead off and all infielders play in. Statement II establishes that one of the two conditions is met (some runners are leading off), but denies that all batters are bunting. This can only be because the other condition is not met: It is false that "All infielders are playing in." Recalling our discussion of direct inferences in the Instructional Overview, we know that this means "Some infielders are not playing in," or answer (E). We cannot conclude (C), that none of the infielders are playing in, only that some are not. Nor can we deduce (D), that all are playing in——for that is logically impossible. Then, recalling our discussion of the meaning of *some* in the Instructional Overview, we eliminate both (A) and (B). Some means "at least one" without regard to the remaining population. That some runners are leading off does not imply that some are not leading off (B). And that some batters are not bunting does not imply that some are bunting.

33. **(B)** The author's attitude toward the bankruptcy law is expressed by his choice of the terms "folly," "protectionism," "conned." He apparently believes that the debtor who has incurred these debts ought to bear the responsibility for them and that the government should not help him get off the hook. (B) properly expresses this attitude: You have created for yourself a situation by your own actions; now you must accept it. The author may share (A) as well, but (A) is not a judgment he would make about the bankrupt, that is, a person who does not have a penny to save. (C) is completely unrelated to the question at hand; the bankrupt has no power to wield. The author may believe (D)——in fact, he opposes at least this one instance of government interference and hints that he is, in general, opposed to government interference for the protection of people from themselves——but the question stem asks for the author's attitude about the bankrupt debtor, not the government. (D) would be appropriate to the latter, but it has no bearing on the question at hand. Finally, (E) would be applicable if the government were giving money to pay a ransom to terrorists or some similar situation. The assistance it provides to the bankrupt debtor is not such a program. It does not pay tribute to the debtor.

34. **(A)** For the author's conclusion to follow from his premises——the debtor will make out like a bandit with the goods he procured with credit—— it must be the case that after the proceedings are

completed the debtor will be left with those goods. At least the author leads us to believe this is the way the law works. As a matter of fact, that implication is incorrect (in part) and is a serious defect in the author's position; but for present purposes we do not need to worry what the "real" law is nor whether the suggestion is *mis*-leading or not——only that the author does lead in that direction. (B) is incorrect because it attributes more to the author than he actually claims. He is making an argument about people who abuse credit; he never even hints that most persons who can obtain credit through use of a card abuse their credit. (C), too, takes us far beyond what the author has specifically claimed. The author argues only that the bankruptcy laws are too favorable to the debtor; he never extends his argument to say what sort of substitute he would advocate. And we certainly do not, without evidence, want to attribute to the author anything so drastic as imprisonment of the debtor as an appropriate remedy. (D) fails for it is highly speculative. Such a conclusion finds no support in the passage because the author is silent about how many debtors take advantage of the law; and, in any event, if there is such an implication in the paragraph, it must surely be that the debtors and not the creditors are the ones to initiate the proceedings. (E) fails for the same reasons that (B) and (C) fail. The author never even hints at such a position.

35. **(D)** The argument commits several errors. One obvious point is that the first premise is very much an oversimplification. Complicated questions about punishment and child rearing are hardly ever easily reduced to "either-or" propositions. Thus, (C) is a good objection. Beyond that, the terms "severely punish" and "bad" are highly ambiguous. It would be legitimate to ask the speaker just what he considered to be bad behavior, (B), and severe punishment, (A). Also, since the speaker has alleged the child has been "bad," and since the term is ambiguous, we can also demand clarification on that score, (E). The one objection it makes no sense to raise is (D). The premises have the very simple logical structure: If a child is bad and not punished, then he becomes a criminal. Child X is bad. There is absolutely no inconsistency between those two statements.

SECTION III

Questions 1–6

This is a linear ordering set. We begin by summarizing the information for easy reference:

O ≠ 1st or 6th

L ≠ J](We know that L > M, so this means
L ≠ K∫L cannot be next to J or K in the line.)

L→M

1. **(D)** For this question, we simply check each choice against the initial conditions. On the ground that O does not finish first or last, we eliminate (C). On the ground that L cannot be next in line to either J or K, we eliminate (A) and (E). Finally, since L must finish immediately ahead of M, we eliminate (B). Only (D) satisfies all of the restrictions.

2. **(E)** We begin by processing the additional information:

1	2	3	4	5	6
J				K	

   This places the L-M combination in positions 3 and 4, respectively (to avoid the J-L conflict). And O must be in position 2, with N in position 6:

1	2	3	4	5	6
J	O	L	M	K	N

   This shows that only (E) is true.

3. **(C)** We begin by processing the additional information:

1	2	3	4	5	6
N	L	M			

   We put N in first because J, K, and O cannot be there. We know further that either J or K must be sixth, since O cannot finish last. But there are four possible arrangements using these restrictions:

1	2	3	4	5	6
N	L	M	O	J	K
N	L	M	O	K	J
N	L	M	K	O	J
N	L	M	J	O	K

Testing the statements, we see that I is merely possible but not necessary. II is definitely not possible. Finally, III is true under the assumptions given, so III alone is the correct choice.

4. **(D)** For this question, we test each arrangement against the initial conditions. We know that four of the five will be acceptable and that only one will not be acceptable. The exception is the correct choice. (D) is not acceptable since we have the impermissible arrangement of J in second and L in third.

5. **(E)** For this question, we must treat each statement as providing additional information. As for statement I, we get

```
1   2   3   4   5   6
N   J   K   O   L   M
```

With J and K in 2 and 3, respectively, we must put L in 5 and therefore M in 6. But O must then be in 4, with N in 1. So there is only one possible arrangement using this information. As for II, we have

```
1   2   3   4   5   6
L   M   J   K   O   N
```

With K in 4, we must put the L-M combination in 1 and 2. This means that N finishes last with O in position 5. So, again, the statement guarantees only one arrangement. Finally, III:

```
1   2   3   4   5   6
L   M   O   J   K   N
```

With J and K in 4 and 5, L and M must be in 1 and 2 or 2 and 3. But they cannot be in 2 and 3 for this would require O to be first or last. So L and M must be in 1 and 2; N must be in 6; and O must be in 3.

6. **(D)** For J and K to be separated by exactly three runners they must finish in 1 and 5 or 2 and 6, though not necessarily in that order. We test each:

```
1     2   3   4    5    6
J/K   O   L   M   J/K   N
```

With either J or K in 1, L and M must be in 3 and 4, with O in 2 and N in 6.

```
1   2     3   4   5    6
N   J/K   O   L   M   J/K
```

With J or K in 2, L and M must be in 4 and 5, with N in 1 and O in 3. Now we are looking for the answer choice which *cannot* be true. (A) is true since O does not finish fourth. (B) is true since only J, K, or N can finish last. (C) is true since L finishes either third or fourth. (E) is true since O in third means that either J or K is last. (D) is not true however: When O is second, N is sixth.

Questions 7–12

Here we have an ordering set which is not strictly linear, that is, the individuals are not aligned in a single file. We begin by summarizing the information:

$$(Q \& R) = 3$$
$$P < M$$
$$K < N$$
$$K < L$$
$$J = L$$

A moment's study will lead us to one or two further conclusions. If K is lower than L, then, of course, K cannot occupy the top floor. Further, since J and L occupy the same floor, and since the fifth floor has only one room, J and L cannot occupy a floor higher than the fourth floor, which means that K cannot occupy a floor higher than the second floor. (Remember that Q and R must occupy the third floor.) With these preliminary conclusions in mind, we can turn to the questions.

7. **(A)** Since K must stay below J, J cannot occupy the first floor. (A), as the exception, must be the correct answer. The other choices could be true, as illustrated by the diagram:

```
5 M/N              5 O
4 J L              4 M N
3 Q R      or      3 Q R
2 O(N/M)           2 J L
1 K P              1 K P
```

8. **(C)** We begin by processing the additional information. With M entered on the second floor, we deduce

```
5
4   J L
3   Q R
2   M
1   P
```

With M on the second floor, P must be on the first floor. Then, with floors 1, 2, and 3 occupied, J and L must occupy floor 4 because the fifth floor has only one room. This seems as far as we can go. We know that K must occupy either 2 or 1, but that is not very helpful. So we look to the choices. We see that (A) is definitely incorrect, since (C) is proved by the diagram. (B) is possibly, though not necessarily, true. As we just noted, (D) is also only possible. Finally, (E) is also just a possibility, since O might also be on floor 5 or 2.

9. **(E)** We have the list of people, J, K, L, M, N, O, P, Q, R, and we eliminate people as first-floor occupants as follows. Q and R must occupy the third floor. J and L occupy a floor together above that of K. M occupies a floor above P, and so cannot occupy floor 1. And the same reasoning applies to N. So we eliminate J, L, M, N, Q, and R, leaving K, O, and P.

10. **(B)** We begin by assimilating the additional information. With M on floor 4 we have:

    5
    4   M
    3   Q and R
    2   J and L
    1   K and P

With M on 4, we must put J and L on 2 for that is the only floor above floor 1 which remains open and has two rooms. Then, K must be on 1 (below L) and P must be on 1 (to be below M). As for N and O, they must occupy floors 4 and 5, though not necessarily in that order. We turn to the Roman-numeral statements. Statement I is possibly, though not necessarily, true. Statement II is definitely not true. So I and II are not part of the correct answer. This leaves only III. We see from the diagram that III is true, that is, K must be on floor 1, so the correct answer is (B).

11. **(B)** We know that K and M, if they are together, cannot occupy floor 3 (because of Q and R) nor floor 5 (which has only one room). Nor can M occupy floor 1. K must be below J and L so it cannot occupy 4. The only floor for K and M together is 2.

12. **(C)** The additional information provided in (C) proves the following:

    5   N
    4   J and L
    3   Q and R
    2   K and M
    1   P and O

With K on 2, J and L must be on 4 (since L must be above K). Then, since K is lower than N, N must occupy 5. Next, since P < M, P must occupy 1 and M must occupy 2. And this leaves only O to occupy the other room on 1. The other answers will not do the trick. As for (A), putting P on 1 does not force J and L onto a floor. They might occupy either 2 or 4. As for (B), putting M on 2 means that J and L will occupy 4 and that P will occupy 1, but this leaves several individuals unplaced. As for (D), see Question 10, above. Finally, placing N on the top floor does not place J and K, and that is critical to fixing a definite order.

Questions 13-18

Here we have a selection problem, and we begin by using a notational system to summarize the information:

(1) $\sim$ (N & T & U)
(2) $\sim$ (M & N & R)
(3) Q ≠ V
(4) V ⊃ [(M & S) v (M & U) v (S & U) v (M & S & U)]
(5) R = Q
(6) S ⊃ (N & V)

Perhaps (4) requires some clarification. The statement given in the problem structure is logically equivalent to: If V is selected, then either (a) M and S are selected or (b) M and U are selected, or (c) S and U are selected, or (d) all three are selected.

13. **(D)** If R appears, then Q must appear (5). And if Q appears, then V cannot appear (3). But if V does not appear, then S cannot appear (6). So (D) is the correct answer. As for the remaining choices, we could have:
    (A) R, Q, and M
    (B) R, Q, and N
    (C) R and Q
    (E) R, Q, and T

14. **(D)** There are four professors who must be accompanied by other professors: V (4), R and Q

(5), and S (6). Every other professor, M, N, T, and U, can appear without the necessity of including any other professor.

15. **(B)** If S appears, then both N and V must also appear (6). And if V appears, then two of the three, M, S and U, must appear. Since S is already included (by stipulation), we need choose only one of the pair M and U. Thus, at minimum we have S, N, V, and either M or U, for a total of four.

16. **(B)** We handle this question by the process of elimination, checking each of the available choices against the restrictions established in the initial set of conditions. (A) can be eliminated because it violates (2). (C) violates (5) since Q is not there to accompany R. (D) can be eliminated because we have S without N, in violation of (6). And (E) violates (5) because we have R without Q.

17. **(A)** This question, too, is solved in a manner similar to that used for the preceding question. But here we must check each choice against the initial conditions in an effort to add exactly one more professor to obtain a permissible grouping. (A) can be turned into an acceptable grouping just by adding Q: M, R, T and Q. (B) can be eliminated since Q requires R (5), but N, M, and R cannot appear together (2). (C) can be eliminated since S will require the addition of both N and V (6), two professors, not just one. (D) can be eliminated since V requires the addition of two out of three from the trio M, S, and U (4). Finally, (E) is incorrect since R requires Q (5) and V requires other professors (4).

18. **(C)** Removing T from the group eliminates the violation of (1), without violating any other restriction. As for (A), removing N eliminates the violation of (1), but this places the group in violation of (6) (S without N). As for (D), removing U corrects the violation of (1), but the resulting group violates (4) because V is included without two out of three from the group M, S, or U. Finally, eliminating V runs afoul of (5).

Questions 19-25

With a set such as this, the main task is organizing the information. We will use a matrix:

Cars

	1	2	3	4	5
Meteor	C	C	D	D	C
Comet	D	C	C	D	D
Flash	D	C	D	D	D
Streak	D	D	C	C	D
Rocket	C	C	C	C	C

D=Deluxe   C=Coach

19. **(A)** This is seen to be true by our matrix. Three of the five trains use deluxe cars in the first position. The matrix shows that (B) is false since the ratio of deluxe to coach here is only one to four. (C) is also seen to be false since the Meteor and the Rocket have coach cars in the fifth position. (D) is proved false by a quick count. In a typical day, 12 deluxe cars and 13 coach cars are used. Finally, (E) is incorrect since the Rocket and the Streak together use only three deluxe cars, while the Flash and the Comet use seven deluxe cars.

20. **(C)** No train has deluxe cars in positions 2 and 3. As for (A), the Streak has deluxe cars first and second. As for (B), the Flash has deluxe cars first and third. As for (D), the Flash has deluxe cars third and fourth. And as for (E), the Flash also has deluxe cars fourth and fifth.

21. **(B)** If we know correctly that the second car of a train is a deluxe car, this establishes that train as the Streak——as shown by the matrix. As for (A), knowing the first car to be deluxe does not distinguish the Streak from the Comet or the Flash. As for (C), knowing the third car to be a coach car leaves open the possibility that the train might be the Comet, the Streak, or the Rocket. As for (D), although the Streak has deluxe as its first and fifth cars, this is also true of the Comet and the Flash. Finally, as for (E), the Streak has coach and deluxe in places 3 and 5, but this is also true of the Comet.

22. **(D)** As the matrix shows, the Meteor, the Comet, the Flash, and the Rocket all have coach cars as the second car. Only the Streak has a deluxe car in the second position.

23. **(C)** A quick look at the matrix shows that only one train, the Flash, has deluxe cars as the first and third cars of the train.

24. **(D)** Again, a quick glance at the matrix gives us the needed information. For the Streak, of the last three cars, only the fifth is a deluxe car. For the Meteor, two of the three last cars are deluxe cars. The same is true for the Comet. For the Flash, the last three cars are all deluxe cars, while for the Rocket none of the last three cars is a deluxe car.

25. **(B)** As for statement I, after the suggested change, the two trains would have the following configurations:

  Meteor: C-D-D-D-C
  Flash: D-C-D-D-D

  As for the second statement, the result would be:

  Comet: D-C-C-C-D
  Streak: D-D-C-C-D

  And the third statement:

  Meteor: D-D-C-C-D
  Streak: D-D-C-C-D

Questions 26-30

This is an unusual problem set, and it is serves a good reminder of a point made in the analytical reasoning lecture. While many problem sets fall into identifiable patterns, there is always the possibility that the test writers will add a new twist. So be on your toes.

You might summarize the initial information as follows:

  At least 1 on FC, OC, and SC
  At least 1 on OC, FC, and MC
  At least 1 on MC, OC, and SC

There are no further conclusions to be drawn, so we'll go to the questions.

26. **(A)** Test each of the statements. I is not necessarily true. The initial conditions could be satisfied by three different individuals, so it is not necessarily the case that anyone is a member of all four committees. II is not necessarily true. Although the first condition establishes that at least one person is a member of the Finance Committee and the Service Committee, that person need not be a member of the Membership Committee. Similarly, though the second condition establishes that at least one person is a member of the Finance Committee and the Membership Committee, that person need not be a member of the Service Committee. And though the third condition establishes that at least one person is a member of the Service Committee and the Membership Committee, that person need not be a member of the Finance Committee. III, however, is necessarily true, as established by the second condition.

27. **(C)** Test each statement. As for I, as noted above, the three conditions may be describing three different individuals—or they may be describing the same individual. So it is possible that one or more persons could be on all four committees. So I is not part of the correct answer. As for II, the initial conditions do not state whether or not there is a person who is a member of the Service Committee, the Finance Committee, and the Membership Committee. So II is not necessarily false, and II is not part of the correct answer. As for III, the first condition establishes that there is at least one person who is a member of the Finance Committee, the Operations Committee, and the Service Committee. So III is definitely false.

28. **(D)** If Jack is the only member of both the Finance Committee and the Operations Committee, then Jack is the only person who can satisfy the first initial condition and he is the only person who can satisfy the second initial condition. So Jack must also be on the Service Committee and on the Membership Committee.

29. **(E)** The additional information for this question stipulates that there is only one person who is a member of all four committees, but that stipulation implies nothing about the members of any group of three committees. There could be other persons who have memberships on three out of the four committees. So none of the statements is necessarily true.

30. **(E)** The additional information provided for this question stipulates that Ellen is the only person on the Membership Committee who is NOT also on the Services Committee. But the initial conditions all make affirmative statements about shared membership. So there is no further conclusion that can be drawn from this information. Thus, none of the three statements is necessarily true.

SECTION IV

1. **(D)** This is a fairly easy inference question. We are asked to determine which of the problems mentioned by the author is the most important. (B) can be eliminated because the author's criticism is not that such courses are not offered, nor even that such courses are not required. So we eliminate (E) as well. The most important shortcoming, according to the author, is that students have not been encouraged to apply the principles learned in the humanities. The support for this conclusion is to be found at the end of the second paragraph. As for (C), this is not mentioned by the author as a weakness in the present curriculum structure. Rather, he anticipates that this is a possible objection to his proposal to require students to devote part of their time to the study of primary problems. (A) is indeed a weakness of the university, and the author does admit that the university has not yet achieved equal opportunity for all. But this he discusses in the first paragraph, where he is outlining the university's successes. Only in the second paragraph does he begin the discussion of the university's failure. This indicates that the author does not regard the university's failure to achieve complete equality of opportunity as a serious problem.

2. **(A)** This is an inference question as well, though of a greater degree of difficulty. It seems possible to eliminate (C) and (E) as fairly implausible. The author's remarks about literature (at the end of the second paragraph), addressed to us as readers, do not suggest that we believe literature is required, nor that it is used to teach writing. As for (D), the author apparently presupposes that we, the readers, do not see the relevance of literature to real problems, for that it is relevant is at least part of the burden of his argument. (B) is perhaps the second best answer. It may very well be that most people regard literature as something scholarly, but that does not prove that (B) is a presupposition of the argument. When the author mentions literature, he states that it is a source of real and vicarious experience. What is the value of that? The author states that it relieves us of the necessity of living everyone else's life. He is trying to show that literature has a real, practical value. The crucial question, then, is why the author is attempting to prove that literature has real value. The answer is because he presupposes

that we disagree with this conclusion. There is a subtle but important difference between a presupposition that literature is scholarly and a presupposition that literature has no practical value. After all, there are many non-scholarly undertakings which may lack practical value.

3. **(D)** This is an explicit idea question. It is important to keep in mind that an explicit idea question is almost always answerable on the basis of information actually stated in the text. With a format of this sort, this means that the question should be readily answerable without speculation, and that this answer should be fairly complete. (D) is correct because the author himself raises a possible objection in the final paragraph. (A) is incorrect because the author never gives any such examples. (B) is incorrect because the author never addresses the issue of political society. That is mentioned only as a point of reference in his introductory remarks. (C) is not answered since no university is ever named. And (E) is incorrect since the author makes the assertion, without elaborating, that the university is a better teacher today than in the past. There is a further point to be made. It is possible to argue that (B) is partially answered. After all, if we improve our students' ability to pose and answer questions, is this not also a way to improve the performance of our political society? But that is clearly more attenuated than the answer we find to question (D). The same reasoning may be applied to other incorrect answers as well. It may be possible to construct arguments in their favor, but this is a standardized exam. And there is a clear, easy answer to (D) in the text, indicating that this is the answer the test writer is looking for.

4. **(B)** This is an application question. The author uses the term "primary problems" to refer to questions of grave importance which are not susceptible to an easy answer. Each of the incorrect answers poses a question which can be answered with a short answer. (A) can be answered with a yes or no. (C) can be answered with a name. (D) can be answered with a date. (E) can be answered with a series of proposals. And even if the answers are not absolutely indisputable, the questions will soon become dead issues. The only problem which is likely to still be around after "we are all dead" is the one of capital punishment.

5. **(A)** This is an application question—with a thought reverser. The question asks us to identify the statement with which the author would be *least* likely to agree. In the fourth paragraph, the author introduces an example of a primary problem. What makes this a primary problem is that there are competing arguments on both sides of the issue: There are benefits to the individual and to society, but there are dangers as well. (A) is not likely to get the author's agreement since he acknowledges that the question is an open one. He implies that society may have such a right, but he points out also that the use of such measures must be studied very carefully. That same paragraph strongly suggests that the author would accept statements (B) and (C). As for (D) and (E), these are strands which are woven into the text as several points.

6. **(A)** This is a main idea question. The author does describe a problem, and he does propose a solution. (B) is incorrect since the analysis of the system leads the author to propose a reform. (C) is incorrect since the author makes a definite recommendation. (D) is incorrect since the new idea the author outlines is defended in the text, not criticized. (E) is incorrect since the author does not develop the passage by raising questions.

7. **(B)** This, too, is a main idea question in that the question asks, What is the general topic? (B) is the best answer since the author is speaking about the university and he is addressing fundamental questions of educational philosophy. (A) and (C) are incorrect since politics and science are only tangentially related to the argument. (D) and (E) can be eliminated on the same ground and on the additional ground that though the author wants to make education practical, the decision to do that will be a decision based on philosophical concerns.

8. **(B)** This is obviously a main idea question. The main purpose of the passage is to review the findings of some research on animal behavior and suggests that this may have implications for the study of depression in humans. (B) neatly restates this. (A) can be overruled since the author proposes no such cure; indeed, he concludes by noting that there are complex issues remaining to be solved. (C) is incorrect since the author does not criticize any experiments. It is important to recognize that in the second paragraph the author is not being critical of any study in which rats were immersed in cold water; it is just that he anticipates a possible interpretation of those results and moves to block it. So, to the extent that the author criticizes anything at that juncture, he criticizes a possible interpretation of the experiment, not the experiment or results. In any event, that can in no way be interpreted as the main theme of the passage. (D) is wide of the mark. Though one might object to the use of animals for experimentation, that is not a burden the author has elected to carry. Finally, (E) is incorrect because the author mentions this only in closing, almost as a qualification on the main theme of the passage.

9. **(D)** This is a logical detail question. As we have just noted, the author introduces the question in the second paragraph to anticipate a possible objection: Maybe the animal's inability to act was caused by the trauma of the shock rather than the fact that it could not escape the shock. The author then lists some experiments the conclusions of which he believes refute this alternative explanation. (A) is incorrect since the question represents an interruption of the flow of the argument, not a continuation of the first paragraph. (B) is incorrect and might be just a confusion of answer and question. (C) can be eliminated since that is not the reason for raising the question, though it may be the overall theme of the passage. Here we cannot answer a question about a specific logical detail by referring to the main point of the text. Finally, (E) is incorrect since the author does not criticize the experiments; he defends them.

10. **(B)** This is an inference question. We are referred by the question stem to lines 36–60. There we find that stimulation of the septal region inhibits behavior while ''rats with septal lesions do not show learned helplessness.'' We infer that the septum somehow sends ''messages'' which tell the action centers not to act. If ordinary rats learn helplessness, and rats with septal lesions do not, this suggests that the communication between the two areas of the brain has been interrupted. This idea is captured by answer (B). (A) is incorrect and confuses the indicated reference with the discussion of ''immunized'' dogs at line 30. (C) seems to offer an explanation, but the text never suggests that rats have ''understanding.'' (D) is incorrect since it does not offer an explanation: Why do rats with septal lesions not learn helplessness? Finally, (E) is irrelevant to the question asked.

11. **(A)** This is an inferred idea question. The author contrasts the inescapable shock experiment with a "nonaversive parallel" in order to demonstrate that inescapability rather than trauma caused inaction in the animals. So the critical difference must be the trauma——it is present in the shock experiments and not in the nonaversive parallels. This is further supported by the example of a nonaversive parallel: the uncontrollable delivery of food. So the relevant difference is articulated by (A). (B) is incorrect since the author specifically states that the nonaversive parallels did succeed in inducing learned helplessness. (C) is incorrect for the same reason. (D) is incorrect since the value of the nonaversive parallel to the logical structure of the argument is that it was not traumatic at all. Finally, (E) is incorrect. Even if one experiment used rats and the other dogs, that is not the defining difference between the shock experiments and the nonaversive parallel experiments.

12. **(A)** This is a logical detail question and is related to the matters discussed immediately above. The author raises the question in paragraph 2 in order to anticipate a possible objection: The shock, not the unavoidability, caused inaction. The author then offers a refutation of this position by arguing that we get the same results using similar experiments with nonaversive stimuli. Moreover, if trauma or shock caused the inaction, we would expect to find learned helplessness induced in rats by the shock, regardless of prior experience with shock. The "mastery effect," however, contradicts this expectation. This is essentially the explanation provided in (A). (B) is incorrect since the author does not mention this until the end of the passage. (C) can be eliminated since the "mastery effect" reference is not included to support the conclusion that neurochemical changes cause the learned helplessness. (D) is incorrect, for though the author makes such an assertion, the "mastery effect" data is not adduced to support that particular assertion. Finally, (E) is the point against which the author is arguing when he mentions the "mastery effect" experiments.

13. **(E)** This is a further application question. The author closes with a disclaimer that the human cognitive makeup is more complex than that of laboratory animals and that for this reason the findings regarding learned helplessness and induced neurosis may or may not be applicable to humans. He does not, however, explain what the differences are between the experimental subjects and humans. A logical continuation would be to supply the reader with this elaboration. By comparison, the other answer choices are less likely. (B) is unlikely since the author begins and ends with references to human depression, and that is evidently the motivation for writing the article. (C) is not supported by the text since it is nowhere indicated that any such experiments have been undertaken. (D) fails for a similar reason. We cannot conclude that the author would want to test the animal model in human cases by experimentation. Finally, (A) is perhaps the second best answer. Its value is that it suggests the mechanism should be studied further. But the most important question is not how the mechanism works in rats but whether that mechanism also works in humans.

14. **(E)** This is an explicit idea question. (A) is mentioned in the final paragraph; (B) is mentioned on several occasions; (C) is mentioned in the second paragraph; (D) is mentioned in the first paragraph. Nowhere, however, does the author mention programs to cure humans of learned helplessness.

15. **(B)** This is a main idea question. In the very first paragraph the author presents the distinction between unlabeled and prohibited uses and then proceeds to develop the important implications of the distinction. (B) correctly describes this form of argument. (A) must be incorrect since no theory is cited for refutation. (C) is incorrect since no opponent is mentioned. (D) can be eliminated since there is no evidence that the practice of unlabeled uses is a recent development. (E) can be eliminated for either of two reasons. First, if one interprets "error" here to mean the practice of forbidden uses, then that is not the main point of the argument. Or if one interprets "error" to mean the conflating of unlabeled with prohibited uses, then (E) is eliminated because "condemn" is inappropriate. The author may wish to correct a misconception, but that is not the wording of (E). Moreover, the method he uses to accomplish that end is drawing a distinction. Thus, (B) stands as correct.

16. **(C)** This is an explicit idea question. The reference we need is to be found in paragraph 1. There the author explains that he uses the term "unlabeled use" to refer to any medically valuable use

of an already approved drug which has not yet been specifically recognized by the FDA. (A) is incorrect because this is a prohibited use, as that term is used in the text. (B) is incorrect because an unlabeled use is one which was not considered when the drug was originally labeled. It is one discovered later, not one proposed, tested, and rejected. (D) is incorrect because this use the author would term a labeled use. Finally, (E) is incorrect since this refers to research designed to determine whether a drug has labeled uses because it meets the legal standard of substantial evidence of such uses.

17. **(C)** This is an inference question which requires that we collate information from two parts of the passage. In paragraph 2 the author refers to physicians who persist in prohibited uses for one of two reasons: ignorance or refusal to accept evidence. Then, in paragraph 3 the author refers to physicians who use drugs in violation of labeling instructions as either uninformed or intransigent. The parallelism here tells us that the intransigent physician is the one who rejects the evidence that the drug is ineffective. This is neatly captured by (C). (A) is incorrect since the intransigent physician prescribes the drug in violation of the labeling provision because he or she believes that the drug is effective. (B) is incorrect for this would be a physician who is anything but intransigent. As for (D), an intransigent physician might take such actions, but this is not the defining characteristic of an intransigent physician. Finally, (E) can be eliminated since the author specifically expresses reservations as to whether such behavior is illegal.

18. **(A)** This is an explicit idea question. The danger that a medical benefit might be otherwise denied to a patient during the period between the discovery of a new use and its approval is mentioned in paragraph 3 as a reason for allowing unlabeled uses. So both (B) and (C) receive explicit mention. (D) is mentioned in paragraph 1: The use may never be researched. Finally, (E) is also mentioned in that paragraph as a further justification for the practice. (A) is incorrect since the author never relates cost to unlabeled uses.

19. **(E)** This is an application question, and we must find the statement which is most likely to be acceptable to the author. (E) would likely be embraced by the author since he explains in the first paragraph that unlabeled uses are created by

the time lag between the discovery of the use and the accumulation of data needed to prove that use. (A) is an attractive answer, but it fails upon careful reading. The distinction referred to there is that between approved and unlabeled uses. The distinction which the author attempts to draw is between two types of unapproved uses: unlabeled and prohibited. This is the distinction which has been blurred, says the author, not the distinction between approved and unlabeled. (B) is incorrect for the same reason. The blurred distinction is between unlabeled and prohibited uses (both types of unapproved uses), not between approved and unlabeled uses. (C) is incorrect since the distinction between unlabeled and approved uses is a matter of practice, not categorization. The unlabeled use exists because a physician *uses* the drug in a beneficial but not yet approved way, not because the physician or government decides that the use is unlabeled versus approved. (D) is incorrect since the author calls for caution in unlabeled use in the final paragraph.

20. **(A)** This is an attitude question. In our discussion of question 18, above, we mentioned several points in the passage which argue for the value of unlabeled uses. But the author's support for this practice is not unqualified. He does recognize the value of FDA regulation. His attitude toward the practice is one of acceptance, as suggested by (A). (B) is incorrect because the author argues for the practice, given the strictness of the FDA regulations. (C) is incorrect since the author does not imply that unlabeled use is illegal (as opposed to the disapproved use). (D) is incorrect because it overstates the case. Though the author sees the value of unlabeled uses, the practice receives only a qualified endorsement. Finally, (E) must be incorrect because the author sees unlabeled use as a practice inherent in the regulatory framework.

21. **(E)** This is a main idea question, and the main idea of this passage, already discussed at some length, is neatly summarized by (E). Answer (B) is surely the second best answer, but (B) must fail by comparison to (E) because (B) is too narrow. To be sure, one point the author makes is that the physician who prescribes unlabeled uses should not be subject to legal liability, but that is only part of the argument. That recommendation depends upon the distinction between the two types of unapproved uses. (E) makes reference to this additional point. Notice also that in a way (B) is

included in (E), so (E) is broad enough to describe the overall point of the author. (A) is incorrect since the author is cautioning against overzealous enforcement of laws against unlabeled uses. (C) is incorrect because it is never mentioned in the passage. Finally, (D) is incorrect for this is at best a minor part of the argument.

22. **(B)** This is a main idea question. The author begins by acknowledging that there exists an actual differential between the earnings of whites and blacks, but then the author moves quickly to block the automatic presupposition that this is attributable to "racial discrimination in employment." The author then examines the effect of various productivity variables on the differentials between black and white men and between black and white women, with particular emphasis on the latter. The conclusion of the argument is that there is little difference in the adjusted earnings of black and white women and the reason for this is the overpowering influence of *sexual* discrimination. (B) captures this analysis. (A) is incorrect since the author's primary focus is the black woman. He studies workers who are both black and female by comparing them with white female workers. The differentials between men and women generally are only incidentally related to this analysis. (C) fails because this is a subordinate level of argumentation. To be sure, the author does introduce productivity factors to adjust actual earnings, but that is so he can better evaluate the effects of discrimination. (D) is incorrect since no history is offered aside from casual references to distribution of workers. Finally, (E) is incorrect since the author makes no such recommendations.

23. **(E)** This is an explicit idea question, the answer to which is found in paragraphs 1 and 2. There the author states that the actual ratio is not an accurate measure of discrimination *in employment* because it fails to take account of productivity factors. (A) is incorrect because of the word "include"—the gross ratio fails to *adjust* for distribution. (B) is not mentioned and so cannot be an answer to a question which begins with the phrase "According to the passage. . . ," (C), too, is never mentioned in the passage, and so it fails for the same reason, as does (D).

24. **(E)** This is an explicit detail question, and our needed reference is the third paragraph. That paragraph gives us comparisons or ratios of earnings by black men to earnings by white men and of earnings by black women to earnings by white women. Notice that the comparisons are relative. We never get actual dollar amounts, nor do we get comparisons between women and men. (E) recognizes that the only conclusion which can be drawn on that basis is that the differential between black and white women is less than the differential between black and white men. The first is a difference of only 2 to 5 percent (before adjustment for productivity factors), while the second is about 20 percent (before adjustment). (A), (C), and (D) can be eliminated on the ground that no such male/female comparison is possible. (B) can be eliminated since no such information is supplied.

25. **(A)** This is a logical structure question. The author states that there are two explanations to be considered: (1) black men are found in jobs characterized by greater discrimination, and (2) sexual discrimination renders insignificant the racial discrimination against black women. But each of these could be true since both could contribute to the phenomenon being studied. There is only an empirical, not a logical, connection between the two, that is, the extent to which each does have explanatory power is a matter of fact. On this ground we can eliminate every other answer choice.

26. **(C)** This is a tone question, and the best description of the treatment of the subject matter is provided by (C). (A) can be eliminated, for the treatment, while confident, is not offensive. (B) can be eliminated for the same reason. (D) is incorrect since there is nothing tentative or inconclusive about the treatment. To acknowledge that one is unable to determine which of two competing theories is preferable is not to be inconclusive or tentative. Finally, though some readers may find in the author's discussion reason for hope or optimism, we cannot say that the author himself shows us these attitudes.

27. **(A)** This is an application question. What would happen if sexual discrimination against women were no longer a factor? On the assumption that the second hypothesis is correct, racial discrimination for women is not a significant factor because it is overpowered by sexual discrimination. The author acknowledges the existence of racial discrimination, so elimination of the sexual

discrimination should result in the manifestation of increased racial discrimination against black women (on the assumption that the second theory is correct). The result should be a greater disparity between white and black female workers, with white female workers enjoying the higher end of the ratio. This is articulated by (A). (B) is contradicted by this analysis and must be incorrect. (C) is inconsistent with the stipulation in the question stem. Finally, there is nothing to suggest that (D) or (E) would occur.

28. **(B)** This is a tone question. Notice that this question asks not about the tone of the presentation but about the author's attitude toward a particular subject. We must take our cue from the first paragraph, where the author refers to the efforts of ''responsible employers.'' This indicates that the author is sympathetic to the situation of workers who are victims of discrimination. (B) is the best way of describing this attitude. (E) is much too strong, for concern is not anxiety. Further, (C) is much too weak, for the reference to ''responsible employers'' indicates the author is not indifferent. (D), like (E), overstates the case. Finally, (A) is incorrect since the author offers no apology.

29. **(D)** This is a main idea question. The author does two things in the passage: He describes the problem of increasing thermal pollution and he suggests that solar energy will solve the problem. (D) neatly describes this double development. (A) is incorrect, for though the author does describe the phenomenon of thermal pollution and its causes, he also proposes a solution. (B) is incorrect since it fails to make reference to the fact that an important part of the passage is the description of a problem. It must be admitted that it can be argued that (B) does make an attempt to describe the development of the passage, but it does not do as nicely as (D) does. (C) is easily eliminated since no ambiguity is mentioned. Finally, (E) is incorrect since whatever objection the author may implicitly try to refute (opponents of solar energy), he never cites and then refutes a counter-argument.

30. **(E)** This is an explicit idea question. (A), (B), and (C) are mentioned in the second paragraph as factors contributing to thermal pollution. (D) is mentioned in the third paragraph as a pressure increasing thermal pollution. (E) is mentioned in the third paragraph—but not as a factor contrib-

uting to thermal pollution. Unpredictable weather patterns make it difficult to predict when the thermal pollution problem will reach the critical stage, but the patterns do not contribute to thermal pollution.

31. **(C)** This is an inference question. In discussing the melting of the polar ice caps, the author notes that there is a positive feedback mechanism: Since the ice caps reflect sunlight and therefore dissipate solar energy which would otherwise be absorbed by the earth, the melting of the ice caps increases the amount of energy captured by the earth, which in turn contributes to the melting of the ice caps, and so on. (C) correctly describes this as intensifying the effects of thermal pollution. (A) is easily eliminated since this feedback mechanism has nothing to do with a possible reduction in per capita energy consumption. (B) is incorrect, for though this feedback loop increases the problem, and thereby the urgency for the changeover to solar energy, the loop itself will not cause a change in policy. (D) is incorrect for the same reason. Finally, though the melting of the polar ice caps will result in flooding, this flooding is not an explanation of the feedback loop. Rather it is the result of the general phenomenon of the melting of the ice caps.

32. **(A)** This is a logical detail question. Why does the author discuss energy conservation? Conservation may appear as a possible alternative to solar energy. The author argues, however, that a closer examination shows that conservation cannot avert but only postpone the crisis. In terms of tactics, the author's move is to raise a possible objection and give an answer to it—as stated in (A). (B) is incorrect, for the refutation of a possible objection does not support the central thesis directly, only indirectly by eliminating a possible counter-argument. (C) is incorrect since the author never acknowledges he has fallen into any contradiction. (D) is incorrect since it overstates the case. The author admits that conservation has a beneficial effect, but he denies that conservation obviates the need for solar energy. Finally, (E) is incorrect since the point is argumentative and not merely informational.

33. **(B)** This is an inference question. In the final paragraph the author makes references to the possibility of ''air-conditioning'' the earth, a word placed in quotation marks, which indicates that he is using it in non-standard way. Ordinarily, we

use the word "air-condition" to mean to cool, say, a room or an entire building. Obviously, the author is not referring to some gigantic Carrier air-conditioning unit mounted, say, on top of the earth. But the general idea of removing heat seems to be what the term means in this context. This is consonant with the passage as well. Thermal pollution is the build-up of energy, and we are showing a positive build-up because fossil fuel and other sources of energy release energy which was only stored. So this, coupled with the sun's energy which comes in each moment, gives us a positive (though not desirable) balance of energy retention over loss. The idea of air-conditioning the earth, though not feasible according to the passage, must refer to schemes to get rid of this energy, say, into outer space. This is the idea presented in (B). As for (A), redistribution of thermal energy within the earth's energy system will not solve the problem of accumulated energy, so that cannot be what proponents of "air-conditioning" have in mind. (C) is a good definition of conservation, but not "air-conditioning." (D) is the recommendation given by the author, but that is not a response to this question. Finally, (E) is incorrect for the reason that burning wood is not going to cool the earth.

34. **(B)** This is a tone question. The author describes a very dangerous situation, but he also shows the way to solve the problem. The author does not necessarily believe that the battle for solar energy has been won; otherwise, he would not be advocating a shift to solar energy. On balance, the tone of the passage is hope or optimism, qualified by the realization that solar energy is not yet a high priority. This qualified hope is best described by (B). (A) is incorrect since this is not the tone of the passage. Though the author may be distressed at what he perceives to be the short-sightedness of policy makers, this distress does not color the writing in the passage. (C) is totally inappropriate since the author is analytical. (D) is inconsistent with the author's concern. Finally, (E) overstates the case. Though the author is concerned, he is not in a panic.

35. **(C)** This is an application question. We are looking for the *most* logical continuation. Since the author has urged us to adopt solar energy, an appropriate continuation would be a discussion of how to implement solar energy. And (C) would be a part of this discussion. (B) can be eliminated since the proposal depends upon the cost and feasibility of solar energy, not on its history. (A) and (E) can be eliminated since the author has explicitly asserted that *only* solar energy will solve the problem of thermal pollution. Finally, (D) is incorrect since the author need not regale us with the gory details of this situation. He has already made the point. As readers, we will want to see the practical details of his plan to avoid disaster.

Use a No. 2 pencil only. Be sure each mark is dark and completely fills the intended oval. Completely erase any errors or stray marks.

A R C O

Start with number 1 for each new section. If a section has fewer than 50 questions, leave the extra answer spaces blank.

SECTION 1		SECTION 2		SECTION 3		SECTION 4	
1	A B C D E	1	A B C D E	1	A B C D E	1	A B C D E
2	A B C D E	2	A B C D E	2	A B C D E	2	A B C D E
3	A B C D E	3	A B C D E	3	A B C D E	3	A B C D E
4	A B C D E	4	A B C D E	4	A B C D E	4	A B C D E
5	A B C D E	5	A B C D E	5	A B C D E	5	A B C D E
6	A B C D E	6	A B C D E	6	A B C D E	6	A B C D E
7	A B C D E	7	A B C D E	7	A B C D E	7	A B C D E
8	A B C D E	8	A B C D E	8	A B C D E	8	A B C D E
9	A B C D E	9	A B C D E	9	A B C D E	9	A B C D E
10	A B C D E	10	A B C D E	10	A B C D E	10	A B C D E
11	A B C D E	11	A B C D E	11	A B C D E	11	A B C D E
12	A B C D E	12	A B C D E	12	A B C D E	12	A B C D E
13	A B C D E	13	A B C D E	13	A B C D E	13	A B C D E
14	A B C D E	14	A B C D E	14	A B C D E	14	A B C D E
15	A B C D E	15	A B C D E	15	A B C D E	15	A B C D E
16	A B C D E	16	A B C D E	16	A B C D E	16	A B C D E
17	A B C D E	17	A B C D E	17	A B C D E	17	A B C D E
18	A B C D E	18	A B C D E	18	A B C D E	18	A B C D E
19	A B C D E	19	A B C D E	19	A B C D E	19	A B C D E
20	A B C D E	20	A B C D E	20	A B C D E	20	A B C D E
21	A B C D E	21	A B C D E	21	A B C D E	21	A B C D E
22	A B C D E	22	A B C D E	22	A B C D E	22	A B C D E
23	A B C D E	23	A B C D E	23	A B C D E	23	A B C D E
24	A B C D E	24	A B C D E	24	A B C D E	24	A B C D E
25	A B C D E	25	A B C D E	25	A B C D E	25	A B C D E
26	A B C D E	26	A B C D E	26	A B C D E	26	A B C D E
27	A B C D E	27	A B C D E	27	A B C D E	27	A B C D E
28	A B C D E	28	A B C D E	28	A B C D E	28	A B C D E
29	A B C D E	29	A B C D E	29	A B C D E	29	A B C D E
30	A B C D E	30	A B C D E	30	A B C D E	30	A B C D E
31	A B C D E	31	A B C D E	31	A B C D E	31	A B C D E
32	A B C D E	32	A B C D E	32	A B C D E	32	A B C D E
33	A B C D E	33	A B C D E	33	A B C D E	33	A B C D E
34	A B C D E	34	A B C D E	34	A B C D E	34	A B C D E
35	A B C D E	35	A B C D E	35	A B C D E	35	A B C D E
36	A B C D E	36	A B C D E	36	A B C D E	36	A B C D E
37	A B C D E	37	A B C D E	37	A B C D E	37	A B C D E
38	A B C D E	38	A B C D E	38	A B C D E	38	A B C D E
39	A B C D E	39	A B C D E	39	A B C D E	39	A B C D E
40	A B C D E	40	A B C D E	40	A B C D E	40	A B C D E
41	A B C D E	41	A B C D E	41	A B C D E	41	A B C D E
42	A B C D E	42	A B C D E	42	A B C D E	42	A B C D E
43	A B C D E	43	A B C D E	43	A B C D E	43	A B C D E
44	A B C D E	44	A B C D E	44	A B C D E	44	A B C D E
45	A B C D E	45	A B C D E	45	A B C D E	45	A B C D E
46	A B C D E	46	A B C D E	46	A B C D E	46	A B C D E
47	A B C D E	47	A B C D E	47	A B C D E	47	A B C D E
48	A B C D E	48	A B C D E	48	A B C D E	48	A B C D E
49	A B C D E	49	A B C D E	49	A B C D E	49	A B C D E
50	A B C D E	50	A B C D E	50	A B C D E	50	A B C D E

EXAMINATION FORECAST

Section Number	Type	Minutes	Questions
	Writing Sample	30	—
I	Reading Comprehension	35	28
II	Logical Reasoning	45	30
III	Analytical Reasoning	45	35
IV	Reading Comprehension	45	35

WRITING SAMPLE

Time: 30 minutes

The Board of Trustees of State University has recently received an anonymous gift to the University in the amount of $100,000 for the construction of a memorial dedicated to students and graduates of the university who lost their lives in the service of their country. The Board is considering proposals by Ann Gerson and Phil Maxwell. Write an argument in favor of one of the two proposals. The following criteria should be taken into consideration:

——The $100,000 must be spent on a memorial, but the Board would like the memorial to have some additional function.

——The board wants a memorial that will assist students in understanding and appreciating the sacrifice made by others.

ANN GERSON is an artist with a substantial national reputation but no particular ties to the University. Many of her sculptures, such as the Plaza Fountain she designed for the Federal Government Center, combine function and art. Ann proposes to build an "oasis" in the center of the campus: a fountain surrounded by greenery and marble benches. The center of the fountain will be a shrouded figure sculpted from stone that is intended to symbolize death, and on the containing wall of the fountain will be engraved the names of university students and graduates who died and the dates and places of their deaths.

PHIL MAXWELL, a graduate of State University, is a local architect who paints and sculpts as a hobby. Several of Phil's paintings are on display in the University museum in the special wing devoted to student alumni work. Additionally, Phil teaches a course in the History of Architecture in the University's continuing education division. Phil proposes a simple memorial, a wall on which will be inscribed the names of the students and graduates who died, the dates of their actual or intended graduation, and brief personal notes to be supplied by relatives such as major area of study, career plans, or outside interests. Phil has designed the wall so that it can be the outside wall of the main entrance of the new student union now being planned for the University.

PRACTICE EXAMINATION 3

SECTION I

Time—35 Minutes
28 Questions

Directions: Below each of the following passages, you will find questions or incomplete statements about the passage. Each statement or question is followed by lettered words or expressions. Select the word or expression that most satisfactorily completes each statement or answers each question in accordance with the meaning of the passage. After you have chosen the best answer, blacken the corresponding space on the answer sheet.

The high unemployment rates of the early 1960's occasioned a spirited debate within the economics profession. One group found the primary cause of unemployment in slow growth and the solution in eco-
5 nomic expansion. The other found the major explanation in changes which had occurred in the supply and demand for labor and stressed measures for matching demand with supply.

The expansionist school of thought, with the Coun-
10 cil of Economic Advisers as its leading advocates, attributed the persistently high unemployment level to a slow rate of economic growth resulting from a deficiency of aggregate demand for goods and services. The majority of this school endorsed the position of
15 the Council that tax reduction would eventually reduce the unemployment level to 4 percent of the labor force with no other assistance. At 4 percent, bottlenecks in skilled labor, middle-level manpower and professional personnel were expected to retard growth
20 and generate wage-price pressures. To go beyond 4 percent, the interim goal of the Council, it was recognized that improved education, training and retraining and other structural measures would be required. Some expansionists insisted that the demand for goods
25 and services was nearly satiated and that it was impossible for the private sector to absorb a significant increase in output. In their estimate, only the lower-income fifth of the population and the public sector offered sufficient outlets for the production efforts of

30 the potential labor force. The fact that the needs of the poor and the many unmet demands for public services held higher priority than the demands of the marketplace in the value structure of this group no doubt influenced their economic judgments.

35 Those who found the major cause of unemployment in structural features were primarily labor economists, concerned professionally with efficient functioning of labor markets through programs to develop skills and place individual workers. They maintained that in-
40 creased aggregate demand was a necessary but not sufficient condition for reaching either the CEA's 4 percent target or their own preferred 3 percent. This pessimism was based, in part, on the conclusion that unemployment among the young, the unskilled, mi-
45 nority groups and depressed geographical areas is not easily attacked by increasing general demand. Further, their estimate of the numbers of potential members of the labor force who had withdrawn or not entered because of lack of employment opportunity
50 was substantially higher than that of the CEA. They also projected that increased demand would put added pressure on skills already in short supply rather than employ the unemployed, and that because of technological change, which was replacing manpower,
55 much higher levels of demand would be necessary to create the same number of jobs.

The structural school, too, had its hyperenthusiasts: fiscal conservatives who, as an alternative to expansionary policies, argued the not very plausible posi-
60 tion that a job was available for every person provided only that he or she had the requisite skills or would relocate. Such extremist positions aside, there was actually considerable agreement between two main groups, though this was not recognized at the time.
65 Both realized the advisability of a tax cut to increase demand, and both realized that structural rigidities

would be needed to reduce unemployment below a point around 4 percent. In either case, the policy implications differed in emphasis and not in con-
70 tent.

1. The primary purpose of the passage is to
   (A) suggest some ways in which tools to manipulate aggregate demand and eliminate structural deficiencies can be used to reduce the level of unemployment
   (B) demonstrate that there was a good deal of agreement between the expansionist and structuralist theories on how to reduce unemployment in the 1960s
   (C) explain the way in which structural inefficiencies prevent the achievement of a low rate of unemployment without wage-price pressures
   (D) discuss the disunity within the expansionist and structuralist schools to show its relationship to the inability of the government to reduce unemployment to 4 percent
   (E) describe the role of the Council of Economic Advisers in advocating expansionist policies to reduce unemployment to 4 percent

2. Which of the following is NOT mentioned in the passage as a possible barrier to achieving a 4 percent unemployment rate through increased aggregate demand?
   (A) Technological innovation reduces the need for workers, so larger increases in demand are needed to employ the same number of workers.
   (B) The increase in output necessary to meet an increase in aggregate demand requires skilled labor, which is already in short supply, rather than unskilled labor, which is available.
   (C) An increase in aggregate demand will not create jobs for certain subgroups of unemployed persons such as minority groups and young and unskilled workers.
   (D) Even if the tax reduction increases aggregate demand, many unemployed workers will be unwilling to relocate to jobs located in areas where there is a shortage of labor.
   (E) An increase in the number of available jobs will encourage people not in the labor market to enter it, which in turn will keep the unemployment rate high.

3. The author's treatment of the "hyperenthusiasts" (lines 57–62) can best be described as one of

(A) strong approval
(B) light-hearted appreciation
(C) summary dismissal
(D) contemptuous sarcasm
(E) malicious rebuke

4. Which of the following best describes the difference between the position taken by the Council of Economic Advisers and that taken by dissenting expansionists (lines 24–27)?
   (A) Whereas the Council of Economic Advisers emphasized the need for a tax cut to stimulate general demand, the dissenters stressed the importance of structural measures such as education and training.
   (B) Although the dissenters agreed that an increase in demand was necessary to reduce unemployment, they argued government spending to increase demand should fund programs for lower income groups and public services.
   (C) The Council of Economic Advisers set a 4 percent unemployment rate as its goal, and dissenting expansionists advocated a goal of 3 percent.
   (D) The Council of Economic Advisers rejected the contention, advanced by the dissenting expansionists, that a tax cut would help to create increased demand.
   (E) The dissenting expansionists were critical of the Council of Economic Advisers because members of the Council advocated politically conservative policies.

5. The passage contains information that helps to explain which of the following?
   I. The fact that the economy did not expand rapidly in the early 1960s.
   II. The start of wage-price pressures as the employment rate approaches 4 percent.
   III. The harmful effects of unemployment on an individual worker.
   (A) I only
   (B) II only
   (C) I and II only
   (D) I and III only
   (E) I, II, and III

6. Which of the following best describes the author's attitude toward the expansionists mentioned in line 9?
   (A) The author doubts the validity of their conclusions because they were not trained economists.

(B) The author discounts the value of their judgment because it was colored by their political viewpoint.

(C) The author refuses to evaluate the value of their contention because he lacks sufficient information.

(D) The author accepts their viewpoint until it can be demonstrated that it is incorrect.

(E) The author endorses the principles upon which their conclusions are based but believes their proposal to be impractical.

7. It can be inferred from the passage that the hyperenthusiasts (lines 57–62) contended

(A) the problem of unemployment could be solved without government retraining and education programs

(B) the number of persons unemployed was greatly overestimated by the Council of Economic Advisers

(C) a goal of 3 percent unemployment could not be reached unless the government enacted retraining and education programs

(D) the poor had a greater need for expanded government services than the more affluent portion of the population

(E) fiscal policies alone were powerful enough to reduce the unemployment rate to 4 percent of the work force

In the art of the Middle Ages, we never encounter the personality of the artist as an individual; rather, it is diffused through the artistic genius of centuries embodied in the rules of religious art. Art of the Middle Ages is first a sacred script, the symbols and meanings of which were well settled. The circular halo placed vertically behind the head signifies sainthood, while the halo impressed with a cross signifies divinity. By bare feet, we recognize God, the angels, Jesus Christ and the apostles, but for an artist to have depicted the Virgin Mary with bare feet would have been tantamount to heresy. Several concentric, wavy lines represent the sky, while parallel lines represent water or the sea. A tree, which is to say a single stalk with two or three stylized leaves, informs us that the scene is laid on earth. A tower with a window indicates a village; and should an angel be watching from the battlements, that city is thereby identified as Jerusalem. Saint Peter is always depicted with curly hair, a short beard and a tonsure, while Saint Paul has always a bald head and a long beard.

A second characteristic of this iconography is obedience to a sacred mathematics. "The Divine Wisdom," wrote Saint Augustine, "reveals itself everywhere in numbers," a doctrine attributable to the neo-Platonists who revived the genius of Pythagoras. Twelve is the master number of the Church and is the product of three, the number of the Trinity, and four, the number of material elements. The number seven, the most mysterious of all numbers, is the sum of four and three. There are the seven ages of man, seven virtues, seven planets. In the final analysis, the seven-tone scale of Gregorian music is the sensible embodiment of the order of the universe. Numbers require also a symmetry. At Chartres, a stained glass window shows the four prophets Isaac, Ezekiel, Daniel, and Jeremiah carrying on their shoulders the four evangelists Matthew, Mark, Luke, and John.

A third characteristic of this art is to be a symbolic language, showing us one thing and inviting us to see another. In this respect, the artist was called upon to imitate God, who had hidden a profound meaning behind the literal, and who wished nature itself to be a moral lesson to man. Thus, every painting is an allegory. In a scene of the final judgment, we see the foolish virgins at the left hand of Jesus and the wise at his right, and we understand that this symbolizes those who are lost and those who are saved. Even seemingly insignificant details carry hidden meaning: The lion in a stained glass window is the figure of the Resurrection.

These, then, are the defining characteristics of the art of the Middle Ages, a system within which even the most mediocre talent was elevated by the genius of the centuries. The artists of the early Renaissance broke with tradition at their own peril. When they are not outstanding, they are scarcely able to avoid insignificance and banality in their religious works; and even when they are great, they are no more than the equals of the old masters who passively followed the sacred rules.

8. The primary purpose of the passage is to

(A) theorize about the immediate influences on art of the Middle Ages

(B) explain why artists of the Middle Ages followed the rules of a sacred script

(C) discuss some of the important features of art of the Middle Ages

(D) contrast the art of the Middle Ages with that of the Renaissance

(E) explain why the Middle Ages had a passion for order and numbers

9. It can be inferred that a painting done in the Middle Ages is most likely to contain

(A) elements representing the numbers 3 and 4

(B) a moral lesson hidden behind the literal figures

(C) highly stylized buildings and trees

(D) figures with halos and bare feet

(E) a signature of the artist and the date of execution

10. Which of the following best describes the attitude of the author toward art of the Middle Ages?

(A) He understands it and admires it.

(B) He regards it as the greatest art of all time.

(C) He prefers music of the period to its painting.

(D) He realizes the constraints placed on the artist and is disappointed that individuality is never evident.

(E) He regards it generally as inferior to the works produced during the period preceding it.

11. The author refers to Saint Augustine in order to

(A) refute a possible objection

(B) ridicule a position

(C) present a suggestive analogy

(D) avoid a contradiction

(E) provide proof by illustration

12. All of the following are mentioned in the passage as elements of the sacred script EXCEPT

(A) abstract symbols such as lines to represent physical features

(B) symbols such as halos and crosses

(C) clothing used to characterized individuals

(D) symmetrical juxtaposition of figures

(E) use of figures to identify locations

13. The passage would most likely be found in a

(A) sociological analysis of the Middle Ages

(B) treatise on the influence of the Church in the Middle Ages

(C) scholarly analysis of art in the Middle Ages

(D) preface to a biography of Saint Augustine

(E) pamphlet discussing religious beliefs

14. By the phrase "diffused through the artistic genius of centuries," the author most likely means

(A) the individual artists of the Middle Ages did not have serious talent

(B) great works of art from the Middle Ages have survived until now

(C) an artist who faithfully followed the rules of religious art was not recognized during his lifetime

(D) the rules of religious art, developed over time, left little freedom for the artist

(E) religious art has greater value than the secular art of the Renaissance

The most damning thing that can be said about the world's best-endowed and richest country is that it is not only not the leader in health status, but that it is so low in the ranks of the nations. The United States ranks 18th among nations of the world in male life expectancy at birth, 9th in female life expectancy at birth, and 12th in infant mortality. More importantly, huge variations are evident in health status in the United States from one place to the next and from one group to the next.

The forces that affect health can be aggregated into four groupings that lend themselves to analysis of all health problems. Clearly the largest aggregate of forces resides in the person's environment. His own behavior, in part derived from his experiences with his environment, is the next greatest force affecting his health. Medical care services, treated as separate from other environmental factors because of the special interest we have in them, make a modest contribution to health status. Finally, the contributions of heredity to health are difficult to judge. We are templated at conception as to our basic weaknesses and strengths; but many hereditary attributes never become manifest because of environmental and behavioral forces which act before the genetic forces come to maturity, and other hereditary attributes are increasingly being palliated by medical care.

No other country spends what we do per capita for medical care. The care available is among the best technically, even if used too lavishly and thus dangerously, but none of the countries which stand above us in health status have such a high proportion of medically disenfranchised persons. Given the evidence that medical care is not that valuable and access to care not that bad, it seems most unlikely that our bad showing is caused by the significant proportion who are poorly served. Other hypotheses have greater explanatory power: excessive poverty, both actual and relative, and excessive affluence.

Excessive poverty is probably more prevalent in the U.S. than in any of the countries that have a better infant mortality rate and female life expectancy at birth. This is probably true also for all but four or five of the countries with a longer male life expectancy. In the notably poor countries that exceed us in male survival, difficult living conditions are a more accepted way of life and in several of them, a good basic diet, basic medical care and basic education, and lifelong employment opportunities are an everyday fact of life. In the U.S. a national unemployment level of 10 percent may be 40 percent in the ghetto while less than 4 percent elsewhere. The countries that have surpassed us in health do not have such severe or entrenched problems. Nor are such a high proportion of their people involved in them.

Excessive affluence is not so obvious a cause of ill health, but, at least until recently, few other nations could afford such unhealthful ways of living. Excessive intake of animal protein and fats, dangerous imbibing of alcohol and use of tobacco and drugs (prescribed and proscribed), and dangerous recreational sports and driving habits are all possible only because of affluence. Our heritage, desires, opportunities, and our machismo, combined with the relatively low cost of bad foods and speedy vehicles, make us particularly vulnerable to our affluence. And those who are not affluent try harder. Our unacceptable health status, then, will not be improved appreciably by expanded medical resources nor by their redistribution so much as by a general attempt to improve the quality of life for all.

15. Which of the following would be the most logical continuation of the passage?
    (A) suggestions for specific proposals to improve the quality of life in America
    (B) a listing of the most common causes of death among male and female adults
    (C) an explanation of the causes of poverty in America, both absolute and relative
    (D) a proposal to ensure that residents of central cities receive more and better medical care
    (E) a study of the overcrowding in urban hospitals serving primarily the poor

16. All of the following are mentioned in the passage as factors affecting the health of the population EXCEPT
    (A) the availability of medical care services
    (B) the genetic endowment of individuals
    (C) overall environmental factors
    (D) the nation's relative position in health status
    (E) an individual's own behavior

17. The author is primarily concerned with
    (A) condemning the U.S. for its failure to provide better medical care to the poor
    (B) evaluating the relative significance of factors contributing to the poor health status in the U.S.
    (C) providing information which the reader can use to improve his or her personal health
    (D) comparing the general health of the U.S. population with world averages

(E) advocating specific measures designed to improve the health of the U.S. population

18. The passage best supports which of the following conclusions about the relationship between per capita expenditures for medical care and the health of a population?
    (A) The per capita expenditure for medical care has relatively little effect on the total amount of medical care available to a population.
    (B) The genetic makeup of a population is a more powerful determinant of the health of a population than the per capita expenditure for medical care.
    (C) A population may have very high per capita expenditures for medical care and yet have a lower health status than other populations with lower per capita expenditures.
    (D) The higher the per capita expenditure on medical care, the more advanced is the medical technology; and the more advanced the technology, the better is the health of the population.
    (E) Per capita outlays for medical care devoted to adults are likely to have a greater effect on the status of the population than outlays devoted to infants.

19. The author refers to the excessive intake of alcohol and tobacco and drug use in order to
    (A) show that some health problems cannot be attacked by better medical care
    (B) demonstrate that use of tobacco and intoxicants is detrimental to health
    (C) cite examples of individual behavior which have adverse consequences for health status
    (D) refute the contention that poor health is related to access to medical care
    (E) illustrate ways in which affluence may contribute to poor health status

20. The passage provides information to answer which of the following questions?
    (A) What is the most powerful influence on the health status of a population?
    (B) Which nation in the world leads in health status?
    (C) Is the life expectancy of males in the U.S. longer than that of females?
    (D) What are the most important genetic factors influencing the health of an individual?
    (E) How can the U.S. reduce the incidence of unemployment in the ghetto?

21. In discussing the forces that influence health, the author implies that medical care services are
    (A) the least important of all
    (B) a special aspect of an individual's environment
    (C) a function of an individual's behavior pattern
    (D) becoming less important as technology improves
    (E) too expensive for most people

Nitroglycerin has long been famous for its relief of angina attacks but ruled out for heart attacks on the theory that it harmfully lowers blood pressure and increases heart rate. A heart attack, unlike an angina
5 attack, always involves some localized, fairly rapid heart muscle death, or myocardial infarction. This acute emergency happens when the arteriosclerotic occlusive process in one of the coronary arterial branches culminates so suddenly and completely that
10 the local myocardium—the muscle area that was fed by the occluded coronary—stops contracting and dies over a period of hours, to be replaced over a period of weeks by a scar, or "healed infarct."

In 1974, in experiments with dogs, it was discov-
15 ered that administration of nitroglycerin during the acute stage of myocardial infarction consistently reduced the extent of myocardial injury, provided that the dogs' heart rate and blood pressure were maintained in the normal range. Soon after, scientists made
20 a preliminary confirmation of the clinical applicability of nitroglycerin in acute heart attack in human patients. Five of twelve human subjects developed some degree of congestive heart failure. Curiously, the nitroglycerin alone was enough to reduce the magni-
25 tude of injury in these five patients, but the other seven patients, whose heart attacks were not complicated by any congestive heart failure, were not consistently helped by the nitroglycerin until another drug, phenylephrine, was added to abolish the nitroglycerin-
30 induced drop in blood pressure. One explanation for this is that the reflex responses in heart rate, mediated through the autonomic nervous system, are so blunted in congestive heart failure that a fall in blood pressure prompts less of the cardiac acceleration which other-
35 wise worsens the damage of acute myocardial infarction.

It appears that the size of the infarct that would otherwise result from a coronary occlusion might be greatly reduced, and vitally needed heart muscle thus
40 saved, by the actions of certain drugs and other measures taken during the acute phase of the heart attack. This is because the size of the myocardial infarct is not really determined at the moment of the coronary occlusion as previously thought. The fate of the strick-
45 en myocardial segment remains largely undetermined, hanging on the balance of myocardial oxygen supply and demand which can be favorably influenced for many hours after the coronary occlusion. So it is possible to reduce the myocardial injury during acute
50 human heart attacks by means of nitroglycerin, either alone or in combination with phenylephrine.

Other drugs are also being tested to reduce myocardial infarct size, particularly drugs presumed to affect myocardial oxygen supply and demand, including not
55 only vessel dilators such as nitroglycerin but also antihypertensives which block the sympathetic nerve reflexes that increase heart rate and work in response to exertion and stress. Such measures are still experimental, and there is no proof of benefit with regard to
60 the great complications of heart attack such as cardiogenic shock, angina or mortality. But the drugs for reducing infarct size now hold center stage in experimental frameworks.

22. According to the passage, the primary difference between a heart attack and an angina attack is that a heart attack
    (A) involves an acceleration of the heart beat
    (B) cannot be treated with nitroglycerin
    (C) generally results in congestive heart failure
    (D) takes place within a relatively short period of time
    (E) always results in damage to muscle tissue of the heart

23. In the study referred to in lines 19–22, the patients who developed congestive heart failure did not experience cardiac acceleration because
    (A) the nitroglycerin was not administered soon enough after the onset of the heart attack
    (B) the severity of the heart attack blocked the autonomic response to the nitroglycerin-induced drop in blood pressure
    (C) administering phenylephrine mitigated the severity of the drop in blood pressure caused by nitroglycerin
    (D) doctors were able to maintain blood pressure, and thus indirectly pulse rate, in those patients
    (E) those patients did not experience a drop in blood pressure as a result of the heart attack

24. The passage provides information to answer all of the following questions EXCEPT
    (A) What are some of the physiological manifestations of a heart attack?
    (B) What determines the size of a myocardial infarct following a heart attack?

(C) What effect does nitroglycerin have when administered to a patient experiencing a heart attack?

(D) What are the most important causes of heart attacks?

(E) What is the physiological effect of phenylephrine?

25. It can be inferred from the passage that nitroglycerin is of value in treating heart attacks because it
(A) lowers the blood pressure
(B) stimulates healing of an infarct
(C) causes cardiac acceleration
(D) dilates blood vessels
(E) counteracts hypertension

26. The author's attitude toward the use of nitroglycerin and other drugs to treat heart attack can best be described as one of
(A) concern
(B) resignation
(C) anxiety
(D) disinterest
(E) optimism

27. It can be inferred that the phenylephrine is administered in conjunction with nitroglycerin during heart attack in order to
(A) prevent the cardiac acceleration caused by a drop in blood pressure
(B) block sympathetic nerve reflexes that increase the pulse rate
(C) blunt the autonomic nervous system, which accelerates the pulse rate
(D) reduce the size of a myocardial infarct by increasing oxygen supply
(E) prevent arteriosclerotic occlusion in the coronary arterial branches

28. The author is primarily concerned with
(A) explaining a predicament
(B) evaluating a study
(C) outlining a proposal
(D) countering an argument
(E) discussing a treatment

It would be enormously convenient to have a single, generally accepted index of the economic and social welfare of the people of the United States. A glance at it would tell us how much better or worse off we had become each year, and we would judge the desirability of any proposed action by asking whether it would raise or lower this index. Some recent discussion implies that such an index could be constructed. Articles in the popular press even criticize the Gross National Production (GNP) because it is not such a complete index of welfare, ignoring, on the one hand, that it was never intended to be, and suggesting, on the other, that with appropriate changes it could be converted into one.

The output available to satisfy our wants and needs is one important determinant of welfare. Whatever want, need, or social problem engages our attention, we ordinarily can more easily find resources to deal with it when output is large and growing than when it is not. GNP measures output fairly well, but to evaluate welfare we would need additional measures which would be far more difficult to construct. We would need an index of real costs incurred in production, because we are better off if we get the same output at less cost. Use of just man-hours for welfare evaluation would unreasonably imply that to increase total hours by raising the hours of eight women from 60 to 65 a week imposes no more burden that raising the hours of eight men from 40 to 45 a week, or even than hiring one involuntarily unemployed person for 40 hours a week. A measure of real costs of labor would also have to consider working conditions. Most of us spend almost half our waking hours on the job and our welfare is vitally affected by the circumstances in which we spend those hours.

To measure welfare we would need a measure of changes in the need our output must satisfy. One aspect, population change, is now handled by converting output to a per capita basis on the assumption that, other things equal, twice as many people need twice as many goods and services to be equally well off. But an index of needs would also account for differences in the requirements for living as the population becomes more urbanized and suburbanized; for the changes in national defense requirements; and for changes in the effect of weather in our needs. The index would have to tell us the cost of meeting our needs in a base year compared with the cost of meeting them equally well under the circumstances prevailing in every other year.

Measures of "needs" shade into measure of the human and physical environment in which we live. We all are enormously affected by the people around us. Can we go where we like without fear of attack? We are also affected by the physical environment—purity of water and air, accessibility of park land and other conditions. To measure this requires accurate data, but such data are generally deficient. Moreover, weighting is required: to combine robberies and murders in a crime index; to combine pollution of the Potomac and pollution of Lak Erie into a water pollution index; and then to combine crime and water pollution into some general index. But there is no basis for weighting these beyond individual preference.

There are further problems. To measure welfare we would need an index of the "goodness" of the distribution of income. There is surely consensus that given the same total income and output, a distribution with fewer families in poverty would be the better, but what is the ideal distribution? Even if we could construct indexes of output, real costs, needs, state of the environment, we could not compute a welfare index because we have no system of weights to combine them.

29. The author is primarily concerned to
    (A) refute arguments for a position
    (B) make a proposal and defend it
    (C) attack the sincerity of an opponent
    (D) show defects in a proposal
    (E) review literature relevant to a problem

30. The author implies that man-hours is not an appropriate measure of real cost because it
    (A) ignores the conditions under which the output is generated
    (B) fails to take into consideration the environmental costs of production
    (C) overemphasizes the output of real goods as opposed to services
    (D) is not an effective method for reducing unemployment
    (E) was never intended to be a general measure of welfare

31. It can be inferred from the passage that the most important reason a single index of welfare cannot be designed is
    (A) the cost associated with producing the index would be prohibitive
    (B) considerable empirical research would have to be done regarding output and needs
    (C) any weighting of various measures into a general index would be inherently subjective and arbitrary

(D) production of the relevant data would require time, thus the index would be only a reflection of past welfare
(E) accurate statistics on crime and pollution are not yet available

32. The author regards the idea of a general index of welfare as
    (A) an unrealistic dream
    (B) a scientific reality
    (C) an important contribution
    (D) a future necessity
    (E) a desirable change

33. According to the passage, the GNP is
    (A) a fairly accurate measure of output
    (B) a reliable estimate of needs
    (C) an accurate forecaster of welfare
    (D) a precise measure of welfare
    (E) a potential measure of general welfare

34. According to the passage, an adequate measure of need must take into account all of the following EXCEPT
    (A) changing size of the population
    (B) changing effects on people of the weather
    (C) differences in needs of urban and suburban populations
    (D) changing requirements for governmental programs such as defense
    (E) accessibility of park land and other amenities

35. The passage is most likely
    (A) an address to a symposium on public policy decisions
    (B) a chapter in a general introduction to statistics
    (C) a pamphlet on government programs to aid the poor
    (D) the introduction to a treatise on the foundations of government
    (E) a speech by a university president to a graduating class

STOP

SECTION II

Time—45 Minutes
30 Questions

Directions: Each group of questions is based on a set of propositions or conditions. Drawing a rough picture or diagram may help in answering some of the questions. Choose the best answer for each question and blacken the corresponding space on your answer sheet.

Questions 1–6

Ten pennants are to be hung side by side on a rope which will then be stretched parallel to the ground between two poles. The positions are numbered consecutively 1 through 10, starting at the left.

There are two green, two blue, three red, and three yellow pennants.
The two green pennants are next to each other.
The two blue pennants are not next to each other.
The three red pennants are next to each other.
A blue pennant is at one end of the rope and a red pennant is at the other.

1. If the fourth and fifth pennants are green, and if the ninth pennant is red, which of the following must be true?
   (A) A blue pennant is next to a green pennant.
   (B) A blue pennant is next to a red pennant.
   (C) Each blue pennant is next to a yellow pennant.
   (D) The sixth pennant is a blue pennant.
   (E) The sixth pennant is a yellow pennant.

2. If a blue pennant is in position 7 and a yellow pennant in position 8, which of the following positions must be a green pennant?
   (A) 3
   (B) 4
   (C) 5
   (D) 6
   (E) 7

3. If each blue pennant is next to a green pennant, then which of the following pennants must be yellow?
   I. The fifth
   II. The sixth
   III. The seventh
   IV. The eighth

   (A) I and II only
   (B) I and III only
   (C) II and III only
   (D) I, II, and III only
   (E) II, III, and IV only

4. If a yellow pennant is in position 9, and the yellow pennants are next to each other, which of the following must be true?
   (A) A blue pennant is in position 1.
   (B) A green pennant is in position 3.
   (C) A green pennant is in position 4.
   (D) A yellow pennant is in position 5.
   (E) A green pennant is in position 5.

5. If yellow pennants are in positions 3 and 5, all of the following must be true EXCEPT
   (A) A yellow pennant is in position 4.
   (B) A green pennant is in position 6.
   (C) A green pennant is in position 7.
   (D) Each blue pennant is next to at least one yellow pennant.
   (E) Exactly one yellow pennant is not next to another yellow pennant.

6. If one green pennant is next to a blue pennant and the other green pennant is next to a red pennant, which of the following must be true?
   (A) The first pennant is a red pennant.
   (B) The first pennant is a blue pennant.
   (C) The third pennant is a red pennant.
   (D) A yellow pennant is flanked by blue pennants.
   (E) A yellow pennant is flanked by yellow pennants.

Questions 7–12

A winery is conducting a tasting of seven wines: J, K, L, M, N, O, and P. Each wine will be tasted in succession according to the following conditions:

J must be tasted either third or seventh.
If J is tasted seventh, then N must be tasted fourth; otherwise N is not tasted fourth.
If J is tasted seventh, then L is tasted sixth.
If J is tasted third, then O is tasted sixth.
N must be the third wine tasted after K.

7. If L is tasted fourth, which wine must be tasted third?
   (A) J
   (B) K
   (C) M
   (D) N
   (E) O

8. If M is tasted immediately following L, which of the following must be true?
   (A) K is tasted first.
   (B) L is tasted second.
   (C) M is tasted third.
   (D) P is tasted fourth.
   (E) P is tasted fifth.

9. M CANNOT be which wine in the tasting sequence?
   (A) second
   (B) third
   (C) fourth
   (D) fifth
   (E) sixth

10. Which of the following must be true?
    (A) J is tasted earlier than K.
    (B) J is tasted earlier than L.
    (C) K is tasted earlier than L.
    (D) K is tasted earlier than O.
    (E) M is tasted earlier than O.

11. If P is tasted earlier than N but later than O, which of the following must be true?
    (A) O is tasted first.
    (B) L is tasted third.
    (C) O is tasted third.
    (D) M is tasted fifth.
    (E) P is tasted fifth.

12. If M is the second wine tasted after P, in how many different orders can the wines be tasted?
    (A) 1
    (B) 2
    (C) 3
    (D) 4
    (E) 5

Questions 13–18

The principal of a high school is selecting a committee of students to attend an annual student leadership conference. The students eligible for selection are P, Q, R, S, T, U, and V. The committee must be selected in accordance with the following considerations:

If V is selected, R must be selected.
If both R and Q are selected, then P cannot be selected.
If both Q and P are selected, then T cannot be selected.
If P is selected, then either S or U must be selected; but S and U cannot both be selected.
Either S or T must be selected, but S and T cannot both be selected.

13. If neither S nor U is selected, what is the largest number of students who can be selected for the conference?
    (A) 2
    (B) 3
    (C) 4
    (D) 5
    (E) 6

14. If both P and V are selected, what is the smallest number of students who can be selected for the conference?
    (A) 3
    (B) 4
    (C) 5
    (D) 6
    (E) 7

15. If both P and U are selected, which of the following must be true?
    (A) Q must be selected.
    (B) S must be selected.
    (C) T must be selected.
    (D) R cannot be selected.
    (E) V cannot be selected.

16. Which of the following is an acceptable delegation to the conference if only three students are selected?
    (A) P, Q, and S
    (B) P, Q, and T
    (C) P, R, and V
    (D) R, S, and T
    (E) R, S, and U

17. If both P and T are chosen, which of the following CANNOT be true?
    I. R is chosen.
    II. Q is chosen.
    III. U is not chosen.

(A) I, but not II or III
(B) II, but not I or III
(C) III, but not I or II
(D) II and III, but not I
(E) I, II, and III

18. If U and three other students are selected, which of the following groups can accompany U?
    (A) P, Q, and T
    (B) P, R, and T
    (C) P, Q, and V
    (D) P, V, and S
    (E) R, S, and V

Questions 19–24

A musical scale contains seven notes—J, K, L, M, N, O, and Q—ranked from first (lowest) to seventh (highest), though not necessarily in that order.

The first note of the scale is O and the last note of the scale is Q.

L is lower than M.

N is lower than J.

K is somewhere between J and M on the scale.

19. If N is the fifth note on the scale, which of the following must be true?
    (A) J is the sixth note and M is the fourth note.
    (B) K is the fourth note and L is the third note.
    (C) M is the third note and L is the second note.
    (D) M is the fourth note and L is the third note.
    (E) L is the fourth note and J is the second note.

20. If M is the sixth note, then J and N could be which of the following notes on the scale, respectively?
    I. fifth and third
    II. fourth and third
    III. third and second

    (A) I, but not II or not III
    (B) II, but not I or not II
    (C) I or II, but not III
    (D) II or III, but not I
    (E) I or II or III

21. If there are exactly two notes on the scale between K and N, which of the following must be true?

(A) K is the fifth note on the scale.
(B) L is between J and K on the scale.
(C) M is the sixth note on the scale.
(D) M is above J on the scale.
(E) L and M are separated by exactly one note on the scale.

22. Which of the following CANNOT be true?
    (A) J is the fourth note on the scale.
    (B) J is the third note on the scale.
    (C) K is the third note on the scale.
    (D) K is the fourth note on the scale.
    (E) K is the fifth note on the scale.

23. If N and O are separated by exactly two notes, which of the following must be true?
    (A) J is the sixth note on the scale.
    (B) L is the fifth note on the scale.
    (C) K is below M on the scale.
    (D) K is between N and O on the scale.
    (E) M is above N on the scale.

24. If N is one note above L on the scale, the number of logically possible orderings of all seven notes from the bottom of the scale to the top of the scale is
    (A) 1
    (B) 2
    (C) 3
    (D) 4
    (E) 5

Questions 25–30

Nine people—P, Q, R, S, T, U, V, W, and X—are to be seated at three tables with three different colored table cloths—red, blue, and green. Exactly three of the people will be seated at each table.

W and V must sit at the same table.
X and T must sit at the same table.
R and U cannot sit at the same table.
Either R or S must sit at the same table as Q.
S must sit at the green table.

25. Which of the following people could sit at the same table?
    (A) P, R, S
    (B) P, U, V
    (C) S, W, X
    (D) T, X, R
    (E) U, X, R

26. Which of the following CANNOT be true?
    (A) Q sits at the red table.
    (B) U sits at the red table.
    (C) X sits at the green table.
    (D) P sits at the red table, and W sits at the blue table.
    (E) R sits at the red table, and Q sits at the blue table.

27. All of the following groups of persons could sit at the blue table EXCEPT
    (A) P, Q, R
    (B) P, R, X
    (C) R, T, X
    (D) R, V, W
    (E) U, V, W

28. All of the following could sit at the same table as W EXCEPT
    (A) P
    (B) R

(C) S
(D) U
(E) X

29. If R and W sit at the blue table, then which of the following must sit at the green table?
    (A) P
    (B) Q
    (C) U
    (D) V
    (E) X

30. If S and T sit at the same table, and if Q sits at the red table, which of the following must sit at the blue table?
    (A) R, V
    (B) R, X
    (C) U, X
    (D) P, V, W
    (E) U, V, W

STOP

IF YOU FINISH BEFORE TIME IS CALLED, CHECK YOUR WORK ON THIS SECTION ONLY. DO NOT WORK ON ANY OTHER SECTION IN THE TEST.

SECTION III

Time——45 Minutes
35 Questions

Directions: In this section, the questions ask you to analyze and evaluate the reasoning in short paragraphs or passages. For some questions, all of the answer choices may conceivably be answers to the question asked. You should select the *best* answer to the question, that is, an answer which does not require you to make assumptions which violate commonsense standards by being implausible, redundant, irrelevant or inconsistent. After choosing the best answer, blacken the corresponding space on the answer sheet.

Questions 1 and 2

On his trip to the People's Republic of China, a young U.S. diplomat of very subordinate rank embarrassed himself by asking a Chinese official how it was that Orientals managed to be so inscrutable. The Chinese official smiled and then gently responded that he preferred to think of the inscrutability of his race in terms of a want of perspicacity in Occidentals.

1. Which of the following best describes the point of the comment made by the Chinese official?
   (A) It is not merely the Chinese, but all Oriental people who are inscrutable.
   (B) Most Americans fail to understand Chinese culture.
   (C) What one fails to perceive may be attributable to carelessness in observation rather than obscurity inherent in the object.
   (D) Since the resumption of diplomatic relations between the United States and Communist China, many older Chinese civil servants have grown to distrust the Americans.
   (E) If the West and the East are ever to truly understand one another, there will have to be considerable cultural exchange between the two.

2. Which of the following best characterizes the attitude and response of the Chinese official?
   (A) angry
   (B) fearful
   (C) emotional
   (D) indifferent
   (E) compassionate

3. People waste a surprising amount of money on gadgets and doodads that they hardly ever use. For example, my brother spent $25 on an electric ice-cream maker two years ago, but he has used it on only three occasions. Yet, he insists that regardless of the number of times he actually uses the ice-cream maker, the investment was a good one because ——————.

   Which of the following best completes the thought of the paragraph?
   (A) The price of ice cream will go up in the future.
   (B) He has purchased the ice-cream maker for the convenience of having it available if and when he needs it.
   (C) In a society that is oriented toward consumer goods, one should take every opportunity to acquire things.
   (D) Today $25 is not worth what it was two years ago on account of the inflation rate.
   (E) By using it so infrequently he has conserved a considerable amount of electrical energy.

4. A poet was once asked to interpret a particularly obscure passage in one of his poems. He responded, ''When I wrote that verse, only God and I knew the meaning of that passage. Now, only God knows.''

   What is the point of the poet's response?
   (A) God is infinitely wiser than man.
   (B) Most men are unable to understand poetry.
   (C) Poets rarely know the source of their own creative inspiration.
   (D) A great poem is inspired by the muse.
   (E) He has forgotten what he had originally meant by the verse.

5. A recent survey by the economics department of an Ivy League university revealed that increases in the salaries of preachers are accompanied by increases in the nationwide average of rum consumption. From 1965 to 1970 preachers' salaries increased on the average of 15% and rum sales grew by 14.5%. From 1970 to 1975 average preachers' salaries rose by 17% and rum sales by

17.5%. From 1975 to 1980 rum sales expanded by only 8% and average preachers' salaries also grew by only 8%.

Which of the following is the most likely explanation for the findings cited in the paragraph?
(A) When preachers have more disposable income, they tend to allocate that extra money to alcohol.
(B) When preachers are paid more, they preach longer; and longer sermons tend to drive people to drink.
(C) Since there were more preachers in the country, there were also more people; and a larger population will consume greater quantities of liquor.
(D) The general standard of living increased from 1965 to 1980, which accounts for both the increase in rum consumption and preachers' average salaries.
(E) A consortium of rum importers carefully limited the increases in imports of rum during the test period cited.

6. Since all four-door automobiles I have repaired have eight-cylinder engines, all four-door automobiles must have eight-cylinder engines.
The author argues on the basis of
(A) special training
(B) generalization
(C) syllogism
(D) ambiguity
(E) deduction

7. Two women, one living in Los Angeles, the other living in New York City, carried on a lengthy correspondence by mail. The subject of the exchange was a dispute over certain personality traits of Winston Churchill. After some two dozen letters, the Los Angeles resident received the following note from her New York City correspondent: "It seems you were right all along. Yesterday I met someone who actually knew Sir Winston, and he confirmed your opinion."

The two women could have been arguing on the basis of all of the following EXCEPT
(A) published biographical information
(B) old news film footage
(C) direct personal acquaintance
(D) assumption
(E) third party reports

8. The protection of the right of property by the Constitution is tenuous at best. It is true that the Fifth Amendment states that the government may not take private property for public use without compensation, but it is the government that defines private property.

Which of the following is most likely the point the author is leading up to?
(A) Individual rights that are protected by the Supreme Court are secure against government encroachment.
(B) Private property is neither more nor less than that which the government says is private property.
(C) The government has no authority to deprive an individual of his liberty.
(D) No government that acts arbitrarily can be justified.
(E) The keystone of American democracy is the Constitution.

9. *Daily Post* newspaper reporter Roger Nightengale let it be known that Andrea Johnson, the key figure in his award-winning series of articles on prostitution and drug abuse, was a composite of many persons and not a single, real person, and so he was the subject of much criticism by fellow journalists for having failed to disclose that information when the articles were first published. But these were the same critics who voted Nightengale a prize for his magazine serial *General*, which was a much dramatized and fictionalized account of a Korean War military leader whose character was obviously patterned closely after that of Douglas MacArthur.

In which of the following ways might the critics mentioned in the paragraph argue that they were NOT inconsistent in their treatment of Nightengale's works?

I. Fictionalization is an accepted journalistic technique for reporting on sensitive subject matter such as prostitution.
II. Critic disapproval is one of the most important ways members of the writing community have for ensuring that reporting is accurate and to the point.
III. There is a critical difference between dramatizing events in a piece of fiction and presenting distortions of the truth as actual fact.

(A) I only
(B) I and II only
(C) II and III only
(D) III only
(E) I, II, and III

10. Why pay outrageously high prices for imported sparkling water when there is now an inexpensive water carbonated and bottled here in the United States at its source—Cold Springs, Vermont. Neither you nor your guests will taste the difference, but if you would be embarrassed if it were learned that you were serving a domestic sparkling water, then serve Cold Springs Water—but serve it in a leaded crystal decanter.

The advertisement rests on which of the following assumptions?

  I. It is difficult if not impossible to distinguish Cold Springs Water from imported competitors on the basis of taste.
  II. Most sparkling waters are not bottled at the source.
  III. Some people may purchase an imported sparkling water over a domestic one as a status symbol.

(A) I only
(B) II only
(C) III only
(D) I and II only
(E) I and III only

11. Choose the best completion of the following paragraph.

Parochial education serves the dual functions of education and religious instruction, and church leaders are justifiably concerned to impart important religious values regarding relationships between the sexes. Thus, when the administrators of a parochial school system segregate boys and girls in separate institutions, they believe they are helping to keep the children pure by removing them from a source of temptation. If the administrators realized, however, that children would be more likely to develop the very attitudes they seek to engender in the company of the opposite sex, they would _____.

(A) put an end to all parochial education
(B) no longer insist upon separate schools for boys and girls
(C) abolish all racial discrimination in the religious schools
(D) stop teaching foolish religious tripe, and concentrate instead on secular educational programs
(E) reinforce their policies of isolating the sexes in separate programs

12. Professor Branch, who is chairman of the sociology department, claims she saw a flying saucer the other night. But since she is a sociologist instead of a physicist, she cannot possibly be acquainted with the most recent writings of our finest scientists that tend to discount such sightings, so we can conclude her report is unreliable.

Which of the following would be the most appropriate criticism of the author's analysis?
(A) He makes an irrelevant attack on Professor Branch's credentials.
(B) He himself may not be a physicist, and therefore may not be familiar with the writings he cites.
(C) Even the U.S. Air Force cannot explain all of the sightings of UFOs which are reported to them each year.
(D) A sociologist is sufficiently well educated that he can probably read and understand scientific literature in a field other than his own.
(E) It is impossible to get complete agreement on matters such as the possibility of life on other planets.

13. INQUISTOR: Are you in league with the devil?
VICTIM: Yes.
INQUISITOR: Then you must be lying, for those in league with the "Evil One" never tell the truth. So you are not in league with the devil.

The inquisitor's behavior can be described as paradoxical because he
(A) charged the victim with being in a league with the devil but later recanted
(B) relies on the victim's answer to reject the victim's response
(C) acts in accordance with religious law but accuses the victim of violating that law
(D) questions the victim about his ties with the devil but does not himself believe there is a devil
(E) asked the question in the first place, but then refused to accept the answer that the victim gave

14. "Whom did you pass on the road?" the King went on, holding his hand out to the messenger for some hay.
"Nobody," said the messenger.
"Quite right," said the King. "This young lady saw him, too. So, of course, Nobody walks slower than you."

The King's response shows that he believes
(A) the messenger is a very good messenger
(B) "Nobody" is a person who might be seen
(C) the young lady's eyesight is better than the messenger's
(D) the messenger is not telling him the truth
(E) there was no person actually seen by the messenger on the road

15. MARY: All of the graduates from Midland High School go to State College.

    ANN: I don't know. Some of the students at State College come from North Hills High School.

Ann's response shows that she has interpreted Mary's remark to mean that
(A) most of the students from North Hills High School attend State College
(B) none of the students at State College are from Midland High School
(C) only students from Midland High School attend State College
(D) Midland High School is a better school than North Hills High School
(E) some Midland High School graduates do not attend college

16. Total contributions by individuals to political parties were up 25 percent in this most recent presidential election over those of four years earlier. Hence, it is obvious that people are no longer as apathetic as they were, but are taking a greater interest in politics.

Which of the following, if true, would considerably weaken the preceding argument?
(A) The average contribution per individual actually declined during the same four-year period.
(B) Per capita income of the population increased by 15 percent during the four years in question.
(C) Public leaders continue to warn citizens against the dangers of political apathy.
(D) Contributions made by large corporations to political parties declined during the four-year period.
(E) Fewer people voted in the most recent presidential election than in the one four years earlier.

17. The harmful effects of marijuana and other drugs have been considerably overstated. Although parents and teachers have expressed much concern over the dangers which widespread usage of marijuana and other drugs pose for high school and junior high school students, a national survey of 5,000 students of ages 13 to 17 showed that fewer than 15% of those students thought such drug use was likely to be harmful.

Which of the following is the strongest criticism of the author's reasoning?
(A) The opinions of students in the age group surveyed are likely to vary with age.
(B) Alcohol use among students of ages 13 to 17 is on the rise, and is now considered by many to present greater dangers than marijuana usage.
(C) Marijuana and other drugs may be harmful to users even though the users are not themselves aware of the danger.
(D) A distinction must be drawn between victimless crimes and crimes in which an innocent person is likely to be involved.
(E) The fact that a student does not think a drug is harmful does not necessarily mean he will use it.

18. AL: If an alien species ever visited Earth, it would surely be because they were looking for other intelligent species with whom they could communicate. Since we have not been contacted by aliens, we may conclude that none have ever visited this planet.

    AMY: Or, perhaps, they did not think human beings intelligent.

How is Amy's response related to Al's argument?
(A) She misses Al's point entirely.
(B) She attacks Al personally rather than his reasoning.
(C) She points out that Al made an unwarranted assumption.
(D) She ignores the detailed internal development of Al's logic.
(E) She introduces a false analogy.

19. I maintain that the best way to solve our company's present financial crisis is to bring out a new line of goods. I challenge anyone who disagrees with this proposed course of action to show that it will not work.

A flaw in the preceding argument is that it
(A) employs group classifications without regard to individuals

(B) introduces an analogy which is weak

(C) attempts to shift the burden of proof to those who would object to the plan

(D) fails to provide statistical evidence to show that the plan will actually succeed

(E) relies upon a discredited economic theory

20. If quarks are the smallest subatomic particles in the universe, then gluons are needed to hold quarks together. Since gluons are needed to hold quarks together, it follows that quarks are the smallest subatomic particles in the universe.

The logic of the above argument is most nearly paralleled by which of the following?

(A) If this library has a good French literature collection, it will contain a copy of *Les Conquerants* by Malraux. The collection does contain a copy of *Les Conquerants;* therefore, the library has a good French literature collection.

(B) If there is a man-in-the-moon, the moon must be made of green cheese for him to eat. There is a man-in-the-moon, so the moon is made of green cheese.

(C) Either helium or hydrogen is the lightest element of the periodic table. Helium is not the lightest element of the periodic table, so hydrogen must be the lightest element of the periodic table.

(D) If Susan is taller than Bob, and if Bob is taller than Elaine, then if Susan is taller than Bob, Susan is also taller than Elaine.

(E) Whenever it rains, the streets get wet. The streets are not wet. Therefore, it has not rained.

21. In the earliest stages of the common law, a party could have his case heard by a judge only upon the payment of a fee to the court, and then only if his case fit within one of the forms for which there existed a writ. At first the number of such formalized cases of action was very small, but judges invented new forms which brought more cases and greater revenues.

Which of the following conclusions is most strongly suggested by the paragraph above?

(A) Early judges often decided cases in an arbitrary and haphazard manner.

(B) In most early cases, the plaintiff rather than the defendant prevailed.

(C) The judiciary at first had greater power than either the legislature or the executive.

(D) One of the motivating forces for the early expansion in judicial power was economic considerations.

(E) The first common law decisions were inconsistent with one another and did not form a coherent body of law.

22. If Martin introduces an amendment to Evans' bill, then Johnson and Lloyd will both vote the same way. If Evans speaks against Lloyd's position, Johnson will defend anyone voting with him. Martin will introduce an amendment to Evans' bill only if Evans speaks against Johnson's position.

If the above statements are true, each of the following can be true EXCEPT

(A) if Evans speaks against Johnson's position, Lloyd will not vote with Johnson.

(B) if Martin introduces an amendment to Evans' bill, then Evans has spoken against Johnson's position.

(C) if Evans speaks against Johnson's position, Martin will not introduce an amendment to Evans' bill.

(D) if Martin introduces an amendment to Evans' bill, then either Johnson will not vote with Lloyd or Evans did not speak against Johnson's position.

(E) if either Evans did not speak against Lloyd's position or Martin did not introduce an amendment to Evans' bill, then either Johnson did not defend Lloyd or Martin spoke against Johnson's position.

23. Once at a conference on the philosophy of language, a professor delivered a lengthy and tiresome address the central thesis of which was that ''yes'' and related slang words such as ''yeah'' can only be used to show agreement with a proposition. At the end of the paper, a listener in the back of the auditorium stood up and shouted in a sarcastic voice, ''Oh, yeah?'' This constituted a complete refutation of the paper.

The listener argued against the paper by

(A) offering a counter-example

(B) pointing out an inconsistency

(C) presenting an analogy

(D) attacking the speaker's character

(E) citing additional evidence

24. If military aid to Latin American countries is to be stopped because it creates instability in the region, then all foreign aid must be stopped.

Which of the following is most like the argument above in its logical structure?
(A) If a war in Central America is to be condemned because all killing is immoral, then all war must be condemned.
(B) If charitable donations are obligatory for those who are rich, then it is certain that the poor will be provided for.
(C) If the fascist government in Chile is to be overthrown because it violates the rights of the people, then all government must be overthrown.
(D) If a proposed weapons system is to be rejected because there are insufficient funds to pay for it, then the system must be purchased when the funds are available.
(E) If a sociological theory is widely accepted but later proven wrong by facts, then a new theory should be proposed which takes account of the additional data.

Questions 25–26

The blanks in the following passage indicate deletions from the text. Select the completion that is most appropriate to the context.

Contemporary legal positivism depends upon the methodological assumption that a theory of law may be conceptual without, at the same time, being normative. In point of fact this assumption is a composite principle. It makes the fairly obvious claim that a conceptual theory, which strives to be descriptive rather than normative, says what the law is—not what it ought to be. A conceptual theory must be supplemented by a normative theory, and the arguments in favor of a particular content for law are couched in terms of the results which are expected to flow from proposed legal acts. It is never a part of an argument for what the law ought to be, in the positivist's view, that to be a law it must have a certain content. While the normative argument refers ultimately to agreed-upon ends, it does not assert that these ends——(25)——. Rather, that they are accepted and acted upon is merely a contingent matter. The second part of the methodological premise is more subtle: A conceptual theory such as legal positivism does not claim that the particular description it offers is uniquely correct. Proponents of legal positivism regard their study of law as analogous to the physicists' study of the universe: They have one theory of legal institutions, ——(26)——.

25. (A) must be pursued as a matter of logical necessity

(B) are not the best ends for any modern legal system
(C) would not be adopted by courts in a democratic society
(D) could be undermined by dissident elements in the community
(E) are shared by everyone

26. (A) and that is the only possible correct theory of law
(B) and someday, with sufficient work, that theory will be able to generate societal goals for us to pursue
(C) but that theory may, someday, be displaced by a better one
(D) although no theory of the physical universe is as reliable as the positivistic theory of law
(E) which is, however, strongly supported by the findings of modern science

27. The Supreme Court's recent decision is unfair. It treats non-resident aliens as a special group when it denies them some rights ordinary citizens have. This treatment is discriminatory, and we all know that discrimination is unfair.

Which of the following arguments is most nearly similar in its reasoning to the above argument?
(A) Doing good would be our highest duty under the moral law, and that duty would be irrational unless we had the ability to discharge it; but since a finite, sensuous creature could never discharge that duty in his lifetime, we must conclude that if there is moral law, the soul is immortal.
(B) Required core courses are a good idea because students just entering college do not have as good an idea about what constitutes a good education as do the professional educators; therefore, students should not be left complete freedom to select coursework.
(C) This country is the most free nation on earth largely as a result of the fact that the founding fathers had the foresight to include a Bill of Rights in the Constitution.
(D) Whiskey and beer do not mix well; every evening that I have drunk both whiskey and beer together, the following morning I have had a hangover.
(E) I know that this is a beautiful painting because Picasso created only beautiful works of art, and this painting was done by Picasso.

28. Creativity must be cultivated. Artists, musicians, and writers all practice, consciously or unconsciously, interpreting the world from new and interesting viewpoints. A teacher can encourage his pupils to be creative by showing them different perspectives for viewing the significance of events in their daily lives.

Which of the following, if true, would most undermine the author's claim?

(A) In a well-ordered society, it is important to have some people who are not artists, musicians, or writers.
(B) A teacher's efforts to show a pupil different perspectives may actually inhibit development of the student's own creative process.
(C) Public education should stress practical skills, which will help a person get a good job, instead of creative thinking.
(D) Not all pupils have the same capacity for creative thought.
(E) Some artists, musicians, and writers "burn themselves out" at a very early age, producing a flurry of great works and then nothing after that.

29. Opponents to the mayor's plan for express bus lanes on the city's major commuter arteries objected that people could not be lured out of their automobiles in that way. The opponents were proved wrong; following implementation of the plan, bus ridership rose dramatically, and there was a corresponding drop in automobile traffic. Nonetheless, the plan failed to achieve its stated objective of reducing average commuting time.

Which of the following sentences would be the most logical continuation of this argument?

(A) The plan's opponents failed to realize that many people would take advantage of improved bus transportation.
(B) Unfortunately, politically attractive solutions do not always get results.
(C) The number of people a vehicle can transport varies directly with the size of the passenger compartment of the vehicle.
(D) Opponents cited an independent survey of city commuters showing that before the plan's adoption only one out of every seven used commuter bus lines.
(E) With the express lanes closed to private automobile traffic, the remaining cars were forced to use too few lanes and this created gigantic traffic tie-ups.

30. Last year, Gambia received $2.5 billion in loans from the International Third World Banking Fund, and its Gross National Product grew by 5%. This year Gambia has requested twice as much money from the ITWBF, and its leaders expect that Gambia's GNP will rise by a full 10%.

Which of the following, if true, would undermine the expectations of Gambia's leaders?

I. The large 5% increase of last year is attributable to extraordinary harvests due to unusually good weather conditions.
II. Gambia's economy is not strong enough to absorb more than $3 billion in outside capital each year.
III. Gambia does not have sufficient heavy industry to fuel an increase in its GNP of more than 6% per year.

(A) I only
(B) II only
(C) I and II only
(D) II and III only
(E) I, II, and III

31. Efficiency experts will attempt to improve the productivity of an office by analyzing production procedures into discrete work tasks. They then study the organization of those tasks and advise managers on techniques to speed production, such as rescheduling of employee breaks or relocating various equipment such as the copying machines. I have found a way to accomplish increases in efficiency with much less to do. Office workers grow increasingly productive as the temperature drops, so long as it does not fall below 68°F.

The passage leads most naturally to which of the following conclusions?
(A) Some efficiency gains will be short-term only.
(B) To maintain peak efficiency, an office manager must occasionally restructure office tasks.
(C) Employees are most efficient when the temperature is 68°F.
(D) The temperature-efficiency formula is applicable to all kinds of work.
(E) Office workers will be equally efficient at 67°F and 69°F.

Questions 32–34

PRO-ABORTION SPEAKER: Those who oppose abortion upon demand make the foundation of their arguments the sanctity of human life, but this seeming bedrock assumption is actually as weak as shifting sand. And it is not necessary to invoke the red herring that many anti-abortion speakers would allow that human life must sometimes be sacrificed for a great good, as in the fighting of a just war. There are counter-examples to the principle of sanctity of life which are even more embarrassing to pro-life advocates. It would be possible to reduce the annual number of traffic fatalities to virtually zero by passing federal legislation mandating a nationwide fifteen-mile-per-hour speed limit on *all* roads. You see, implicitly we have always been willing to trade off quantity of human life for quality.

ANTI-ABORTION SPEAKER: The analogy my opponent draws between abortion and traffic fatalities is weak. No one would propose such a speed limit. Imagine people trying to get to and from work under such a law, or imagine them trying to visit a friend or relatives outside their own neighborhoods, or taking in a sports event or a movie. Obviously such a law would be a disaster.

32. Which of the following best characterizes the anti-abortion speaker's response to the pro-abortion speaker?
    (A) His analysis of the traffic fatalities case actually supports the argument of the pro-abortion speaker.
    (B) His analysis of the traffic fatalities case is an effective rebuttal of the pro-abortion argument.
    (C) His response provides a strong affirmative statement of the anti-abortionist position.
    (D) His response is totally irrelevant to the issue raised by the pro-abortion speaker.
    (E) His counter-argument attacks the character of the pro-abortion speaker instead of the merits of his argument.

33. Which of the following represents the most logical continuation of the reasoning contained in the pro-abortion speaker's argument?
    (A) Therefore, we should not have any laws on the books to protect human life.

(B) We can only conclude that the anti-abortionist is also in favor of strengthening enforcement of existing traffic regulations as a means to reducing the number of traffic fatalities each year.
(C) So the strongest attack on the anti-abortionist position is that he contradicts himself when he agrees that we should fight a just war even at the risk of considerable loss of human life.
(D) Even the laws against contraception are good examples of this tendency.
(E) The abortion question just makes explicit that which for so long has remained hidden from view.

34. In his argument, the pro-abortionist makes which of the following assumptions?
    I. It is not a proper goal of a society to protect human life.
    II. The human fetus is not a human life.
    III. The trade-off between the number of human lives and the quality of those lives is appropriately decided by society.

    (A) I only
    (B) II only
    (C) I and II only
    (D) III only
    (E) I, II, and III

Some Alphas are not Gammas.
All Betas are Gammas.

35. Which of the following conclusions can be deduced from the two statements above?
    I. Some Alphas are not Betas.
    II. No Gammas are Alphas.
    III. All Gammas are Betas.

    (A) I only
    (B) II only
    (C) I and II only
    (D) I and III only
    (E) I, II, and III

STOP

SECTION IV

Time—45 Minutes
35 Questions

Directions: Below each of the following passages, you will find questions or incomplete statements about the passage. Each statement or question is followed by lettered words or expressions. Select the word or expression that most satisfactorily completes each statement or answers each question in accordance with the meaning of the passage. After you have chosen the best answer, blacken the corresponding space on the answer sheet.

Desertification in the arid United States is flagrant. Groundwater supplies beneath vast stretches of land are dropping precipitously. Whole river systems have dried up; others are choked with sediment washed
5 from denuded land. Hundreds of thousands of acres of previously irrigated cropland have been abandoned to wind or weeds. Several million acres of natural grassland are eroding at unnaturally high rates as a result of cultivation or overgrazing. All told, about 225 million
10 acres of land are undergoing severe desertification.

Federal subsidies encourage the exploitation of arid land resources. Low-interest loans for irrigation and other water delivery systems encourage farmers, industry, and municipalities to mine groundwater. Fed-
15 eral disaster relief and commodity programs encourage arid-land farmers to plow up natural grassland to plant crops such as wheat and, especially, cotton. Federal grazing fees that are well below the free market price encourage overgrazing of the commons. The
20 market, too, provides powerful incentives to exploit arid land resources beyond their carrying capacity. When commodity prices are high relative to the farmer's or rancher's operating costs, the return on a production-enhancing investment is invariably greater
25 than the return on a conservation investment. And when commodity prices are relatively low, arid land ranchers and farmers often have to use all their available financial resources to stay solvent.

The incentives to exploit arid land resources are
30 greater today than ever. The government is now offering huge new subsidies to produce synfuel from coal or oil shale as well as alcohol fuel from crops. Moreover, commodity prices are on the rise; and they will provide farmers and agribusiness with powerful in-
35 centive to overexploit arid land resources. The existing federal government cost-share programs designed to help finance the conservation of soil, water, and vegetation pale in comparison to such incentives.

In the final analysis, when viewed in the national
40 perspective, the effects on agriculture are the most troublesome aspect of desertification in the United States. For it comes at a time when we are losing over a million acres of rain-watered crop and pasture land per year to "higher uses"—shopping centers, indus-
45 trial parks, housing developments, and waste dumps—heedless of the economic need of the United States to export agricultural products or of the world's need for U.S. food and fiber. Today the arid West accounts for 20 percent of the nation's total agricul-
50 tural output. If the United States is, as it appears, well on its way toward overdrawing the arid land resources, then the policy choice is simply to pay now for the appropriate remedies or pay for more later, when productive benefits from arid land resources
55 have been both realized and largely terminated.

1. The author is primarily concerned with
   (A) discussing a solution
   (B) describing a problem
   (C) replying to a detractor
   (D) finding a contradiction
   (E) defining a term

2. The passage mentions all of the following as effects of desertification EXCEPT
   (A) increased sediment in rivers
   (B) erosion of land
   (C) overcultivation of arid land
   (D) decreasing groundwater supplies
   (E) loss of land to wind or weeds

3. The author most likely encloses the phrase "higher uses" (line 44) in quotations marks in order to
   (A) alert the reader to the fact that the term is very important
   (B) minimize the importance of desertification in non-arid land
   (C) voice his support for expansion of such programs
   (D) express concern over the extent of desertification
   (E) indicate disagreement that such uses are more important

4. The passage mentions which of the following as tending to encourage desertification?
   I. high prices for certain commodities which provide incentives for farmers to use arid lands
   II. low government fees for grazing on public lands
   III. the world's need for food and fiber produced by the United States
   (A) I only
   (B) II only
   (C) III only
   (D) I and II only
   (E) I, II, and III

5. According to the passage, the most serious long-term effect of desertification would be the reduced ability of
   (A) the United States to continue to export agricultural products
   (B) municipalities to supply water to meet the needs of residents
   (C) farmers to cover their expenses
   (D) the United States to meet the food needs of its own people
   (E) the United States to produce sufficient fuel for energy from domestic sources

6. The passage leads most logically to discussion of a proposal for
   (A) reduced agricultural output in the United States
   (B) direct government aid to farmers affected by desertification
   (C) curtailing the conversion of land to shopping centers and housing
   (D) government assistance to develop improved farming methods to increase exploitation of arid land
   (E) increased government assistance to finance the conservation of arid land

7. The author's attitude toward desertification can best be described as one of
   (A) alarm
   (B) optimism
   (C) understanding
   (D) conciliation
   (E) concern

The need for solar electricity is clear. It is safe, ecologically sound, efficient, continuously available, and it has no moving parts. The basic problem with the use of solar photovoltaic devices is economics, but

5 until recently very little progress had been made toward the development of low-cost photovoltaic devices. The larger part of research funds has been devoted to study of single-crystal silicon solar cells, despite the evidence, including that of the leading
10 manufacturers of crystalline silicon, that this technique holds little promise. The reason for this pattern is understandable and historical. Crystalline silicon is the active element in the very successful semiconductor industry, and virtually all of the solid state devices
15 contain silicon transistors and diodes. Crystalline silicon, however, is particularly unsuitable to terrestrial solar cells.

Crystalline silicon solar cells work well and are successfully used in the space program, where cost is not
20 an issue. While single crystal silicon has been proven in extraterrestrial use with efficiencies as high as 18 percent, and other more expensive and scarce materials such as gallium arsenide can have even higher efficiencies, costs must be reduced by a factor of more
25 than 100 to make them practical for commercial uses. Beside the fact that the starting crystalline silicon is expensive, 95 percent of it is wasted and does not appear in the final device. Recently, there have been some imaginative attempts to make polycrystalline
30 and ribbon silicon which are lower in cost than high-quality single crystals; but to date the efficiencies of these apparently lower-cost arrays have been unacceptably small. Moreover, these materials are cheaper only because of the introduction of disordering in
35 crystalline semiconductors, and disorder degrades the efficiency of crystalline solar cells.

This dilemma can be avoided by preparing completely disordered or amorphous materials. Amorphous materials have disordered atomic structure as
40 compared to crystalline materials: that is, they have only short-range order rather than the long-range periodicity of crystals. The advantages of amorphous solar cells are impressive. Whereas crystals can be grown as wafers about four inches in diameter, amor-
45 phous materials can be grown over large areas in a single process. Whereas crystalline silicon must be made 200 microns thick to absorb a sufficient amount of sunlight for efficient energy conversion, only 1 micron of the proper amorphous materials is neces-
50 sary. Crystalline silicon solar cells cost in excess of $100 per square foot, but amorphous films can be created at a cost of about 50¢ per square foot.

Although many scientists were aware of the very low cost of amorphous solar cells, they felt that they
55 could never be manufactured with the efficiencies necessary to contribute significantly to the demand for electric power. This was based on a misconception about the feature which determines efficiency. For

example, it is not the conductivity of the material in
60 the dark which is relevant, but only the photoconductivity, that is, the conductivity in the presence of sunlight. Already, solar cells with efficiencies well above
6 percent have been developed using amorphous materials, and further research will doubtless find even
65 less costly amorphous materials with higher efficiencies.

8. The author is primarily concerned with
   (A) discussing the importance of solar energy
   (B) explaining the functioning of solar cells
   (C) presenting a history of research on energy sources
   (D) describing a possible solution to the problem of the cost of photovoltaic cells
   (E) advocating increased government funding for research on alternative energy sources

9. According to the passage, which of the following encouraged use of silicon solar cells in the space program?
   I. the higher cost of materials such as gallium arsenide
   II. the fairly high extraterrestrial efficiency of the cells
   III. the relative lack of cost limitations in the space program
   (A) I only
   (B) II only
   (C) I and II only
   (D) II and III only
   (E) I, II, and III

10. The author mentions recent attempts to make polycrystalline and ribbon silicon (lines 28–31) primarily in order to
    (A) minimize the importance of recent improvements in silicon solar cells
    (B) demonstrate the superiority of amorphous materials over crystalline silicon
    (C) explain why silicon solar cells have been the center of research
    (D) contrast crystalline silicon with polycrystalline and ribbon silicon
    (E) inform the reader that an alternative type of solar cell exists

11. Which of the following pairs of terms does the author regard as most nearly synonymous?
    (A) solar and extraterrestrial
    (B) photovoltaic devices and solar cells
    (C) crystalline silicon and amorphous materials

   (D) amorphous materials and higher efficiencies
   (E) wafers and crystals

12. The material in the passage could best be used in an argument for
    (A) discontinuing the space program
    (B) increased funding for research on amorphous materials
    (C) further study of the history of silicon crystals
    (D) increased reliance on solar energy
    (E) training more scientists to study energy problems

13. The author mentions which of the following as advantages of amorphous materials for solar cells over silicon crystals?
    I. the relative thinness of amorphous materials
    II. the cost of the amorphous material
    III. the size of solar cells which can be made of amorphous material
    (A) I only
    (B) II only
    (C) I and II only
    (D) II and III only
    (E) I, II, and III

14. The tone of the passage can best be described as
    (A) analytical and optimistic
    (B) biased and unprofessional
    (C) critical and discouraged
    (D) tentative and inconclusive
    (E) concerned and conciliatory

   According to legend, Aesculapius bore two daughters, Panacea and Hyegeia, who gave rise to dynasties of healers and hygienists. The schism remains today, in clinical training and in practice; and because of the
5 imperative nature of medical care and the subtlety of health care, the former has tended to dominate. Preventive medicine has as its primary objective the maintenance and promotion of health. It accomplishes this by controlling or manipulating environmental factors
10 which affect health and disease. For example, in California presently there is serious suffering and substantial economic loss because of the failure to introduce controlled fluoridation of public water supplies. Additionally, preventive medicine applies prophylactic
15 measures against disease by such actions as immunization and specific nutritional measures. Third, it

attempts to motivate people to adopt healthful life-styles through education.

For the most part, curative medicine has as its pri-
20 mary objective the removal of disease from the patient. It provides diagnostic techniques to identify the presence and nature of the disease process. While these may be applied on a mass basis in an attempt to "screen" out persons with preclinical disease, they
25 are usually applied after the patient appears with a complaint. Second, it applies treatment to the sick patient. In every case, this is, or should be, individu-alized according to the particular need of each patient. Third, it utilizes rehabilitation methodologies to re-
30 turn the treated patient to the best possible level of functioning.

While it is true that both preventive medicine and curative medicine require cadres of similarly trained personnel such as planners, administrators, and edu-
35 cators, the underlying delivery systems depend upon quite distinctive professional personnel. The require-ments for curative medicine call for clinically trained individuals who deal with patients on a one-to-one basis and whose training is based primarily on an
40 understanding of the biological, pathological, and psychological processes which determine an individu-al's health and disease status. The locus for this train-ing is the laboratory and clinic. Preventive medicine, on the other hand, calls for a very broad spectrum of
45 professional personnel, few of whom require clinical expertise. Since their actions apply either to environ-mental situations or to population groups, their train-ing takes place in a different type of laboratory or in a community not necessarily associated with the clinical
50 locus.

The economic differences between preventive med-icine and curative medicine have been extensively dis-cussed, perhaps most convincingly by Winslow in the monograph *The Cost of Sickness and the Price of*
55 *Health*. Sickness is almost always a negative, non-productive, and harmful state. All resources expended to deal with sickness are, therefore, fundamentally economically unproductive. Health, on the other hand, has a very high value in our culture. To the
60 extent that healthy members of the population are replaced by sick members, the economy is doubly burdened. Nevertheless, the per capita cost of preven-tive measures for specific diseases is generally far lower than the per capita cost of curative medicine
65 applied to treatment of the same disease. Prominent examples are dental caries, poliomyelitis and phenyl-ketonuria.

There is an imperative need to provide care for the sick person within a single medical care system, but
70 there is no overriding reason why a linkage is neces-

sary between the two components of a health care sys-tem, prevention and treatment. A national health and medical care program composed of semi-autonomous systems for personal health care and medical care
75 would have the advantage of clarifying objectives and strategies and of permitting a more equitable division of resources between prevention and cure.

15. The author is primarily concerned to
    (A) refute a counter-argument
    (B) draw a distinction
    (C) discuss a dilemma
    (D) isolate causes
    (E) describe new research

16. The author mentions which of the following as differences between curative and preventive medicine?
    I. Curative medicine is aimed primarily at peo-ple who are already ill while preventive medicine is aimed at healthy people.
    II. Curative medicine is focused on an individ-ual patient while preventive medicine is ap-plied to larger populations.
    III. The per capita cost of curative medicine is generally much higher than the per capita cost of preventive medicine.
    (A) I only
    (B) II only
    (C) I and II
    (D) II and III only
    (D) I, II, and III

17. It can be inferred that the author regards a pro-gram of controlled fluoridation of public water supplies as
    (A) an unnecessary government program which wastes economic resources
    (B) a potentially valuable strategy of preventive medicine
    (C) a government policy which has relatively lit-tle effect on the health of a population
    (D) an important element of curative medicine
    (E) an experimental program the health value of which has not been proved

18. Which of the following best explains the author's use of the phrase "doubly burdened" (lines 61–62)?
    (A) A person who is ill not only does not con-tribute to production, but his treatment con-sumes economic resources.
    (B) The per capita cost of preventive measures is

only one-half of the per capita cost of treatment.

(C) The division between preventive medicine and curative medicine requires duplication of administrative expenses.

(D) The individual who is ill must be rehabilitated after the cure has been successful.

(E) The person who is ill uses economic resources which could be used to finance prevention rather than treatment programs.

19. It can be inferred that the author regards Winslow's monograph (lines 54–55) as
(A) ill conceived
(B) incomplete
(C) authoritative
(D) well organized
(E) highly original

20. The author cites dental caries, poliomyelitis, and phenylketonuria in order to prove that
(A) some diseases can be treated by preventive medicine
(B) some diseases have serious consequences if not treated
(C) preventive medicine need not be linked to treatment
(D) the cost of preventing some diseases is less than the cost for treatment
(E) less money is allocated to prevention of some diseases than to treating them

21. The main reason the author advocates separating authority for preventive medicine from that for curative medicine is
(A) the urgency of treatment encourages administrators to devote more resources to treatment than to prevention
(B) the cost of treating a disease is often much greater than the cost of programs to prevent the disease
(C) the professionals who administer preventive health care programs must be more highly trained than ordinary doctors
(D) curative medicine deals primarily with individuals who are ill while preventive medicine is applied to healthy people
(E) preventive medicine is a relatively recent development while curative medicine has a long history

From the time they were first proposed, the 1962 Amendments to the Food, Drug and Cosmetic Act have been the subject of controversy among some elements of the health community and the pharmaceutical industry. The Amendments added a new requirement for Food and Drug Administration approval of any new drug: The drug must be demonstrated to be effective by substantial evidence consisting of adequate and well-controlled investigations. To meet this effectiveness requirement, a pharmaceutical company must spend considerable time and effort in clinical research before it can market a new product in the United States. Only then can it begin to recoup its investment. Critics of the requirement argue that the added expense of the research to establish effectiveness is reflected in higher drug costs, decreased profits, or both, and that this has resulted in a "drug lag."

The term "drug lag" has been used in several different ways. It has been argued that the research required to prove effectiveness creates a lag between the time when a drug could theoretically be marketed without proving effectiveness and the time when it is actually marketed. "Drug lag" has also been used to refer to the difference between the number of new drugs introduced annually before 1962 and the number of new drugs introduced each year after that date. It is also argued that the Amendments resulted in a lag between the time when the new drugs are available in other countries and the time when the same drugs are available in the United States. And "drug lag" has also been used to refer to a difference in the number of new drugs introduced per year in other advanced nations and the number introduced in the same year in the United States.

Some critics have used "drug lag" arguments in an attempt to prove that the 1962 Amendments have actually reduced the quality of health care in the United States and that, on balance, they have done more harm than good. These critics recommend that the effectiveness requirements be drastically modified or even scrapped. Most of the specific claims of the "drug lag" theoreticians, however, have been refuted. The drop in new drugs approved annually, for example, began at least as early as 1959, perhaps five years before the new law was fully effective. In most instances, when a new drug was available in a foreign country but not in the United States, other effective drugs for the condition were available in the country and sometimes not available in the foreign country used for comparison. Further, although the number of new chemical entities introduced annually dropped from more than 50 in 1959 to about 12 to 18 in the 1960's and 1970's, the number of these that can be termed important—some of them of "breakthrough" caliber—has remained reasonably close to 5 or 6 per year. Few, if any, specific examples have actually been offered to show how the effectiveness requirements have done significant harm to the health of Americans. The requirement does ensure that a patient exposed to a drug has the likelihood of benefiting from it, an assessment that is most important, considering the possibility, always present, that adverse effects will be discovered later.

22. The author is primarily concerned with
    (A) outlining a proposal
    (B) evaluating studies
    (C) posing a question
    (D) countering arguments
    (E) discussing a law

23. The passage states that the phrase "drug lag" has been used to refer to all of the following situations EXCEPT
    (A) a lag between the time when a new drug becomes available in a foreign country and its availability in the United States
    (B) the time period between which a new drug would be marketed if no effectiveness research were required and the time it is actually marketed
    (C) the increased cost of drugs to the consumer and the decreased profit margins of the pharmaceutical industry
    (D) the difference between the number of drugs introduced annually before 1962 and the number introduced after 1962
    (E) the difference between the number of new drugs introduced in a foreign country and the number introduced in the United States

24. The author would most likely agree with which of the following statements?
    (A) Whatever "drug lag" may exist because of the 1962 Amendments is justified by the benefit of effectiveness studies.
    (B) The 1962 Amendments have been beneficial in detecting adverse effects of new drugs before they are released on the market.
    (C) Because of the requirement of effectiveness studies, drug consumers in the United States pay higher prices than consumers in foreign countries.
    (D) The United States should limit the number of new drugs which can be introduced into this country from foreign countries.
    (E) Effectiveness studies do not require a significant investment of time or money on the part of the pharmaceutical industry.

25. The author points out the drop in new drugs approved annually before 1959 in order to
    (A) draw an analogy between two situations
    (B) suggest an alternative causal explanation
    (C) attack the credibility of an opponent
    (D) justify the introduction of statistics
    (E) show an opponent misquoted statistics

26. The author implies that the non-availability of a drug in the United States and its availability in a foreign country is not necessarily proof of a drug lag because this comparison fails to take into account
    (A) the number of new drugs introduced annually before 1959
    (B) the amount of research done on the effectiveness of drugs in the United States
    (C) the possible availability of another drug to treat the same condition
    (D) the seriousness of possible unwanted side effects from untested drugs
    (E) the length of time needed to accumulate effectiveness research

27. The author attempt to respond to the claim that the number of new chemical entities introduced annually since the Amendments has dropped by
    (A) denying that the total number of new chemical entities has actually dropped
    (B) analyzing the economic factors responsible for the drop
    (C) refining terminology to distinguish important from non-important chemical entities
    (D) proposing that further studies be done to determine the effectiveness of new chemical entities
    (E) listing the myriad uses to which each new chemical entity can be put

28. The comparisons made by proponents of the "drug lag" theory between the availability of drugs in foreign countries and their availability in the United States logically depend upon which of the following presuppositions?

    I. The pharmaceutical industry in the foreign country is roughly as sophisticated as that in the United States.
    II. The pharmaceutical industry in the foreign country is more profitable than that of the United States.
    III. New drugs in the United States are subject to a more rigorous testing requirement than new drugs in the foreign country.

(A) I only
(B) II only
(C) III only
(D) I and III only
(E) I, II, and III

What we expect of translation is a reasonable facsimile of something that might have been said in our language, but there is involved in this notion of reasonable facsimile a debate between critics as to what constitutes a reasonable facsimile. Most of us at heart belong to the "soft-line" party: a given translation may not be exactly "living language," but the facsimile is generally reasonable. The "hard-line" party aims only for the good translation. The majority of readers never notice the difference, as they read passively, often missing stylistic integrity so long as the story holds them. Additionally, a literature like Japanese may even be treated to an "exoticism handicap."

Whether or not one agrees with Roy A. Miller's postulation of an attitude of mysticism by the Japanese toward their own language, it is true that the Japanese have special feelings toward the possibilities of their language and its relation to life and art, and these feelings have an effect on what Japanese writers write about and how they write. Many of the special language relationships are not immediately available to the non-Japanese (which is only to say that the Japanese language, like every other, has some unique features). For example, in my own work on Dazai Osamu, I have found how close to the sense of the rhythms of spoken Japanese his writing is, and how hard that is to duplicate in English. Judas's cackling hysterically, "Heh, heh, heh" (in *Kakekomi uttae*), or the coy poutings of a schoolgirl (in *Joseito*) have what Masao Miyoshi has called, in *Accomplices of Silence,* an "embarrassing" quality. It is, however, the embarrassment of recognition that the reader of Japanese feels. The moments simply do not work in English.

Even the orthography of written Japanese is a resource not open to us. Tanizaki Jun'ichirō, who elsewhere laments the poverty of "indigenous" Japanese vocabulary, writes in *Bunshō tokuhon* of the contribution to literary effect——to "meaning," if you will——made simply by the way a Japanese author chooses to "spell" a word. In Shiga Naoya's *Kinosaki nite,* for example, the onomatopoeic "bu——n" with which a honeybee takes flight has a different feeling for having been written in *hiragana* instead of *katakana*. I read, and I am convinced. Arishima Takeo uses onomatopoeic words in his children's story *Hitofusa no budō,* and the effect is not one of baby talk, but of gentleness and intimacy that automatically pulls the reader into the world of childhood fears, tragedies, and consolations, memories of which lie close under the surface of every adult psyche.

This, of course, is hard to reproduce in translation, although translators labor hard to do so. George Steiner speaks of an "intentional strangeness," a "creative dislocation," that sometimes is invoked in the attempt. He cites Chateaubriand's 1836 translation of Milton's *Paradise Lost,* for which Chateaubriand "created" a Latinate French to approximate Milton's special English as an example of just such a successful act of creation. He also laments what he calls the " 'moon in pond like blossom weary' school of instant exotica," with which we are perhaps all too familiar.

29. The author is primarily concerned with
    (A) criticizing translators who do not faithfully reproduce the style of works written in another language
    (B) suggesting that Japanese literature is more complex than English literature
    (C) arguing that no translation can do justice to a work written in another language
    (D) demonstrating that Japanese literature is particularly difficult to translate into English
    (E) discussing some of the problems of translating Japanese literature into English

30. It can be inferred that *Accomplices of Silence* is
    (A) an English translation of Japanese poetry
    (B) a critical commentary on the work of Dazai Osamu
    (C) a prior publication by the author on Japanese literature
    (D) a text on Japanese orthography
    (E) a general work on the problem of translation

31. The author cites Shiga Naoya's *Kinosaki nite* in order to
    (A) illustrate the effect that Japanese orthography has on meaning
    (B) demonstrate the poverty of indigenous Japanese vocabulary
    (C) prove that it is difficult to translate Japanese into English
    (D) acquaint the reader with an important work of Japanese literature
    (E) impress upon the reader the importance of faithfully translating a work from one language into another

32. With which of the following statements would the author most likely agree?
    (A) The Japanese language is the language best suited to poetry.
    (B) English is one of the most difficult languages into which to translate any work written in Japanese.
    (C) It is impossible for a person not fluent in Japanese to understand the inner meaning of Japanese literature.
    (D) Most Japanese people think that their language is uniquely suited to conveying mystical ideas.
    (E) Every language has its own peculiar potentialities which present challenges to a translator.

33. It can be inferred that the Japanese word "bu——n" is most like which of the following English words?
    (A) bee
    (B) honey
    (C) buzz
    (D) flower
    (E) moon

34. The author uses all of the following EXCEPT
    (A) examples to prove a point
    (B) citation of authority
    (C) analogy
    (D) personal knowledge
    (E) contrasting two viewpoints

35. It can be inferred that the "exoticism handicap" mentioned by the author is
    (A) the tendency of some translators of Japanese to render Japanese literature in a needlessly awkward style
    (B) the attempt of Japanese writers to create for their readers a world characterized by mysticism
    (C) the lack of literal, word-for-word translational equivalents for Japanese and English vocabulary
    (D) the expectation of many English readers that Japanese literature can only be understood by someone who speaks Japanese
    (E) the difficulty a Japanese reader encounters in trying to penetrate the meaning of difficult Japanese poets

STOP

END OF SECTION! IF YOU HAVE ANY TIME LEFT, GO OVER YOUR WORK IN THIS SECTION ONLY. DO NOT WORK IN ANY OTHER SECTION OF THE TEST.

PRACTICE EXAMINATION 3
ANSWER KEY

SECTION I

1.	B	8.	C	15.	A	22.	E	29.	D
2.	D	9.	B	16.	D	23.	B	30.	A
3.	C	10.	A	17.	B	24.	D	31.	C
4.	B	11.	E	18.	C	25.	D	32.	A
5.	B	12.	D	19.	E	26.	E	33.	A
6.	B	13.	C	20.	A	27.	A	34.	E
7.	A	14.	D	21.	B	28.	E	35.	A

SECTION II

1.	C	7.	A	13.	C	19.	C	25.	D
2.	C	8.	E	14.	B	20.	D	26.	E
3.	A	9.	E	15.	C	21.	A	27.	B
4.	E	10.	D	16.	A	22.	C	28.	E
5.	A	11.	D	17.	D	23.	A	29.	B
6.	E	12.	A	18.	B	24.	B	30.	E

SECTION III

1.	C	8.	B	15.	C	22.	D	29.	E
2.	E	9.	D	16.	E	23.	A	30.	E
3.	B	10.	E	17.	C	24.	C	31.	C
4.	E	11.	B	18.	C	25.	A	32.	A
5.	D	12.	A	19.	C	26.	C	33.	E
6.	B	13.	B	20.	A	27.	E	34.	D
7.	C	14.	B	21.	D	28.	B	35.	A

SECTION IV

1.	B	8.	D	15.	B	22.	D	29.	E
2.	C	9.	D	16.	E	23.	C	30.	B
3.	E	10.	A	17.	B	24.	A	31.	A
4.	D	11.	B	18.	A	25.	B	32.	E
5.	A	12.	B	19.	C	26.	C	33.	C
6.	E	13.	E	20.	D	27.	C	34.	C
7.	E	14.	A	21.	A	28.	D	35.	A

EXPLANATORY ANSWERS

SECTION I

1. **(B)** This is a main idea question presented in the format of a sentence completion. We are looking for the answer choice which, when added to the question stem, produces a sentence that summarizes the main thesis of the passage. Insofar as the verbs are concerned, that is, the first words of each choice, each choice seems acceptable. One could say that the author is concerned to "suggest," "demonstrate," "explain," "discuss," or "describe." So we must look at the fuller content of each choice. The author begins the passage by noting that there were two schools of thought on how to reduce unemployment, and then proceeds to describe the main ideas of both schools of thought. Finally, the author concludes by noting that, for all of their avowed differences, both schools share considerable common ground. This development is captured very well by (B). (A) is perhaps the second best choice. It is true that the author does mention some economic tools which can be used to control unemployment, but the main thesis is not that such ways exist. Rather, the main thesis, as pointed out by (B), is that the two groups, during the 1960s, had seemingly different yet ultimately similar views on how the tools could best be used. (C) is incorrect since the discussion of structural inefficiencies is only a minor part of the development. (D) is incorrect because the discussion of disunity is included simply to give a more complete picture of the debate and not to show that this prevented the achievement of full employment. Finally, the CEA is mentioned as a matter of historical interest, but its role is not the central focus of the passage.

2. **(D)** This is an explicit idea question. Each of the incorrect answers is mentioned as a possible barrier to achieving 4 percent unemployment in the discussion of structural inefficiencies of the third paragraph. There reference is made to the effect of technological innovation, the shortage of skilled labor, the problem of minority and un-skilled labor, and the reserve of workers not yet counted as being in the labor force. There is no mention, however, of the need to relocate workers to areas of labor shortage. The only reference to relocation is in the final paragraph. Since (D) is never mentioned as a possible barrier to achieving the 4 percent goal, it is the correct answer.

3. **(C)** This is an attitude or tone question. The author refers to the position of the hyperenthusiasts as "not very plausible," which indicates he does not endorse the position. On this ground we can eliminate (A). (B) can be eliminated on the same ground, and on the further ground that "light-hearted" is not a good description of the tone of the passage. (D) and (E), however, are overstatements. Though the author obviously rejects the position of the hyperenthusiasts, there is no evidence that he holds so negative an attitude as those suggested by (D) and (E). (C) describes well the author's mood. He mentions the position and then does not even bother to discuss it.

4. **(B)** This is an explicit idea question. The needed reference is found in the second paragraph. The difference between the CEA and the dissenting expansionists grew out of the question of where to spend the money that would be used to stimulate the economy. The dissenting faction wanted to target the expansionary spending for public services and low-income groups. (B) presents this difference very well. (A) is incorrect and conflates the dissenting expansionists (paragraph 2) and the structuralists (paragraph 3). (C) commits the same error. (D) represents a misreading of the second paragraph: The CEA were expansionists. (E) is incorrect since the passage does not state that the CEA were conservatives.

5. **(B)** This is an explicit idea question. Information which would bear on the issue raised by statement II is included in the third paragraph. As for statement I, there is no such information in the passage. In the first paragraph, the author mentions that the economy failed to expand rapidly in

the early 1960's, but he offers no explanation for that phenomenon. And III is never mentioned at any point in the text. So our correct answer must be II only.

6. **(B)** The author mentions a dissenting group of expansionists in the closing lines of paragraph 2. This question asks about his attitude toward those economists. The author remarks of their arguments that their commitment to certain political ideals likely interfered with their economic judgments. For this reason he places very little faith in their arguments. (B) nicely brings out this point. (A) is incorrect. Though the author does discount the value of their conclusions, he does not do so because they were not trained as economists. As for (C), there is nothing which suggests that the author lacks information. Rather, it seems from the passage that the author has what he believes is sufficient information to discount the position. (D) is clearly in contradiction to this analysis and must be incorrect, and (E) can be eliminated on the same ground.

7. **(A)** Here we have a relatively easy inference question. The hyperenthusiasts used structuralist-type arguments to contend that jobs were already available. That being the case, the hyperenthusiasts dissented from both the positions of the expansionists and the structuralists who believed unemployment to be a problem. We may infer, then, that the essence of the hyperenthusiasts' position was that no government action was needed at all—at least no government action of the sort being discussed by the main camps described by the author. As for (B), nowhere in the passage does the author state or even hint that anyone overestimated the number of people out of work. As for (C), this represents a reading which confuses the hyperenthusiasts (paragraph 4) with the main-line structuralists (paragraph 3). (D) is incorrect and conflates the hyperenthusiasts of the expansionary school of thought with those of the structuralist school. Finally, (E) is incorrect since it describes the position of the main group of expansionists.

8. **(C)** This is obviously a main idea question. The author discusses three important characteristics of art of the Middle Ages—the sacred script, the sacred mathematics, and sacred symbolic language. At the close of his remarks, the author mentions in passing the Renaissance, primarily as a way of praising the art of the Middle Ages. (C) does a fair job of describing this development.

(A) can be eliminated because the discussion focuses upon the art of the Middle Ages, not upon the art preceding the Middle Ages. And to the extent that the author does mention what might be called influences, e.g., the revival of certain views of Pythagoras, he does so in passing. They do not constitute the focus of the passage. (D) is incorrect for the same sort of reason. The reference in closing to the art of the Renaissance cannot be considered the overall theme of the passage. Finally, (B) and (E) are incorrect because the author never takes on the "why."

9. **(B)** This is an inference question. In essence, the question is asking which of the five features listed was most likely to be found in a painting. (E) can be eliminated since that is inconsistent with the concept of the artist who recedes into the background of the sacred rules. As for (A), the author's only example of numbers was their use in music. This does not lead us to conclude that numbers might not be important in painting as well, but we cannot conclude, on the other hand, that every painting was likely to use the numbers 3 and 4. (C) and (D) are mentioned as characteristics of certain subjects. But the author does not imply that the subjects were treated in every painting. (B), however, has the specific support of paragraph 3. There the author states that "Every painting is an allegory." So, though the specific content of paintings of the period would vary from work to work, the overarching idea of a literal and hidden meaning pervaded the work of the period.

10. **(A)** The tone of the passage is clearly one of appreciation—both in the sense that the author understands and in the sense that he admires what he understands. This is further supported by the contrast between art of the Middle Ages and religious art of the Renaissance at the end of the passage. (B) overstates the case. The author is only discussing the one period, with only casual reference to the period following it. We cannot conclude from the fact that he discusses art of the Middle Ages in this text, that he considers this art the greatest of all art. (C) cannot be deduced from the passage; the reference to music will not support such a judgment. (D) is inconsistent with the author's opening and closing remarks. Finally, (E) too must be incorrect given the general approving treatment of the passage.

11. **(E)** This is a question about a logical detail: Why does the author quote Saint Augustine? At that

point, the author has just asserted that the art of the Middle Ages also is characterized by a passion for numbers. Then he quotes a statement from Augustine which makes that very point. The reason for the quotation must be to give an example of the general attitude toward numbers. Answer choice (E) describes this move. (A) is incorrect since no objection is mentioned. (B) is incorrect for the same reason, and for the further reason that "ridicule" is inconsistent with the tone of the passage. (C) is incorrect because the author is not attempting to demonstrate the similarities between two things. Finally, (D) is incorrect since it does not appear that the author is in any danger of falling into a contradiction.

12. **(D)** This is an explicit idea question. Each of the incorrect answers is mentioned in paragraph 1 as an element of the sacred script. As for (A), lines may be used to represent water or the sky. As for (B), these indicate sainthood or divinity. As for (C), shoes are mentioned as an identifying characteristic. And (E) also is mentioned (a tree represents earth). (D), however, is not mentioned as an element of the sacred script. Symmetry is discussed in conjunction with numbers, and that has to do with another characteristic altogether.

13. **(C)** This is an application question. Of course, we do not know where the passage actually appeared, and the task is to pick the most likely source. We stress this because it is always possible to make an argument for any of the answer choices to a question of this sort. But the fact that a justification is possible does not make that choice correct; the strongest possible justification makes the choice correct. (C) is the most likely source. The passage focuses on art and is scholarly in tone. (A) can be eliminated, for the passage casts no light on social conditions of the period. (B) can be eliminated for a similar reason. The author treats art in and of itself—not as a social force. And we certainly cannot conclude that by discussing religious art the author wants to discuss the church. (D) is incorrect because the reference to Saint Augustine is incidental and illustrative only. (E) is incorrect because it is inconsistent with the scholarly and objective tone of the passage.

14. **(D)** This is an inferred idea question, one asking for an interpretation of a phrase. The idea of the first paragraph is that the rules of art in the Middle Ages placed constraints on the artist so that

his artistic effort had to be made within certain conventions. As a result, painting was not individualistic. This is most clearly expressed by (D). (A) is incorrect since the author is saying that the artist's talent just did not show as individual talent. (B) is incorrect, for though this is a true statement, it is not a response to the question. (C) is perhaps the second best answer because it at least hints at what (D) says more clearly. But the author does not mean to say the artist was not recognized in his lifetime. Perhaps he was. What the author means to say is that we do not now see the personality of the artist. Finally, (E) is just a confused reading of a part of the passage not relevant here.

15. **(A)** This is an application. As we have noted before, application questions tend to be difficult because the correct answer can be understood as correct only in context. With an explicit idea question, for example, an answer can be understood as right or wrong—either the author said it or he did not. With a question such as this, the *most logical continuation* depends upon the choices available. Here the best answer is (A). The author concludes the discussion of the causes of our poor showing on the health status index by asserting that the best way to improve this showing is a general improvement in the quality of life. This is an intriguing suggestion, and an appropriate follow-up would be a list of proposals that might accomplish this. As for (B), this could be part of such a discussion, but a listing of the most common causes of death would not, in and of itself, represent an extension of the development of the argument. (C), too, has some merit. The author might want to talk abut the causes of poverty as a way of learning how to improve the quality of life by eliminating the causes. But this argument actually cuts in favor of (A), for the justification for (C) then depends on (A)—that is, it depends on the assumption that the author should discuss the idea raised in (A). (D) is incorrect because the author specifically states in his closing remarks that redistribution of medical resources is not a high priority. (E) can be eliminated on the same ground.

16. **(D)** This is an explicit idea question, and we find mention of (A), (B), (C), and (E) in the second paragraph. (D), too, is mentioned, but (D) is not a factor "affecting the health of the population." (D) is a measure of, or an effect of, the health of the population, not a factor causing it.

17. **(B)** This is a main idea question. (A) can be eliminated because the author actually minimizes the importance of medical care as a factor affecting the health of a population. (C) can be eliminated because this is not the author's objective. To be sure, an individual may use information supplied in the passage to improve in some way his or her health, but that is not why the author wrote the passage. (D) is incorrect because this is a small part of the argument, a part which is used to advance the major objective outlined in (B). Finally, (E) is incorrect since the author leaves us with a pregnant suggestion but no specific recommendations. (B), however, describes the development of the passage. The author wishes to explain the causes of the poor health status of the U.S. It is not, he argues, lack of medical care or even poor distribution of medical care, hypotheses which, we can infer from the text, are often proposed. He then goes on to give two alternative explanations: affluence and poverty.

18. **(C)** This is an application question. (C) is strongly supported by the text. In paragraph 3, the author specifically states that we have the highest per capita expenditure for medical care in the world. Yet, as he notes in the first paragraph, we rank rather low in terms of health. (A) is not supported by the arguments given in the passage. Though medical care may not be the most important determinant of health, the author never suggests that expenditure is not correlated with overall availability. (B) is incorrect and specifically contradicted by the second paragraph, where the author states that genetic problems may be covered over by medical care. (D) is incorrect since the author minimizes the importance of technology in improving health. Finally, (E) is simply not supported by any data or argument given in the passage.

19. **(E)** This is a logical detail question. The author refers to excess consumption to illustrate the way in which affluence, one of his two hypotheses, could undermine an individual's health. As for (A), while it is true that such problems may not be susceptible to medical treatment, the author does not introduce them to prove that. He introduces them at the particular point in the argument to prove that affluence can undermine health. (B) is incorrect for a similar reason. The author does not introduce the examples to prove that drinking and smoking are unhealthful activities. He presupposes his readers know that already. Then, on the assumption that the reader already believes that, the author can say, "See, affluence causes smoking and drinking—which we all know to be bad." (C) must fail for the same reason. Finally (D) is incorrect since this is not the reason for introducing the examples. Although the author does argue that medical care and health are not as tightly linked as some people might think, this is not the point he is working on when he introduces smoking and drinking. With a logical detail question of this sort, we must be careful to select an answer which explains why the author makes the move he does at the particular juncture in the argument. Neither general reference to the overall idea of the passage, (e.g., to prove his main point) nor a reference to a collateral argument will turn the trick.

20. **(A)** The answer to the question posed in answer choice (A) is explicitly provided in the second paragraph: environment. As for (B), though some information is given about the health status of the U.S., no other country is mentioned by name. As for (C), though some statistics are given about life expectancies in the U.S., no comparison of male and female life expectancies is given. As for (D), though genetic factors are mentioned generally in paragraph 2, no such factors are ever specified. Finally, the author offers no recommendations, so (E) must be incorrect.

21. **(B)** This is an inferred idea based on a specific reference. In the second paragraph, the author lists four groups of factors that influence health. In referring to medical services, he says they are treated separately from environmental factors because of our special interest in them. This implies that he would actually consider them to be just another, although important, factor in the environment. As for (A), the least important group of factors is specifically stated to be genetic factors. As for (C), there is no support for such a conclusion in that paragraph. The same reason allows us to eliminate both (D) and (E).

22. **(E)** This is an explicit idea question. The answer can be found in the first paragraph, where the author notes that a heart attack is unlike an angina attack because the heart attack always involves the death of heart muscle. As for (A), although a heart attack may involve acceleration of the heart beat, this is not what distinguishes it from angina. (B) is incorrect since the author describes the way in which nitroglycerin may be used to treat heart

attack. (C) is incorrect both because this is not a statement which can be justified by the text (generally?) and because it is not the defining characteristic of a heart attack. Finally, (D) is incorrect, for though the heart attack involves rapid muscle death, it is the death of tissue and not the length of time of the attack that is the distinguishing feature.

23. **(B)** This, too, is an explicit idea question, but it is more difficult than the preceding question. The author cites the "curious" result that the nitroglycerin helped the most seriously stricken patients but did not help the less seriously stricken patients. He explains that in the more seriously stricken patients the ordinary autonomic response to a drop in blood pressure, which would be a faster heart rate, did not occur. Apparently, the congestive heart failure effectively blocked this reaction. Consequently, the drop in blood pressure caused by the nitroglycerin did not invite the normal increase in heart rate. This explanation is presented by choice (B). (A) is incorrect since no mention is made of any delay in administering drugs. (C) is incorrect since phenylephrine was not available to the 12 patients at the time of the study. Phenylephrine was later used to counter the drop in blood pressure caused by nitroglycerin. (D) is incorrect since the passage states that blood pressure did drop in those patients with congestive heart failure. The difference between those patients and the less seriously stricken ones was that the drop in blood pressure did not cause an increase in heart rate. For the same reason, (E) must also be eliminated.

24. **(D)** This is an explicit idea question. As for (A), several results of heart attack are mentioned at various points in the text. The answer to (B) is explicitly provided in the third paragraph. As for (C), the author mentions the effect of nitroglycerin at various points, e.g., dilates blood vessels, reduces blood pressure. Finally, (E) is answered in the second paragraph. (D), however, is not answered in the passage. Though the author discusses the effects of heart attack, he does not discuss the causes of heart attack.

25. **(D)** The answer to this inference question can be found in the final paragraph. There the author states that research is being done on drugs which affect myocardial oxygen supply and demand "including . . . vessel dilators such as nitroglycerin. . . . From this we can infer that nitroglycerin dilates blood vessels and this somehow affects the oxygen balance in the heart muscle. This is

the value of the drug. (A) is incorrect because the lowering of blood pressure is an unwanted side effect of nitroglycerin, not its medical value. (B) is incorrect since the value of nitroglycerin is to prevent damage, not to aid in healing. (C) is incorrect for the same reason that (A) is incorrect. Finally, (E) is incorrect because nitroglycerin is mentioned as a vessel dilator in the final paragraph, not a drug that counters hypertension.

26. **(E)** This is a tone question. The author's attitude is best studied in the final paragraph. Having described the possibility of treating heart attack with nitroglycerin, he adds the disclaimer that there is no proof yet of the value of the treatment in very serious cases. From this we may infer, however, that the author believes it has some value in less serious cases. Moreover, since he refers to research being done, he apparently believes that the treatment may prove to have value in other cases as well. This attitude is best described as one of optimism. Since the passage has, on balance, a positive tone, we can eliminate (B), (C), and (D). As for (A), though the author may be concerned about the treatment of heart attacks, the overall tone of the discussion is not concern or worry, but rather hope or optimism.

27. **(A)** This is an inference question the answer to which is found in the second paragraph. There it is stated that phenylephrine is used to maintain blood pressure; but that simple statement is not enough to answer the question. We must dig deeper. Why is it important to maintain blood pressure? The final sentence of the paragraph states that a drop in blood pressure causes the heart to speed up. It is this increase in heart rate which "worsens the damage." So the value of phenylephrine is that it prevents cardiac acceleration by maintaining blood pressure. This is the explanation given in choice (A). As for (B) and (C), these answers make essentially the same statement using language drawn from different parts of the passage. But they describe something other than the effect of phenylephrine. (D) is incorrect since the phenylephrine has a particular use that complements nitroglycerin. Although the effect of both drugs taken together may be something like that described in (D), this is not an answer to the question asked. Finally, (E) is just language taken from the first paragraph and is not an answer to the question asked.

28. **(E)** This is a main idea question. The best way of describing the development of the passage is giv-

en in (E). The author is discussing a treatment for heart attack. As for (A), the only suggestion of a predicament is contained in paragraph 1: Nitroglycerin has beneficial effects, but it also lowers blood pressure. But once that has been stated, the author proceeds to explain how the dilemma has been resolved. So the passage, if anything, explains not a predicament but how a predicament has been solved. As for (B), though the author does evaluate the results of a study, that evaluation is incidental to the larger goals of describing a treatment. As for (C), though we, the readers, may see implicit in the treatment some sort of proposal, it cannot be said that the author's intention is to outline a proposal. Finally, (D) is the least effective choice since there is no argument presented.

29. **(D)** This is a main idea question. The author begins by stating that it would be useful to have a general index to measure welfare and notes that some have even suggested the GNP might be adapted for that purpose. He then proceeds to demonstrate why such an index cannot be constructed. Generally, then, the author shows the defects in a proposal for a general index of welfare, and (D) nicely describes this development. (A) is incorrect for the author never produces any arguments for the position he is attacking. And even when the author raises points such as the suggestion that hours worked might be a measure of cost of production, he is not citing arguments for that position; he is only mentioning the position to attack it. (B) is incorrect since the author is attacking and not defending the proposal discussed. (C) is easily eliminated because the author never attacks the sincerity of those he opposes. Finally, (E) is wrong, for the author never reviews any literature on the subject he is discussing.

30. **(A)** This is an inference question. We turn to the second paragraph. There the author mentions that a general index of welfare would have to include some measure of the cost of producing the output. He suggests that someone might think hours worked would do the trick. He rejects that position by noting that hours worked, as a statistic, does not take account of the quality of the worktime, e.g., long-hours versus short-hours, working conditions, satisfaction of workers. Answer (A) best describes this argument. (B) is incorrect, for the author discusses environmental costs in connection with another aspect of a general index. (C) is incorrect since this distinction is never

used by the author. (D) is incorrect since this is not mentioned as a goal of such a measure. Finally, (E) confuses the GNP, mentioned in the first part of the paragraph, with the index to measure real costs.

31. **(C)** This is an inference question which asks about the main point of the passage. The author adduces several objections to the idea of a general index of welfare. Then the final blow is delivered in the last paragraph: Even if you could devise measures for these various components of a general index, any combination or weighting of the individual measures would reflect only the judgment (personal preference) of the weighter. For this reason alone, argues the author, the entire idea is unworkable. (C) makes this point. (A) and (D) can be eliminated since the author never uses cost or time as arguments against the index. (B) can be eliminated on similar ground. The author may recognize that considerable research would be needed to attempt such measures, yet he does not bother to use that as an objection. (E) can be eliminated for a similar reason. The author may have some arguments against the way such statistics are gathered now, but he does not bother to make them. His argument has the structure: Even assuming there are such data, we cannot combine these statistics to get a general measure of the quality of the environment.

32. **(A)** This is a tone question, and the justification for (A) is already implicit in the discussion thus far. The author sees fatal theoretical weaknesses inherent in the idea of an index of welfare. So we might say that he regards such a notion as an unrealistic, that is, unachievable, dream. (B) is incorrect because the author does not believe the idea can ever be implemented. (C), (D), and (E) can be eliminated on substantially the same ground.

33. **(A)** This is an explicit idea question. In the second paragraph, the author acknowledges that the GNP is a fairly accurate measure of output. He never suggests that the GNP can estimate needs, predict welfare, or measure welfare generally. So we can eliminate the remaining choices.

34. **(E)** This is an explicit idea question, with a thought reverser. (A), (B), (C), and (D) are all mentioned in the third paragraph as aspects of a needs index. The fourth paragraph does not treat the idea of a needs index but the idea of a physical

environment index. That is where the author discusses the items mentioned in (E). So the author does mention the items covered by (E), but not as part of a needs index.

35. **(A)** This is an application question. We are looking for the most likely place for the passage. To be sure, it is possible that the passage might appear in any of the five suggested locations, but the most likely place is that suggested by (A). This could easily be one of a series of papers addressed to a group meeting to discuss public policy decisions. As for (B), it is not likely that the passage would be an introduction to a general text on statistics. It is too firmly dedicated to a particular idea, and the use of statistics is in a way subordinate to the theoretical discussion. (C) is inappropriate since the discussion bears only remotely on programs to aid the poor. (D) is even less likely since the passage does not discuss the foundations of government. Finally, (E) is to a certain extent plausible, but (A) is more closely connected to the content of the passage.

SECTION II

Questions 1–6

Here we have a linear ordering problem involving ten individuals. Since the number of individuals is so large, we will probably do better to sketch a diagram for each problem; after all, the diagram is nothing more than a series of positions numbered 1 through 10. We should also summarize the particular restrictions placed on each color pennant:

2 Green, 2 Blue, 3 Red, 3 Yellow
G = G (Greens are next to each other.)
B ≠ B (Blues are not next to each other.)
R = R = R (Reds are next to each other.)
B/R = ends (Blue at one end; red at the other.)

1. **(C)** We begin by entering the additional information:

```
1  2  3  4  5  6  7  8  9  10
         G  G           R
```

And since the red pennants are together, and one of the pennants on the end is red and the other blue, we know

```
1  2  3  4  5  6  7  8  9  10
B        G  G        R  R  R
```

The only condition remaining to be observed is to separate the blue penants. This means the remaining blue pennant can be placed in positions 3, 6, and 7, and that yellow pennants will fill the remaining places. Now we turn to the answer choices. (A), (B), (D), and (E) are all incorrect since the other blue pennant can occupy positions 3 or 6 or 7, though precisely which is not determined. In any event, no matter which position the remaining blue pennant occupies, position 2 will be occupied by a yellow pennant, so both blue pennants will be next to yellow penants.

2. **(C)** We enter the additional information on a diagram:

```
1  2  3  4  5  6  7  8  9  10
                  B  Y
```

Then, since the red pennants are together, with one on one end and a blue pennant on the other end, we deduce

```
1  2  3  4  5  6  7  8  9  10
R  R  R           B  Y     B
```

We now must place two yellow and two green pennants; since the green pennants must go next to each other, they must occupy position 4 and 5, or 5 and 6:

```
1 2 3 4 5 6 7 8 9 10
R R R G G Y B Y Y B
```

or: R R R Y G G B Y Y B

We can see from the diagram that position 5 is necessarily occupied by a green pennant.

3. **(A)** We begin by entering the additional information on a diagram:

```
1 2 3 4 5 6 7 8 9 10
B G G B Y Y Y R R R
```

or: R R R Y Y Y B G G B

There are only two possible arrangements given all of the restrictions. Since the question stem stipulates that the blue pennants are next to green pennants, we know those four pennants form a bloc, BGGB, at one end or the other. Further, at the opposite end will be the bloc RRR, which means that the yellow pennants will be adjacent to each other. It is not determined from the information at which end the blue pennants will be and at which end the red pennants will be. But we can see that under either scenario, both the fifth and sixth positions are occupied by yellow pennants.

4. **(E)** We begin by entering the additional information on a diagram:

1 2 3 4 5 6 7 8 9 10
                           Y

So, we deduce

1 2 3 4 5 6 7 8 9 10
R R R   Y Y Y B

for we know that the three red pennants are in a row at one end or the other, and that a blue pennant occupies the other end. The only pennants left to place are the two green pennants, which must be next to each other, and the remaining blue pennant:

1 2 3 4 5 6 7 8 9 10
R R R G G B Y Y Y B

or: R R R B G G Y Y Y B

Then we look to the answer choices. We can see that (A), (B), and (D) are false. Further, (C) is only possibly true. Under either scenario, however, (E) is necessarily true.

5. **(A)** We enter the additional information on a diagram:

1 2 3 4 5 6 7 8 9 10
  Y Y

So we know:

1 2 3 4 5 6 7 8 9 10
B Y Y   R R R

given the restrictions on the red pennants and the end pennants. Now we may also deduce

1 2 3 4 5 6 7 8 9 10
B Y Y B Y G G R R R

because position 2 may not be blue and position 6 and 7 must be green. Now we can see that (B), (C), (D), and (E) are necessarily true and that (A) is necessarily false.

6. **(E)** Given the restriction that one end pennant is blue and that at the other end we have three red pennants, we can deduce the following since the question stem stipulates that one green pennant is next to a blue pennant and the other next to a red pennant:

1 2 3 4 5 6 7 8 9 10
R R R G G B Y Y Y B

or: B Y Y Y B G G R R R

So there are only two possible arrangements given the stipulation of the question stem. We can see that (A) and (B) are possibly, though not necessarily, true. (D) is impossible. (E) is, as the diagram proves, necessarily true.

Questions 7–12

This set is an ordering set with a twist: There are two main orders, depending on whether J is tasted third or seventh. We begin then with the following:

1 2 3 4 5 6 7
     J

or: J

Then we enter the second condition:

1 2 3 4 5 6 7
     J (~N)

or: N   J

Then comes the third condition:

1 2 3 4 5 6 7
     J (~N)

or: N   L J

And the fourth condition:

1 2 3 4 5 6 7
     J (~N)
                      O
or: N   L J

and finally:

1 2 3 4 5 6 7
(~K)   J (~N) O

or: K   N   L J

7. **(A)** L can only be tasted fourth if we use the upper order. In that case, it will be J that is tasted third.

8. **(E)** For M to follow L, we cannot use the lower arrangement, for there L is already scheduled as the sixth wine followed immediately by J. We must therefore use the upper arrangement. The key to the solution is to see that there is a further conclusion to be drawn about the scheduling of K

and N. Our original diagram shows positions 1 and 4, 2 and 5, and 4 and 7 as open and available for the K ? ? ? N schedule. A closer look shows that we can eliminate the 1–4 arrangement, because N cannot be the fourth wine tasted in that sequence. So K and N are either 2 and 5, or 4 and 7, respectively. If, however, M must be tasted immediately following the tasting of L, then K cannot be in position 2. Only if K and N are in positions 4 and 7 can we put L and M together in sequence. So the entire sequence is:

$$1 \quad 2 \quad 3 \quad 4 \quad 5 \quad 6 \quad 7$$
$$L \quad M \quad J \quad K \quad P \quad O \quad N$$

The only position left for P is fifth, and (E) is necessarily true. The other choices are necessarily false.

9. **(E)** M is under no particular restriction with regard to another wine, so M can be inserted in any open position. Positions 1, 2, and 4 are open under the first order. Positions 2, 3, and 5 are open under the second order. So depending on when J is tasted, M could be tasted second, third, fourth, or fifth. M cannot be tasted sixth, however, since either O or L is tasted sixth (depending on when J is tasted).

10. **(D)** This question must be answered on the basis of the information provided in the initial set of conditions. In spite of the fact that these conditions leave considerable flexibility in the scheduling of wines, it is necessarily true that K will be tasted earlier than O. In the second possible order, K is tasted first and necessarily ahead of every other wine. In the first order, K must be tasted either second or fourth (so that N can follow as the third wine after K). So (D) is the correct answer. (A) is incorrect because K could be tasted second under the first arrangement. (B) is incorrect since the second arrangement places L before J. (C) is incorrect since K could follow L under the first arrangement. Finally, (E) is incorrect since M is under no restriction and could be tasted in every position except sixth (see explanation for question 9).

11. **(D)** In order for P to be tasted earlier than N and yet later than O, we must use the second possible sequence, placing O in the second tasting position and P in the third. This means that M will be tasted fifth:

$$1 \quad 2 \quad 3 \quad 4 \quad 5 \quad 6 \quad 7$$
$$K \quad O \quad P \quad N \quad M \quad L \quad J$$

(D) is proved by the diagram to be true, while the other choices are shown by the diagram to be false.

12. **(A)** If M is to be the second wine after P, the first arrangement cannot be used. Under the first arrangement, M and P would have to be tasted second and fourth or fifth and seventh, but K must be second or fourth and N fifth or seventh. Under the second arrangement one sequence is possible: K, O, P, N, M, L, J.

Questions 13–18

This is a selection set, and we begin by setting up the information in more usable form:

(1) V→R
(2) (R & Q)→~P
(3) (Q & P)→~T
(4a) P→(S v U)
(4b) ~(S & U)
(5a) (S v T)
(5b) ~(S & T)

The numbered statements (1) through (5b) correspond to the five conditions given in the set. We have broken the fourth and fifth conditions down into two statements because each of those conditions is actually two conditions. So (4a) corresponds to "If P is selected, then either S or U must be selected," and (4b) corresponds to "S and U cannot both be selected." (5) is treated in similar fashion.

13. **(C)** If neither S nor U is selected, then we know by (5a) that T is selected and by (4a) that P is not selected. Thus far we have eliminated S and U (by stipulation) and P, and we have selected T, which leaves Q, R, and V for consideration. Since P is not selected, we may include both R and Q without violating (2). And having chosen R, we may include V without violating (1). So, on the assumption that neither S nor U is selected, the largest delegation would consist of T, R, Q, and V.

14. **(B)** If V is selected, then by (1) R must also be selected. Further, if P is selected, by (4a) either S or U must be selected. But we also have (5a), and either S or T must be selected. Since we have both (S or U) and (S or T), we will minimize the number selected if we choose S rather than U or T. So the smallest delegation which includes both P and V will also include R and S.

15. **(C)** If P is selected, then by (4a) either S or U must be selected. Since by (4b) we cannot choose both S and U, S cannot be selected. But we know by (5a) that either S or T must be chosen, so we must pick T. As for the incorrect answers, this reasoning eliminates (B) as definitely false. As for (A), we cannot choose Q, for to choose Q along with P would mean we could not select T [by (3)]. But we have already learned that we must choose T because S cannot be chosen. As for (D) and (E), it is possible to choose R or V and R: since Q cannot be selected [see rejection of (A)], this effectively isolates R and V from the other students by breaking the only connection with R and V, which is (2).

16. **(A)** P, Q, and S are a possible three-student delegation. Selecting P requires that we have either S or U (4a), and that condition is satisfied by including S. Having P and Q together means only that we may not have T (3), but that can be avoided if we choose S to satisfy (5a). As for (B), P, Q, and T are not a possible delegation, since Q and P together require that T not be chosen, by (3). As for (C), P, R, and V are not acceptable because, by (5a), we must have either S or T. As for (D), R, S, and T are not permissible because this violates (5b). Finally, (E) is incorrect since the group R, S, and U violates (4b).

17. **(D)** If P is selected, then either S or U must also be selected, by (4a). But if T is chosen, then S cannot be chosen, by (5b), which means that U must be chosen. So it is not possible that U is not chosen. Hence, III must be part of the correct choice. Then, since T and P are chosen, we cannot choose Q, by (3), so II is part of the correct choice. As for statement I, R may or may not be chosen.

18. **(B)** P, R, and T accompanied by U will satisfy all of the requirements. Choosing T satisfies (5a). Then, P and U together satisfy (4a). We do not have S, so both (4b) and (5b) are respected. And since we do not have Q, (2) and (3) are satisfied. Finally, without V, we have no problem with (1). As for (A), P and Q cannot accompany T; that is a violation of (3). As for (C), V must be accompanied by R, by (1); and (D) can be eliminated on the same ground. Finally, as for (E), S and U violates (4b).

Questions 19–24

For this ordering set, the order is so highly undetermined that a single overall diagram is not likely to be of much assistance. Instead, for each problem we will simply sketch the scale using dashes and numbers. To conserve space, we will render the scale horizontally:

$$\underline{1}\ \underline{2}\ \underline{3}\ \underline{4}\ \underline{5}\ \underline{6}\ \underline{7}$$

though a more intuitive approach would use a vertical arrangement:

$$
\begin{array}{c}
7 \\
6 \\
5 \\
4 \\
3 \\
2 \\
1
\end{array}
$$

We know:

$$
\begin{array}{c}
L < M \\
N < J \\
J < K < M \text{ or } M < K < J
\end{array}
$$

We can effectively ignore O and Q since they are placed in positions 1 and 7 and will not change.

19. **(C)** With N as the fifth note, we know that J, in order to be higher than N, must be the sixth note. Then, to keep M higher than L while keeping K between M and J, we must have the order:

1	2	3	4	5	6	7
O	L	M	K	N	J	Q

which demonstrates that (C) is necessarily true, while each other choice is clearly false.

20. **(D)** If M is the sixth note, then J can be no higher than the fourth note, for K must come between J and M. Further, K could be no lower than the third since N must be below J. So we have the following:

1	2	3	4	5	6	7
O	N	J	K	L	M	Q

or: O L N J K M Q

These are not the only possible arrangements with M as note 6, but this does prove that J and N can be third and second, respectively, and fourth and third, respectively. So II and III form the correct answer, since J cannot be in fifth position.

21. **(A)** For K and N to be separated by two notes, they must occupy positions 2 and 5 or 3 and 6. Ignoring the other restrictions we would have four possibilities:

```
1   2   3   4   5   6   7
O   N           K       Q

O       N           K   Q

O   K           N       Q

O       K           N   Q
```

The second and third possibilities are not permissible because K could not be between J and M. The fourth also can be eliminated since N must be lower than M. Only the first is possible, and this proves that K must be the fifth note on the scale. As for (B), though L might be between J and K;

```
1   2   3   4   5   6   7
O   N   J   L   K   M   Q
```

it is not necessarily true that L is between J and K:

```
1   2   3   4   5   6   7
O   N   L   J   K   M   Q
```

As for (C), we have just seen it is possible for M to be the sixth note, but that is not necessarily the case:

```
1   2   3   4   5   6   7
O   N   L   M   K   J   Q
```

As for (D), our diagrams show this is possibly, though not necessarily, the case. Similarly, (E) is incorrect since the diagrams show that L and M may or may not be separated by exactly one note.

22. **(C)** Since K must be between J and M, either J or M must be lower on the scale than K. Additionally, some other note must be lower than whichever note is lower than K; that is, if J is lower than K, then N is lower than K as well, and if M is lower than K, then L is lower than K as well. This means that K can be no lower than the fourth note. The other choices are possibilities:

```
   (A) and (E)      |      (B) and (D)
1 2 3 4 5 6 7       |  1 2 3 4 5 6 7
O N L J K M Q       |  O N J K L M Q
```

23. **(A)** If N is separated by two notes from O, then N must be note 4; and we know J must be above N. Since K can be no lower than fourth, this means K must be note 5, and J note 6, leaving L and M as 2 and 3, respectively.

```
1   2   3   4   5   6   7
O   L   M   N   K   J   Q
```

The diagram confirms that (A) is necessarily true, while each of the other choices is necessarily false.

24. **(B)** If L and N are together, they must be notes 2 and 3, respectively, for both J and M must be higher than L and N, and K must be between J and M on the scale. This means that J, K, and M are notes 4, 5, and 6, though not necessarily in that order. So we have two possibilities:

```
1   2   3   4   5   6   7
O   L   N   J   K   M   Q
```

or: O   L   N   M   K   J   Q

Questions 25–30

Start by summarizing the information:

$$
\begin{aligned}
&W = V \\
&X = T \\
&R \neq U \\
&(R \text{ or } S) = Q \\
&S = \text{Green}
\end{aligned}
$$

25. **(D)** Use the initial conditions to eliminate choices. Using the first condition, eliminate (B) and (C). Using the second condition, eliminate (E). And using the fourth condition, eliminate (A). (D) is a possible seating arrangement:

RED	GREEN	BLUE
TXR	QSU	WVP

26. **(E)** Since S sits at the green table, if R sits at the red table and Q at the blue table, then neither R nor S sits with Q—a violation of the fourth condition.

27. **(B)** X must sit with T. Since only three people can be accommodated at each table, (B) is not a possible arrangement.

28. **(E)** Since W must sit with V and X sit with T, those pairs cannot be seated at the same table.

29. **(B)** If R and W sit at the blue table, then V is also seated at the blue table. Thus, since Q must sit with either S or R, Q is left to sit at the green table with S.

30. **(E)** S and T must be joined at the green by X, and this means that R and Q must sit at the same table, the red table. Therefore, V and W sit at the blue table:

Red	Green	Blue
RQ—	STX	VW—

And since U will not sit with R, the blue table consists of U, V, and W.

SECTION III

1. **(C)** The point of the Chinese official's comment is that the Chinese may appear to some Westerners to be "inscrutable" because those Westerners simply do not pay very careful attention to what is directly before them. Thus, (C) is the best answer. (A) is misleading. The Chinese official refers to Occidentals in general, but he never mentions Orientals in general. Even so, (A) misses the main point of the anecdote. (B) is better than (A) since it is at least generally related to the point of the Chinese official, but the precise point is not that Americans (rather then Occidentals) fail to understand Chinese culture, but rather that they suffer from a more specific myopia: They find they are not able to penetrate the motivations of the Chinese. In any event, the point of the passage is not just that there is such a failure, but that such failure is attributable to the lack of insight of Westerners—not any real inscrutability of the Chinese. (E) mentions the problem of understanding, but the difficulty described in the passage is one way only. Nowhere is it suggested that the Chinese have difficulty in understanding Westerners. Finally, (D) would be correct only if the passage had contained some key word to qualify the official's response, such as *hesitatingly* or *cautiously*.

2. **(E)** Once it is seen that the passage is humorous, this question is fairly easy. The official "smiles" and he "gently" responds. Further, the scenario is set by the first sentence: a *junior* official *embarrassed* himself. This shows the situation is uncomfortable for the American, but it is not a serious international incident. And the Chinese official's response is kind—not angry (A), not fearful (B), not indifferent (D). (C) requires an assumption of malice on the part of the Chinese official. By comparison, "compassion" better fits the description of the official's action—smiling and gentle.

3. **(B)** Here the problem is to make sense out of the brother's claim that a device he rarely used and may never use again is still a good investment. It is not land, a work of art, or some similar thing, so it does not appear as though it will appreciate in value. The advantage, then, of owning must come from merely being able to possess it. Thus, answer (B), which cites the convenience of having the item to use if and when he should decide to do so, is best. (A) can be disregarded because the brother regards the investment as a good one *even if* he never again uses the device. To save money on ice cream, he would have to use it. (C) is highly suggestive—is the brother saying that it is a good idea to have things around in case one needs them? If so, then (C) sounds a bit like (B). But (C) is not nearly so direct as (B), and it requires some work to make it into (B). (D) is wrong because saving money by having purchased earlier would be worthwhile only if the item is actually needed. After all, a great deal you made by buying a ton of hay is not a great deal just because the price of hay is going up—you need an elephant (or a horse, or a plan to resell, or something) to make it worthwhile. Just buying hay because it's a "bargain" is no bargain at all. (E) is fairly silly. It is like saying: "The bad news is you are to be executed tomorrow morning; the good news is you would have had liver for lunch." Or perhaps closer to this example would be: "The bad news is that someone stole your car; the good news is that the price of gasoline went up by 25¢ a gallon this morning." The point is that you will avoid some trivial injury or cost at the expense of something more serious.

4. **(E)** Again, the passage is somewhat lighthearted. The poet is saying that the poem is obscure: When he wrote it only he and the Almighty could understand it, and now (it is so difficult) even he has forgotten the point of the verse. (A) is somewhat attractive because the passage does state that God knows what man does not. Of course, once one understands the point of the passage, (A) can be discarded. Even so, there is something about (A) that lets you know it is wrong—"infinitely." One might infer from the poet's comments that man is not as wise as God, but it is not

possible to conclude, on the basis of the one example, that God is infinitely wiser than man. (B) is also attractive, for the poet is saying that it is difficult to understand this particular poem. But (B) is wrong because he is not saying that men cannot understand poetry in general. (C) and (D) are distractions. They play on the term "God" in the paragraph. The poet cites God as the one who understands the verse——not the one who inspired it.

5. **(D)** Here we have one final humorous passage. Now this should not lead you to conclude that *many* LSAT paragraphs are amusing——to generalize to that conclusion on the basis of three examples would be a fallacy in and of itself—— but taken individually each is reflective of the LSAT. And even if the LSAT does not string together three or four in a row, we hope that you have found them diverting. After all, study for this test is not the most enjoyable pastime available to human beings. But back to the task at hand. . . . You must always be careful of naked correlations. Sufficient research would probably turn up some sort of correlation between the length of skirts and the number of potatoes produced by Idaho, but such a correlation is obviously worthless. Here, too, the two numbers are completely unrelated to one another at any concrete cause-and-effect level. What joins them is the very general movement of the economy. The standard of living increases; so, too, does the average salary of a preacher, the number of vacations taken by factory workers, the consumption of beef, the number of color televisions, and the consumption of rum. (D) correctly points out that these two are probably connected only this way. (A) is incorrect for it is inconceivable that preachers, a small portion of the population, could account for so large an increase in rum consumption. (B) is wildly implausible. (C), however, is more likely. It strives for that level of generality of correlation achieved by (D). The difficulty with (C) is that it focuses upon *total* preachers, not the *average* preacher; and the passage correlated not *total* income for preachers with rum consumption, but *average* income for preachers with consumption of rum. (E) might be arguable if only one period had been used, but the paragraph cites three different times during which this correlation took place.

6. **(B)** This is a relatively easy question. The argument is similar to "All observed instances of S are P; therefore, all S must be P." (All swans I have seen are white; therefore, all swans must be white.) There is little to suggest the author is a mechanic or a factory worker in an automobile plant; therefore, (A) is incorrect——and would be so even if the author were an expert because he does not argue using that expertise. A syllogism is a formal logical structure such as: "All S are M; all M are P; therefore, all S are P," and the argument about automobiles does not fit this structure——so (C) is wrong. By the same token, (E) is wrong since the author generalizes——he does not deduce, as by logic, anything. Finally, (D) is incorrect because the argument is not ambiguous, and one could hardly argue on the basic of ambiguity anyway, especially on the LSAT.

7. **(C)** The key phrase here——and the problem is really just a question of careful reading——is "who actually knew." This reveals that neither of the two knew the person whom they were discussing. There are many ways, however, of debating about the character of people with whom one is not directly acquainted. We often argue about the character of Napoleon or even fictional characters such as David Copperfield. When we do, we are arguing on the basis of indirect information. Perhaps we have read a biography of Napoleon (A), or maybe we have seen a news film of Churchill (B). We may have heard from a friend, or a friend of a friend, that so and so does such and such (E). Finally, sometimes we just make more or less educated guesses, (D). At any event, the two people described in the paragraph could have done all of these things. What they could not have done——since they finally resolved the problem by finding someone who actually knew Churchill——was to have argued on the basis of their own personal knowledge.

8. **(B)** Here we have a question which asks us to draw a conclusion from a set of premises. The author points out that the Constitution provides that the government may not take private property. The irony, according to the author, is that government itself defines what it will classify as private property. We might draw an analogy to a sharing practice among children: You divide the cake and I will choose which piece I want. The idea behind this wisdom is that this ensures fairness to both parties. The author would say that the Constitution is set up so that the government not only divides (defines property), it chooses

(takes what and when it wants). (A) is contradicted by this analysis. (C) is wide of the mark since the author is discussing property rather than liberty. While the two notions are closely connected in the Constitution, this connection is beyond the scope of this argument. (D) is also beyond the scope of the argument. It makes a broad and unqualified claim that is not supported by the text. (E) is really vacuous and, to the extent that we try to give it content, it must fail for the same reason as (A).

9. **(D)** The insight required to solve this problem is that the apparent contradiction can be resolved by observing that the two cases are essentially different. The one is supposed to be a factual story; the other is a fictional account. Only III properly expresses this distinction, and II is simply irrelevant. While it may be true that disapproval is one way of trying to keep members of the profession honest, that has nothing to do with the seeming contradiction in the behavior of the critics. Finally, I contradicts the explicit wording of the passage, which stated that the critics rejected the fictionalization.

10. **(E)** The main point of the advertisement is that you should not hesitate to buy Cold Springs Water even though it is not imported. According to the ad, you will not be able to taste the difference. Thus, I is an assumption of the ad: "Neither you nor your guests will taste the difference," and it is explicitly mentioned. We know it is an assumption because if there were a taste difference, the appeal of the ad would be seriously undermined. III is an assumption, too—but it is hidden or suppressed. Implicit in the ad is a rebuttal to the objection: "Yes, but it is not imported." Whether it is imported or not can have only to do with status since the ad also states (assumes) that the tastes of Cold Springs and imported waters are indistinguishable. II is not an assumption. Although it is mentioned that Cold Springs is bottled at the source, the ad does not depend on where other imported or domestic waters are bottled. They could be bottled 50 miles away from the source, and that would not affect the appeal of the ad.

11. **(B)** Careful reading of the paragraph shows that the author's attitude toward parochial education is that he believes the insistence on instruction in religious values is *justifiable;* he disagrees, however, on the question of how best to inculcate those values. He believes that the proper attitude toward relations between the sexes could best be learned by children in the company of the other sex. Thus, (E) is diametrically opposite to the policy the author would recommend. (A) and (D) must be wrong because the passage clearly indicates that the author supports parochial schools and the religious instruction they provide. (C) is a distraction. It plays on the association of segregation and racial discrimination. Racial segregation is not the only form of segregation. The word *segregation* means generally to separate or to keep separate.

12. **(A)** In this story, the identity of the person who reports the incident is irrelevant. So long as it is not someone with a special infirmity (very poor eyesight, for example) or poor credibility (an inveterate liar), the person is quite capable of reporting what he saw——or what he thought he saw. The most serious weakness of the analysis presented is that it attacks Professor Branch's credentials. To be sure, one might want to question the accuracy of the report: At what time did it occur? What were the lighting conditions? Had the observer been drinking or smoking? But these can be asked independently of attacking the qualifications of the source. Thus, (D) must be wrong, for special credentials are just not needed in this case, so the wrong way to defend Professor Branch is to defend those. By the same token, it makes no sense to defend Branch by launching a counter-*ad hominem* attack on her attacker, so (B) is incorrect. (C) and (E) may or may not be true, but they are surely irrelevant to the question of whether this particular sighting is to be trusted.

13. **(B)** The inquisitor's behavior is paradoxical—that is, internally inconsistent or contradictory. The victim tells him that he is in league with the devil, so the inquisitor refuses to believe him because those in league with the devil never tell the truth. In other words, the inquisitor refuses to believe the victim because he accepts the testimony of the victim. Thus, (B) is correct. (A) is incorrect because the inquisitor does not *withdraw* anything he has said; in fact, he lets everything he has said stand, and that is how he manages to contradict himself. (E) is a bit more plausible, but it is incomplete. In a certain sense, the inquisitor does not accept the answer, but the real point of the passage is that his basis for *not* accepting the answer is that he *does* accept the

answer: He believes the victim when he says he is in league with the devil. (C) and (D) find no support in the paragraph. Nothing suggests that the inquisitor is violating any religious law, and nothing indicates that the inquisitor does not himself believe in the devil.

14. **(B)** The key here is that the word ''nobody'' is used in a cleverly ambiguous way and, as many of you probably know, the ''young lady'' in the story is Lewis Carroll's Alice. This is fairly representative of his word play. (E) must be incorrect since it misses completely the little play on words: ''I saw Nobody,'' encouraging a response such as ''Oh, is he a handsome man?'' (D) is beside the point, for the King is not interested in the messenger's veracity. He may be interested in his reliability (A); but, if anything, we should conclude the King finds the messenger unreliable since ''nobody walks slower'' than the messenger. (C) is wrong because the question is not a matter of eyesight. The King does not say, ''If you had better eyes, you might have seen Nobody.''

15. **(C)** Ann's response would be appropriate only if Mary had said, ''All of the students at State College come from Midland High.'' That is why (C) is correct. (D) is wrong, because they are talking about the background of the students, not the reputations of the schools. (E) is wrong, for the question is from where the students at State College come. (B) is superficially relevant to the exchange, but it, too, is incorrect. Ann would not reply to this statement, had Mary made it, in the way she did reply. Rather, she would have said, ''No, there are some Midland students at State College.'' Finally, Ann would have correctly said (A) only if Mary had said, ''None of the students from North Hills attend State College,'' or ''Most of the students from North Hills do not attend State College.'' But Ann makes neither of these responses, so we know that (A) cannot have been what she thought she heard Mary say.

16. **(E)** If you wanted to determine how politically active people are, what kind of test would you devise? You might do a survey to test political awareness; you might do a survey to find out how many hours people devote to political campaigning each week or how many hours they spend writing letters, etc.; or you might get a rough estimate by studying the voting statistics. The paragraph takes contributions as a measure of political activity. (E) is correct for two reasons. One, the paragraph says nothing about individual activity. It says total contributions were up, not average or per person contributions. Second, (E) cites voting patterns which seem as good as or better an indicator of political activity than giving money. This second reason explains why (A) is wrong. (A) may weaken the argument, but a stronger attack would use voting patterns. (D) confuses individual and corporate contributions, so even if campaign giving were a strong indicator of activity, (D) would still be irrelevant. (B) does not even explain why contributions *in toto* rose during the four years, nor does it tell us anything about the pattern of giving by individual persons. Finally, (C) seems the worst of all the answers, for it hardly constitutes an attack on the author's reasoning. It seems likely that even in the face of increased political activity, public leaders would continue to warn against the dangers of political apathy.

17. **(C)** If you want to determine whether or not drug use is harmful to high school students, you surely would not conduct a survey of the students themselves. This is why (C) is correct. That a student does not *think* a drug is harmful does not mean that it *is not* actually harmful. (E) misses the point of the argument. The author is not attempting to prove that drug use is not widespread; he is trying to show it is not dangerous. (D) is part of an argument often used in debates over legalization of drugs by proponents of legalization. Here, however, it is out of place. The question is whether the drugs are harmless, that is, whether they are, in fact, victimless. (D) belongs to some other part of the debate. (A) sounds like the start of an argument. One might suggest that students change their minds as they get older, and eventually many acknowledge the danger of such drugs. But (A) does not get that far; and, even if it did, (C) would be stronger for it gives us the final statement up to which that argument would only be leading. Finally, (B) is irrelevant. The question here is the harm of drugs, and that issue can be resolved independent of whether other things are harmful, e.g., alcohol or drag-racing.

18. **(C)** Amy points out that Al assumes that any extraterrestrial visitors to Earth, seeking intelligent life, would regard human beings here on Earth as intelligent, and therefore contact us. Amy hints that we might not be intelligent enough to interest them in contacting us. This is

why (C) is the best answer. (A) is wrong. Amy does not miss Al's point: She understands it very well and criticizes it. (B) is wrong since Amy is not suggesting that Al is any less intelligent than any other human being, just that the aliens might regard us all as below the level of intelligence which they are seeking. (D) is more nearly correct than any other choice save (C). The difficulties with it are threefold: One, there really is not all that much internal development of Al's argument, so (D) does not seem on target; two, in a way she does examine what internal structure there is—she notes there is a suppressed assumption which is unsound; finally, even assuming that what (D) says is correct, it really does not describe the point of Amy's remark nearly so well as (C) does. Finally, (E) is incorrect because Amy does not offer an analogy of any sort.

19. **(C)** The problem with this argument is that it contains no argument at all. Nothing is more frustrating than trying to discuss an issue with someone who will not even make an attempt to prove his case, whose only constructive argument is: "Well, that is my position; if I am wrong, you prove I am wrong." This is an illegitimate attempt to shift the burden of proof. The person who advances the argument naturally has the burden of giving some argument for it. (C) points out this problem. (A) is incorrect because the author uses no group classifications. (B) is incorrect because the author does not introduce any analogy. (D) is a weak version of (C). It is true that the author does not provide statistical evidence to prove his claim, but then again he provides no kind of argument at all to prove his claim. So if (D) is a legitimate objection to the paragraph (and it is), then (C) must be an even stronger objection. So any argument for answer (D)'s being the correct choice ultimately supports (C) even more strongly. The statement contained in (E) may or may not be correct, but the information in the passage is not sufficient to allow us to isolate the theory upon which the speaker is operating. Therefore, we cannot conclude that it is or is not discredited.

20. **(A)** Let us assign letters to represent the complete clauses of the sentence from which the argument is built. "If quarks . . . universe" will be represented by the letter P, the rest of the sentence by Q. The structure of the argument is therefore: "If P then Q. Q. Therefore, P." The argument is obviously not logically valid. If it

were, it would work for any substitutions of clauses for the letters, but we can easily think up a case in which the argument will not work: "If this truck is a fire engine, it will be painted red. This truck is painted red; therefore, it is a fire engine." Obviously, many trucks which are not fire engines could also be painted red. The argument's invalidity is not the critical point. Your task was to find the answer choice that paralleled it—and since the argument first presented was incorrect, you should have looked for the argument in the answer choices which makes the same mistake: (A). It has the form: "If P then Q. Q. Therefore, P" (B) has the form: "If P, then Q. P. Therefore, Q," which is both different from our original form and valid to boot. (C) has the form: "P or Q. Not P. Therefore, Q." (D) has the form: "If P, then Q. If Q, then R. Therefore, if P, then R." Finally, (E) has the form: "If P then Q. Not Q. Therefore, not P."

21. **(D)** The author explains that the expansion of judicial power by increasing the number of causes of action had the effect of filling the judicial coffers. A natural conclusion to be drawn from this information is that the desire for economic gain fueled the expansion. (A) is not supported by the text since the judges may have made good decisions—even though they were paid to make them. (E) is incorrect for the same reason. (C) is not supported by the text since no mention is made of the other two bodies (even assuming they existed at the time the author is describing). (B) is also incorrect because there is nothing in the text to support such a conclusion.

22. **(D)** As we did in question 20, let us use letters to represent the form of the argument. The first sentence is our old friend: "If P, then Q." Now we must be careful not to use the same letter to stand for a different statement. No part of the second sentence is also a part of the first one, so we must use a new set of letters: "If R, then S." Do not be confused by the internal structure of the sentences. Though the second clause of the first sentence speaks about Johnson and Lloyd voting the same way, the second clause of the second sentence speaks about Johnson's defending someone. So the two statements are different ideas and require different letters. The first clause of the third sentence is the same idea as the first clause of the first sentence, so we use letter P again, but the second clause is different, T. The third sen-

tence uses the phrase "only if," "P only if T," which can also be written: "If P, then T." Our three sentences are translated as:

1. If P, then Q.
2. If R, then S.
3. If P, then T.

Now we can find which of the answers cannot be true.

(A) "If R, then not Q." That is a possibility. While it cannot be deduced from our three assumptions, nothing in the three assumptions precludes it. So (A) could be true.

(B) "If P, then T." This is true, a restatement of the final assumption.

(C) "If T, then not-P." This is possibly true. Sentence 3 tells us, "If P then T," which is the same thing as "if not-T, then not-P"; but it does not dictate consequences when the antecedent clause (the if-clause) is T.

(D) "If P, then either not-Q or not-T." This must be false, since sentences 1 and 3 together tell us that from P must follow both Q and T.

(E) "If not-T or not-P, then either not-S or U." We have to add a new letter: U. In any event, this is possible for the reasons mentioned in (C).

23. **(A)** The listener's comment constitutes a counter-example. He shows by his sarcasm that "yeah" can be used to show disagreement. Obviously, the listener does not point out an inconsistency within the speaker's address (even though the listener's remark is inconsistent with the speaker's position). There is no analogy developed by the listener, whose remark is very brief, so (C) is incorrect. The argument is directed against the speaker's contention, not his character, so (D) is incorrect. Finally, though the listener's comment is high evidence that the speaker is wrong, the comment itself does not cite evidence, so (E) is incorrect.

24. **(C)** The argument in the question stem commits the fallacy of hasty generalization in two respects. It reasons from *military* aid to *Latin America* (a particular type of aid to a certain region) to the general conclusion that *all* aid must be stopped, regardless of type or of recipient. (C) parallels this. From a particular conclusion about one form of government in one country, it moves to a general conclusion about all government—regardless of form or of society. Although (A), (B), and (D) have superficial similarities of con-

tent (war, donation, military), the logical structures of these arguments differ from that of the stem paragraph. (A) is a valid argument: Given anything that is a war, if any war is to be condemned, then all wars are to be condemned. (B) is not a valid argument but a nonsequitur. It does not follow that an obligation on one party guarantees a benefit to any other. For example, there may not be enough rich to provide for all the poor. (D) is also a nonsequitur. That we reject a system now because we lack the money to buy it does not imply we should buy it when we have funds. Finally, (E) is not really an argument but only a statement. Not all "If . . ., then . . . ." statements mean "P, therefore Q." For example, "If you do not do the assignment, you will fail the course" is not an argument with a premise and a conclusion but a single statement which describes a causal relation.

25. **(A)** The ends of law, according to legal positivism, are to be agreed upon—"accepted as a contingent matter." They are values which the community adopts; they are not handed down by God, nor are they dictated by logic. (B) actually reverses the point. The legal positivist probably would say he does not claim these ends are the best for all modern legal systems. He does not want to commit himself to anything beyond a mere factual description of things as they are. The normative theory ultimately reduces to a question of practical politics—whatever succeeds. (C) can be rejected because the question raised by the normative theory is what values the law ought to generally embody, not just what values the courts ought to promote. (D) is incorrect because while it is perhaps true, it does not address itself to the *status* of the normative values: Are they universally held and dictated by logic? Are they given by God? etc. (E) is similar to (D) in that it may be true simply as a matter of fact, but, again, (E) does not address itself to the status of the values. It is true that the values are those the community chooses, but that such status is *selected* rather than dictated is not undermined because there is not complete agreement on the values. Whatever values are selected will be chosen by more or less unanimous agreement.

26. **(C)** The analogy to physical theory is highly suggestive. The physicist advances a theory which represents an improvement on existing theories, but he is aware that tomorrow another theory may be proposed which is more correct than his. So

the legal positivist advances a descriptive theory, that is, a description of existing legal institutions, but new information or advances in theory may displace that theory. (A) is directly contrary to the legal positivist's position that no one theory is uniquely correct. (B) ignores the radical and complete divorce of description and normative recommendation upon which the legal positivist insists. (D) just confuses the point of the analogy to physics. The author introduces the analogy to explain how the legal positivist views his theory—in the same way the physicist views his—not to compare the reliability of physics with jurisprudence. (E) makes a mistake similar to that committed by (D).

27. **(E)** The argument given in the question stem is circular, that is, it begs the question. It tries to prove that the decision is unfair by claiming that it singles out a group, which is the same thing as discriminating, and then concludes that *since* all discrimination is unfair, so, too, is the court's decision unfair. Of course, the real issue is whether singling out this particular group is unfair. After all, we do make distinctions, e.g., adults are treated differently than children, businesses differently than persons, soldiers differently than executives. The question of fairness cannot be solved by simply noting that the decision singles out some persons. (E) also is circular: It tries to prove this is a beautiful painting because all paintings of this sort are beautiful. (A) is perhaps the second best answer, but notice that it is purely hypothetical in its form: *If* this were true, *then* that would be true. As a consequence, it is not as similar to the question stem as (E), which is phrased in categorical assertions rather than hypothetical statements. (B) moves from the premise that students are not good judges of their needs to a conclusion about the responsibility for planning course work. The conclusion and the premise are not the same so the argument is not circular. (C) is not, technically speaking, even an argument. Remember from our instructional material at the beginning of the book, an argument has premises and a conclusion. These are separate statements. (C) is one long statement, not two short ones. It reads: ''A because B''; not ''A; therefore B.'' For example, the statement ''I am late because the car broke down'' is not an inference but a causal statement. In (D), since the premise (everything after the semicolon) is not the same as the conclusion (the statement before the semicolon), the argument is

not a circular argument and so does not parallel the stem argument.

28. **(B)** The author's claim depends in a very important way on the assumption that the assistance he advocates will be successful. After all, any proposed course of action which just won't work clearly ought to be rejected. (B) is just this kind of argument: Whatever else you say, your proposed plan will not work; therefore, we must reject it. (A) opens an entirely new line of argument. The author has said only that there is a certain connection between guidance and creativity; he never claims that everyone can or should be a professional artist. Thus, (A) is wrong, as is (E) for the same reason. (C) is wrong for a similar reason. The author never suggests that all students should be professional artists; and, in fact, he may want to encourage students to be creative no matter which practical careers they may choose. (E) is probably the second best answer; it does, to a certain extent, try to attack the workability of the proposal. Unfortunately, it does not address the general connection the author says exists between training and creativity. In other words, (E) does not say the proposal will not work at all; it merely says it may work too well. Further, (E) is wrong because it does not attribute the ''burn out'' to the training of the sort proposed by the author.

29. **(E)** What we are looking for here is an intervening causal link which caused the plan to be unsuccessful. The projected train of events was: (1) Adopt express lanes, (2) fewer cars, and (3) faster traffic flow. Between the first and the third steps, however, something went wrong. (E) alone supplies that unforeseen side effect. Since the cars backed up on too few lanes, total flow of traffic was actually slowed, not speeded up. (A) is irrelevant since it does not explain what went wrong *after* the plan was adopted. (B) does not even attempt to address the sequence of events which we have just outlined. Although (C) is probably true and was something the planners likely considered in their projections, it does not explain the plan's failure. Finally, (D) might have been relevant in deciding whether or not to adopt the plan, but given that the plan was adopted, (D) cannot explain why it then failed.

30. **(E)** We have all seen arguments of this sort in our daily lives, and perhaps if we have not been very careful, we have even made the same mis-

takes made by the leaders of Gambia. For example, last semester, which was fall, I made a lot of money selling peanuts at football games. Therefore, this spring semester I will make even more money. All three propositions point out weaknesses in the projections made by Gambia's leaders. I: Of course, if the tremendous increase in GNP is due to some unique event (my personal income increased last semester when I inherited $2,000 from my aunt), it would be foolish to project a similar increase for a time period during which that event cannot repeat itself. II: This is a bit less obvious, but the projection is based on the assumption that Gambia will receive additional aid, and will be able to put that aid to use. If they are not in a position to use that aid (I cannot work twice as many hours in the spring), they cannot expect the aid to generate increases in GNP. Finally, III also is a weakness in the leaders' projections. If there are physical limitations on the possible increases, then the leaders have made an error. Their projections are premised on the existence of physical resources which are greater than those they actually have.

31. **(C)** The conclusion of the paragraph is so obvious that it is almost difficult to find. The author says office workers work better the cooler the temperature—provided the temperature does not drop below 68°. Therefore, we can conclude, the temperature at which workers will be most efficient will be precisely 68°. Notice that the author does not say what happens once the temperature drops below 68° except that workers are no longer as efficient. For all we know, efficiency may drop off slowly or quickly compared with improvements in efficiency as the temperature drops to 68°. So (E) goes beyond the information supplied in the passage. (D) also goes far beyond the scope of the author's claim. His formula is specifically applicable to *office* workers. We have no reason to believe the author would extend his formula to non-office workers. (B) is probably not a conclusion the author would endorse since he claims to have found a way of achieving improvements in efficiency in a different and seemingly permanent way. Finally, (A) is not a conclusion the author seems likely to reach since nothing indicates that his formula yields only short-term gains which last as long as the temperature is kept constant. To be sure, the gains will not be repeatable, but then they will not be short-run either.

32. **(A)** The anti-abortion speaker unwittingly plays right into the hands of the pro-abortion speaker. The "pro" speaker tries to show that there are many decisions regarding human life in which we allow that an increase in the quality of life justifies an increase in the danger to human life. All that the "anti" speaker does is to help prove this point. He says the quality of life would suffer if we lowered the speed limits to protect human life. Given this analysis, (B) must be incorrect, for the "anti" speaker's position is completely ineffective as a rebuttal. Moreover, (C) must be incorrect, for his response is not a strong statement of an anti-abortion position. (D) is incorrect, for while his response is of no value to the position he seeks to defend, it cannot be said that it is irrelevant. In fact, as we have just shown, his position is very relevant to that of the "pro" speaker's because it supports that position. Finally, (E) is not an appropriate characterization of the "anti" speaker's position, for he tries, however ineptly, to attack the merits of the "pro" speaker's position, not the character of that speaker.

33. **(E)** The "pro" speaker uses the example of traffic fatalities to show that society has always traded the quality of life for the quantity of life. Of course, he says, we do not always acknowledge that is what we are doing, but if we were honest we would have to admit that we were making a trade-off. Thus, (E) is the best conclusion of the passage. The author's defense of abortion amounts to the claim that abortion is just another case in which we trade off one life (the fetus) to make the lives of others (the survivors) better. The only difference is that the life being sacrificed is specifiable and highly visible in the case of abortion, whereas in the case of highway fatalities no one knows in advance on whom the ax will fall. (A) certainly goes far beyond what the author is advocating. If anything, he probably recognizes that sometimes the trade-off will be drawn in favor of protecting lives, and thus we need some such laws. (B) must be wrong, first, because the "anti" speaker claims this is not his position, and second, because the "pro" speaker would prefer to show that the logical consequence of the "anti" speaker's response is an argument in favor of abortion. (C) is not an appropriate continuation because the author has already said this is a weak counter-example and that he has even stronger points to make. Finally,

the author might be willing to accept contraception, (D), as yet another example of the trade-off, but his conclusion can be much stronger than that. The author wants to defend abortion, so the conclusion of his speech ought to be that abortion is an acceptable practice—not that contraception is an acceptable practice.

34. **(D)** This is a very difficult question. That III is an assumption the author makes requires careful reading. The author's attitude about the just war tips us off. He implies that this is an appropriate function of government and, further, that there are even clearer cases. Implicit in his defense of abortion is that a trade-off must be made and that it is appropriately a collective decision. I is not an assumption of the argument. Indeed, the author seems to assume, as we have just maintained, that the trade-off is an appropriate goal of society. Finally, the author does not assume II; if anything, he almost states that he accepts that the fetus is a life but it may be traded off in exchange for an increase in the quality in the lives of others.

35. **(A)** You might attack this item using a circle diagram. To show the possible relationships of three categories, use three overlapping circles:

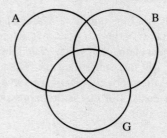

Now enter the information provided by the second statement:

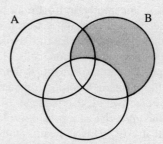

The area that is not logically possible given the second statement is shaded. Now enter the information provided by the first statement:

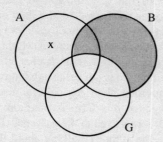

The "x" shows that there is at least one individual which is an Alpha but not a Gamma.

The diagram shows that statement I must be true. There is at least one individual which is an Alpha but not a Beta. II, however, is not necessarily true. The overlap between the Alpha-circle and the Gamma-circle, which represents the possibility that an individual might have both characteristics Alpha and Gamma, is left open. Finally, III is not necessarily true for a similar reason. There is a portion of the Gamma-circle not contained in the Beta-circle, and this part represents the logical possibility that some individuals could have characteristic Gamma but not characteristic Beta.

SECTION IV

1. **(B)** This is a main idea question. The author's primary concern is to discuss the problem of desertification. So choice (B) is correct. A natural extension of the discussion would be a proposal to slow the process of desertification, but that is not included in the passage as written, so (A) must be incorrect. (C), (D), and (E) are each incorrect because we find no elements in the passage to support those choices. Even admitting that the author intends to define, implicitly, the term "desertification," that is surely not the main point of the passage. The author also dwells at length on the causes of the problem.

2. **(C)** This is an explicit idea question. In the first paragraph, the author mentions (A), (B), (D), and (E) as features of desertification. (C), however, is one of the *causes* of desertification mentioned in the second paragraph.

3. **(E)** This is an inference question. The author places the phrase "higher uses" in quotation marks. In essence, this is similar to prefacing the

phrase with the disclaimer "so called." This impression is reinforced by the final entry in the list of examples of "higher uses": waste dumps. This is not to say that the author would argue that such uses are not important. Rather, this is to say that the author does not believe that those uses are more important than agricultural uses. (A) is incorrect since this term is no more important than other terms used in the passage. (B) is incorrect since the author is talking about the conversion of non-arid land to higher uses. (C) is incorrect since the author is clearly opposed to such expansion. Finally, (D) is a sentiment expressed in the passage, but that is not the reason for placing this phrase in quotation marks.

4. **(D)** This is an explicit idea question. In the second paragraph, the author mentions that high commodity prices encourage farmers to expand production of arid lands, so statement I is part of the correct answer. Also, relatively low government fees for grazing on common lands are mentioned in that same paragraph, so statement II is part of the correct answer. The world's need for U.S. agricultural exports, however, is not mentioned as a factor encouraging desertification. It is mentioned in the final paragraph as being connected with the ultimate danger of desertification. To be sure, it is possible to argue that the demand creates the need to produce, but that is an argument that demand creates production—not that demand creates desertification. Indeed, the author believes it is possible to meet that demand without sacrificing land. So statement III is not part of the correct answer. Moreover, as a matter of test-taking wisdom, since this is an explicit idea question, it is better to prefer a fairly obvious answer, something stated on the face of the text, and not to dig for some possible connection.

5. **(A)** This is an explicit idea question, and the answer is found in the last paragraph. There the author states that the most serious long-term effect of desertification will be on the U.S.'s ability to export agricultural products. This will be harmful to the U.S. economically and to the rest of the world in terms of meeting the demand for food and fiber. As for (B) and (C), though these are plausible as effects of desertification, the author does not mention them specifically, and he certainly does not describe them as the most serious effects of desertification. (D) is incorrect because the author's concern is over the ability of the U.S. to continue to export agricultural products, not the ability of the U.S. to meet domestic

demand. Finally, (E) fails for the same reason that (B) and (C) are incorrect. Though it might arguably be one result of desertification (and that is an issue we need not address), the author never mentions it as a possible effect.

6. **(E)** This is an application question. In the passage the author indicates that government programs which encourage exploitation of arid land are in large measure responsible for the rapid rate of desertification. A natural extension of the discussion would be a proposal for government spending to conserve arid lands. And this receives specific support in the third paragraph, where the author mentions that government conservation incentives are inadequate. With regard to (A), the author seems to believe that it is necessary for the U.S. to continue to export agricultural products to meet the world demand; he favors conserving arid land while meeting this demand. (B) is surely incorrect, for the author argues that aid to farmers is one cause of the rapid rate of desertification. (D) is incorrect for the same reason. As for (C), the conversion of land to "higher uses" is mentioned as a factor complicating the process of desertification. It is not a cause of desertification. The most natural extension of the passage would be a discussion of how to combat desertification.

7. **(E)** This is a tone question. We can surely eliminate (B), (C), and (D) as not expressing the appropriate element of worry. Then, between (A) and (E), (A) overstates the case. The author says we solve the problem now or we solve it later (at a higher cost). But that is an expression of concern, not alarm.

8. **(D)** This is a main idea question. The author begins by noting that solar energy is very important and, further, that the problem of the cost of solar cells, apparently an important part of solar energy technology, has not yet been solved. The author then discusses research on solar cells and the difficulties with silicon cells. In the third paragraph, the author states that there is a solution to this problem: amorphous materials. So the overall objective of the passage is to present amorphous material as a possible solution to the problem of cost. This is neatly summarized by choice (D). (A) is incorrect since the author discusses the importance of solar energy only by way of introduction. (B) is incorrect because the author never explains how solar cells work. (C) is incorrect because the only reference to history is

included to explain the bias in favor of silicon solar cells. (E) is incorrect because the author never mentions such funding. To be sure, the arguments contained in the passage might be very useful in making the further point suggested by (E), but then that is to admit that (E) is not the main point of the passage as written.

9. **(D)** This is an explicit idea question. In the second paragraph, the author discusses why silicon solar cells are used in the space program. The passages states that extraterrestrial efficiency is fairly high, so statement II is part of the correct answer choice. Moreover, the author mentions casually, but explicitly, that cost is not a factor in developing materials for the space program, so statement III is part of the correct choice. The extra cost of scarce materials, however, is not mentioned as a factor encouraging the use of silicon solar cells in the space program. Though it is stated that materials such as gallium arsenide are more efficient and more costly, these factors are not reasons why silicon solar cells are used in the space program. So the correct answer is II and III only.

10. **(A)** This is a logical structure question: Why does the author mention polycrystalline and ribbon silicon? In a way, the mention of these techniques could undermine the case for amorphous materials, since these are recent developments in crystalline substances which improve silicon solar cells. The author surely does not intend to weaken his argument. The logical move is to acknowledge the existence of a possible objection and to attempt to demonstrate that it is not really a very important objection. This is described by (A). (B) is incorrect, for though this is the general idea of the passage, (B) is not a proper response to the question asked. (C) is a point raised in the passage, but this is not the reason for the reference to polycrystalline and ribbon silicon. (D) is incorrect because the author never elaborates on the distinction between crystalline silicon and other forms of silicon. He only mentions that the latter are further developments on crystalline silicon. As for (E), though we infer from the mention of polycrystalline and ribbon silicon that other forms of solar cells exist, this is not the reason the author has introduced them into the discussion.

11. **(B)** This is an inference question. In the first paragraph, the author mentions that the basic problem with solar energy is the economics of solar photovoltaic devices. The rest of the passage discusses solar cells. We may infer from the juxtaposition of these terms that the author uses them synonymously. In any event, none of the other pairs are used interchangeably. As for (A), from the passage we may infer that "extraterrestrial" refers to space and that "solar" refers to the sun. As for (C), these terms are used as opposites. As for (D), though the author claims that amorphous materials are more efficient than silicon materials, he does not equate amorphous materials and efficiency. Finally, (E) is incorrect since a wafer is apparently a big crystal of silicon. But that means the terms are not used interchangeably.

12. **(B)** This is a further application question. We noted earlier, in question 8, that though the author does not specifically advocate greater funding for research on amorphous materials, the passage might be used in such an argument. Since there is an historical bias in favor of silicon cells, and since such cells have been the focus of most research, and amorphous materials offer an alternative, the natural conclusion is that further research should be done on amorphous materials. This is answer choice (B). (A) must be incorrect since the author never condemns the space program. He only notes that silicon cells were appropriate for the space program since cost was no object. (C) must be incorrect since the author advocates amorphous materials as opposed to silicon crystals for solar cells. (D) has some merit. To the extent that the entire passage advocates further research for solar energy, it could be used for the purpose suggested by (D). With an application question, however, the task is to find the answer choice most closely tied to the text, and that is (B). Logically, then, there is nothing "wrong" with (D); it is just that it is not so closely related to the passage as (B). Finally, (E) is incorrect for the same reason: One could conceivably use the passage in the service of this goal, but (B) is a more obvious choice.

13. **(E)** This is an explicit idea question. All three statements are mentioned in paragraph 3 as being advantages which amorphous material has over silicon.

14. **(A)** This is a tone question. The tone of the passage is clearly analytical. The final paragraph is the warrant for the "optimistic" part of choice (A). The author implies that the problem of the cost of solar cells can be solved by further

research on amorphous materials. (B) is incorrect since though the passage advocates a position, it cannot be termed biased. (C) is correct insofar as the passage is critical, but the author does not seem to be discouraged. (D) is incorrect because the passage is argumentative and the author seems to be confident. Finally, (E) is correct in that it states that the author is concerned, but there is nothing mentioned in the passage about which the author could be conciliatory.

15. **(B)** This is a main idea question. The author draws a distinction between preventive health care and curative health care. Using this distinction, he suggests that there should be established separate authorities for each. So the primary method of developing the argument is the drawing of a distinction, as correctly stated by (B). (A) is incorrect since the author does not cite any counter-arguments to his position. (C) is incorrect, for a dilemma is a "damned if you do and damned if you don't" argument. To draw a distinction is not necessarily to set up a dilemma. (D) is incorrect, for whatever causes of poor health are discussed in the passage are not the main focus of the discussion. (E) is incorrect for a similar reason. Whatever new research we may try to read into the passage, e.g., the Winslow monograph, is surely not the main point of the passage.

16. **(E)** This is an explicit idea question. In the first sentence of the second paragraph, the author notes that treatment is aimed at a patient already ill, but we have been told in the first paragraph that preventive care is just that, aimed at people who are healthy in order to keep them that way. So statement I is part of the correct answer. Similarly, statement II is supported by the first two paragraphs, particularly the sentence of the second paragraph which reads, "While these may be applied on a mass basis . . . , they are usually applied after the patient appears with a complaint," thus distinguishing preventive care from curative care. Finally, per capita differences in cost are discussed in paragraph 4.

17. **(B)** This is an inference question. In the first paragraph, the author is discussing the basic strategy of preventive medicine. He then states that in California there is needless suffering and economic harm due to the failure of authorities to implement controlled fluoridation. The development of the argument leads us to conclude that the author regards the failure of the authorities to flu-

oridate water as a failure to implement a preventive health care program. (B) explains this reasoning. (A) is incorrect since the author holds a positive attitude about fluoridation. (C) is incorrect because the author cites the failure to fluoridate as an example of a failure to adopt a potentially valuable preventive strategy. (D) is incorrect because fluoridation is a preventive, rather than a treatment, strategy. Finally, (E) is incorrect since the author recommends the fluoridation of water as a valuable preventive strategy.

18. **(A)** This is an inference question. In paragraph 4, the author remarks that expenditure of resources on treatment is an expenditure that is lost, that is, produces nothing positive (eliminating the negative is not regarded as producing a positive result). Then, the sick person is also not contributing anything positive while he or she is sick. So the economy is doubly disadvantaged because of the burden on or drain on resources to cure an ill person and because production is lost. (A) neatly captures this idea. (B) is incorrect because the author never quantifies the cost difference between the two types of care. He says only that prevention is less costly than treatment. (C) is incorrect because the author eventually will support such a division on the ground that the two activities are sufficiently dissimilar to warrant a division of authority. (D) is incorrect since both rehabilitation and cure belong to curative medicine, so that will not explain why the economy is doubly burdened. Finally, (E) is attractive because it is at least consistent with the general theme of the passage. But (E) is not responsive to the question. It does not explain why the economy is doubly burdened by the person who requires treatment.

19. **(C)** This is an attitude, or tone, question. Two clues support answer choice (C). First, the author refers to the monograph and then continues to make points made by Winslow. This indicates he agrees with Winslow. Second the author refers to the analysis by Winslow as "convincing." (A) and (B) can be eliminated because of the negative connotations associated with both terms. (D) can be eliminated because style is not relevant to the point under discussion. Finally, (E) is the second best answer. We eliminate (E) because the author states that the economics of prevention have been widely discussed, indicating that the uniqueness of Winslow's contribution is not necessarily originality. Further, the reference to the persuasive-

ness of Winslow's analysis makes (C) a better descriptive phrase to apply to the author's attitude than (E).

20. **(D)** This is a logical detail question. The author introduces these three diseases in the paragraph discussing the economics of prevention, and following the statement that the cost of prevention is less than the cost of treatment when averaged out on a per capita basis. (D) makes this point. (A) is incorrect, for while this is a statement the author would surely accept, it is not the reason for introducing the examples. (B) is incorrect for a similar reason. This may very well be true, but it is not an answer to the question. (C) must be wrong, for though this is one of the main points of the discussion, it will not answer this particular question. Finally, (E) is also a statement which the author could accept, but it is not responsive to the question.

21. **(A)** This is a question about the logical structure of the argument. The author mentions several differences between preventive and curative medicines: cost, personnel, persons addressed. But these differences are not compelling reasons for creating a division of authority. The need to separate authority for the two strategies is discussed in the first and last paragraphs. The value of the division will be to clarify objectives and redress the inequitable division of resources. These are problems, so says the first paragraph, because "the imperative nature of medical care" will allow it to dominate health care. In other words, the urgency of treatment attracts attention. This is the explanation provided in (A). And for this reason it is not cost, (B), personnel, (C), or persons addressed, (D), which is the important difference. Finally, (E) is directly contradicted by the opening sentences of the passage.

22. **(D)** This is a main idea question. The author cites several arguments in favor of the "drug lag" theory, then offers refutations of at least some of them. He concludes that the arguments for "drug lag" are not conclusive and that, contrary to the view of the "drug lag" theoreticians, the 1962 Amendments are not, on balance, harmful. The main technique of development is refutation of arguments cited. (D) is therefore the best answer to this question. (A) can be eliminated since the author does not outline a proposal. Discussing the effectiveness of some past action is not outlining a proposal. (B) has some merit because the author does analyze the evidence pre-

sented by the "drug lag" theoreticians. This analysis, however, is not the final objective of the passage. It is presented in order to further the goal of refuting the general position of that group. (C) is incorrect since the author poses no question, and indeed seems to answer any question which might be implicit in the passage regarding the value of the Amendments. (E) has some merit since the focus of the passage is a law. But the intent of the author is not to discuss the law per se. Rather, the intent of the passage is to refute objections to the law. On balance, (D) more precisely describes the main idea than the other choices.

23. **(C)** (A), (B), (D), and (E) are all mentioned as "drug lag" arguments in the second paragraph. As for (C), the argument that effectiveness studies cost money is mentioned in the first paragraph. But "drug lag" results from the time and cost of effectiveness studies. "Drug lag" is not the increased cost itself.

24. **(A)** This is an application question. Support for (A) is found in the closing sentences of the passage. In the final paragraph, the author insists that there are few, if any, examples of harm done by the requirements of effectiveness studies. Then he says that we are at least assured that the drug, which might actually prove harmful, does have some benefit. The qualified nature of the claim suggests that the author would acknowledge that some "drug lag" does exist but that, on balance, it is justified. This thought is captured by choice (A). (B) is incorrect because the author never states the effectiveness studies are designed to determine whether the drug has unwanted effects. Apparently, effectiveness studies, as the name implies, are designed to test the value of the drug. This is not to say that such studies may not, in fact, uncover unwanted side effects, but given the information in the passage, (B) is a more tenuous inference than (A). (C) is incorrect for two reasons. First, the passage never states that the cost of drugs is higher in the United States than in other countries. The passage states only that the proponents of the "drug lag" theory argue that the effectiveness study requirement increases the cost of drugs here. That makes no comparison with a foreign country. Second, the author seems to discount the significance of the increased cost. (D) is incorrect because there is no basis for such a recommendation in the passage. Finally, (E) is incorrect because the passage never states that the studies do not cost money or time. The author

only doubts whether the cost or time create profit pressures serious enough to cause "drug lag."

25. **(B)** This is a logical structure question. In the final paragraph the author states that the drop in new drugs introduced annually began before the Amendments took effect. He does not deny that the drop occurred; rather, he points out that it predated the supposed cause. In other words, the author is suggesting that there must be some other reason for the drop. Answer (B) correctly describes the author's logical move. (E) is directly contradicted by this analysis. The author does not deny that there was a drop in the number of new drugs introduced every year. As for (A), the author does not point to any similarity between two situations. He says only that the situation being studied existed even before the Amendments took effect. (C) is incorrect because the author never questions the credibility of an opponent, only the value of his opponent's arguments. Finally, (D) is incorrect because the author's use of statistics is not an attempt to justify his use of those statistics. He uses statistics to prove some further conclusion.

26. **(C)** This is a logical structure question. In the second paragraph, the author cites, as one argument for the existence of "drug lag," the non-availability in the U.S. of a drug which is available in a foreign country. In the third paragraph, he offers a refutation of this argument. The simple availability–non-availability comparison is not valid because consumers may not suffer from the non-availability of that particular drug if another drug is available to treat the same condition. Answer (C) correctly describes the structure of this argument. The remaining answer choices are in various ways related to the overall argument of the passage, but they are not answers to this particular question.

27. **(C)** Again, we have a logical structure question. We have already noted that the author does not deny that fewer drugs were introduced each year after the Amendments than before the Amendments. But he argues that the total number of new chemical entities is not necessarily a measure of the value of new drugs introduced. By redefining terms so that we speak not just of new chemical entities but of unimportant, important, and breakthrough chemical entities, he minimizes the significance of the argument. The relevant comparison, he claims, is between important and

breakthrough chemical entities, not total new chemical entities introduced. Answer (C) correctly points out that the essence of this logical move is redefining terminology. (A) is incorrect because the author does not deny that the total number had dropped. (B) is incorrect because the author does not explain why that number has dropped. (D) is incorrect because the author makes no such proposal. Finally, (E) is only remotely related to the correct answer. While it may be true that an important or breakthrough chemical has many more uses than an unimportant chemical entity, the author does not list the uses of any chemical.

28. **(D)** This is an application question. What are the logical underpinnings of the comparison? Notice that the author's description of the arguments he attacks includes reference to "advanced" nations. Apparently, the proponents of the "drug lag" theory realize that a comparison between the United States and a non-advanced country would not be relevant. They want a situation in which the only important difference is the strictness of the laws on new drugs. For this reason both I and III are presuppositions of the argument. II is not a presupposition of the argument since proponents of the theory do not have to make any assumption about profitability. The opponents of the Amendments claim only that the testing required increases the cost of drugs in the U.S., not that it makes drugs more costly in the U.S. than elsewhere, nor that the pharmaceutical industry here is less profitable than elsewhere.

29. **(E)** This is a main idea question. (A) is not correct because although the author discusses the difficulty of making a translation, he does not criticize translators. In fact, he seems sympathetic to their problems since he is a translator himself. (B) is not correct since he mentions the fact that all languages have their particular difficulties and uses the poetry of Milton—an English poet—as an example of a difficult text to translate. (C) is wrong because although the author says it is difficult to do justice to a work in another language, he refers to some translations that are successful—those that please the "hard-liners," for instance. He also mentions Chateaubriand's translation of *Paradise Lost* as a successful translation. (D) is incorrect because although the author mentions some of the difficulties of translating Japanese into English, the point of the passage is not that Japanese is particularly diffi-

cult—just that it is difficult in some particular ways. (E) is the correct answer.

30. **(B)** This is an implied idea question. The author mentions the fact that he has done some translating of work by Dazai Osamu. He then mentions another book, *Accomplices of Silence,* which talks about certain aspects of Osamu's work. We may infer, then, that the book mentioned is a critical commentary on the work of Osamu. It is certainly not an English translation of Japanese poetry since it is clear that this book talks *about* the literature. It is not a prior publication by the author because the author names another author—Masao Miyoshi; thus, (C) is incorrect. (D) is wrong because the author gives examples of the things mentioned in Miyoshi's book and they have nothing to do with orthography. Finally, (E) is wrong because it is clear that Miyoshi's comments as quoted by the author are about Osamu's effects *in Japanese,* not in English; therefore, he is not talking about the problems of translation.

31. **(A)** This is a logical detail question. The author uses an example taken from *Kinosaki nite* to illustrate the onomatopoeic effect of writing a word in one system of orthography rather than another. (B) is incorrect because although the author mentions the fact that a Japanese writer laments the poverty of indigenous Japanese vocabulary, this is not the point of his example. In fact, the example actually demonstrates a certain richness of the Japanese language. (C) is incorrect because the example has nothing to do with translation. It is an example of an effect rendered in Japanese. (D) is not correct since the reader actually learns nothing at all about this work of literature except that this literary device appears in it. Finally, (E) is wrong because, again, the example has nothing to do with translation.

32. **(E)** This is a further application question. (A) is incorrect because although the author says that the Japanese people have special feelings about the possibilities of their language, he does not say that he shares these feelings. (B) is wrong because although the author discusses the difficulties of translating Japanese, he says that the difficulty stems from the peculiarities of the Japanese language, not from the limitations of the English. There is no reason to assume that the

author thinks it would be easier to translate Japanese into any other language. (C) is wrong because it overstates the case. The author might say that it is difficult, but not necessarily impossible, for someone not fluent in Japanese to understand Japanese literature. (D) is wrong because the author specifically brackets the question of the truth of this hypothesis. (E) is correct because the author states that although Japanese has "special language relationships," he just means that like any other language, it has unique features. Thus, the author seems to feel that all languages have special qualities and they all present special challenges to a translator.

33. **(C)** This is an implied idea question. Since the author cites this word as an example of onomatopoeia (a poetic device in which the word used to describe an action *sounds* like the action itself), the answer can only be (C): buzz. In English, the word "buzz" sounds like the flight of a bee.

34. **(C)** This is a logical structure question. The author uses many examples to illustrate his points. He cites the example of onomatopoeia in *Kinosaki nite,* for instance. He also cites the particular effects which are difficult to translate in the work of Osamu. He cites several authorities. He cites Miyoshi on the subject of Osamu, and George Steiner on the subject of translation. As for (D), the author discusses his personal experience in translating the work of Osamu. Finally, as for (E), the author contrasts two viewpoints in the first paragraph (the hard line and the soft line).

35. **(A)** This is an implied idea question. (B) cannot be correct since the handicap referred to is the result of translating the poetry, not the result of the Japanese writer's intention. (C) is incorrect because although there may be no word-for-word equivalents, that is a general problem of translation, not just a problem of translating Japanese into English. (D) is incorrect because the handicap is not related to the expectations of the reader. (E) is obviously incorrect since the problem is related to translation and has nothing to do with the problems of a Japanese reader reading in Japanese. The example quoted by the author is obviously a translator's attempt to make the English sound "oriental," or what a Western audience thinks "oriental" sounds like. So (A) is the correct response.

Use a No. 2 pencil only. Be sure each mark is dark and completely fills the intended oval. Completely erase any errors or stray marks.

☐ A R C O ☐

Start with number 1 for each new section. If a section has fewer than 50 questions, leave the extra answer spaces blank.

SECTION 1	SECTION 2	SECTION 3	SECTION 4

Each section contains numbered rows 1 through 50, with answer ovals labeled Ⓐ Ⓑ Ⓒ Ⓓ Ⓔ for each question.

1 Ⓐ Ⓑ Ⓒ Ⓓ Ⓔ
2 Ⓐ Ⓑ Ⓒ Ⓓ Ⓔ
3 Ⓐ Ⓑ Ⓒ Ⓓ Ⓔ
4 Ⓐ Ⓑ Ⓒ Ⓓ Ⓔ
5 Ⓐ Ⓑ Ⓒ Ⓓ Ⓔ
6 Ⓐ Ⓑ Ⓒ Ⓓ Ⓔ
7 Ⓐ Ⓑ Ⓒ Ⓓ Ⓔ
8 Ⓐ Ⓑ Ⓒ Ⓓ Ⓔ
9 Ⓐ Ⓑ Ⓒ Ⓓ Ⓔ
10 Ⓐ Ⓑ Ⓒ Ⓓ Ⓔ
11 Ⓐ Ⓑ Ⓒ Ⓓ Ⓔ
12 Ⓐ Ⓑ Ⓒ Ⓓ Ⓔ
13 Ⓐ Ⓑ Ⓒ Ⓓ Ⓔ
14 Ⓐ Ⓑ Ⓒ Ⓓ Ⓔ
15 Ⓐ Ⓑ Ⓒ Ⓓ Ⓔ
16 Ⓐ Ⓑ Ⓒ Ⓓ Ⓔ
17 Ⓐ Ⓑ Ⓒ Ⓓ Ⓔ
18 Ⓐ Ⓑ Ⓒ Ⓓ Ⓔ
19 Ⓐ Ⓑ Ⓒ Ⓓ Ⓔ
20 Ⓐ Ⓑ Ⓒ Ⓓ Ⓔ
21 Ⓐ Ⓑ Ⓒ Ⓓ Ⓔ
22 Ⓐ Ⓑ Ⓒ Ⓓ Ⓔ
23 Ⓐ Ⓑ Ⓒ Ⓓ Ⓔ
24 Ⓐ Ⓑ Ⓒ Ⓓ Ⓔ
25 Ⓐ Ⓑ Ⓒ Ⓓ Ⓔ
26 Ⓐ Ⓑ Ⓒ Ⓓ Ⓔ
27 Ⓐ Ⓑ Ⓒ Ⓓ Ⓔ
28 Ⓐ Ⓑ Ⓒ Ⓓ Ⓔ
29 Ⓐ Ⓑ Ⓒ Ⓓ Ⓔ
30 Ⓐ Ⓑ Ⓒ Ⓓ Ⓔ
31 Ⓐ Ⓑ Ⓒ Ⓓ Ⓔ
32 Ⓐ Ⓑ Ⓒ Ⓓ Ⓔ
33 Ⓐ Ⓑ Ⓒ Ⓓ Ⓔ
34 Ⓐ Ⓑ Ⓒ Ⓓ Ⓔ
35 Ⓐ Ⓑ Ⓒ Ⓓ Ⓔ
36 Ⓐ Ⓑ Ⓒ Ⓓ Ⓔ
37 Ⓐ Ⓑ Ⓒ Ⓓ Ⓔ
38 Ⓐ Ⓑ Ⓒ Ⓓ Ⓔ
39 Ⓐ Ⓑ Ⓒ Ⓓ Ⓔ
40 Ⓐ Ⓑ Ⓒ Ⓓ Ⓔ
41 Ⓐ Ⓑ Ⓒ Ⓓ Ⓔ
42 Ⓐ Ⓑ Ⓒ Ⓓ Ⓔ
43 Ⓐ Ⓑ Ⓒ Ⓓ Ⓔ
44 Ⓐ Ⓑ Ⓒ Ⓓ Ⓔ
45 Ⓐ Ⓑ Ⓒ Ⓓ Ⓔ
46 Ⓐ Ⓑ Ⓒ Ⓓ Ⓔ
47 Ⓐ Ⓑ Ⓒ Ⓓ Ⓔ
48 Ⓐ Ⓑ Ⓒ Ⓓ Ⓔ
49 Ⓐ Ⓑ Ⓒ Ⓓ Ⓔ
50 Ⓐ Ⓑ Ⓒ Ⓓ Ⓔ

(The same numbered answer grid, 1–50 with ovals Ⓐ Ⓑ Ⓒ Ⓓ Ⓔ, is repeated for Section 2, Section 3, and Section 4.)

EXAMINATION FORECAST

Section Number	Type	Minutes	Questions
	Writing Sample	30	—
I	Logical Reasoning	45	30
II	Reading Comprehension	45	35
III	Analytical Reasoning	45	35
IV	Reading Comprehension	45	35

WRITING SAMPLE

Time: 30 minutes

ASHLEY REEVE has just inherited $50,000. Ashley wants to invest the $50,000 in a business that she can operate herself. She is considering two possibilities, a fast food franchise and a clothing store. Write an argument in favor of one of the two proposals. The following criteria should be considered:

——Ashley recently received her M.B.A. and wants a business that will give her an opportunity to apply her theoretical knowledge in a practical setting.

——Ashley has considerable students loans and no substantial assets, so the $50,000 must cover the start-up costs of the business.

Ashley is considering buying a Hearty Burger franchise. Hearty Burger is a regional company with 5 company owned and 20 franchise stores. The cost of the franchise is $10,000, and the estimated cost of the physical plant is another $25,000, depending on whether the franchisee buys or leases a building and on the extent of renovation required. A franchisee must attend a two-week ''Hearty Burger Orientation'' and is required to purchase all supplies from the company's commissary. The main company does regional advertising and special promotional campaigns and supplies franchisees with everything they need to run their restaurants, including cooking equipment, employee time sheets, tax forms, cooking procedure booklets, and technical assistance. Ashley is also considering purchasing an existing clothing store. The owner of the store, which has been in operation for over 50 years, is retiring and is willing to sell the store

PRACTICE EXAMINATION 4

SECTION I

Time——45 Minutes
30 Questions

Directions: Each group of questions is based on a set of propositions or conditions. Drawing a rough picture or diagram may help in answering some of the questions. Choose the best answer for each question and blacken the corresponding space on your answer sheet.

Questions 1-6

The programming manager of a television station is scheduling movies for the upcoming week. She has seven films, J, K, L, M, N, O, and P. Exactly one of the films will be shown each day, and no film will be shown more than once. The films must be shown in accordance with the following programming restrictions:

K must be shown either Monday or Saturday.
O must be shown on Thursday.
P must be shown on Sunday.
J and L must be shown on consecutive days.
J and N must not be shown on consecutive days.

1. If M is shown on Tuesday, which of the following must be true?
   (A) N is shown on Monday.
   (B) N is shown on Wednesday.
   (C) L is shown on Friday.
   (D) J is shown on Saturday.
   (E) K is shown on Saturday.

2. If J and K are shown on consecutive days, which of the following must be true?
   (A) J is shown on Wednesday.
   (B) K is shown on Saturday.
   (C) L is shown on Wednesday.
   (D) M is shown on Saturday.
   (E) N is shown on Friday.

3. If N is shown on Tuesday, which of the following must be true?

   I. K is shown on Saturday.
   II. L is shown on Friday.
   III. M is shown on Wednesday.

   (A) I only
   (B) II only
   (C) III only
   (D) I and II only
   (E) II and III only

4. If K is shown on Saturday, which of the following must be true?
   (A) M is shown on Monday.
   (B) N is shown on Tuesday.
   (C) If N and L are shown on consecutive days, J is shown on Wednesday.
   (D) If J and M are shown on consecutive days, L is shown on Wednesday.
   (E) If K and M are shown on consecutive days, L is shown on Tuesday.

5. If J is not shown on Monday, Tuesday, or Wednesday, which of the following must be true?
   (A) If J is shown on Saturday, M is shown on Wednesday.
   (B) If L is shown on Friday, N is shown on Tuesday.
   (C) If M is shown on Tuesday, J is shown on Friday.
   (D) If M is shown on Wednesday, L is shown on Saturday.
   (E) If N is shown on Wednesday, M is shown on Tuesday.

275

6. If L is shown on Tuesday, which of the following must be true?

 I. If M is shown on Monday, N is shown on Friday.
 II. If K is shown on Monday, M is shown on Friday.
 III. If K is shown on Saturday, J is shown on Wednesday.

 (A) I only
 (B) II only
 (C) III only
 (D) I and II only
 (E) II and III only

Questions 7-12

Nine people, G, H, J, K, L, M, N, O, and P, are taking part in a parade. They will ride in three cars, the cars forming a line. Three people will sit in each car.

G and H must ride in the same car.
J must ride in the second car.
N and P must ride in the same car.
K and O must not ride in the same car.
M must ride in the same car with either O or J or both.

7. Which of the following groups of people could ride together in the same car?
 (A) G, J, and N
 (B) J, L, and O
 (C) K, H, and L
 (D) K, N, and O
 (E) O, N, and P

8. Which of the following CANNOT be true?
 (A) K rides in the first car.
 (B) M rides in the first car.
 (C) N rides in the second car.
 (D) O rides in a car two cars behind M's car.
 (E) L rides in a car two cars behind G's car.

9. If P rides in the second car and O rides in the third car, which of the following must be true?
 (A) G rides in the third car.
 (B) L rides in the first car.
 (C) L rides in the third car.
 (D) M rides in the first car.
 (E) M rides in the second car.

10. All of the following people could ride in the same car as G EXCEPT
 (A) J

 (B) K
 (C) L
 (D) N
 (E) O

11. If G and O are riding in the first car, which of the following people must ride in the second car?
 (A) H
 (B) K
 (C) L
 (D) M
 (E) N

12. If P rides in the same car as J, and if M rides in the third car, who must ride in the first car?
 (A) H and O
 (B) K and N
 (C) O and N
 (D) H, K, and G
 (E) H, L, and O

Questions 13-18

Seven children, J, K, L, M, N, O, and P, are students at a certain grammar school with grades 1 through 7.

One of these children is in each of the seven grades.
N is in the first grade, and P is in the seventh grade.
L is in a higher grade than K.
J is in a higher grade than M.
O is in a grade somewhere between K and M.

13. If there are exactly two grades between J and O, which of the following must be true?
 (A) K is in the second grade.
 (B) J is in the sixth grade.
 (C) M is in a higher grade than K.
 (D) L is in a grade between M and O.
 (E) K and L are separated by exactly one grade.

14. If J is in the third grade, which of the following must be true?
 (A) K is in grade 4 and L is in grade 5.
 (B) K is in grade 5 and L is in grade 6.
 (C) L is in grade 4 and M is in grade 6.
 (D) M is in grade 2 and K is in grade 4.
 (E) O is in grade 4 and L is in grade 5.

15. If K is in the second grade, in which of the following grades, respectively, could J and M be?

   I. 3 and 4
  II. 4 and 5
 III. 4 and 6

  (A) I, but not II and not III
  (B) II, but not I and not III
  (C) I or III, but not II
  (D) II or III, but not I
  (E) I, II, or III

16. If J and N are separated by exactly one grade, which of the following must be true?
  (A) L is in grade 6.
  (B) L is in grade 3.
  (C) K is in a lower grade than J.
  (D) K is in a lower grade than O.
  (E) O is in a grade between J and N.

17. Which of the following CANNOT be true?
  (A) O is in the third grade.
  (B) O is in the fourth grade.
  (C) O is in the fifth grade.
  (D) M is in the fourth grade.
  (E) M is in the fifth grade.

18. If L is in the grade immediately ahead of J, the number of logically possible orderings of all seven children, from the lowest grade to the highest grade, is
  (A) 1
  (B) 2
  (C) 3
  (D) 4
  (E) 5

Questions 19-24

Ten sports car enthusiasts, J, K, L, M, N, O, P, Q, R, and T, participate in a sports car rally in which a series of races are held. Five cars participate in each race, finishing first through fifth, with no ties. Exactly two people ride in each car.

P and M always ride together and never finish last.
L and Q never ride in the same car.
N and O always ride in the same car.
R's car always finishes exactly one place ahead of L's.

19. All of the following lists of pairs of participants, in order of finish from first to last, are possible EXCEPT

  (A) J, T; R, Q; K, L; M, P; O, N
  (B) P, M; R, T; L, K; J, Q; O, N
  (C) K, T; R, Q; J, L; P, M; N, O
  (D) O, N; P, M; R, J; L, Q; K, T
  (E) O, N; P, M; R, Q; L, T; K, J

20. If the car in which L is riding finishes somewhere ahead of the car in which M is riding and somewhere behind the car in which O is riding, which of the following must be true?
  (A) R rides in the first-place car.
  (B) J rides in the first-place car.
  (C) R rides in the second-place car.
  (D) Q rides in the second-place car.
  (E) Q rides in the fifth-place car.

21. If N's car finishes second and R's car finishes third, which of the following must be true?
  (A) M's car finishes first.
  (B) Q's car finishes second.
  (C) Q's car finishes fourth.
  (D) J's car finishes ahead of K's car.
  (E) O's car finishes exactly two places ahead of Q's car.

22. If J and T ride together in a car, and if L's car finishes fourth, which of the following must be true?

   I. P's car finishes first.
  II. N's car finishes second.
  III. Q's car finishes third.

  (A) I only
  (B) II only
  (C) III only
  (D) I and II only
  (E) I and III only

23. If L, O, and T ride in cars finishing second, third, and last, respectively, and if J and R ride in the same car, which of the following must be true?
  (A) P's car finishes first.
  (B) L's car finishes first.
  (C) N's car finishes second.
  (D) P's car finishes third.
  (E) Q's car finishes last.

24. If P's car finishes third and K and T ride in the same car, Q could be riding in a car which finishes either
  (A) first or second
  (B) first or fourth
  (C) first or last

(D) second or fourth
(E) second or last

Questions 25-30

The personnel director of a firm must interview six job applicants—M, N, O, P, Q, and R—during a certain week, Monday through Friday. At least one applicant must be interviewed each day.

P must be interviewed on a day before N is interviewed.

M must be interviewed on a day before O is interviewed.

Q must be interviewed on a day before R is interviewed.

25. Which of the following is a possible schedule for the interviews?

	M	Tu	W	Th	F
(A)	P	O,N	Q	M	R
(B)	P	M	O,R	Q	N
(C)	M	O	Q	P,R	N
(D)	M,Q	N	P	R	O
(E)	Q	R	M	O	P,N

26. Which is the earliest day on which both N and O could be interviewed?
    (A) Monday
    (B) Tuesday
    (C) Wednesday
    (D) Thursday
    (E) Friday

27. What is the latest day in the week on which both M and Q could be interviewed?
    (A) Monday
    (B) Tuesday
    (C) Wednesday
    (D) Thursday
    (E) Friday

28. If M and R are interviewed on the same day, sometime after the day on which N is interviewed, which of the following must be true?
    (A) P is interviewed on Monday.
    (B) Q is interviewed on Monday.
    (C) N is interviewed on Tuesday.
    (D) M is interviewed on Friday.
    (E) O is interviewed on Friday.

29. If N is interviewed on the day after O and R are interviewed together, all of the following could be true EXCEPT
    (A) P is interviewed on Monday.
    (B) M is interviewed on Tuesday.
    (C) Q is interviewed on Tuesday.
    (D) Q is interviewed on Wednesday.
    (E) N is interviewed on Thursday.

30. If P and Q are both interviewed on Wednesday, how many different schedules are possible for the six interviews?
    (A) 1
    (B) 2
    (C) 3
    (D) 4
    (E) 6

STOP

IF YOU FINISH BEFORE TIME IS CALLED, CHECK YOUR WORK ON THIS SECTION ONLY. DO NOT WORK ON ANY OTHER SECTION IN THE TEST.

Directions: Below each of the following passages, you will find questions or incomplete statements about the passage. Each statement or question is followed by five lettered words or expressions. Select the word or expression that most satisfactorily completes each statement or answers each question in accordance with the meaning of the passage. After you have chosen the best answer, blacken the corresponding space on the answer sheet.

Reverse discrimination, minority recruitment, racial quotas and, more generally, affirmative action are phrases that carry powerful emotional charges. But why should affirmative action, of all government pol-
5 icies, be so controversial? In a sense, affirmative action is like other governmental programs, e.g., defense, conservation and public schools. Affirmative action programs are designed to achieve legitimate government objectives such as improved economic
10 efficiency, reduced social tension and general betterment of the public welfare. While it cannot be denied that there is no guarantee that affirmative action will achieve these results, neither can it be denied that there are plausible, even powerful, sociological and
15 economic arguments pointing to its likely success.

Government programs, however, entail a cost, that is, the expenditure of social or economic resources. Setting aside cases in which the specific user is charged a fee for service (toll roads and tuition at state
20 institutions), the burdens and benefits of publicly funded or mandated programs are widely shared. When an individual benefits personally from a government program, it is only because she or he is one member of a larger beneficiary class, e.g., a farmer;
25 and most government revenue is obtained through a scheme of general taxation to which all are subject.

Affirmative action programs are exceptions to this general rule, though not, as might at first seem, because the beneficiaries of the programs are specific
30 individuals. It is still the case that those who ultimately benefit from affirmative action do so only by virtue of their status as a member of a larger group, a particular minority. Rather, the difference is the location of the burden. In affirmative action, the burden of
35 "funding" the program is not shared universally, and that is inherent in the nature of the case, as can be seen clearly in the case of affirmative action in employment. Often job promotions are allocated along a single dimension, seniority; and when an employer

40 promotes a less senior worker from a minority group, the person disadvantaged by the move is easily identified: the worker with greatest seniority on a combined minority–non-minority list passed over for promotion.

45 Now we are confronted with two competing moral sentiments. On the one hand, there is the idea that those who have been unfairly disadvantaged by past discriminatory practices are entitled to some kind of assistance. On the other, there is the feeling that no
50 person ought to be deprived of what is rightfully his, even for the worthwhile service of his fellow humans. In this respect, disability due to past racial discrimination, at least insofar as there is no connection to the passed-over worker, is like a natural evil. When a vil-
55 lainous man willfully and without provocation strikes and injures another, there is not only the feeling that the injured person ought to be compensated but there is consensus that the appropriate party to bear the cost is the one who inflicted the injury. Yet, if the same
60 innocent man stumbled and injured himself, it would be surprising to hear someone argue that the villainous man ought to be taxed for the injury simply because he might have tripped the victim had he been given the opportunity. There may very well be agreement that
65 he should be aided in his recovery with money and personal assistance, and many will give willingly; but there is also agreement that no one individual ought to be singled out and forced to do what must ultimately be considered an act of charity.

1. The passage is primarily concerned with
   (A) comparing affirmative action programs to other government programs
   (B) arguing that affirmative action programs are morally justified
   (C) analyzing the basis for moral judgments about affirmative action programs
   (D) introducing the reader to the importance of affirmative action as a social issue
   (E) describing the benefits which can be obtained through affirmative action programs

2. The author mentions toll roads and tuition at state institutions (lines 19–20) in order to
   (A) anticipate a possible objection on counter-examples

(B) avoid a contradiction between moral sentiments
(C) provide illustrations of common government programs
(D) voice doubts about the social and economic value of affirmative action
(E) offer examples of government programs which are too costly

3. With which of the following statements would the author most likely agree?
   (A) Affirmative action programs should be discontinued because they place an unfair burden on non-minority persons who bear the cost of the programs.
   (B) Affirmative action programs may be able to achieve legitimate social and economic goals such as improved efficiency.
   (C) Affirmative action programs are justified because they are the only way of correcting injustices created by past discrimination.
   (D) Affirmative action programs must be redesigned so that society as a whole rather than particular individuals bears the cost of the programs.
   (E) Affirmative action programs should be abandoned because they serve no useful social function and place unfair burdens on particular individuals.

4. The author most likely places the word "funding" in quotation marks (line 35) in order to remind the reader that
   (A) affirmative action programs are costly in terms of government revenues
   (B) particular individuals may bear a disproportionate share of the burden of affirmative action
   (C) the cost of most government programs is shared by society at large
   (D) the beneficiaries of affirmative action are members of larger groups
   (E) the cost of affirmative action is not only a monetary expenditure

5. The "villainous man" discussed in lines 54–69 functions primarily as
   (A) an illustration
   (B) a counter-example
   (C) an authority
   (D) an analogy
   (E) a disclaimer

6. According to the passage, affirmative action programs are different from most other government programs in which of the following ways?

I. the goals the programs are designed to achieve
II. the ways in which costs of the programs are distributed
III. the ways in which benefits of the programs are allocated

(A) I only
(B) II only
(C) III only
(D) II and III only
(E) I, II, and III

7. It can be inferred that the author believes the reader will regard affirmative action programs as
   (A) posing a moral dilemma
   (B) based on unsound premises
   (C) containing self-contradictions
   (D) creating needless suffering
   (E) offering a panacea

8. The primary purpose of the passage is to
   (A) reconcile two conflicting points of view
   (B) describe and refute a point of view
   (C) provide a historical context for a problem
   (D) suggest a new method for studying social problems
   (E) analyze the structure of an institution

The number of aged in Sweden is one of the largest in the world, close to 14 percent of the total population, and the need for health and social support for them has been intensified by improvements in the standard of living. Life expectancy has increased and at the same time there is a greater unwillingness on the part of adult offspring to care for aged parents living in their households. The percentage of aged persons living with their children a decade ago was approximately 10 in Sweden (3 in Stockholm), contrasted with 20 in Denmark, 30 in the United States, 40 in England, 70 in Poland, and 90 in the USSR. Sweden placed a moratorium on the construction of new acute beds in favor of long-term beds, but that has foundered because care in a long-stay facility, if done correctly, while less costly than an acute facility, may still be prohibitively expensive.

Payroll is the single most important budgetary component in all branches of hospital service, accounting for over 60 percent of total costs; and the staff-bed ratio requirements for the chronic aged are higher than for acute patients, especially with respect to nursing and rehabilitation personnel. Payroll expenditures have grown sizably as the result of advancing standards of industrial justice which challenge the validity of the traditional idea that health workers other than doctors should work for lower wages than persons doing comparable work elsewhere in the economy because of the eleemosynary and humanitarian ethic of patient care. The progress of women in securing greater parity with men in income and employment opportunities are especially notable in the health field where women who comprise roughly three-fourths of the labor force have been concentrated disproportionately in low-paying and low-status jobs.

In nearly all highly developed countries recently the policy has been to bring the wages of low-income hospital workers into line with those in industry and manufacturing. Even so, the conditions of employment are unattractive and staffing remains a problem, especially during off hours, weekends, and summers when people prefer to be with their families or on vacation. The magnitude of these problems is greater in long-stay than in short-stay facilities, because of the differences in prestige and responsiveness of patients to intervention.

Paradoxically, the cutbacks in long-term care spending in Sweden may have contributed to an improvement in treatment outcomes. Patients have been required to take maximum responsibility for their own care, and this has lessened dependency and fostered rehabilitation. A similar principle of self-care applies to the treatment of the mentally retarded and the aged. In addition to the patient care benefits, significant economies can be obtained, demonstrating that the two objectives are not necessarily incompatible. The medical director of a large-sized long-term care facility has found that in the case of the aged over 80, multiple-patient rooms are better than single-patient rooms. Older and mentally disoriented patients are much quieter when they have roommates, and because of the tendency of people to help one another, they require less staff time. Staff time per patient is directly correlated to the number of beds in the room, decreasing from 217 minutes for single room to 99 minutes for four-bed rooms. Many new long-term hospitals for the psychogeriatrics of advanced age are being designed for four to five beds per room. The reaction to resource scarcity has resulted in unexpected contributions to patient welfare.

9. It can be inferred from the passage that the increasing number of aged requiring care prompted Sweden to
   (A) shift funds from construction of facilities for care of the acutely ill to projects to build facilities for long-term care
   (B) restructure its tax laws to penalize families who refused to provide in-house care for their aging relatives
   (C) attempt to reduce long-term care costs by

depressing salaries of hospital workers and delaying wage increases
   (D) crowding four or five patients into a room designed for only one patient in order to reduce payroll costs
   (E) discontinue construction of long-term hospitals for the psychogeriatrics of the aged

10. All of the following are mentioned in the passage as difficulties in staffing long-stay facilities EXCEPT
    (A) the low prestige of such jobs
    (B) the relatively low rate of pay
    (C) the character of the patient population
    (D) the inconvenient work schedules
    (E) the large number of weekly hours

11. It can be inferred from the passage that pay rates in the health field have historically been lower than those for manufacturing and industry because
    (A) jobs in the health field have a lower status
    (B) service in the health field was considered charitable work
    (C) doctors insisted on receiving higher salaries than other workers
    (D) labor costs are the greatest category of expenditures for hospitals
    (E) aged people are not able to pay high fees for long-term care

12. It can be inferred from the passage that the staff/bed cost of long-stay care in Sweden is
    (A) greater than that for acute care
    (B) increasing less rapidly than that for acute care
    (C) unrelated to the number of persons being cared for
    (D) borne primarily by the individual patient
    (E) less than in other countries such as England and the United States

13. The author refers to the results of cutbacks in long-term care spending as "paradoxical" because
    (A) cutbacks in expenditures ordinarily result in better care
    (B) the longer a patient lives, the greater is his or her need for care
    (C) fewer adult offspring are willing to care for aged parents in their own homes
    (D) reduced staffing needs means fewer positions for hospital workers
    (E) reductions in spending placed a moratorium on new construction

14. Which of the following, if true, would most strengthen the author's contention that improvements in the standard of living increase the reluctance of adults to care for aged parents?
    (A) The United States has a higher standard of living than Sweden.
    (B) Stockholm has a substantially higher standard of living than the rest of Sweden.
    (C) The number of long-term care beds in England has not increased appreciably in the past five years.
    (D) Sweden has fewer aged persons than Denmark.
    (E) Sweden has a higher acute to long-term beds ratio than the USSR.

Can computers reason? Reasoning requires the individual to take a given set of facts and draw correct conclusions. Unfortunately, errors frequently occur, and we are not talking about simple carelessness as occurs when two numbers are incorrectly added, nor do we mean errors resulting from simple forgetfulness. Rather, we have in mind errors of a logical nature—those resulting from faulty reasoning. Now, or at least soon, computers will be capable of error-free logical reasoning in a variety of areas. The key to avoiding errors is to use a computer program that relies on the last two decades' research in the field of automated theorem proving. AURA (Automated Reasoning Assistant) is the program that best exemplifies this use of the computer.

AURA solves a problem by drawing conclusions from a given set of facts about the problem. The program does not learn, nor is it self-analytical, but it reaches logical conclusions flawlessly. It uses various types of reasoning and, more important, has access to very powerful and sophisticated logical strategies. AURA seldom relies on brute force to find solutions. Instead it solves almost all problems by using sophisticated techniques to find a contradiction. One generally starts with a set of assumptions and adds a statement that the goal is unreachable. For example, if the problem is to test a safety system that automatically shuts down a nuclear reactor when instruments indicate a problem, AURA is told that the system will not shut the reactor down under those circumstances. If AURA finds a contradiction between the statement and the system's design assumptions, then this aspect of the reactor's design has been proved satisfactory. This strategy, known as the set of support strategy, lets AURA concentrate on the problem at hand and avoid the many fruitless steps required to explore the entire theory underlying the problem. Almost never does the program proceed by carrying out an exhaustive search.

The chief use for AURA at this time is for electronic circuit design validation, but a number of other uses will arise. For example, there already exist "expert systems" that include a component for reasoning. An expert system is a special-purpose program designed to automate reasoning in a specific area such as medical diagnosis. These expert programs, unlike human experts, do not die. Such systems continue to improve and have an indefinite life span. Moreover, they can be replicated for pennies. A human who can expertly predict where to drill for oil is in great demand. A program that can predict equally well would be invaluable and could be duplicated any number of times.

Will the computer replace the human being? Certainly not. It seems likely that computer programs will reproduce—that is, design more clever computer programs and more efficient, more useful components. Reasoning programs will also analyze their own progress, learn from their attempts to solve a problem, and redirect their attack on a problem. Such programs will assist, rather than replace, humans. Their impact will be felt in design, manufacturing, law, medicine, and other areas. Reasoning assistants will enable human minds to turn to deeper and far more complex ideas. These ideas will be partially formulated and then checked for reasoning flaws by a reasoning program. Many errors will be avoided.

15. According to the passage, the primary purpose of AURA is to
    (A) design new and easily replicated programs
    (B) function as a safety mechanism in nuclear reactors
    (C) detect contradictions and other faults in computer programs
    (D) develop expert human programs for technical fields
    (E) check human reasoning for possible errors

16. Which of the following titles best describes the content of the passage?
    (A) Scientific Applications of Computers
    (B) Theories of Artificial Intelligence
    (C) Some Suggested Applications for AURA
    (D) Using Computers to Assist Human Reasoning
    (E) The Dangers of Automated Reasoning Assistants

17. According to the passage, all of the following are advantages of expert programs EXCEPT

(A) they have an indefinite life span
(B) they cost little to reproduce
(C) many copies can be made available
(D) they are self-analytical
(E) more knowledges can be added to them

18. The author mentions which of the following as areas for applying AURA?

   I. electronic engineering
   II. nuclear engineering
   III. mathematic and formal logic
   IV. medical diagnosis

   (A) I and II only
   (B) II and IV only
   (C) I, II, and IV only
   (D) II, III, and IV only
   (E) I, II, III, and IV

19. If the design of an electronic circuit were tested by AURA, and the conclusion that under certain circumstances a switching device would remain open generated a contradiction, this would lead to the conclusion that
   (A) the circuit was properly designed
   (B) the switch would remain closed under the circumstances
   (C) the switch would remain open under the circumstances
   (D) an error in human reasoning invalidated the design
   (E) the circuit was incorrectly designed

20. The author's attitude toward the developments he describes can best be described as
   (A) enthusiastic
   (B) reluctant
   (C) cautious
   (D) skeptical
   (E) worried

21. The author is primarily concerned to
   (A) discuss recent developments
   (B) correct a misconception
   (C) propose a theory
   (D) refute an objection
   (E) recommend a solution

Until Josquin des Prez, 1440–1521, Western music was liturgical, designed as an accompaniment to worship. Like the intricately carved gargoyles perched atop medieval cathedrals beyond sight of any human, music was composed to please God before anybody else; its dominant theme was reverence. Emotion was there, but it was the grief of Mary standing at the foot of the Cross, the joy of the faithful hailing Christ's resurrection. Even the secular music of the Middle Ages was tied to predetermined patterns that sometimes seemed to stand in the way of individual expression.

While keeping one foot firmly planted in the divine world, Josquin stepped with the other into the human. He scored magnificent masses, but also newly expressive motets such as the lament of David over his son Absalom or the "Deploration d'Ockeghem," a dirge on the death of Ockeghem, the greatest master before Josquin, a motet written all in black notes, and one of the most profoundly moving scores of the Renaissance. Josquin was the first composer to set psalms to music. But alongside *Benedicite omnia opera Domini Domino* ("Bless the Lord, all ye works of the Lord") he put *El Grillo* ("The cricket is a good singer who manages long poems") and *Allegez moy* ("Solace me, sweet pleasant brunette"). Josquin was praised by Martin Luther, for his music blends respect for tradition with a rebel's willingness to risk the horizon. What Galileo was to science, Josquin was to music. While preserving their allegiance to God, both asserted a new importance for man.

Why then should Josquin languish in relative obscurity? The answer has to do with the separation of concept from performance in music. In fine art, concept and performance are one; both the art lover and the art historian have thousands of years of paintings, drawings and sculptures to study and enjoy. Similarly with literature: Poetry, fiction, drama, and criticism survive on the printed page or in manuscript for judgment and admiration by succeeding generations. But musical notation on a page is not art, no matter how lofty or excellent the composer's conception; it is, crudely put, a set of directions for producing art. Being highly symbolic, musical notation requires training before it can even be read, let alone performed. Moreover, because the musical conventions of other days are not ours, translation of a Renaissance score into modern notation brings difficulties of its own. For example, the Renaissance notation of Josquin's day did not designate the tempo at which the music should be played or sung. It did not indicate all flats or sharps; these were sounded in accordance with musicianly rules, which were capable of transforming major to minor, minor to major, diatonic to chromatic sound, and thus affect melody, harmony, and musical expression. A Renaissance composition might include several parts—but it did not indicate which were to be sung, which to be played, nor even whether instruments were to be used at all.

Thus, Renaissance notation permits of several interpretations and an imaginative musician may give an interpretation that is a revelation. But no matter how imaginative, few modern musicians can offer any interpretation of Renaissance music. The public for it is small, limiting the number of musicians who can afford to learn, rehearse, and perform it. Most of those who attempt it at all are students organized in *collegia musica* whose memberships have a distressing habit of changing every semester, thus preventing directors from maintaining the year-in, year-out continuity required to achieve excellence of performance. Finally, the instruments used in Renaissance times—drummhorns, recorders, rauschpfeifen, shawms, sackbuts, organettos—must be specially procured.

22. The primary purpose of the passage is to
    (A) introduce the reader to Josquin and account for his relative obscurity
    (B) describe the main features of medieval music and show how Josquin changed them
    (C) place Josquin's music in an historical context and show its influence on later composers
    (D) enumerate the features of Josquin's music and supply critical commentary
    (E) praise the music of Josquin and interest the reader in further study of medieval music

23. The passage contains information which would help answer all of the following questions EXCEPT
    (A) What are the titles of some of Josquin's secular compositions?
    (B) What are the names of some Renaissance musical instruments?
    (C) Who was the greatest composer before Josquin?
    (D) Where might it be possible to hear Renaissance music performed?
    (E) What are the names of some of Josquin's most famous students?

24. It can be inferred from the passage that modern musical notation has which of the following characteristics?

    I. The tempo at which a composition is to be played is indicated in the notation.
    II. Whether a note is sharp or a flat is indicated in the notation.
    III. The notation indicates which parts of the music are to be played by which instruments.

    (A) I only

(B) II only
(C) I and III only
(D) II and III only
(E) I, II, and III

25. The author would most likely agree with which of the following statements?
    (A) Music is a more perfect art form than painting or sculpture.
    (B) Music can be said to exist only when it is being performed.
    (C) Josquin was the greatest composer of the Middle Ages.
    (D) Renaissance music is superior to music produced in modern times.
    (E) Most people dislike Josquin because they do not understand his music.

26. The passage leads most logically to a proposal to
    (A) establish more *collegia musica*
    (B) study Josquin's compositional techniques in greater detail
    (C) include Renaissance music in college studies
    (D) provide funds for musicians to study and play Josquin
    (E) translate Josquin's music into modern notation

27. The author cites all of the following as reasons for Josquin's relative obscurity EXCEPT
    (A) the difficulty one encounters in attempting to read his musical notation
    (B) the inability of modern musicians to play instruments of the Renaissance
    (C) the difficulty of procuring unusual instruments needed to play the music
    (D) the lack of public interest in Renaissance music
    (E) problems in finding funding for the study of Renaissance music

28. The author's attitude toward Galileo can best be described as
    (A) admiring
    (B) critical
    (C) accepting
    (D) analytical
    (E) noncommittal

Our current system of unemployment compensation has increased nearly all sources of adult unemploy-

ment: season and cyclical variations in the demand for labor, weak labor force attachment, and unnecessarily
5 long durations of unemployment. First, for those who are already unemployed, the system greatly reduces the cost of extending the period of unemployment. Second, for all types of unsteady work—seasonal, cyclical and casual—it raises the net wage to the employ-
10 ee, relative to the cost of the employer.

As for the first, consider a worker who earns $500 per month or $6,000 per year if she experiences no unemployment. If she is unemployed for one month, she loses $500 in gross earnings but only $116 in net
15 income. How does this occur? A reduction of $500 in annual earnings reduces her federal, payroll and state tax liability by $134. Unemployment compensation consists of 50 percent of her wage or $250. Her net income therefore falls from $366 if she is employed,
20 to $250 paid as unemployment compensation. Moreover, part of the higher income from employment is offset by the cost of transportation to work and other expenses associated with employment; and in some industries, the cost of unemployment is reduced fur-
25 ther or even made negative by the supplementary unemployment benefits paid by employers under collective bargaining agreements. The overall effect is to increase the duration of a typical spell of unemployment and to increase the frequency with which indi-
30 viduals lose jobs and become unemployed.

The more general effect of unemployment compensation is to increase the seasonal and cyclical fluctuations in the demand for labor and the relative number of short-lived casual jobs. A worker who accepts such
35 work knows she will be laid off when the season ends. If there were no unemployment compensation, workers could be induced to accept such unstable jobs only if the wage rate were sufficiently higher in those jobs than in the more stable alternative. The higher cost of
40 labor, then, would induce employers to reduce the instability of employment by smoothing production through increased variation in inventories and delivery lags, by additional development of off-season work and by the introduction of new production tech-
45 niques, e.g., new methods of outdoor work in bad weather.

Employers contribute to the state unemployment compensation fund on the basis of the unemployment experience of their own previous employees. Within
50 limits, the more benefits that those former employees draw, the higher is the employer's tax rate. The theory of experience rating is clear. If an employer paid the full cost of the unemployment benefits that his former employees received, unemployment compensation
55 would provide no incentive to an excess use of unstable employment. In practice, however, experience

rating is limited by a maximum rate of employer contribution. For any firm which pays the maximum rate, there is no cost for additional unemployment and no
60 gain from a small reduction in unemployment.

The challenge at this time is to restructure the unemployment system in a way that strengthens its good features while reducing the harmful disincentive effects. Some gains can be achieved by removing the
65 ceiling on the employer's rate of contribution and by lowering the minimum rate to zero. Employers would then pay the full price of unemployment insurance benefits and this would encourage employers to stabilize employment and production. Further improve-
70 ment could be achieved if unemployment insurance benefits were taxed in the same way as other earnings. This would eliminate the anomalous situations in which a worker's net income is actually reduced when he returns to work.

29. The author is primarily concerned to
   (A) defend the system of unemployment compensation against criticism
   (B) advocate expanding the benefits and scope of coverage of unemployment compensation
   (C) point to weaknesses inherent in government programs which subsidize individuals
   (D) suggest reforms to eliminate inefficiencies in unemployment compensation
   (E) propose methods of increasing the effectiveness of government programs to reduce unemployment

30. The author cites the example of a worker earning $500 per month in order to
   (A) show the disincentive created by unemployment compensation for that worker to return to work
   (B) demonstrate that employers do not bear the full cost of worker compensation
   (C) prove that unemployed workers would not be able to survive without unemployment compensation
   (D) explain why employers prefer to hire seasonal workers instead of permanent workers for short-term jobs
   (E) condemn workers who prefer to live on unemployment compensation to taking a job

31. The author recommends which of the following changes be made in the unemployment compensation?

   I. taxing unemployment compensation to lower net benefits received by workers

II. shortening the length of time during which a worker is eligible to receive benefits to force the worker to seek work

III. eliminating any maximum rate of employer contribution to increase the amount of money paid by employers into the unemployment compensation fund

(A) I only
(B) I and II only
(C) I and III only
(D) II and III only
(E) I, II, and III

32. The author mentions all of the following as ways by which employers might reduce seasonal and cyclical unemployment EXCEPT
(A) developing new techniques of production not affected by weather
(B) slowing delivery schedules to provide work during slow seasons
(C) adopting a system of supplementary benefits for workers laid off in slow periods
(D) manipulating inventory supplies to require year-round rather than short-term employment
(E) finding new jobs to be done by workers during the off-season

33. With which of the following statements about experience rating would the author most likely agree?
(A) Experience rating is theoretically sound, but its effectiveness in practice is undermined by maximum contribution ceilings.
(B) Experience rating is an inefficient method of computing employer contribution because an employer has no control over the length of an employee's unemployment.
(C) Experience rating is theoretically invalid and should be replaced by a system in which the employee contributes the full amount of benefits he will later receive.
(D) Experience rating is basically fair, but its performance could be improved by requiring large firms to pay more than small firms.
(E) Experience rating requires an employer to pay a contribution which is completely unrelated to the amount his employees draw in unemployment compensation benefits.

34. The author makes which of the following criticisms of the unemployment compensation system?

I. It places an unfair burden on firms whose production is cyclical or seasonal.
II. It encourages out-of-work employees to extend the length of time they are unemployed.
III. It constitutes a drain on state treasuries which must subsidize unemployment compensation funds.

(A) I only
(B) II only
(C) III only
(D) I and II only
(E) II and III only

35. It can be inferred that the author regards the unemployment compensation system as
(A) socially necessary
(B) economically efficient
(C) inherently wasteful
(D) completely unnecessary
(E) seriously outdated

STOP

IF YOU FINISH BEFORE TIME IS CALLED, CHECK YOUR WORK ON THIS SECTION ONLY. DO NOT WORK ON ANY OTHER SECTION IN THE TEST.

SECTION III

Time——45 Minutes
35 Questions

Directions: In this section, the questions ask you to analyze and evaluate the reasoning in short paragraphs or passages. For some questions, all of the answer choices may conceivably be answers to the question asked. You should select the *best* answer to the question, that is, an answer which does not require you to make assumptions which violate commonsense standards by being implausible, redundant, irrelevant or inconsistent. After choosing the best answer, blacken the corresponding space on the answer sheet.

1. All of the following conclusions are based upon accurate expense vouchers submitted by employees to department heads of a certain corporation in 1989. Which of them is LEAST likely to be weakened by the discovery of additional 1989 expense vouchers?
   (A) The accounting department had only 15 employees and claimed expenses of at least $500.
   (B) The sales department had at least 25 employees and claimed expenses of at least $35,000.
   (C) The legal department had at least 2 employees and claimed no more than $3,000 in expenses.
   (D) The public relations department had no more than 1 employee and claimed no more than $200 in expenses.
   (E) The production department had no more than 500 employees and claimed no more than $350 in expenses.

2. Mr. Mayor, when is the city government going to stop discriminating against its Hispanic residents in the delivery of critical municipal services?

   The form of the question above is most nearly paralleled by which of the following?
   (A) Mr. Congressman, when is the Congress finally going to realize that defense spending is out of hand?
   (B) Madam Chairperson, do you anticipate the committee will take luncheon recess?
   (C) Dr. Greentree, what do you expect to be the impact of the Governor's proposals on the economically disadvantaged counties of our state?

   (D) Gladys, since you're going to the grocery store anyway, would you mind picking up a quart of milk for me?
   (E) Counselor, does the company you represent find that its affirmative action program is successful in recruiting qualified minority employees?

3. The main ingredient in this bottle of Dr. John's Milk of Magnesia is used by nine out of ten hospitals across the country as an antacid and laxative.

   If this advertising claim is true, which of the following statements must also be true?

   I. Nine out of ten hospitals across the country use Dr. John's Milk of Magnesia for some ailments.
   II. Only one out of ten hospitals in the country do not treat acid indigestion and constipation.
   III. Only one out of ten hospitals across the country does not recommend Dr. John's Milk of Magnesia for patients who need a milk of magnesia.

   (A) I only
   (B) II only
   (C) I and III only
   (D) I, II, and III
   (E) None of the statements is necessarily true.

Questions 4 and 5

   I. All wheeled conveyances which travel on the highway are polluters.
   II. Bicycles are not polluters.
   III. Whenever I drive my car on the highway, it rains.
   IV. It is raining.

4. If the above statements are all true, which of the following statements must also be true?
   (A) Bicycles do not travel on the highway.
   (B) Bicycles travel on the highway only if it is raining.

287

(C) If my car is not polluting, then it is not raining.

(D) I am now driving on the highway.

(E) My car is not a polluter.

5. The conclusion "my car is not polluting" could be logically deduced from statements I–IV if statement

    (A) II were changed to: "Bicycles are polluters."

    (B) II were changed to: "My car is a polluter."

    (C) III were changed to: "If bicycles were polluters, I would be driving my car on the highway."

    (D) IV were changed to: "Rainwater is polluted."

    (E) IV were changed to: "It is not raining."

6. Statistics published by the U.S. Department of Transportation show that nearly 80 percent of all traffic fatalities occur at speeds of under 50 miles per hour and within 25 miles of home. Therefore, you are safer in a car if you are driving at a speed over 50 miles per hour and not within a 25-mile radius of your home.

Which of the following, if true, most weakens the conclusion of the argument above?

    (A) Teenage drivers are involved in 75 percent of all traffic accidents resulting in fatalities.

    (B) 80 percent of all persons arrested for driving at a speed over the posted speed limit are intoxicated.

    (C) 50 percent of the nation's annual traffic fatalities occur on six weekends which are considered high-risk weekends because they contain holidays.

    (D) The Department of Transportation statistics were based on police reports compiled by the 50 states.

    (E) 90 percent of all driving time is registered within a 25-mile radius of the driver's home and at speeds less than 50 miles per hour.

7. Usually when we have had an inch or more of rain in a single day, my backyard immediately has mushrooms and other forms of fungus growing in it. There are no mushrooms or fungus growing in my backyard.

Which of the following would logically complete an argument with the premises given above?

  I. Therefore, there has been no rain here in the past day.

  II. Therefore, there probably has been no rain here in the past day.

  III. Therefore, we have not had more than an inch of rain here in the past day.

  IV. Therefore, we probably have not had more than an inch of rain here in the past day.

    (A) I only

    (B) II only

    (C) III only

    (D) IV only

    (E) II and IV only

Questions 8–9

Can you really have that body you want without a monotonous program of daily exercise? Is there really an exercise routine that will help you to shed that fat quickly and painlessly? Now, a university study shows that this is possible. Surely, you would not want to miss a chance to find out whether you can have that body once again. Try the new Jack Remain's twice-a-week workout—and judge for yourself.

8. Which of the following conclusions can be completely justified assuming that the statements made are true?

    (A) Only Jack Remain's program offers the possibility for effortless weight loss.

    (B) Exercise experts have developed a program to help people of all ages lose weight.

    (C) Following Jack Remain's twice-a-week workout program might help you to lose weight.

    (D) If you follow Jack Remain's twice-a-week workout program, you will lose weight.

    (E) Most people must exercise in order to lose weight.

9. The method of persuasion used by the advertisement can be described as

    (A) providing evidence and allowing the listener to arrive at his or her own conclusions

    (B) presenting the reader with a logical set of premises and inviting the reader to draw his or her own conclusion

    (C) presenting both sides of an issue while carefully avoiding influencing the reader's decision

    (D) asking that the reader provide evidence to test the truth of the claims made in the advertisement

(E) attempting to convince the reader that similar claims made by others are false

10. I recently read a book by an author who insists that everything man does is economically motivated. Leaders launch wars of conquest in order to capture the wealth of other nations. Scientists do research in order to receive grants or find marketable processes. Students go to college to get better jobs. He even maintains that people go to museums to become better informed on the off-chance that some day they will be able to turn that knowledge to their advantage. So persuaded was I by the author's evidence that, applying his theory on my own, I was able to conclude that he had written the book _____.

Which of the following provides the most logical completion of the above paragraph?
(A) as a labor of love
(B) in order to make money
(C) as a means of reforming the world by calling man's attention to his greed
(D) as an exercise in scientific research
(E) in response to a creative urge to be a novelist

11. In our investigation of this murder, we are guided by our previous experience with the Eastend Killer. You will recall that in that case, the victims were also carrying a great deal of money when they were killed but the money was not taken. As in this case, the murder weapon was a pistol. Finally, in that case also, the murders were committed between six in the evening and twelve midnight. So we are probably after someone who looks very much like the Eastend Killer, who was finally tried, convicted, and executed: 5'11" tall, a mustache, short, brown hair, walks with a slight limp.

The author makes which of the following assumptions?

I. Crimes similar in detail are likely to be committed by perpetrators who are similar in physical appearance.
II. The Eastend Killer has apparently escaped from prison and has resumed his criminal activities.
III. The man first convicted as the Eastend Killer was actually innocent, and the real Eastend Killer is still loose.

(A) I only

(B) II only
(C) III only
(D) I and II only
(E) I and III only

12. I. Everyone who has not read the report either has no opinion in the matter or holds a wrong opinion about it.
II. Everyone who holds no opinion in the matter has not read the report.

Which of the following best describes the relationship between the two above propositions?
(A) If II is true, I may be either false or true.
(B) If II is true, I must also be true.
(C) If II is true, I is likely to be true.
(D) If I is true, II must also be true.
(E) If I is false, II must also be false.

13. The idea that women should be police officers is absurd. After all, women are on the average three to five inches shorter than men and weigh 20 to 50 pounds less. It is clear that a woman would be less effective than a man in a situation requiring force.

Which of the following, if true, would most weaken the above argument?
(A) Some of the female applicants for the police force are larger than some of the male officers presently on the force.
(B) Police officers are required to go through an intensive 18-month training program.
(C) Police officers are required to carry pistols and are trained in the use of their weapons.
(D) There are a significant number of desk jobs in the police force which women could fill.
(E) Many criminals are women.

14. No sophomores were selected for Rho Rho Phi. Some sophomores are members of the Debating Society. Therefore, some members of the Debating Society were not selected for Rho Rho Phi.

Which of the following is logically most similar to the argument given above?
(A) Everyone who exercises in the heat will get ill. I never exercise in the heat, so I will probably never be ill.
(B) Drivers who wish to avoid expensive automobile repairs will have their cars tuned up

regularly. My uncle refuses to have his car tuned up regularly. Therefore, he enjoys paying for major repairs.

(C) Some books which are beautiful were written in French, and French literature is well respected. Therefore, any book which is beautiful is well respected.

(D) All pets are excluded from this apartment complex. But many pets are valuable. Therefore, some valuable animals are excluded from this apartment complex.

(E) St. Paul is a long way from London. Minneapolis is a long way from London. Therefore, St. Paul is a long, long way from Minneapolis.

15. All Burrahobbits are Trollbeaters, and some Burrahobbits are Greeblegrabbers.

If these statements are true, which of the following must also be true?

   I. If something is neither a Trollbeater nor a Greeblegrabber, it cannot be a Burrahobbit.

   II. It is not possible to be a Trollbeater without being a Greeblegrabber.

   III. An elf must be either a Trollbeater or a Greeblegrabber.

(A) I only
(B) II only
(C) III only
(D) I and II only
(E) I, II, and III

16. If the batteries in my electric razor are dead, the razor will not function. My razor is not functioning. Therefore, the batteries must be dead.

Which of the following arguments is most similar to that presented above?

(A) If Elroy attends the meeting, Ms. Barker will be elected club president. Ms. Barker was not elected club president; therefore, Elroy did not attend the meeting.

(B) All evidence is admissible unless it is tainted. This evidence is inadmissible. Therefore, it is tainted.

(C) If John committed the crime, his fingerprints will be found at the scene. John's fingerprints were found at the scene; therefore, John committed the crime.

(D) Grant is my uncle. Sophie is Grant's niece. Therefore, Sophie is my sister.

(E) Jonathan will wear his dark glasses if the coast is clear. The coast is clear. Therefore, Jonathan will wear his dark glasses.

17. All general statements are based solely on observed instances of a phenomenon. That the statement has held true up to a certain point in time is no guarantee that it will remain unexceptionless. Therefore, no generalization can be considered free from possible exception.

The logic of the above argument can best be described as
(A) self-defeating
(B) circular
(C) ill defined
(D) valid
(E) inductive

Questions 18–19

The films of Gonzalez have had a lasting impact on motion pictures in this country. By showing what a Mexican-American woman could accomplish as a director, she paved the way for other, more commercially acceptable movie makers of similar backgrounds. Furthermore, by firmly resisting pressure to abandon the political and social themes that are central to her work she --(18)--.

18. Which of the following best completes the paragraph above?
(A) demonstrated the remarkable popularity that politically engaged films can have
(B) set an example of integrity for younger, socially conscious filmmakers
(C) revealed the underlying ethnic and social bias so pervasive in the film industry
(D) weakened the chances for later filmmakers to develop similar themes
(E) overcame the obstacles she faced as a member of an oppressed minority group

19. The passage implies that the films of Gonzalez
(A) deal mainly with feminist issues
(B) have become widely popular
(C) are generally regarded with favor by film critics and historians
(D) portray Mexican-Americans in a positive light
(E) were not extremely profitable

20. Hospital administrators and medical officials often say that bringing spiralling health care costs under control will require a reduction in the levels of care expected by many groups in our society,

particularly the elderly and the chronically ill. And it is true that recent increases in health care costs have been caused partly by improved levels of care for these groups. But the basic causes of the uncontrolled growth of health care costs lie elsewhere. Duplication of the most costly services within regions; inefficient allocation of medical expertise and resources; excessive salaries for some groups of health care professionals—these are some of the more fundamental problems that must be addressed.

Which of the following conclusions is most strongly supported by the paragraph above?
(A) Controlling the growth of health care costs need not involve a significant reduction in the level of services for the elderly and chronically ill.
(B) Duplication and inefficient allocation of medical resources are important factors contributing to the increasing cost of health care services for the elderly and chronically ill.
(C) To control costs in the health care sector it will be necessary to reduce the levels of services provided to certain groups.
(D) People who are elderly and/or chronically ill are forced to pay higher prices in order to receive the same quality of health care services once purchased at a lower price.
(E) Unless immediate action is taken to slow the rate of inflation in the health care sector, health care services will be beyond the means of most elderly and chronically ill people.

21. A recent study ranked American cities according to ten different criteria, including among others, the incidence of crime, cost of living, ease of transportation, and cultural amenities. Since San Francisco ranked third overall and Detroit sixth, we can conclude that Detroit has a more serious crime problem than San Francisco.

Which of the following, if true, most weakens the argument above?
(A) The cost of living is higher in Detroit than in San Francisco.
(B) San Francisco ranked higher than Detroit on seven of the ten criteria.
(C) Both Atlanta and Houston, which have more serious crime problems than Detroit, ranked higher than Detroit on the overall index.
(D) Seattle, which has a more serious crime problem than Boston, also ranked below Boston in seven other categories.

(E) San Francisco and Detroit both have more serious crime problems than Washington, D.C., which ranked first in overall desirability.

22. Adults often assume that the emotional lives of children are radically different from those of adults, while their thinking is basically the same (though less accurate and skillful). In fact, psychologists who have studied children carefully, know that the very opposite is true.

Which of the following conclusions can be most reliably drawn from the statements above?
(A) Children react to the world around them in ways that clearly prefigure the adult personalities they will develop.
(B) Children's feelings are much like those of adults, but their ways of reasoning are often very different.
(C) Differences between individuals of the same age are more important than differences between groups of different ages.
(D) Emotional responses and thought patterns are established at a very early age and continue into adulthood.
(E) The reactions of children are the mirror images of those that would be expected of adults in the same situation.

23. Whenever it is sunny, Hector either goes fishing or goes swimming. When Hector goes swimming, Sharon plays tennis. On Saturday, Sharon did not play tennis.

If the statements above are true, then which of the following must also be true?

   I. Hector did not go swimming on Saturday.
  II. It was not sunny on Saturday.
 III. Hector did not go fishing on Saturday.

(A) I only
(B) III only
(C) I and II only
(D) I and III only
(E) I, II, and III

John: I oppose spending more money on the space program. Those tax dollars should be spent right here on Earth rather than being used to construct satellites and spaceships to be sent to the heavens.

Joan: Well, then you should support the space program, for those dollars are spent right here on Earth, creating jobs for thousands of scientific and technical workers in the aerospace and other industries.

24. Which of the following best describes Joan's response to John?
    (A) It points out that John's position is inherently contradictory.
    (B) It attempts to force John into choosing between two horns of a dilemma.
    (C) It exploits an ambiguity in a key phrase in John's statement of his position.
    (D) It tries to refute John's position by attacking John personally rather than by analyzing the merits of John's claim.
    (E) It uncovers a hidden assumption in John's position that is highly questionable.

25. I am perfectly capable of driving home safely from this party. I drank only wine and scrupulously avoided all hard liquor.
    The statement above presupposes that
    (A) someone who has been drinking hard liquor is drunk
    (B) drinking hard liquor impairs driving more than drinking wine
    (C) the police are less likely to arrest someone who has been drinking wine than someone who has been drinking hard liquor
    (D) only someone who has had no alcohol to drink is fit to drive
    (E) drinking wine will impair driving ability only if the person has also been drinking hard liquor

26. Senator Allen has admitted to having an illicit affair and lying to her husband about it. Although the affair ended several years ago, and Allen and her husband are now reconciled, this episode should disqualify Allen from seeking higher office. How could world leaders be expected to negotiate with a president who has admitted lying to her spouse?

    Which of the following assumptions underlies the argument above?
    (A) A president who has committed adultery might be subject to blackmail or other pressures.
    (B) Many voters would not vote for Allen because she admitted to having an affair.
    (C) The personal life of a political leader may affect that leader's ability to make correct decisions.
    (D) A person who would tell an untruth in a personal situation is likely to tell a lie in public.

    (E) A public leader has an extraordinary obligation to set an example of high moral standards.

Questions 27–28
    (A) The safety of the new drug Zorapan has yet to be clearly demonstrated. Only one study of its effects has been conducted, and the results were inconclusive.
    (B) George is unlikely to make a good class president. He is hot-tempered and extremely critical of all those around him.
    (C) Mayor Warren favors the new zoning law for one reason only: her husband is a building contractor who stands to profit from the increased construction the law will encourage.
    (D) It's almost impossible to get good repair service nowadays. I brought my camera to the local camera shop for repair, and it still doesn't work properly.
    (E) Helen probably got her interest in medicine from her family. Both of her parents, as well as two of her uncles, are physicians.

27. Which of the arguments above is a generalization that could be criticized because it is based upon a limited sampling?

28. Which of the arguments above attempts to discredit an opponent rather than attack the merits of a position?

29. Spokespeople for the nations of the West boast of the freedoms their people enjoy, yet how much freedom do they really have? Housing, medical care, and other basic needs are increasingly costly, and no one is guaranteed a job. It is the people living in the nations of the communist bloc who enjoy true freedom since they are free from the fear that the constant threat of poverty brings.

    The persuasive force of the argument above depends largely upon the ambiguous use of which of the following pairs of terms?
    (A) basic needs and job
    (B) poverty and fear
    (C) free and freedom
    (D) guarantee and poverty
    (E) spokespeople and people

30. French painting during the first half of the 19th century was characterized by a lack of imagina-

tion. The Ecole des Beaux Arts, the quasi-governmental agency that controlled the dissemination of lucrative government scholarships and commissions, effectively stifled creativity. A student who hoped to achieve any fame or financial success was well advised to paint in the style of the Ecole. It is a small wonder then that the Impressionist painters initially earned only the scorn of their colleagues and empty bellies for their efforts.

The passage above implies that
(A) Impressionist painters did not paint in the style of the Ecole des Beaux Arts
(B) the Impressionist painters eventually gained control of the Ecole des Beaux Arts
(C) the Ecole des Beaux Arts promulgated rules defining the permissible subject matter of paintings
(D) the Ecole des Beaux Arts determined licensing standards for those who wanted to become professional artists
(E) French painting during the second half of the 19th century was less creative than during the first half of the 19th century

31. TEACHER: Some students have received passing marks on the test, but you were not one of them.
STUDENT: I sure hate to tell my parents that I failed a test.
TEACHER: That is not yet necessary.

Which of the following, if true, best explains the teacher's second remark?
(A) The student should lie to his parents about his mark.
(B) One low test mark will not result in a failing mark for the course.
(C) The student should wait for an opportune time to tell his parents.
(D) The teacher has not finished grading the test papers.
(E) The student will have to take other exams before the course is over.

32. Most arguments in favor of legalizing marijuana focus attention on the lack of evidence of harmful effects of the drug. The purpose of such contentions is to neutralize the negative effect of arguments supporting prohibition because of a supposed correlation between the use of marijuana and violent antisocial behavior. Thus far, the burden of constructive argumentation has been borne by the doctrine of individual rights. "Liberty"

has been the rallying cry of those who favor legalization. No serious proponent of legislative change has yet advanced the obvious proposition that the sale of marijuana should be legal because smoking marijuana is pleasurable.

The author of the paragraph implies that
(A) smoking marijuana can, in some cases, lead to criminal behavior
(B) the sale of marijuana is illegal because the smoking of marijuana is pleasurable
(C) the fact that an activity is pleasurable is a reason for allowing people to engage in it
(D) advocates of the legalization of marijuana are not really concerned about individual liberty
(E) opponents of the legalization of marijuana deny that smoking marijuana is a pleasurable activity

33. DAVID: Every painting by Kissandra should be displayed in the National Art Museum.
MARAT: I disagree. I have seen some very fine works by Electra and Bluesina that should be displayed in the Museum.

Marat's response indicates that he has understood David to mean that
(A) paintings by Electra and Bluesina should be displayed in the Museum
(B) only Kissandra's paintings should be displayed in the Museum
(C) every painting by Kissandra should be displayed in the Museum
(D) not every Kissandra painting should be displayed in the Museum
(E) Kissandra's paintings should only be displayed in the Museum

Questions 34–35

Paul is older than Sally.
Sally is older than Fred.
Mike is older than Paul.
Ralph is younger than Mike but older than Fred.

34. If the statements above are true, which of the following must also be true?

I. Mike is older than Sally.
II. Ralph is older than Sally.
III. Fred is the youngest member of the group.

(A) I only
(B) III only

(C) I and II only
(D) I and III only
(E) I, II, and III

35. If a sixth person, Chuck, is younger than Ralph, all of the following could be true EXCEPT

(A) Chuck is younger than Sally.
(B) Chuck is older than Sally.
(C) Fred is younger than Chuck.
(D) Chuck is younger than Fred.
(E) Mike is younger than Chuck.

STOP

IF YOU FINISH BEFORE TIME IS CALLED, CHECK YOUR WORK ON THIS
SECTION ONLY. DO NOT WORK ON ANY OTHER SECTION IN THE
TEST.

SECTION IV

Time—45 Minutes
35 Questions

Directions: In this section, the questions ask you to analyze and evaluate the reasoning in short paragraphs or passages. For some questions, all of the answer choices may conceivably be answers to the question asked. You should select the *best* answer to the question, that is, an answer which does not require you to make assumptions which violate commonsense standards by being implausible, redundant, irrelevant or inconsistent. After choosing the best answer, blacken the corresponding space on the answer sheet.

1. Which of the following activities would depend upon an assumption which is inconsistent with the judgment that you cannot argue with taste?
   (A) a special exhibition at a museum
   (B) a beauty contest
   (C) a system of garbage collection and disposal
   (D) a cookbook filled with old New England recipes
   (E) a movie festival

2. If George graduated from the University after 1974, he was required to take Introductory World History.

   The statement above can be logically deduced from which of the following?
   (A) Before 1974, Introductory World History was not a required course at the University.
   (B) Every student who took Introductory World History at the University graduated after 1974.
   (C) No student who graduated from the University before 1974 took Introductory World History.
   (D) All students graduating from the University after 1974 were required to take Introductory World History.
   (E) Before 1974, no student was permitted to graduate from the University without having taken Introductory World History.

3. Largemouth bass are usually found living in shallow waters near the lake banks wherever minnows are found. There are no largemouth bass living on this side of the lake.

Which of the following would logically complete an argument with the preceding premises given?

   I. Therefore, there are no minnows on this side of the lake.
   II. Therefore, there are probably no minnows on this side of the lake.
   III. Therefore, there will never be any minnows on this side of the lake.

   (A) I only
   (B) II only
   (C) III only
   (D) I and III only
   (E) II and III only

4. TOMMY: That telephone always rings when I am in the shower and can't hear it.

   JUANITA: But you must be able to hear it; otherwise you couldn't know that it was ringing.

Juanita's response shows that she presupposes that
   (A) the telephone does not ring when Tommy is in the shower
   (B) Tommy's callers never telephone except when he is in the shower
   (C) Tommy's callers sometimes hang up thinking he is not at home
   (D) Tommy cannot tell that the telephone has rung unless he actually heard it
   (E) the telephone does not always function properly

5. ADVERTISEMENT: You cannot buy a more potent pain-reliever than RELIEF without a prescription.

Which of the following statements is inconsistent with the claim made by the advertisement?

   I. RELIEF is not the least expensive non-prescription pain-reliever one can buy.
   II. Another non-prescription pain-reliever, TOBINE, is just as powerful as RELIEF.

295

III. Some prescription pain-relievers are not as powerful as RELIEF.

(A) I only
(B) II only
(C) I and II only
(D) I, II, and III
(E) None of the statements is inconsistent with the advertisement.

Questions 6 and 7

A behavioral psychologist interested in animal behavior noticed that dogs who are never physically disciplined (e.g., with a blow from a rolled-up newspaper) never bark at strangers. He concluded that the best way to keep a dog from barking at strange visitors is to not punish the dog physically.

6. The psychologist's conclusion is based on which of the following assumptions?

   I. The dogs he studied never barked.
   II. Dogs should not be physically punished.
   III. There were no instances of an unpunished dog barking at a stranger which he had failed to observe.

   (A) I only
   (B) II only
   (C) III only
   (D) II and III only
   (E) I, II and III

7. Suppose the psychologist decides to pursue his project further, and he studies 25 dogs which are known to bark at strangers. Which of the following possible findings would undermine his original conclusion?

   I. Some of the owners of the dogs studied did not physically punish the dog when it barked at a stranger.
   II. Some of the dogs studied were never physically punished.
   III. The owners of some of the dogs studied believe that a dog which barks at strangers is a good watchdog.

   (A) I only
   (B) II only
   (C) I and II only
   (D) II and III only
   (E) I, II, and III

8. Everything a child does is the consequence of some experience he has had before. Therefore, a child psychologist must study the personal history of his patient.

The author's conclusion logically depends upon the premise that
(A) everything that a child is doing he has already done before
(B) every effect is causally generated by some previous effect
(C) the study of a child's personal history is the best way of learning about that child's parents
(D) a child will learn progressively more about the world because experience is cumulative
(E) it is possible to ensure that a child will grow up to be a mature, responsible adult

9. It is sometimes argued that we are reaching the limits of the earth's capacity to supply our energy needs with fossil fuels. In the past ten years, however, as a result of technological progress making it possible to extract resources from even marginal wells and mines, yields from oil and coal fields have increased tremendously. There is no reason to believe that there is a limit to the earth's capacity to supply our energy needs.

Which of the following statements most directly contradicts the conclusion drawn above?
(A) Even if we exhaust our supplies of fossil fuel, the earth can still be mined for uranium for nuclear fuel.
(B) The technology needed to extract fossil fuels from marginal sources is very expensive.
(C) Even given the improvements in technology, oil and coal are not renewable resources; so we will eventually exhaust our supplies of them.
(D) Most of the land under which marginal oil and coal supplies lie is more suitable to cultivation or pasturing than to production of fossil fuels.
(E) The fuels that are yielded by marginal sources tend to be high in sulphur and other undesirable elements which aggravate the air pollution problem.

Questions 10–12 refer to the following arguments.

(A) The Bible must be accepted as the revealed word of God, for it is stated several times in the Bible that it is the one, true word of God. And since the Bible is the true word of God, we must accept what it says as true.
(B) It must be possible to do something about the

deteriorating condition of the nation's interstate highway system. But the repairs will cost money. Therefore, it is foolish to reduce federal appropriations for highway repair.

(C) The Learner Commission's Report on Pornography concluded that there is a definite link between pornography and sex crimes. But no one should accept that conclusion because the Learner Commission was funded by the Citizens' Committee Against Obscenity, which obviously wanted the report to condemn pornography.

(D) People should give up drinking coffee. Of ten people who died last year at City Hospital from cancer of the pancreas, eight of them drank three or more cups of coffee a day.

(E) Guns are not themselves the cause of crime. Even without firearms crimes would be committed. Criminals would use knives or other weapons.

10. Which of the above arguments contains circular reasoning?

11. Which of the above arguments contains a generalization which is based on a sample?

12. Which of above arguments addresses itself to the source of the claim rather than to the merits of the claim itself?

13. Some sociologists believe that religious sects such as the California-based Waiters, who believe the end of the world is imminent and seek to purify their souls by, among other things, abstaining completely from sexual relations, are a product of growing disaffection with modern, industrialized and urbanized living. As evidence, they cite the fact that there are no other active organizations of the same type which are more than 50 or 60 years old. The evidence, however, fails to support the conclusion for _____ .

Which of the following is the most logical completion of the passage?

(A) the restrictions on sexual relations are such that the only source of new members is outside recruitment, so such sects tend to die out after a generation or two.

(B) it is simply not possible to gauge the intensity of religious fervor by the length of time the religious sect remains viable.

(C) the Waiters group may actually survive beyond the second generation of its existence.

(D) there are other religious sects that emphasize group sexual activity which currently have several hundred members.

(E) the Waiters are a California-based organization and have no members in the Northeast, which is even more heavily urban and industrialized than California.

14. Any truthful auto mechanic will tell you that your standard 5,000-mile checkup can detect only one-fifth of the problems which are likely to go wrong with your car. Therefore, such a checkup is virtually worthless and a waste of time and money.

Which of the following statements, if true, would weaken the above conclusion?

I. Those problems which the 5,000-mile checkup will turn up are the ten leading causes of major engine failure.

II. For a new car, a 5,000-mile checkup is required to protect the owner's warranty.

III. During a 5,000-mile checkup the mechanic also performs routine maintenance which is necessary to the proper functioning of the car.

(A) I only
(B) II only
(C) I and II only
(D) II and III only
(E) I, II, and III

Questions 15 and 16

In recent years, unions have begun to include in their demands at the collective bargaining table requests for contract provisions which give labor an active voice in determining the goals of a corporation. Although it cannot be denied that labor leaders are highly skilled administrators, it must be recognized that their primary loyalty is and must remain to their membership, not to the corporation. Thus, labor participation in corporate management decisions makes about as much sense as _____ .

15. Which of the following represents the best continuation of the passage?

(A) allowing inmates to make decisions about prison security

(B) a senior field officer asking the advice of a junior officer on a question of tactics

(C) a university's asking the opinion of the student body on the scheduling of courses

(D) Chicago's mayor inviting the state legislators for a ride on the city's subway system

(E) the members of a church congregation discussing theology with the minister

16. The author's reasoning leads to the further conclusion that
(A) the authority of corporate managers would be symbolically undermined if labor leaders were allowed to participate in corporate planning
(B) workers have virtually no idea of how to run a large corporation
(C) workers would not derive any benefit from hearing the goals of corporate management explained to them at semiannual meetings
(D) the efficiency of workers would be lowered if they were to divide their time between production line duties and management responsibilities
(E) allowing labor a voice in corporate decisions would involve labor representatives in a conflict of interest

17. DRUGGIST: Seventy percent of the people questioned stated that they would use Myrdal for relief of occasional headache pain. Only 30 percent of those questioned indicated that they would take Blufferin for such pain.

CUSTOMER: Oh, then over twice as many people preferred Myrdal to Blufferin.

DRUGGIST: No, 25 percent of those questioned stated they never took any medication.

In what manner may the seeming inconsistency in the druggist's statements be explained?
(A) The 30 percent who indicated they would take Blufferin are contained within the 70 percent of those who indicated they would take Myrdal.
(B) The questioner asked more than 100 people.
(C) The questioner did not accurately record the answers of at least 25 percent of those questioned.
(D) The sampling population was too small to yield results that were statistically significant.
(E) Some of those questioned indicated that they would take both brands of pain relievers.

18.
I. No student who commutes from home to a university dates a student who resides at a university.
II. Every student who lives at home commutes to his university, and no commuter student ever dates a resident student.

Which of the following best describes the relationship between the two preceding sentences?
(A) If II is true, I must also be true.
(B) If II is true, I must be false.
(C) If II is true, I may be either true or false.
(D) If I is true, II is unlikely to be false.
(E) If II is false, I must also be false.

19. All books from the Buckner collection are kept in the Reserve Room.
All books kept in the Reserve Room are priceless.
No book by Hemingway is kept in the Reserve Room.
Every book kept in the Reserve Room is listed in the card catalogue.

If all of the statements above are true, which of the following must also be true?
(A) All priceless books are kept in the Reserve Room.
(B) Every book from the Buckner collection which is listed in the card catalogue is not valuable.
(C) No book by Hemingway is priceless.
(D) The Buckner collection contains no books by Hemingway.
(E) Every book listed in the card catalogue is kept in the Reserve Room.

20. The new car to buy this year is the Goblin. We had 100 randomly selected motorists drive the Goblin and the other two leading subcompact cars. Seventy-five drivers ranked the Goblin first in handling. Sixty-nine rated the Goblin first in styling. From the responses of these 100 drivers, we can show you that they ranked Goblin first overall in our composite category of style, performance, comfort, and drivability.

The persuasive appeal of the advertisement's claim is most weakened by its use of the undefined word
(A) randomly
(B) handling
(C) first
(D) responses
(E) composite

21. Recently the newspaper published the obituary notice of a novelist and poet that had been written by the deceased in anticipation of the event. The last line of the verse advised the reader that the author had expired a day earlier and gave as the cause of death ''a deprivation of time.''

    The explanation of the cause of the author's death is
    (A) circular
    (B) speculative
    (C) self-serving
    (D) medically sound
    (E) self-authenticating

22. Since Ronnie's range is so narrow, he will never be an outstanding vocalist.

    The statement above is based on which of the following assumptions?

    I. A person's range is an important indicator of his probable success or failure as a professional musician.
    II. Vocalizing requires a range of at least two and one-half octaves.
    III. Physical characteristics can affect how well one sings.

    (A) I only
    (B) II only
    (C) I and II
    (D) III only
    (E) I, II, and III

Questions 23 and 24

During the 1970's the number of clandestine CIA agents posted to foreign countries increased 25 percent and the number of CIA employees not assigned to field work increased by 21 percent. In the same period, the number of FBI agents assigned to case investigation rose by 18 percent, but the number of non-case-working agents rose by only 3 percent.

23. The statistics best support which of the following claims?
    (A) More agents are needed to administer the CIA than are needed for the FBI.
    (B) The CIA needs more people to accomplish its mission than does the FBI.
    (C) The proportion of field agents tends to increase more rapidly than the number of non-field agents in both the CIA and the FBI.
    (D) The rate of change in the number of supervisory agents in an intelligence gathering

agency or a law-enforcement agency is proportional to the percentage change in the results produced by the agency.
    (E) At the end of the 1960's, the CIA was more efficiently administered than the FBI.

24. In response to the allegation that it was more overstaffed with support and supervisory personnel than the FBI, the CIA could best argue that
    (A) the FBI is less useful than the CIA in gathering intelligence against foreign powers
    (B) the rate of pay for a CIA non-field agent is less than the rate of pay for a non-investigating FBI agent
    (C) the number of FBI agents should not rise so rapidly as the number of CIA agents given the longer tenure of an FBI agent
    (D) a CIA field agent working in a foreign country requires more backup support than does an FBI investigator working domestically
    (E) the number of CIA agents is determined by the Congress each year when they appropriate funds for the agency, and the Congress is very sensitive to changes in the international political climate

The following material contains blanks that represent deleted material. For Questions 25 and 26, select the most appropriate completion of the passage.

When we reflect on the structure of moral decisions, we come across cases in which we seem to be subject to mutually exclusive moral demands. But the conflict is just that, a seeming one. We must be careful to distinguish two levels of moral thinking: The *prima facie* and the critical. A *prima facie* moral principle is analogous to a workaday tool, say a(n)___(25)___. It is versatile, that is, useful in many situations, and at your fingertips, to wit, no special skill is needed to use it. Unfortunately, the value of a *prima facie* principle derives from its non-specific language, which means that in some situations it will turn out to be an oversimplification. For example, two fairly straightforward moral rules such as ''keep all promises'' and ''assist others in dire need,'' which work well enough in most cases, seem to clash in the following scenario: ''I have promised a friend I will run a very important errand on his behalf (and he is relying on me); but while en route I happen across a person in need of emergency medical assistance, which I can provide, but only at the cost of leaving my original purpose unaccomplished.'' The appearance of conflict arises from the choice of tools used in analyzing the situation—the two *prima facie* rules do not cut finely enough. What is wanted, therefore, is a more refined analysis which will be applicable to the specific situation. At this, the second level of moral thinking, critical moral thinking employs a finer system of categories so that the end result is—(26)—

25. (A) surgical scalpel
    (B) kitchen knife
    (C) electrical generator
    (D) tuning fork
    (E) library book

26. (A) not two conflicting moral judgments, but a single consistent moral judgment
    (B) an advance for the human species over the savagery of our forebears
    (C) the improvement of medical care for the population in general
    (D) moral principles of higher levels of abstraction which are applicable to larger numbers of cases
    (E) that value judgments will no longer depend on the particulars of any given situation

27. All effective administrators are concerned about the welfare of their employees, and all administrators who are concerned about the welfare of their employees are liberal in granting time off for personal needs; therefore, all administrators who are not liberal in granting time off for their employees' personal needs are not effective administrators.

    If the argument above is valid, then it must be true that
    (A) no ineffective administrators are liberal in granting time off for their employees' personal needs
    (B) no ineffective administrators are concerned about the welfare of their employees
    (C) some effective administrators are not liberal in granting time off for their employees' personal needs
    (D) all effective administrators are liberal in granting time off for their employees' personal needs
    (E) all time off for personal needs is granted by effective administrators

28. CLYDE: You shouldn't drink so much wine. Alcohol really isn't good for you.
    GERRY: You're wrong about that. I have been drinking the same amount of white wine for 15 years, and I never get drunk.

    Which of the following responses would best strengthen and explain Clyde's argument?
    (A) Many people who drink as much white wine as Gerry does get very drunk.
    (B) Alcohol does not always make a person drunk.
    (C) Getting drunk is not the only reason alcohol is not good for a person.
    (D) If you keep drinking white wine, you may find in the future that you are drinking more and more.
    (E) White wine is not the only drink that contains alcohol.

29. In considering the transportation needs of our sales personnel, the question of the relative cost of each of our options is very important. The initial purchase outlay required for a fleet of diesel autos is fairly high, though the operating costs for them will be low. This is the mirror image of the cost picture for a fleet of gasoline-powered cars. The only way, then, of making a valid cost comparison is on the basis of ——————.

    Which of the following best completes the above paragraph?
    (A) projected operating costs for both diesel- and gasoline-powered autos
    (B) the average costs of both fleets over the life of each fleet
    (C) the purchase cost for both diesel-powered and gasoline-powered autos.
    (D) the present difference in the operating costs of the two fleets
    (E) the relative amount of air pollution that would be created by the one type of car compared with the other

30. The Dormitory Canteen Committee decided that the prices of snacks in the Canteen vending machines were already high enough, so they told Vendo Inc., the company holding the vending machine concession for the Canteen, either to maintain prices at the then current levels or to forfeit the concession. Vendo, however, man-

aged to thwart the intent of the Committee's instructions without actually violating the letter of those instructions.

Which of the following is probably the action taken by Vendo referred to in the above paragraph?
(A) The president of Vendo met with the University's administration, and they ordered the Committee to rescind its instructions.
(B) Vendo continued prices at the prescribed levels but reduced the size of the snacks vended in the machines.
(C) Vendo ignored the Committee's instructions and continued to raise prices.
(D) Vendo decided it could not make a fair return on its investment if it held the line on prices, so it removed its machines from the Dormitory Canteen.
(E) Representatives of Vendo met with members of the Dormitory Canteen Committee and offered them free snacks to influence other members to change the Committee's decision.

31. The president of the University tells us that a tuition increase is needed to offset rising costs. That is simply not true. Weston University is an institution approximately the same size as our own University, but the president of Weston University has announced that they will not impose a tuition increase on their students.

The author makes his point primarily by
(A) citing new evidence
(B) proposing an alternative solution
(C) pointing out a logical contradiction
(D) drawing an analogy
(E) clarifying an ambiguity

32. Only White Bear gives you all-day deodorant protection and the unique White Bear scent.

If this advertising claim is true, which of the following cannot also be true?

I. Red Flag deodorant gives you all-day deodorant protection.
II. Open Sea deodorant is a more popular deodorant than White Bear.
III. White Bear after-shave lotion uses the White Bear scent.

(A) I only
(B) II only
(C) III only
(D) I and III only
(E) All of the propositions could be true.

33. Clara prefers English Literature to Introductory Physics. She likes English Literature, however, less than she likes Basic Economics. She actually finds Basic Economics preferable to any other college course, and she dislikes Physical Education more than she dislikes Introductory Physics.

All of the following statements can be inferred from the information given above EXCEPT
(A) Clara prefers Basic Economics to English Literature
(B) Clara likes English Literature better than she likes Physical Education
(C) Clara prefers Basic Economics to Advanced Calculus
(D) Clara likes World History better than she likes Introductory Physics
(E) Clara likes Physical Education less than she likes English Literature

34. In *The Adventure of the Bruce-Partington Plans*, Sherlock Holmes explained to Dr. Watson that the body had been placed on the top of the train while the train paused at a signal.

"It seems most improbable," remarked Watson.

"We must fall back upon the old axiom," continued Holmes, "that when all other contingencies fail, whatever remains, however improbable, must be the truth."

Which of the following is the most effective criticism of the logic contained in Holmes' response to Watson?
(A) You will never be able to obtain a conviction in a court of law.
(B) You can never be sure you have accounted for all other contingencies.
(C) You will need further evidence to satisfy the police.
(D) The very idea of putting a dead body on top of a train seems preposterous.
(E) You still have to find the person responsible for putting the body on top of the train.

35. PROFESSOR: Under the rule of primogeniture, the first male child born to a man's first wife is always first in line to inherit the family estate.

STUDENT: That can't be true; the Duchess of Warburton was her father's only child by his only wife and she inherited his entire estate.

The student has misinterpreted the professor's remark to mean which of the following?

(A) Only men can father male children.
(B) A daughter cannot be a first-born child.
(C) Only sons can inherit the family estate.
(D) Illegitimate children cannot inherit their fathers' property.
(E) A woman cannot inherit her mother's property.

STOP

IF YOU FINISH BEFORE TIME IS CALLED, CHECK YOUR WORK IN THIS SECTION ONLY. DO NOT WORK ON ANY OTHER SECTION IN THE TEST.

PRACTICE EXAMINATION 4
ANSWER KEY

SECTION I

1.	B	7.	E	13.	B	19.	D	25.	C
2.	C	8.	D	14.	D	20.	C	26.	C
3.	C	9.	C	15.	D	21.	A	27.	C
4.	E	10.	D	16.	A	22.	C	28.	E
5.	E	11.	D	17.	C	23.	E	29.	E
6.	A	12.	D	18.	B	24.	B	30.	B

SECTION II

1.	C	8.	E	15.	E	22.	A	29.	D
2.	A	9.	A	16.	D	23.	E	30.	D
3.	B	10.	E	17.	D	24.	E	31.	C
4.	E	11.	B	18.	C	25.	B	32.	C
5.	D	12.	A	19.	B	26.	D	33.	A
6.	B	13.	A	20.	A	27.	B	34.	B
7.	A	14.	B	21.	A	28.	A	35.	A

SECTION III

1.	B	8.	C	15.	A	22.	B	29.	C
2.	A	9.	D	16.	C	23.	A	30.	A
3.	E	10.	B	17.	A	24.	C	31.	D
4.	A	11.	A	18.	B	25.	B	32.	C
5.	E	12.	A	19.	E	26.	D	33.	B
6.	E	13.	A	20.	A	27.	D	34.	D
7.	D	14.	D	21.	C	28.	C	35.	E

SECTION IV

1.	B	8.	B	15.	A	22.	D	29.	B
2.	D	9.	C	16.	E	23.	C	30.	B
3.	B	10.	A	17.	E	24.	D	31.	D
4.	D	11.	D	18.	A	25.	B	32.	E
5.	E	12.	C	19.	D	26.	A	33.	D
6.	C	13.	A	20.	E	27.	D	34.	B
7.	B	14.	E	21.	A	28.	C	35.	C

EXPLANATORY ANSWERS

SECTION I

Questions 1–6

Here we have a linear ordering set. Even though the ordering is temporal, it can be represented spatially like a calendar. We begin by summarizing the given information:

K = (Mon. or Sat.)
O = Th.
P = Sun.
J = L
J ≠ N

1. **(B)** We begin by entering the additional information:

Mon.	Tu.	Wed.	Th.	Fri.	Sat.	Sun.
K	M	N	O	J/L	J/L	P

The only open question, as shown by the diagram, is, of J or L, which is shown on Friday and which on Saturday. With M shown on Tuesday, and O and P on Thursday and Sunday, J and L must be shown on Friday and Saturday, though not necessarily respectively. Then, K must be shown on Monday, which means N must be shown on Wednesday. As the diagram shows, only (B) is necessarily true. (C) and (D) are possibly, though not necessarily, true. (A) and (E) are definitely untrue.

2. **(C)** We begin by processing the additional stipulations:

Mon.	Tu.	Wed.	Th.	Fri.	Sat.	Sun.
K	J	L	O	M/N	M/N	P

If J and K are shown on consecutive days, then to respect the requirement that J and L also be shown on consecutive days, we have a group of either KJL or LJK. With Thursday and Sunday already scheduled, however, this group must be aired on Monday through Wednesday. This

means K must be Monday, J Tuesday, and L Wednesday. As a result, M and N will be scheduled Friday and Saturday, though we cannot establish which one will be shown on which day. Thus, (D) and (E) are only possible, not necessary. (A) and (B) are both impossible. (C), however, makes a necessarily true statement.

3. **(C)** We begin by processing the additional information:

Mon.	Tu.	Wed.	Th.	Fri.	Sat.	Sun.
K	N	M	O	J/L	J/L	P

With N scheduled for Tuesday, this forces the programming manager to air J and L on Friday and Saturday, though which is shown on which day is not established. Then, K must be aired on Monday, which means that M is aired on Wednesday. So we can see that statement I is known to be untrue. Statement II is only possibly true. Statement III is necessarily true. So the correct answer is (C).

4. **(E)** We begin by processing the additional information:

Mon.	Tu.	Wed.	Th.	Fri.	Sat.	Sun.
		O		K	P	

This is not sufficient to establish either (A) or (B). We must then look to the remaining answer choices and process the extra information supplied therein. As for (C), knowing that N and L are aired on consecutive days establishes only that N, L, and J are aired consecutively: NLJ or JLN; but this does not determine which film is shown on Wednesday. As for (D), knowing that J is aired either immediately before or immediately after M sets up a LJM or a JLM sequence. (E) is the correct answer. If K and M are shown on consecutive days, then M is shown on Friday. We are left with J and L, which must be shown on consecutive days, and N, which must not be shown on a day before or after J. There are only

304

two possible schedules for this three-film sequence which must be aired Monday, Tuesday, and Wednesday: JLN or NLJ. Either way we schedule the films, L is scheduled on Tuesday.

5. **(E)** For this question we must use not only the additional stipulation provided in the stem of the question, but the additional information provided in the answer choices as well. If J is not shown on Monday, Tuesday, or Wednesday, we know:

Mon.	Tu.	Wed.	Thu.	Fri.	Sat.	Sun.
K			O	J/L	J/L	P

because K must be shown on either Monday or Saturday. Tuesday and Wednesday must be dedicated to M and N, though not necessarily in that order. As for (A) and (B), fixing the JL combination for Friday and Saturday is not going to affect the showing of films on Tuesday and Wednesday. As for (C) and (D), scheduling M and N will not affect the order of J and L. (E), however, is correct. If N is shown on Wednesday, then M must be scheduled for Tuesday.

6. **(A)** Here we have a similar problem. We must test each statement using all the information available. The stem establishes:

Mon.	Tu.	Wed.	Thu.	Fri.	Sat.	Sun
	L		O			P

As for statement I, knowing the M is shown on Monday allows us to determine that L is shown on Tuesday, K on Saturday, and N on Friday:

Mon.	Tu.	Wed.	Th.	Fri.	Sat.	Sun.
M	L	J	O	N	K	P

So statement I is correct. As for statement II, if K is shown on Monday, we deduce:

Mon.	Tu.	Wed.	Th.	Fri.	Sat.	Sun.
K	L	J	O			P

And we know that M and N must be shown on Friday and Saturday, but we do not know their order. So statement II is not necessarily true. As for III, if K is shown on Saturday, this leaves both Monday and Wednesday open for J, so statement III is not necessarily true. So the correct answer is I only.

Questions 7–12

Here we have a selection problem. The three-cars aspect introduces what seems to be an element of spatial ordering, but in actuality this aspect does nothing more than specify that three groups will be selected. We could as easily have dispensed with spatial ordering in favor of another device, say, three tables at a banquet, the blue table, the green table, and the red table. We begin by summarizing the information for ready reference:

$$G = H$$
$$J = 2$$
$$N = P$$
$$K \neq O$$
$$M = (J) \, v \, (O) \, v \, (J \, \& \, O)$$

7. **(E)** With this question we just check each answer choice against the restrictions given in the initial conditions. Using the requirement that $G = H$, we eliminate both (A) and (C). Then, using the requirement than $N = P$, we eliminate (D). (B) can be eliminated because we have both J and O together with L, but that means M cannot be riding with J or O, as required. Finally, (E) is consistent with all the restrictions. We can show this by example: First (GHL), second (JMK) and third (ONP). But as a matter of test practice we would not do so. Once we have eliminated (A) through (D) for good reasons, we would assume that the test writers had correctly drafted the problem and that (E) could be proved correct by example. Trying to construct such an example will not further the issue of the correct answer: It must, by elimination, be (E).

8. **(D)** For this question, we must again check our choices against the restrictions given, but here we will have to dig a little deeper. As a matter of tactics, we would look at (A), (B), and (C) first, since they are simpler than (D) and (E). On the surface there appears no good reason why those three could not be true. This is not to say that they are possible; rather, since there is no obvious reason for them to be impossible, we look for another, obvious answer. We find it in (D). This asserts that O and M ride in cars 1 and 3, in that order. But this is not possible, for this places M in a car without O or J. (Remember that J must ride in car 2.) (E) is possible, for L is under no such restriction. So, as a matter of tactics, we preview the choices, looking for a good reason to select

one. The point is, there might be some exotic reason why (B) or (A) is impossible, e.g., when K is in the first car, and M is in the third, G cannot be in the second. . . . But for a train of reasoning of this sort to be the key to the correct answer would make a very difficult problem indeed. With a set such as this, we do not expect to see such a difficult problem. So we look for a more obvious answer.

9. **(C)** We begin by using the additional information. With O in the third car and P in the second, we deduce:

1	2	3
G	J	O
H	P	M
K	N	L

for P requires N in the second car. This means M must go with O in the third. Now, for G and H to go together, they must be in the first car. And K must go in the first car as well——not with O in the third car. This means that L will ride in the third car. Our diagram shows that (C) is necessarily true, while (A), (B), (D), and (E) are all false.

10. **(D)** Here we are looking for a reason to disqualify one of the individuals listed from riding with G. We know that G and H must go together, so what might disqualify another individual from riding in the same car? Again, rather than look for very subtle tricks, we look for an obvious disqualification. N and P must ride together, so N cannot ride with G, for that would put a total of four persons in the same car. Thus, (D) is correct. As for (A), we could have J, G, and H in the second car. As for (B), we could have G, K, and H in the first or third cars. Similarly with L, since L is under no restriction at all. Finally, (E) is also possible; with G, O, and H together, we can put M into the second car, so that M rides with J.

11. **(D)** We begin by processing the additional information. With G and O in the first car, we have H in the first car as well, so (A) is incorrect. With that first car full, M must ride in the second car with J, proving (D) is the correct answer. As for (E), this is false, since N and P together would preclude us from placing M with J. Finally, either K or L could ride with J and M in the second car, but that is only possibly and not necessarily true.

12. **(D)** Processing the additional information, we have:

1	2	3
G	J	M
H	N	O
K	P	L

With P in the second car, N must also ride in the second car. And this means that O must accompany M in the third car. This requires that G and H go in the first car, and that they be accompanied by K, who must not ride with O. So L must ride in the remaining spot in the third car. This proves that (D) is the correct answer.

Questions 13–18

Here we have a linear ordering problem, a type now very familiar. We begin by summarizing the information:

N = 1 and P = 7
L > K
J > M
K > O > M or K < O < M

13. **(B)** We begin by processing the additional information. For J and O to be separated by exactly two grades, it must be that they are in grades 2 and 5 or grades 3 and 6, though not necessarily in that order:

1	2	3	4	5	6	7
N	J			O		P
N	O			J		P
N		O			J	P
N		J			O	P

We can eliminate all but the third possibility. The first arrangement is not possible because we cannot honor the requirement J > M. The second is not possible because we cannot place O between K and M. The fourth is not possible for the same reason. Using only the third possibility, we know further:

1	2	3	4	5	6	7
N	K	O	M	L	J	P

or: N K O L M J P

or: N M O K L J P

This proves (B) is necessarily true. The diagram further shows that (A), (C), (D), and (E) are only possibly, though not necessarily, true.

14. **(D)** We begin by processing the additional information:

$$1\ 2\ 3\ 4\ 5\ 6\ 7$$
$$N\ M\ J\ O\ K\ L\ P$$

With J in grade 3, M must be in grade 2. And we know that L must be higher than K and, further, that O must go between K and M. This means that O, K, and L must be in grades 4, 5, and 6, respectively. The diagram shows that (D) is necessarily true, and that each of the remaining choices is necessarily false.

15. **(D)** The proper means of attack on this question is to test each of the three statements. Since there are only three, this can be done in a reasonable amount of time. As for statement I:

$$1\ 2\ 3\ 4\ 5\ 6\ 7$$
$$N\ K\ M\ J\ \ \ \ \ P$$

We see there is no place for O between K and M. So this is not possible. As for statement II:

$$1\ 2\ 3\ 4\ 5\ 6\ 7$$
$$N\ K\ \ \ M\ J\ \ \ P$$

This will allow us to place O between K and M, and placing L in grade 6 ensures that L is in a grade higher than K's grade. So statement II is possible. As for statement III:

$$1\ 2\ 3\ 4\ 5\ 6\ 7$$
$$N\ K\ \ \ M\ \ \ J\ P$$

This allows us to place O in grade 3, and therefore between K and M. And we can place L in grade 5, which respects all other conditions. So statement III is also possible. Our correct answer must therefore be (D), II and III are possible, though I is not possible.

16. **(A)** We begin by processing the additional information:

$$1\ 2\ 3\ 4\ 5\ 6\ 7$$
$$N\ M\ J\ O\ K\ L\ P$$

We separate J from M by one grade by placing J in grade 3, which means that M, to be in a lower grade, must be in grade 2. Next, we reason that for L to be in a grade higher than K's, and yet

allowing that O must be between K and M, we have O, K, and L in grades 4 through 6, respectively. The diagram, therefore, proves that (A) is correct while each of the other choices is necessarily false.

17. **(C)** Looking back over the work we have already done, we learned in our discussion of question 13 that O can be in grade 3, and that M can be in grade 4 or grade 5. Our discussion of question 14 shows that O can be in grade 4. So (A), (B), (D), and (E) are all possible. (C), however, is not possible. If O is in the fifth grade, we cannot place either K or M above O without violating one or the other restriction that L > K and that J > M.

18. **(B)** We begin by processing the additional information.

$$1\quad 2\quad 3\quad 4\quad 5\ 6\ 7$$
$$N\quad K/M\quad O\quad K/M\quad J\ L\ P$$

For L to be in the grade ahead of J, they must be in grades 6 and 5 respectively; otherwise it will not be possible to get O between K and M, since both K and M must be in grades lower than those of L and J, respectively. Then, we must put O between K and M, but there is no reason to place K in grade 2 and M in grade 4, as opposed to K in 4 and M in 2. So there are two possible arrangements, as shown by the diagram.

Questions 19–24

This is an ordering problem in which individuals are aligned two by two. We begin by summarizing the information:

(P & M) ≠ last
L ≠ Q
N = O
R → L

19. **(D)** With this question, we simply apply the initial conditions to each choice. All choices meet the requirement regarding P and M. Further, all choices meet the requirement on N and O. Finally, all choices meet the requirement on R and L. (D), however, fails to meet the requirement that L and Q never ride together. The remaining choices respect this requirement. (D), therefore, is not a possible order.

20. **(C)** We begin by processing the additional infor-

mation. We know that R and L finish so that R is one place ahead of L. This means that the order for this question must be O, R, and L. But with M following L, this means our O, R, L, and M order must be 1 through 4, respectively, for M never finishes last:

```
1   2   3   4   5
ON  R   L   MP
```

There do not appear to be any further deductions of an obvious nature, so we check our choices against the diagram. We can see that (A) is definitely false, that (B) is definitely false, that (D) is only possibly true, and that (E) is only possibly true. (C), however, is necessarily true, as shown by the diagram.

21. **(A)** We begin by processing the additional information.

```
1    2   3 4  5
PM  NO  R L
```

If N finishes second, then O must also finish second. And if R finishes third, then L must finish fourth. Since P and M must finish together in any place but fifth, P and M must finish first. This seems to be as far as we can go, so we look to the choices. (A) is confirmed by our diagram. (B) is shown by the diagram to be false. (C) and (E) are incorrect for similar reasons. Q does not ride with L, so Q cannot finish in fourth place. Finally, (D) is possibly, though not necessarily, true.

22. **(C)** We begin by processing the additional information:

```
1   2   3   4   5
        R   L
```

We have three pairs of participants who must ride together: P and M, N and O, and, by stipulation, J and T. Of course, P and M cannot finish last, but they may finish first or second. This means there are several ways of distributing our pairs. There is, however, one further deduction. Since our pairs, in whatever order they finish, occupy cars 1, 2, and 5, and since Q cannot ride with L, Q must ride in the third-place car and K in the fourth-place car. As for our statements, statements I and II are possibly, though not necessarily, true. Statement III must be true, so our correct answer is III only.

23. **(E)** We begin by processing the additional information:

```
1    2    3    4    5
JR   KL   NO   MP   QT
```

With L in second place, R must finish first. This leaves only place 4 for the pair P and M. Then we know further than N finishes with O in place 3, and by stipulation that J rides with R and finishes first. Q cannot ride with L, so Q rides with T and finishes last, and K rides with L in the second-place car. Thus, the diagram confirms that (E) is correct, and that the other choices are incorrect.

24. **(B)** For the final time, we begin by processing the additional information:

```
        1   2   3   4   5
                MP
    or: R   L       R   L
```

We see that R and L must finish first and second or fourth and fifth, respectively. Since Q cannot ride with L, and since the non-L car not occupied by a pair of participants is the R car, Q must ride with R. This means that Q finishes either first or fourth.

Questions 25–30

This is a simple ordering set. Summarizing the initial conditions:

$$P < N$$
$$M < O$$
$$Q < R$$

25. **(C)** This item provides no additional information, so use the initial conditions to eliminate choices. Using the first condition, you can eliminate (D) and (E). Using the second condition, eliminate (A). And using the third condition, eliminate (B).

26. **(C)** Since N must be interviewed later in the week than P, and O later in the week than M, and since only one pair of applicants can be interviewed on a single day, N and O cannot be interviewed until after both P and M have been interviewed.

27. **(C)** Since M must be interviewed before O, and Q must be interviewed before R, and since only one pair of applicants can be interviewed on any

one day, M and Q must be interviewed on a day before either O or R are interviewed——which means if M and Q are to be interviewed on the same day, they must be interviewed no later than Wednesday.

28. **(E)** Here the question stem isolates part of an order: N,(M&R).

   But on what days does this sequence occur? Since O must be interviewed later in the week than M, the correct sequence must be N,(M&R),O. Since P must be interviewed before N, the sequence must be P,N,(M&R),O. Finally, Q must be interviewed before R and therefore before O as well. Consequently, O is the last person interviewed.

29. **(E)** This question stem establishes the partial order (O&R), N. O, R, and N are the three applicants who must be interviewed after someone else has been interviewed. This means that P, M, and Q must be interviewed before O and R, and so O and R must be interviewed on Thursday and N on Friday. The other applicants, Q, M, and P, must be interviewed on Monday, Tuesday, or Wednesday, but not in any required order.

30. **(B)** Start by entering the new information on a diagram:

   M T W Th F
   P,Q

   Since P is interviewed before N and Q is interviewed before R, N and R must be interviewed on Thursday and Friday, though not necessarily in that order. As for the first two days, M must be interviewed before O:

   M Tu W   Th   F
   M O P,Q N/R N/R

   So there are exactly two possible sequences in which the applicants can be interviewed.

SECTION II

1. **(C)** This is a main idea question. The author begins by posing the question: Why are affirmative action programs so controversial? He then argues that affirmative action is unlike ordinary government programs in the way it allocates the burden of the program. Because of this, he concludes, we are torn between supporting the programs (because they have legitimate goals) and condemning the programs (because of the way the cost is allocated). (C) neatly describes this development. The author analyzes the structure of the moral dilemma. (A) is incorrect since the comparison is but a subpart of the overall development and is used in the service of the larger analysis. (B) is incorrect since the author reaches no such clear-cut decision. Rather, we are left with the question posed by the dilemma. (D) is incorrect since the author presupposes in his presentation that the reader already understands the importance of the issue. Finally, (E) is incorrect since the advantages of the programs are mentioned only in passing.

2. **(A)** This is a logical structure question. In the second paragraph, the author will describe the general structure of government programs in order to set up the contrast with affirmative action. The discussion begins with "Setting aside . . .," indicating the author recognizes such cases and does not wish to discuss them in detail. Tolls and tuition are exceptions to the general rule, so the author explicitly sets them aside in order to preempt a possible objection to his analysis based on claimed counter-examples. (B) is incorrect since the overall point of the passage is to discuss this dilemma, but the main point of the passage will not answer the question about the logical substructure of the argument. (C) is incorrect since tolls and tuition are not ordinary government programs. (D) is incorrect since the author never raises such doubts. Finally, (E) misses the point of the examples. The point is not that they are costly but that the cost is born by the specific user.

3. **(B)** This is an application question. In the first paragraph, the author states affirmative action is designed to achieve social and economic objectives. Although he qualifies his claim, he seems to believe that those arguments are in favor of affirmative action. So (B) is clearly supported by the text. (A) is not supported by the text since the author leaves us with a question; he does not resolve the issue. (C) can be eliminated on the same ground. The author neither embraces nor rejects affirmative action. (D) goes beyond the scope of the argument. While the author might wish that this were possible, nothing in the pas-

sage indicates such restructuring is possible. Indeed, in paragraph 3, the author remarks that the ''funding'' problem seems to be inherent. Finally, (E) can be eliminated on the same ground as (A). Though the author recognizes the unfairness of affirmative action, he also believes that the programs are valuable.

4. **(E)** In paragraph 2, the author mentions that government programs entail both social and economic costs. Then, the cost of the specific example, the passed-over worker, is not a government expenditure in the sense that money is laid out to purchase something. So the author is using the term ''funding''.in a non-standard way, and he wishes to call his readers' attention to this. (E) parallels this explanation. (A) is incorrect since it is inconsistent with the reasoning just provided. (B) is incorrect, for though the author may believe that individuals bear a disproportionate share of the burden, this is not a response to the question asked. (C) is incorrect for the same reason: It is a true but non-responsive statement. Finally, (D) fails for the same reason. Though the author notes that affirmative action programs are similar to other government programs in this respect, this is not an explanation for the author's placing ''funding'' in quotation marks.

5. **(D)** This is a logical structure question. In the final paragraph, the author analyzes another, similar situation. This technique is called arguing from analogy. The strength of the argument depends on our seeing the similarity and accepting the conclusion of the one argument (the ''villainous man'') as applicable to the other argument (affirmative action). (A) is perhaps the second best response, but the author is not offering an illustration, e.g., an example of affirmative action. To be sure, the author is attempting to prove a point, but attempting to prove a conclusion is not equivalent to illustrating a contention. (B) is incorrect since the author adduces the situation to support his contention. (C) is incorrect for the author cites no authority. Finally, (E) can be eliminated since the author uses the case of the villainous man to support, not to weaken, the case.

6. **(B)** This is an explicit idea question. In paragraph 1, the author mentions that affirmative action is like other government programs in that it is designed to achieve certain social and economic goals. So statement I cites a similarity rather than a difference. Statement III can also be eliminated. In paragraph 3, the author states that the relevant difference is not the method of allocating benefits. The salient difference is set forth in the same paragraph, and it is the difference described by statement II.

7. **(A)** This is an inference question. In the first paragraph the author asks why affirmative action is so controversial. In the final paragraph, he reveals the answer: the moral dilemma. The wording of the passage, e.g., ''we are confronted with . . .,'' indicates that the author expects his reader will share this tension. So the passage is addressed to those who think affirmative action has value but who also believe it is unfair to non-minority persons. As for (B), the author believes that affirmative action is based on sound premises, achieving a legitimate social goal, but that the world is built so that we encounter this conflict. As for (C), it is not the programs themselves which contain contradictions. Rather, it is our value structure which creates the conflict. As for (D), the author believes the reader will regard the programs as creating suffering, but not that the suffering is needless. It may very well be the cost that must be paid. (E) is easily eliminated since the author expresses reservations about the programs.

8. **(E)** This is a main idea question, but one which asks about the main idea in the abstract. The discussion thus far makes clear the justification for (E). The author has a sense of this moral dilemma, which he believes will be shared by his readers, and he wants to explain why we experience this as conflict. As for (A), though the author develops a dilemma, he does not suggest that it is possible to slip between the horns of the dilemma. As for (B), he offers no refutation, so we will eliminate this as incorrect. As for (C), any historical references are purely incidental to the overall development of the thesis. And as for (D), though the analysis of affirmative action may suggest to the reader a method of analyzing other social problems, the focus of the passage is a particular problem—not methodology.

9. **(A)** This is an inference question. The material we need is in the first paragraph. There the author discusses the high percentage of aged persons living in Sweden and notes that relatively few live with family. He then states that Sweden placed a moratorium on the *construction of acute beds* in

favor of long-term beds. From the order of presentation, we may infer that the one caused the other. So (A) is inferable from the text. (B) is incorrect since no mention is made of tax laws. (C) is incorrect and represents a confused reading of the second paragraph. Wages in the health field are depressed because of historical circumstances, not government policy. (D) is incorrect and is a confused reading of the final paragraph. The text states that rooms are now designed to accommodate more patients, not that more patients are being crowded into small rooms. (E) is incorrect and is a misreading of the first paragraph. The moratorium halted the building of acute-care beds, not long-term beds.

10. **(E)** This is an explicit idea question. (A), (B), (C), and (D) are all mentioned in paragraph 3 as contributing to staffing problems. (E), however, is not mentioned. Though the author cites irregular hours as a problem, he never cites long hours as contributing to the staffing problem.

11. **(B)** This is an inference question. In the second paragraph, the author notes that wages in the health sector (aside from those of doctors) have traditionally been lower than those for comparable work in non-health care sectors because of a traditional presumption that health care is eleemosynary, or charitable, work. (B) nicely captures this idea. (A) is incorrect since it fails to make this connection. Moreover, it will not do to argue that, generally speaking, low-paying jobs have a lower status. In the first place, that does not respond to the question, which asks about the health field. In the second, that low status and low pay are correlated does not mean that one necessarily causes the other. As for (C), though the passage states that doctors earned acceptable salaries, the passage does not suggest that other workers were paid low wages because of this. It was traditional bias against health care workers other than doctors, who are professionals, which accounted for the low compensation. (D) is incorrect, for while it makes a true statement, the statement is not responsive to the question. Finally, (E) is not suggested by the text.

12. **(A)** This is an inference question. At the beginning of paragraph 2, the author notes that staff costs are the most important budgetary component of health care and, further, that this is higher for chronic aged than for acute patients. Since the author uses long-term care and care for the chron-

ic aged almost interchangeably, we may infer that most long-term care is for the aged. So we conclude that the staff cost for long-term care generally is greater than for acute care. This is stated by (A). Every other answer choice can be eliminated. (B) must be incorrect, for to the extent that staffing requirements are greater for long-term than for acute care, the general inflationary trend in labor costs will cause the cost of long-term care to rise more rapidly than that of acute care. (C) can be eliminated because the last paragraph establishes that there is a connection. (D) cannot be inferred since no mention is ever made of methods of payment. Finally, (E) is not supported by the passage. Though we have information about relative numbers of aged living with family, that will not generate a conclusion about relative cost.

13. **(A)** This is an inference question. The author states in the final paragraph that cutbacks in funding actually lead to better care. He calls this paradoxical. This can only be paradoxical if cutbacks in funding ordinarily result in a decline in the quality of care, and increases improve quality. This is answer (A). As for (B), though this may be true (and that is a question we need not answer), this will not answer the question posed. As for (C), though this is clearly stated in the passage, it does not explain why the cutback in funding led, paradoxically, to an improvement in care. (D) can be eliminated for it, too, does not explain the paradox. Finally, (E) is a confused reading of the first paragraph. The moratorium was placed on construction of acute-care beds, then, later, there was a cutback in funding for long-term care.

14. **(B)** This is an application question of some difficulty. The author states that rising standards of living have decreased the willingness of young adults to care for aging parents in their own homes. The percentage in Sweden is 10 percent as compared with 20 to 30 and even higher percentages in other countries. There is also the intriguing note that it is only 3 percent in Stockholm. Why the large difference between Sweden as a whole and Stockholm? If it were the case that the standard of living is higher in Stockholm than in Sweden as a country, this would add support to the author's explanation. This is articulated in (B). As for (A), if the U.S. has a higher standard of living, this would undermine the author's point. For that would suggest a higher percentage

of aged not cared for in homes; yet the numbers show a higher percentage of aged living with family in the U.S. (C) is incorrect for it is only remotely connected, if at all, with the cause for the percentages under consideration. (D) will not do the trick, for we are interested in percentage of aged living with family, not in the absolute number of aged. Finally, (E) must fail for the same reason that (C) fails: it is only remotely, if at all, connected to the question of why aged parents are not cared for in family homes.

15. **(E)** This is an explicit idea question. According to the passage, automated theorem proving, of which AURA is the best example, is used to check human reasoning. So (E) is the best response to the question. (A) is incorrect, since though this is a feature of programs such as "expert" programs, it is not the primary purpose of a system such as AURA. (B) fails for the same reason; this is one of many possible applications. (C) is incorrect since the function of AURA is to check human reasoning. To the extent that it can be used to analyze other computer programs, an issue we need not resolve, that is not the ultimate or primary purpose. The passage is quite clear on this score. The purpose of AURA is to aid human beings in solving problems by checking logic. Finally, (D) is just one of several possible applications.

16. **(D)** This is a main idea question, cast in the form of a "best title" question. The best title will be neither too broad nor too narrow—that is, just right. (A) is too broad. The author is discussing one limited aspect of computer use. (B) too is wide of the mark. Though AURA programs may have some implications for theories of artificial intelligence, the author does not discuss them. (C) is surely the second best answer, but it is too narrow on two counts. First, AURA is just an example of how computers might be used to assist human reasoning. So (D) is better in this respect. Second, even allowing that AURA is the best example of this possibility, the discussion of AURA is broader than just possible applications. The author sketches some basic theoretical concepts of AURA as well. (E) is wide of the mark since the author seems to endorse the use of AURA.

17. **(D)** This is an explicit idea question. (A), (B), (C), and (E) are all mentioned as advantages of expert programs in paragraph 3. The only reference to self-analytical programs is in paragraph 2. There the author states that AURA is not self-analytical.

18. **(C)** This, too, is an explicit idea question. Both statements I and IV are mentioned in paragraph 3. Statement II is mentioned in paragraph 2. No mention is made, however, of possible applications of AURA to mathematics or formal logic.

19. **(B)** This is a fairly interesting application question. In the second paragraph the author describes the theory of the AURA program. The computer is given the design of the system and then told that the goal cannot be reached given the design. Then, if the computer finds a contradiction in that information, this means the goal will be achieved by the design. In other words, we have a sort of indirect proof. We take the set of premises and the negation of the conclusion we hope to prove. If a contradiction can be found in the premises and negation of the conclusion, then the conclusion itself is proved. Applying this to our question, if the assertion that the switch remains open generates a contradiction, then the opposite conclusion is proved: The switch should be closed. And that answer is (B). (A) is too broad a conclusion. The contradiction does not prove the system was well designed, only that the result described by (B) will occur. That may or may not be the desired result. (C) is incorrect for it is contradicted by our analysis. (D) and (E) make the same error as (A), just in the opposite direction.

20. **(A)** This is a tone question. The author obviously thinks very highly of the development he is describing. The only adjective in the array of choices consistent with this attitude is (A). Every other choice has certain negative connotations. But no reservations are expressed by the author.

21. **(A)** This is a main idea question. (A) nicely describes the approach of the author. He describes recent developments in computer applications. (B) is incorrect for there is no misconception mentioned. To be sure, the author answers the second question (Will computers replace humans?) in the negative. But that is not the same thing as correcting a misconception. (C) is incorrect since the author describes, but does not propose, a theory. (D) is incorrect, for no objections are raised. Finally, (E) is incorrect since the

author does not focus on any particular problem and propose a solution. In general, it is possible to argue that there are elements of (B), (C), (D), or (E) in the passage, but it cannot be said that any one of those is the main point of the passage.

22. **(A)** This is a main idea question. The passage actually makes two points: Who is Josquin, and why have we never heard of him? (A) correctly mentions both of these. (B) is incorrect for the main focus is not to describe medieval music at all. Rather, the author focuses on Josquin, a man of the Renaissance. (C) is incorrect because the author is more concerned to introduce the reader to Josquin than to place Josquin into a context. And in any event, though the author mentions some ways in which Josquin broke with his predecessors, this is not a discussion of his "influence on later composers." (D) is incorrect, for the enumeration of features of Josquin's music is incidental to the task of introducing the reader to Josquin. Moreover, the author does not offer critical commentary. The mere fact that he praises Josquin's music does not constitute critical analysis. Finally, (E) is incorrect because it fails to refer to the second major aspect of the passage: Why is Josquin not better known?

23. **(E)** This is an explicit idea question. (A) is answered in paragraph two ("Solace me, ...). (B) is answered in the final paragraph (sackbut). (C) is answered in the second paragraph (Ockeghem). An answer to (D) is suggested in the final paragraph. (E) must be the correct answer, since the author never makes reference to any students.

24. **(E)** This is an inference question. In the third paragraph the author lists certain difficulties in reading a Renaissance score: no tempo specified, missing flats and sharps, and no instrument/voice indication. Since these are regarded as deficiencies of Renaissance scoring, we may infer that modern music notation contains all of these.

25. **(B)** This is an application question. The support for (B) is found in paragraph 3, where the author discusses the distinction between concept and performance. The author states that music does not exist as printed notes. The notation is just a set of instructions for producing music. So the author would agree with (B). As for (A), it is conceivable that the author might endorse this

statement——though it is also possible that the author would reject it. It is clear, however, that as between the statement in (B) and that in (A) we can be sure that the author would endorse (B). So (B), rather than (A), must be correct. (C) is incorrect because Josquin belongs to the Renaissance, not the Middle Ages. (D) fails for the same reason that (A) fails. Finally, there is no support for the statement in (E).

26. **(D)** Here, too, we have an application question. There is some merit to each of the choices, but we are looking for the one answer that is most closely connected with the text. Since the author discusses the lack of funding as one important reason for Josquin's obscurity, an obscurity the author deplores, the argument might be used to support a proposal for funds to promote Josquin's music. That is (D). (A) is less clearly supported by the text. To the extent that it is read as a device to promote Josquin's music, it would be less effective than (D) since the author states that *collegia musica* have a high turnover of students. Establishing yet another one would not do as much to bring Josquin's music to more people as (D). As for (B) and (E), these do not tie in with the idea of publicizing Josquin's music. Finally, (C) has some plausibility, but (D) has a connection with the passage which (C) lacks.

27. **(B)** This is an explicit idea question. (C), (D), and (E) are mentioned in the final paragraph. (A) is mentioned in the third paragraph. (B) is never mentioned. The author states that musicians who read modern notation have difficulty reading Renaissance notation——not that these musicians lack talent.

28. **(A)** This is a tone question. The author compares Josquin to Galileo in order to praise Josquin. This must mean that the author has a very high opinion of Galileo. So (D) and (E) can be eliminated because they are merely neutral. (B) can be eliminated because of its negative connotations. And (C) can be eliminated as being lukewarm, when the author is clearly enthusiastic about Josquin and therefore Galileo as well.

29. **(D)** This is a main idea question. The main idea of the passage is fairly clear: suggest reforms to correct the problems discussed. Choice (D) is a very good description of this development. (A) is incorrect since the author himself criticizes the system. (B) is incorrect since no recommendation

for expanding benefits and scope is made by the author. (C) overstates the case. The author limits his indictment to unemployment compensation, and even then he believes that the shortcomings of the system can be remedied. (E) is incorrect because the author is discussing unemployment compensation, not government programs designed to achieve full employment generally. We may infer from the passage that unemployment compensation is not a program designed to achieve full employment, but a program designed to alleviate the hardship of unemployment. On balance, (D) is the most precise description given of the development of the passage.

30. **(A)** This is a logical detail question. In the second paragraph the author introduces the example of a worker who loses surprisingly little by being unemployed. The author does this to show that unemployment encourages people to remain unemployed by reducing the net cost of unemployment. (A) makes this point. (B) is incorrect, for the author does not discuss the problem of employer contribution until the fourth paragraph. (C) is incorrect, for this is not the reason that the author introduces the point. (D) is incorrect because this topic is not taken up until the third paragraph. Finally, (E) is incorrect since the author analyzes the situation in a neutral fashion; there is no hint of condemnation.

31. **(C)** This is an explicit idea question. Statement I contains a recommendation made by the author in the final paragraph. Statement III is also recommended in that paragraph. As for statement II, the author never suggests shortening the time an out-of-work person may receive benefits. Though such a change might encourage people to limit the length of their unemployment, this was not mentioned in the passage. And the question is an explicit idea question that asks what recommendations were made by the author.

32. **(C)** Here, too, we have an explicit idea question. (A), (B), (D), and (E) are all mentioned in the third paragraph as ways by which an employer might reduce seasonal and cyclical fluctuations in labor needs. (C), however, was not mentioned as a way to minimize unemployment. Indeed, we may infer from other information supplied by the passage that supplementary benefits actually increase unemployment.

33. **(A)** This is an application question. We are asked to apply the author's analysis of the rating system to conclusions given in the answer choices. The author is critical of the rating system because it does not place the full burden of unemployment on the employer. This is because there is a maximum contribution limit, and in the final paragraph the author recommends the ceiling be eliminated. From these remarks, we may infer that the author believes the rating system is, in theory, sound, but that practically it needs to be adjusted. Choice (A) neatly describes this judgment. (B) can be eliminated since the author implies that the system is, in principle, sound. Moreover, the author implies that the employer does have some control over the time his former employees remain out of work. The maximum limit on employer contribution allows the employer to exploit this control. As for (C), this is contradicted by our analysis thus far and for the further reason that the passage never suggests employee contribution should replace employer contribution. Indeed, the author implies that he regards the system as serving a useful and necessary social function. (D) can be eliminated because the author never draws a distinction between contributions by large firms and contributions by small firms. Finally, (E) is incorrect since the experience rating system is theoretically tied to the amount drawn by employees. The difficulty is not with the theory of the system, but with its implementation.

34. **(B)** This is an explicit detail question. We are looking for criticisms which are made in the passage. Statement II is such a criticism, and it can be found in the very opening sentence. As for statement I, the author actually states the opposite: The system allows firms of this sort to use the unemployment compensation system as a subsidy for their employees, reducing their own costs of production. As for statement III, the author only states that employers contribute to the fund from which benefits are paid. No mention is ever made of a state contribution. So the correct answer is II only.

35. **(A)** This is a tone question. In the final paragraph, as he makes his recommendations, the author states that we must reform the system, preserving its good aspects and correcting its bad effects. (A) describes this judgment. (B) is incorrect since much of the discussion in the passage is an indictment of the system's economic inefficiency. (C) is wrong because the author makes

recommendations which, he states, will correct the wasteful effects. (D) is incorrect, for the author implies that the system has usefulness. Finally, though the author criticizes the system, the objection is that the system is inefficient, not that it is outdated.

SECTION III

1. **(B)** This question requires careful attention to the quantifiers in each claim. An additional expense voucher might indicate additional expenses for an already identified employee or expenses incurred by an additional employee. A claim which states only that there are "at least so many employees" and that they incurred "at least this in expenses" cannot be contradicted by a revision upward in any number. A claim which states "there were exactly so many employees" or which states "there were at most so many employees" is contradicted by the discovery of another employee. The same reasoning applies to expenses. An "at least" claim is not contradicted by an upward revision, but the other claims are. (A) can be contradicted by an upward revision in the number of employees. (C) can be contradicted by an upward revision in the amount of expenses claimed. (D) and (E) can be contradicted on both grounds. (B) cannot be contradicted by any new finding.

2. **(A)** The question stem contains a hidden assumption: It is a loaded question. It presupposes that the person questioned agrees that the city is discriminating against its Hispanic residents. (A) is a pretty nice parallel. The questioner assumes that the Congressman agrees that defense spending is out of hand, which may or may not be true. (B) makes no such assumption. It can be answered with a simple "yes" if the chairperson plans to take a luncheon recess; otherwise a "no" will do the job. (C) requires more than a "yes" or "no" answer, but it still contains no presuppositions. Since the question asks "what," the speaker may respond by saying much, little, or none at all. (D) may be said to make a presupposition—Gladys is going to the store—but here the presupposition is not concealed. It is made an explicit condition of the answer. Finally, (E) is a little like (B) in that a simple "yes" or "no" can communicate the counselor's opinion. It might be objected that (E) presupposes that the company has an affirmative action program, and that this

makes it similar to the question stem. Two responses can be made. First, (E) is in this way like (D): The assumption—if there is one—is fairly explicit. Second, (E) does not have the same loaded tone as (A) does, so by comparison (A) is a better choice.

3. **(E)** The ad is a little deceptive. It tries to create the impression that if hospitals are using Dr. John's Milk of Magnesia, people will believe it is a good product. But what the ad actually says is that Dr. John uses the same *ingredient* which hospitals use (milk of magnesia is a simple suspension of magnesium hydroxide in water). The ad is something like an ad for John's Vinegar which claims it has "acetic acid," which is vinegar. I falls into the trap of the ad and is therefore wrong. II is not inferable since there may be treatments other than milk of magnesia for these disorders. Finally, since I is incorrect, III must certainly also be incorrect. Even if I had been true, III might still be questionable since use and recommendation are not identical.

4. **(A)** Statements I and II combine to give us (A). If all wheeled conveyances which travel on the highway are polluters, and a bicycle does not travel on the highway, then a bicycle cannot be a polluter. If (A) is then correct, (B) must be incorrect because bicycles do not travel on the highways at all. (C) and (D) make the same mistake. III must be read to say, "If I am driving, it is raining," not "If it is raining, I am driving." (E) is clearly false since my car is driven on the highway. Don't make the problem harder than it is.

5. **(E)** Picking up on our discussion of (C) and (D) in the previous question, III must read, "If I am driving, then it is raining." Let that be: "If P, then Q." If we then had not-Q, we could deduce not-P. (E) gives us not-Q by changing IV to "It is not raining." Changing I or II or even both is not going to do the trick, for they don't touch the relationship between my driving my car and rain—they deal only with pollution and we need the car to be connected. Similarly, if we change III to make it deal with pollution, we have not adjusted the connection between my driving and rain, so (C) must be wrong. (D) is the worst of all the answers. Whether rainwater is polluted or not has nothing to do with the connection between my driving and rain. Granted, there is the unstated assumption that my car only pollutes when I drive it, but this is OK.

6. **(E)** The reasoning in the argument is representative of the fallacy of false cause. Common sense tells you that you are not necessarily safer driving at higher speeds. Moreover, the distance you are from your home does not necessarily make you more or less safe. And it will not do to engage in wild speculation, e.g., people suddenly become more attentive at speeds over 45 miles per hour. The exam is just not that subtle. Rather we should look for a fairly obvious alternative explanation, and we find it in (E). The real reason there are fewer fatalities at speeds over 50 miles per hour and at a distance greater than 25 miles from home is that less driving time is logged under such conditions. Most driving originates at home and proceeds at speeds set for residential areas. (A), (B), and (C) all seem to make plausible statements, but they are irrelevant to the claim made in the stem paragraph. It is difficult to see how they could either weaken or strengthen the argument. (D) has the merit of addressing the statistics used to support the argument, but without further information (D) does not weaken the argument—it merely makes an observation. To be sure, if we knew that states were notoriously bad at gathering statistics, (D) could weaken the argument. But that requires speculation, and we always prefer an obvious answer such as (E).

7. **(D)** The author states that a certain amount of rain in a given time *usually* results in mushrooms growing in his backyard. Both I and II are wrong for the same reason. From the fact that there has not been the requisite minimum rainfall required for mushrooms, we would not want to conclude that there has been *no* rain at all. III overstates the author's case and is for that reason wrong. The author specifically qualifies his claim by saying it "usually" happens this way. Thus, he would not want to say that the absence of mushrooms and fungus definitely means that the requisite amount of rain has not fallen—only that it seems likely or probable that there has not been enough rain.

8. **(C)** Given the fairly "soft" information provided in the paragraph, any conclusion which is to be "completely justified" on the basis of that information will have to be a fairly minimal claim. We can eliminate (A) since the paragraph asserts something about the effect of Jack Remain's program but never claims that the Jack Remain program is unique in this respect. (B) goes beyond the scope of the argument by asserting the pro-gram is effective for all ages. The paragraph actually makes only a minimal claim, namely, this is possible. Even if the program is effective only for persons 20 to 25, the claim is not false—it is true though only for that limited age group. (D) over-states the case. The paragraph claims that weight loss is possible—not that it is certain. (E) cannot be justified for that would be to move from the premise "weight loss is possible" to the conclusion "most people need exercise to lose weight." But the conclusion does not follow from the premise. (C), however, can be justified. If it is true, as the stem asks us to assume, that a study shows weight loss is possible, then it must be true that the program is effective for some—even if only for one person. This is all (C) claims: You might be one of the lucky ones.

9. **(D)** In essence, the advertisement attempts to shift the burden of proof to the reader. It is possible—you try it and find out whether it is possible for you. (E) is incorrect since no other claims are cited. (C) is incorrect since the ad is clearly an attempt to influence the reader's decision. (B) should be eliminated in favor of (A) since the paragraph is not a logical set of premises. This leaves (A) as the second best answer. And it can be argued that the paragraph does provide evidence (the study) and, further, that it does allow the reader to reach a conclusion. But what would that conclusion be? If the conclusion mentioned in (A) is to try or not to try the product, then (A) is incorrect since the ad reaches the conclusion that the reader should try it. But if the conclusion is whether or not the product works, then (D) is better because it more accurately describes the attempt to shift the burden of proof.

10. **(B)** The author's claim is self-referential—it refers to itself or includes itself in its own description. The author says that *every* action is economically motivated; therefore, we may conclude that his own motivation in making such a claim and in writing a book about it is also economically motivated. The speaker in our passage says he is going to apply the author's theory to his (the author's) own actions. This is why (B) is correct. Neither (A) nor (E) can be correct inasmuch as the author of the book claims that there are no such motivations. Ultimately, he says, all motivations can be reduced to one, economics. (C) has to be wrong, since the author of the book claims that everything done is economically mo-

tivated. His examples make it clear that even a reformer with some seemingly non-economic motive would be "pure" only on the surface, with a deeper, economic motivation for reforming. Finally, (D) can be rejected since it conflicts with one of the examples given by the author of the book.

11. **(A)** The argument makes the rather outlandish assumption that the physical characteristics of the criminal dictate the kind of crime he will commit. But as unreasonable as that may seem in light of common sense, it *is* an assumption made by the speaker. (We did not make the assumption, he did.) II is not an assumption of the argument, since the paragraph specifically states that the killer was executed—he cannot have escaped. III does not commit the blatant error committed by II, but it is still wrong. Although III might be a better explanation for the crimes now being committed than that proposed by our speaker, our speaker advances the explanation supported by I, not III. In fact, the speaker uses phrases such as "looks very much like" which tell us that he assumes there are two killers.

12. **(A)** The form of the argument can be represented using letters as:

I. All R are either O or W. (All non-Readers are non-Opinion holders or Wrong.)
II. All O are R.

If II is true, I might be either false or true, since it is possible that there are some who have not read the report who hold right opinions. That is, even if II is true and all O are R, that does not tell us anything about all the R's, only about all the O's. The rest of the R's might be W's (wrong-opinion holders) or something else altogether (right-opinion holders). By this reasoning we see that we cannot conclude that I is definitely true, so (B) must be wrong. Moreover, we have no ground for believing I to be more or less likely true, so (C) can be rejected. As for (D), even if we assume that all the R's are *either* O or W, we are not entitled to conclude that all O's are R's. There may be someone without an opinion who has not read the report. Finally (E), if it is false that all the O's (non-opinion holders) are not R's, this tells us nothing about all R's and their distribution among O and W.

13. **(A)** The fallacy in the author's argument is that he takes a group term ("the average size of

women") and applies it to the individual. (A) calls attention to this fallacy. The average size of women is irrelevant in the case of those women who are of sufficient size. (D) concedes too much to the author. We do not have to settle for the conclusion that some women may be suitable for desk jobs. We can win the larger claim that some women may be suitable to be police officers—or at least as suitable as their male counterparts. (B), (C), and (E) are possible arguments to be used against the author's general position. We might want to claim, for example, that training or weapons will compensate for want of size, but again there is no reason even to grant the author that much. We do not even have to concede that the *average* size is relevant. Finally, (E) also gives away too much. Although the use of pistols is sometimes called "deadly force," the author's linkage of size to force specifies force as being a strength or size idea.

14. **(D)** We can use our capital letters to see why (D) is the correct answer. The structure of the stem argument is:

No S are R.
Some S are D.
Therefore, Some D are not R.

(D) shares this form:

All pets are   No P are A.   (A = allowed)
excluded: Some P are V.
Many = Some:
Therefore, some V are not A.

(A) has a very different form since it is presented as a probabilistic, not a deductive or logical, argument. (B)'s conclusion goes beyond the information given in the premises. We cannot conclude that uncle *enjoys* paying the bills, even though he may incur them. (C) has the form:

Some BB are F.
All F is WR.
Therefore, All BB are WR.

This does not parallel our question stem for two reasons. First, our stem argument is valid, while the argument in (C) is not. Second, (D) is more nearly parallel to the stem argument than (C); for even if we rearrange the assumptions in (C) to put the "all" proposition first and the "some" proposition second, the "all's" and the "some's" of (C) do not parallel those of the question stem. (E) does not share the stem form. First, it is not the same argument form (all, some, etc.). Second, (E) is clearly not a proper logical argument.

15. **(A)** Perhaps a little diagram is the easiest way to show this problem.

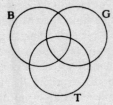

We will show all B are T by eliminating that portion of the diagram where some area of B is not also inside T:

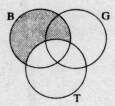

Now, let us put an *x* to show the existence of those B's which are G's:

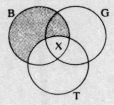

The diagram shows us that I is true. Since the only areas left for B's are within the T circle, the G condition is unimportant. II is not inferable. Although there is some overlap of the G and T circles, there is also some non-overlap. This shows that is may be possible to be a T without also being a G. III is not inferable since our diagrams are restricted to the three categories B, G, and T and say nothing about things outside of those categories.

16. **(C)** The stem argument has the form: "If P, then Q. Q. Therefore, P." The argument is invalid. There may be other reasons that the razor is not functioning, e.g., the switch is not on, it is broken, etc. (C) has this form also. John's fingerprints might have been found at the scene, yet he may not have committed the crime. (A) has the form: "If P, then Q. Not Q. Therefore, not P," which not only is not parallel to the question

stem, but is valid and thus a poor parallel to the invalid original argument as well. (B) has the form: "P or Q. Not P. Therefore, Q." This, too, does not parallel the stem argument, and, like (B), is valid. (D) is invalid, but the fallacy is not the same as what we find in the stem argument. The stem argument is set up using "if, then" statements. (D) does not parallel this form. (E) does use "if, then" statements, but its form is: "If P, then Q. P. Therefore, P." This argument is clearly valid.

17. **(A)** The author's statement is self-contradictory or paradoxical. It says, in effect, "No statement is always correct," but then that statement itself must be false——since it attempts to make a claim about "always." The author's statement is inductive, that is, a generalization; but (E) is not as good an answer as (A) because it fails to pick up on the fact that the statement is internally contradictory. The statement cannot be valid, (D), since the author tries to pass it off as a generalization. Generalizations can be strong or weak, well founded or ill founded, but they cannot be valid or invalid. (C) is incorrect for there is nothing ambiguous or poorly defined in the argument. Finally, the argument is not circular, (B), because the author does not seek to establish his conclusion by assuming it. As we have noted, the statement is self-contradictory, so it could not possibly be circular.

18. **(B)** This item asks you to draw a conclusion from the paragraph. The best answer will be one that is well supported by the text, and this is (B). The initial paragraph sets up a contrast between political commitment and financial reward and indicates that Gonzalez chose political commitment over financial reward. The conclusion of the paragraph should be some consequence of this decision. (B) describes a possible consequence of this decision.

(A) is wrong because the paragraph implies that she did not enjoy popular acclaim. (C) is incorrect because it goes beyond the scope of the selection. Although (C) describes an idea that is generally related to the subject matter of the paragraph, it does not flow as a conclusion from the distinction drawn in the paragraph. (D) must surely be wrong, for Gonzalez's resistance to certain inducements would not be calculated to compromise the chances of those who came later. And finally, (E) makes the same mistake as (C). To be sure, this is an idea that is generally related to the subject of the initial paragraph, but this idea does not follow as a conclusion from the paragraph.

19. **(E)** Again, we are looking for a choice that is strongly supported by the text, and this time it is (E). The paragraph clearly implies a distinction between economic reward and political commitment and that the latter was the course chosen by Gonzalez. As for (A) and (D), these are topics that conceivably were treated by Gonzalez's films, but nothing in the paragraph requires such a conclusion. (C), though possible, is not supported by the text.

20. **(A)** Analyze the argument into its various premises. They are:

    1. Some experts maintain reductions will hurt care of the elderly and chronically ill.
    2. Part of recent increases in costs have helped provide service to these groups.
    3. But the real causes of high costs are duplication, inefficiency, inflated salaries.

    Once the argument is analyzed in this way, you can see that the most likely conclusion is that contained in (A): Efforts to control costs will necessarily hurt the elderly and chronically ill that much.

    (B) is probably the second best response, but a careful reading of (B) shows that it is fatally flawed. (B) asserts that duplication and inefficiency contribute to the rising cost of care for the elderly and the chronically ill. But the passage says (1) that recent increases in the cost of care for those groups reflect improvements in service and (2) that the factors cited inflate health care costs in general, not just those specifically incurred by the elderly or chronically ill.

    (C), of course, is contradicted by the passage. (D), too, is at least in tension with the passage, for the author implies that some of the increase in health care costs for the elderly and chronically ill have come as the result of improvements in services. Finally, (E) goes beyond the scope of the passage. In the first place, you would need to know whether elderly and chronically ill pay their own expenses (as opposed to having them paid by the government or a third-party carrier), and the passage is silent on that question. Additionally, you would need a lot more to support the conclusion that rising costs will make health care unaffordable for those groups, as opposed to just burdensome.

21. **(C)** The logical flaw in the argument is not that difficult to find. The argument assumes that a city

that ranks below another city in any one category (in particular the crime category) cannot rank above that city in the overall category. Now the question becomes which of the choices attacks this assumption.

The best available attack is provided by (C). Although this choice does not state directly that the assumption just isolated is erroneous, it does provide two counter-examples to the assumption. (A), (B), and (E) make assertions not inconsistent with the information provided in the paragraph about Detroit and San Francisco, and they don't attack the hidden premise we have isolated. Finally, (D) is somewhat like the correct answer, but (D) does not attack the hidden assumption in the way that (C) does. (Notice that (D) describes a situation in which the city which ranks lower in the overall standings also ranks lower in other categories as well.)

22. **(B)** This item serves as a good reminder of the importance of reading the answer choices carefully, for some of the choices here are very close. The speaker says that adults often assume that a child feels like a child but thinks like an adult. But, according to the speaker, this is wrong— the opposite is true. But what is the opposite? Children feel not like children but like adults, and children think not like adults but like children. This is the conclusion provided by (B).

As for (A), while the speaker apparently believes that there is some connection between the emotional and mental functions of a child and those of an adult, nothing in the passage supports the conclusion that the one *prefigures* the other. (C), too, goes beyond the scope of the paragraph. The speaker claims that there are some similarities and some differences between children and adults, but that premise will not support the conclusion that the differences are more important than the similarities. The suggestion in (D) seems to be contradicted by the selection, for the speaker clearly says that thought patterns change. Finally, (E) is surely the second best answer, for (E) at least has the merit of suggesting a reversal of a position. But when the speaker asserts "the opposite is true," he means the opposite of the *contention* of many adults (specifically, that children think like adults but feel like children). He does not mean that children and adults have opposite reactions to the same situations.

23. **(A)** Here you can use the same devices you use in solving analytical reasoning items to keep

track of this information. The statements in the initial paragraph can be summarized as follows:

SY→(FG or SG) (Sunny implies Fishing
                or Swimming)
SG→TS   (Swimming implies Tennis)
~TS   (Not tennis)

From this you can infer ~SG (Hector did not go swimming.) But you cannot infer from the fact that Hector did not go swimming that he did or did not go fishing; and since he might have gone fishing, it is possible that Saturday was sunny. So only I is inferable.

24. **(C)** This is a fun little item. John says the dollars should be spent right here on Earth, meaning, of course, they should be spent on practical projects rather than projects such as space exploration. Joan turned John's language around on him by pointing out that—literally—this money is spent right here on Earth (even if it is for space exploration). Notice how the question stem here guides you. It doesn't just ask you to comment on the exchange. It informs you that the exchange is characterized by a shift in meaning and then asks you to identify the critical term.

25. **(B)** The conclusion of the argument is "I am not impaired." The premise is "I drank wine but I did not drink liquor." One possible assumption that could underwrite the conclusion is "It is impossible to become impaired drinking wine." This, however, is not a possible choice. But (B) does articulate a possible hidden assumption. The speaker means to say "I can't be drunk, I have only been drinking wine and not liquor." (An obviously fallacious argument, but for reasons not presently relevant.) This claim depends on the assumption that hard liquor impairs more than wine.

26. **(D)** This item, too, asks you to identify a hidden assumption. First, find the conclusion of the argument. It is contained in the rhetorical question at the end of the paragraph, a question that should be read to assert affirmatively "World leaders would not trust someone who has admitted lying to her spouse." That conclusion rests upon the hidden assumption that a person who would lie to her or his spouse about an affair would also lie to world leaders.

27. **(D)** The only paragraph containing an argument

that makes a generalization is (D). The speaker makes a claim about cameras in general based upon the one incident.

28. **(C)** The only paragraph containing an argument directed toward an opponent instead of the merits of the argument is (C). There the speaker attacks the Mayor by alleging that the Mayor is biased by a financial interest in the issue.

29. **(C)** The speaker uses the word "free" in two different ways. In the first occurrence of the word, it means "liberty"—a general term— meaning freedom from governmental or other constraint. The second occurrence is the use we reserve for being free of some particular problem, e.g., free or rid of a problem.

30. **(A)** The author states that the Ecole was a quasi-governmental agency that controlled the distribution of government money for artists. Since the Impressionist painters were scorned and received no money (only empty bellies) for their efforts, we can infer that they did not paint in the accepted style. (B) goes beyond the scope of what is specifically stated in the initial paragraph. Although you can infer that the Impressionists rejected the standards of the Ecole and further that they were ultimately successful (note the word "initially," which qualifies their lack of success), you cannot infer that they gained control over the Ecole. (C) and (D) also go beyond the scope of the initial paragraph. According to the author, the Ecole exercised its control by the ways in which it distributed money. The passage does not suggest that the Ecole exercised any direct control. Finally, (E) too goes beyond what can be legitimately inferred from the initial paragraph. In fact, if anything can be inferred from the selection about the state of painting in France in the second half of the 19th century, it is that it was more creative than the art of the first half of the century, for you might reasonably infer that the Impressionists constituted a new creative force.

31. **(D)** The task here is to explain why the teacher makes the second remark. (D) provides the best explanation. The teacher's first remark says only that the student to whom he is speaking is not one of the students who has passed the test. You cannot infer from that remark that the student in the conversation has not passed the test. It is possible that his paper has not yet been graded. (Consider

a similar situation: You look into a classroom through a door that is slightly ajar and see three students, all of whom are girls. You then say ''Some of the students in this class are girls''— obviously a true statement. If you later open the door completely and see only female students in the classroom, you can say ''All of the students in this class are girls''—also a true statement. But your first statement is not thereby rendered false. It remains true as well.) The other choices fail to explain why the teacher would say, ''You don't yet need to tell your parents that you failed the test.''

32. **(C)** The author notes that arguments in favor of legalizing marijuana have generally fallen into two categories: those which assert that there is no evidence that marijuana is dangerous and those which assert that laws proscribing the use of marijuana infringe on an individual's liberty. The arguments of the first sort are designed to show that there is no good reason to have laws against marijuana, while arguments of the second sort are intended to show that there is a reason to legalize marijuana. At this point the author says that there is yet another reason to legalize marijuana: smoking marijuana is pleasurable. Thus, the author implies that the fact that an activity is pleasurable is a reason that might be given for allowing people to engage in it. (A) is not inferable from the paragraph. In fact, the author states that there is no evidence to prove such a contention. (B) represents a possible misreading of the paragraph. The author does not state that marijuana is illegal because it is pleasurable but that it should be legal because it is pleasurable. As for (D), the author states that arguments based on claims of individual liberty are not the only ones that could be advanced for the legalization of marijuana, not that those who use such arguments are insincere. Finally, as for (E), opponents of marijuana might not deny that the drug has a pleasurable effect, but they would insist that people are not entitled to that pleasurable effect because the use of marijuana leads to ill effects as well, such as antisocial behavior.

33. **(B)** A neat way to attack problems like this (in which a second speaker evidently misconstrues the remark of a first speaker) is to put each answer choice into the mouth of the first speaker. The correct choice will be the one that creates a meaningful exchange between the two speakers: (A) David: Paintings by Electra and Bluesina

should be displayed in the Museum.
Marat: I disagree. I have seen some very fine works by Electra and Bluesina that should be displayed in the Museum.

(B) David: Only Kissandra's paintings should be displayed in the Museum.
Marat: I disagree. I have seen some very fine works by Electra and Bluesina that should be displayed in the Museum.

(C) David: Every painting by Kissandra should be displayed in the Museum.
Marat: I disagree. I have seen some very fine works by Electra and Bluesina that should be displayed in the Museum.

(D) David: Not every Kissandra painting should be displayed in the Museum.
Marat: I disagree. I have seen some very fine works by Electra and Bluesina that should be displayed in the Museum.

(E) David: Kissandra's paintings should be displayed only in the Museum.
Marat: I disagree. I have seen some very fine works by Electra and Bluesina that should be displayed in the Museum.

Questions 34–35

34. **(D)** A diagram makes it easy to keep track of the relationships:

Younger ————————————> Older

Paul is older than Sally:

Sally is older than Fred:

Mike is older than Paul:

Ralph is younger than Mike but older than Fred:

The diagram shows that both I and III are true. II, however, may or may not be true. Fred could be younger than Sally, so Ralph too could be younger than Sally.

35. **(E)** Since Chuck is younger than Ralph and

Ralph is younger than Mike, Chuck must be younger than Mike.

SECTION IV

1. **(B)** The proposition that you cannot argue with taste says that taste is relative. Since we are looking for an answer choice inconsistent with that proposition, we seek an answer choice that argues that taste. or aesthetic value, is absolute, or at least not relative—that there are standards of taste. (B) is precisely that.

   (C) and (D) are just distractions, playing on the notion of taste in the physical sense and the further idea of the distasteful; but these superficial connections are not strong enough.

   (A), (B), and (E) are all activities in which there is some element of aesthetic judgment or appreciation. In (A), the holding of an exhibition, while implying some selection principle and thus some idea of a standard of taste, does not truly purport to judge aesthetics in the way that (B), precisely a beauty *contest*, does. The exhibition may be of historical or biographical interest, for example. (E) also stresses more of the exhibition aspect than the judging aspect. You should not infer that all movie festivals are contests, since the word "festival" does not require this interpretation and, in fact, there are festivals at which the judging aspect is minimal or non-existent. The Cannes Film Festival, while perhaps the best known, is not the only type of movie festival there is. The questions are not tests of your knowledge of the movie industry.

2. **(D)** Note the question stem very carefully: We are to find the answer choice *from which* we can deduce the sample argument. You must pay very careful attention to the question stem in every problem. (D) works very nicely as it gives us the argument structure: All post-1974 students are required. . . . George is a post-1974 student. Therefore, George is required. . . ." Actually, the middle premise is phrased in the conditional (with an "if"), but our explanation is close enough, even if it is a bit oversimplified. (A) will not suffice, for while it describes the situation before 1974, it just does not address itself to the post-1974 situation. And George is a post-1974 student. (B) also fails. From the fact that all of those who took the course graduated after 1974, we cannot conclude that George was one of them

(any more than we can conclude from the proposition that all airline flight attendants lived after 1900 and that Richard Nixon, who lived after 1900, was one of them). (C) fails for the same reason that (A) fails. (E) is a bit tricky because of the double negative. It makes the sentence awkward. The easiest way to handle such a sentence is to treat the double negative as an affirmative. The negative cancels the negative, just as in arithmetic a negative number times a negative number yields a positive number. So (E) actually says that before 1974 the course was not required. That is equivalent to (A) and must be wrong for the same reason.

3. **(B)** II is the only one of the three which is completely supported by the argument. III is easily dismissed. That there are no minnows on this side of the lake now surely does not mean that there will never be any, any more than the fact that there are no children in the park now means that there never will be any children in the park. I is very close to II and differs only in the qualification introduced by the word "probably," but that is an important qualification. The author states specifically that bass are *usually* found wherever there are minnows. So where there are no bass, he *expects* to find no minnows. But, of course, he cannot be certain. Perhaps there are other reasons for the absence of bass: The water is too cold or too shallow or too muddy for bass, though not for minnows. So I overstates the case. The author apparently allows that you may find minnows without bass—but not usually.

4. **(D)** Juanita wonders how Tommy knows the phone has rung if he couldn't hear it because of the shower. She overlooks the possibility that he learned the phone had rung without actually hearing it himself. Perhaps someone else lives with him who heard it; perhaps Tommy has an answering machine and later learned that the phone rang while he was in the shower; maybe the caller calls back and tells Tommy he called earlier and Tommy says "Oh, I must have been in the shower and didn't hear it." Juanita overlooks these possibilities. (A) is incorrect because Juanita apparently assumes the phone does ring and that Tommy can hear it ringing. (C) and (E) may or may not be true, but they do not address themselves to Juanita's statement. (B) could only underlie Juanita's objection to Tommy's remarks if hearing calls were the only possible way in which Tommy could learn of the call. But as we show, there are other possibilities.

5. **(E)** I is not inconsistent with the advertisement since the ad is touting the strength of the pain-reliever, not its price. III, too, can easily be seen not to be inconsistent. The ad speaks of non-prescription pain-relievers, but III brings up the irrelevant matter of prescription pain-relievers. II is not inconsistent because RELIEF does not claim to be the one strong*est* pain-reliever, only that no other non-prescription pain-reliever is stronger. So none of the statements contradicts the ad.

6. **(C)** III is an assumption of the psychologist. He observed the dogs for a certain period of time, and found that each time a stranger approached they kept silent. From those observed instances he concluded that the dogs never barked at strangers. Obviously his theory would be disproved (or at least it would have to be seriously qualified) if, when he was not watching, the dogs barked their heads off at strangers. I is not assumed, however. The psychologist was concerned only with the dogs' reactions to strangers. As far as we know, he may have seen the dogs barking during a frolic in the park, or while they were being bathed, or at full moon. II is not an assumption the author makes. The author makes a factual claim: Dogs treated in this way do not bark at strangers. We have no basis for concluding that the author does or does not think that dogs ought or ought not to bark at strangers. In fact, it seems as likely that the author thinks a great way to train watchdogs is to hit them with rolled-up newspapers.

7. **(B)** II would undermine the psychologist's thesis that "only a beaten dog barks." It cites instances in which the dog was not beaten and still barked at strangers. This would force the psychologist to reconsider his conclusion about the connection between beating and barking. I is not like II. It does not state the dogs were never beaten; it states only that the dogs were not beaten when they barked at strangers. It is conceivable that they were beaten at other times. If they were, then even though they might bark at strangers (and not be beaten at that moment), they would not be counter-examples to the psychologist's theory. III is not an assumption of the psychologist, as we saw in the preceding question, so denying it does not affect the strength of his argument. The psychologist is concerned with the factual connection between beating a dog and its barking; information about the owners' feelings can hardly be relevant to the factual issue.

8. **(B)** Here the author must assume that every effect which is part of the child's experience has been generated by a cause which was also a part of the child's experience, but that is possible only on the assumption that the cause, which is an effect itself, is the result of some previous cause. In other words, every effect flows from some earlier effect. Now, admittedly, that seems to lead to a pretty absurd conclusion: Therefore, there could be no beginning of experience for the child—it must stretch back infinitely. But the question stem does not ask us to critique the argument, only to analyze it and uncover its premises, (A) is wrong because the author does not say all experiences are alike, only that the one today has its roots in the one yesterday. For example, sometimes the presence of moisture in the atmosphere causes rain, sometimes snow. (C) oversimplifies matters in two respects. One, while the author may agree that a child's experiences may tell us *something* about the parents (assuming the child is in intimate contact with them), we surely would not want to conclude that is the *best* way to learn about the parents. Two, the parents are not the only source of experience the child has, so the later effects would be the result of non-parental causes as well. (D) is incorrect because the author need not assume that experience is cumulative. In some cases, the cause-and-effect sequence may only reiterate itself so that experience is circular rather than cumulative. Finally, (E) is another example of going too far—of extending a simple factual statement beyond the scope the author originally gave it. Here the author says that experience causes experience, but he never suggests that we are in a position to use this principle practically, to manipulate the input to mold the child.

9. **(C)** The author's claim is that we have unbounded resources, and he tries to prove this by showing that we are getting better and better at extracting those resources from the ground. But that is like saying, "I have found a way to get the last little bit of toothpaste out of the tube; therefore, the tube will never run out." (C) calls our attention to this oversight. (A) does not contradict the author's claim. In fact, it seems to support it. He might suggest, "Even if we run out of fossil fuels, we still have uranium for nuclear power." Now, this is not to suggest that he would. The point is only to show that (A) supports rather than undermines the author's contention. (B) is an attack on the author's general stance, but it does not really *contradict* the particular conclusion he

draws. The author says, "We have enough." (B) says, "It is expensive." Both could very well be true, so they cannot contradict one another. (D) is similar to (B). Yes, you may be correct, the technology is expensive, or in this case wasteful, but it will still get us the fuel we need. Finally, (E) is incorrect for pretty much these same reasons. Yes, the energy will have unwanted side effects, but the author claimed only that we could get the energy. The difficulty with (B), (D), and (E) is that though they attack the author's general *position,* though they undermine his general suggestion, they do not *contradict* his *conclusion.*

Questions 10–12

10. **(A)** 11. **(D)** 12. **(C)** Argument (A) is circular. It is like saying, "I never tell a lie; and you must believe that because, as I have just told you, I never tell a lie." So (A) is the answer to question 10. (E) might seem circular: Guns do not cause crimes, people do. But it is not. The author's point is that these crimes would be committed anyway, and he explains how they would be committed. (C) is an *ad hominem* attack. It rejects the conclusion of the argument not because the argument is illogical but because it comes from a particular source. Remember, as we learned in the Test Busters section, not all *ad hominem* are illegitimate. It is perfectly all right to inquire into possible biases of the source, and that is just what occurs here. So (C) is the answer to question 12. (D) is a fairly weak argument. It takes a handful of observed instances and generalizes to a strong conclusion. But even though it may be weak, it does fit the description "generalization," so (D) is the answer to question 11. (B) is just left over and fits none of the descriptions.

13. **(A)** The author places himself in opposition to the sociologists whom he cites. He claims an alternative interpretation of the evidence. In other words, the most logical continuation of the passage will be the one which explains why such sects are not a recent phenomenon even though there are no old ones around. (A) does this neatly. Since the members abstain from sexual relations, they will not reproduce members and the sect will tend to die out. This explains why there are none more than 50 or 60 years old. (C), if anything, supports the position of the sociologists, for it implicitly gives up trying to explain the evidence differently and also undercuts the explanation the author might have given. (B) is irrelevant be-

cause intensity of religious fervor is irrelevant to the length of the sect's existence; it cannot possibly help the author explain away the evidence of the sociologists. (D) is irrelevant for another reason. The author needs to explain why the sects are all relatively young without having recourse to the thesis of the sociologists that they are a recent phenomenon. That there are other organizations which encourage sexual relations of whatever kind cannot help the author explain a phenomenon such as the Waiters. Finally, (E) is a distraction, picking up as it does on a minor detail. The author needs to explain the short-livedness of groups of which the Waiters is only an example.

14. **(E)** The conclusion of the speaker is that the checkup has *no* value, so anything which suggests the checkup does have value will undermine the conclusion. I shows a possible advantage of having the checkup. It says, in effect, while the checkup is not foolproof and will not catch everything, it does catch some fairly important things. II also gives us a possible reason for visiting our mechanic for a 5,000-mile checkup. Even if it won't keep our car in running order, it is necessary if we want to take advantage of our warranty. Finally, III also gives us a good reason to have a checkup: The mechanic will make some routine adjustments. All three of these propositions, then, mention possible advantages of having a checkup. So all three weaken the author's conclusion that the checkup is *worthless* and a waste of money and time.

15. **(A)** Here we are looking for the most perfect analogy. Keep in mind, first, that the author opposes the move, and second, all of the features of the union-management situation, in particular that they are adversaries. (A) captures both elements. The relationship between prison administrators and inmates is adversarial, and the suggestion that inmates make decisions on security is outrageous enough that it captures also the first element. (B) fails on both counts. First, the two are not on opposites of the fence; second, the senior officer is *asking* for advice—not deferring to the opinion of his junior officer. (C) is very similar. First, the administration of the university and the student body are not necessarily adversaries; at least, although they may disagree on the best means for advancing the goals of the university, there is often agreement about those goals. Second, the administration is, as with (B),

asking advice, not abdicating responsibility for the decision. In (D) we lack both elements; the mayor need not be an adversary of the state legislators (he may be seeking their assistance), nor is he giving them his authority to make decisions. Finally, (E) lacks both elements as well; the minister is a leader, not an adversary, who is discussing questions, not delegating authority.

16. **(E)** The author's reason for rejecting the notion of labor participation in management decisions is that the labor leaders first have a responsibility to the people they represent and that the responsibility would color their thinking about the needs of the corporation. His thinking is reflected in the adage (and this could easily have been worked into an LSAT-type question): No man can serve two masters. (B) is incorrect for the author is referring to the labor *leaders,* not the rank-and-file; and he specifically mentions that the leaders are skilled administrators. (D) is incorrect because it, too, fails to respect the distinction between union leader and union member. (A) is a distraction. The notion that the authority would be "symbolically undermined" is edifying but finds no support in the paragraph. In any event, it entirely misses the main point of the paragraph as we have explained it. (C) also fails to observe the distinction between leader and worker, not to mention also that it is only remotely connected with the discussion.

17. **(E)** The question stem advises us that the inconsistency is only "seeming." (E) explains it away. Of the total population, 70 percent take X and 30 percent take Y, yet only 75 percent of the population take anything at all. This means that some people took both X and Y. (A) is close, but it gets no cigar. While we can infer that there must be some overlap, we cannot conclude that the 30 percent is totally contained within the 70 percent. It is possible that only 25 percent of the population take both. In that case, we would have 5 percent who take Y only, 45 percent who take X only, and 25 percent who take both X and Y. This still leaves 25 percent of the population who take neither. (B) seems totally unrelated to the logic of the argument. As for (C) and (D), while these are possible weaknesses in any statistical argument, there is nothing to indicate that they operate here specifically.

18. **(A)** If II is true, then both independent clauses of II must be true. This is because a sentence which has the form "P and Q" (Eddie is tall and John is short) can be true only if both subparts are true. If either is false (Eddie is not tall or John is not short) or if both are false, then the entire sentence makes a false claim. If the second clause of II is true, then I must also be true, for I is actually equivalent to the second clause in II. That is, if "P and Q" is true then Q must itself be true. On this basis, (B) and (C) can be seen to be incorrect. (D) is wrong, for we can actually define the interrelationship of I and II as a matter of logic: We do not have to have recourse to a probabilistic statement; i.e., it is *unlikely.* (E) is incorrect since a statement of the form "P and Q" might be false and Q could still be true—if P is false, "P and Q" is false even though Q is true.

19. **(D)** Again, let us resort to the use of capital letters to make it easier to talk about the propositions. Incidentally, you may or may not find this technique useful under test conditions. Some people do, but others do not. We use it here because it makes explanation easier. Let us render the four premises as:

(1) All B are R.   (All Buckner are Reserve)
(2) All R are P.   (All Reserve are Priceless)
(3) No H is R.   (No Hemingway is Reserve)
(4) All R are C.   (All Reserve are Catalogue)

From this we can deduce: (5) All B are P. (using 1 and 2)
and: (6) No H is B. (using 1 and 3)

Since "no B is H" is equivalent to "no H is B" (there is no overlap between the two categories), (D) must be our correct answer. From (2), we would not want to conclude "all P are R," any more than we would go from "all station wagons are cars" to "all cars are station wagons"; so (A) is not a proper inference and cannot be our answer. As for (B), we can show that "all B are C" (using 1 and 4) and also "all B are P" (5), so we would be wrong in concluding that "no B are not P." As for (C), while we know that "no H is R," we would not want to conclude that "no H is P." After all, books by Hemingway may be priceless, but the Buckner collection and the Reserve Room may just not contain any. Finally, (E) is not deducible from our four propositions. We cannot deduce "all C is R" from "all R is C."

20. **(E)** Now, it must be admitted that a liar can abuse just about any word in the English language, and so it is true that each of the five answer choices is *conceivably* correct. But it is

important to keep in mind that you are looking for the BEST answer, which will be the one word which, more than all the others, is likely to be abused. As for (A), while there may be different ways of doing a random selection, we should be able to decide whether a sample was, in fact, selected fairly. Although the ad may be lying about the selection of participants in the study, we should be able to determine whether they are lying. In other words, though they may not have selected the sample randomly, they cannot escape by saying, "Oh, by *random* we meant anyone who liked the Goblin." The same is true of (C), *first*. That is a fairly clear term. You add up the answers you got, and one will be at the top of the list. The same is true of (D), a "response" is an answer. Now, (B) is open to manipulation. By asking our question correctly, that is, by finagling a bit with what we mean by "handling," we can influence the answers we get. For example, compare: "Did you find the Goblin handled well?" "Did you find the Goblin had a nice steering wheel?" "Did you find the wheel was easy to turn?" We could keep it up until we found a question that worked out to give a set of "responses" from "randomly" selected drivers who would rank the Goblin "first." Now, if the one category itself is susceptible to manipulation, imagine how much easier it will be to manipulate a "composite" category. We have only to take those individual categories in which the Goblin scored well, construct from them a "composite" category, and announce the Goblin "first" in the overall category. There is also the question of how the composite was constructed, weighted, added, averaged, etc.

21. **(A)** The explanation given is no explanation at all. It is like a mechanic saying to a motorist, "Your car did not get over this steep hill because it did not have enough grade climbing power." While the author may have speculated about when and how his death would occur, it cannot be said that his explanation was speculative. So (A) is correct, not (B). Of course, since the explanation is merely circular, it cannot be considered medically sound, any more than our hypothetical mechanic's answer is sound as a matter of automotive engineering, so (D) must be wrong. As for (C), while the author's *announcement* may be self-serving, designed to aggrandize his reputation, the *explanation* he gives in the announcement is not. Finally, the explanation is not self-authenticating, that is, it does not provide that

standard by which its own validity is to be measured. So (E) can be overruled.

22. **(D)** It is important not to attribute more to an author than he actually says or implies. Here the author states only that Ronnie's range is narrow so he will not be an *outstanding vocalist*. *Vocalizing* is only one kind of music career, so I, which speaks of professional *musicians*, takes us far beyond the claim the author actually makes. II also goes beyond what the author says. He never specifies what range an outstanding vocalist needs, much less what range is required to vocalize without being outstanding. Finally, III is an assumption since the author moves from a physical characteristic to a conclusion regarding ability.

23. **(C)** You should remember that there is a very important distinction between "numbers" and "percentages." For example, an increase from one murder per year to two murders per year can be described as a "whopping big 100% increase." The argument speaks only of percentages, so we would not want to conclude anything about the numbers underlying those percentages. Therefore, both (A) and (B) are incorrect. They speak of "more agents," and "more people," and those are numbers rather than percentages. Furthermore, if we would not want to draw a conclusion about numbers from data given in percentage terms, we surely would not want to base on percentages a conclusion about efficiency or work accomplished. Thus, (D) and (E) are incorrect. What makes (C) the best answer of the five is the possibility of making percentage comparisons *within* each agency. Within both agencies, the number of field agents increased by a greater *percentage or proportion* than the non-field agents.

24. **(D)** Keeping in mind our comments about (D) and (E) in the preceding question, (A) must be wrong. We do not want to conclude from sheer number of employees anything about the actual work accomplished. (B) and (E) are incorrect for pretty much the same reason. The question stem asks us to give an argument *defending* the CIA against the *claim* that it is *overstaffed*. Neither rate of pay nor appropriations has anything to do with whether or not there are too many people on the payroll. (C) is the second best answer, but it fails because it does not keep in mind the ratio of non-field agents to field agents. Our concern is

not with the number of agents generally, but with the number of *support* and *supervisory* workers (reread the question stem). (D) focuses on this nicely by explaining why the CIA should experience a faster increase (which is to say, a greater percentage increase) in the number of its supervisory personnel than the FBI.

25. **(B)** This is essentially an analogy question. Argument from analogy is an important form of argument, and the LSAT has many different ways of determining whether or not a student can use that argumentative technique. In this question, we are looking for the tool which is most analogous to a rule-of-thumb moral principle. Our task is made easier by the string of adjectives that follows the blank. We need a tool which is useful in many situations, which rules out a tuning fork (D) and an electrical generator (C), both of which have highly specialized functions. Moreover, we need a tool which requires no special training, so we can eliminate answer (A). Finally, although a library book requires no special training, it has only one use—to be read. Though the knowledge it contains may be generally useful, the book itself, *qua* book, has only one use.

26. **(A)** The point of the passage is that a moral decision sometimes seems difficult because we are using moral principles which are too general. They work most of the time, but sometimes they are too abstract, and as a result, two or more of them give contradictory results. (D) and (E) are wrong, then, for they confuse the value of abstract and particular principles. When a conflict arises, we need principles which are more specific, not more abstract, (D) and particularly (E). (C) is a distraction; the medical character of the example was purely fortuitous and irrelevant to the author's point about moral reasoning. (B) is edifying but hardly a logical completion of the paragraph. The author is not trying to explain advances in moral reasoning; he is explaining two different levels of moral reasoning available to us now.

27. **(D)** Let us use letters to represent the categories. "All effective administrators" will be A. "Concerned about welfare" will be C. "Are liberal" will be L. The three propositions can now be represented as:

1. All A are W.

2. All W are L.
3. All non-L are not A.

Proposition #3 is equivalent to "all A are not non-L," and that is in turn equivalent to "all A are L." Thus, (D) follows fairly directly as a matter of logic. (A) is incorrect, for while we know that "all A are L," we would not want to conclude that "No L are A"—there might be some ineffective administrators who grant time off. They could be ineffective for other reasons. (B) is incorrect for the same reason. Even though all effective administrators are concerned about their employees' welfare, this does not mean that an ineffective administrator could not be concerned. He might be concerned but ineffective for another reason. (C) is clearly false given our propositions; we know that all effective administrators are liberal. Finally, (E) is not inferable. Just because all effective administrators grant time off does not mean that all the time granted off is granted by effective administrators.

28. **(C)** The weakness in Gerry's argument is that he assumes, incorrectly, that getting drunk is the only harm Clyde has in mind. Clyde could respond very effectively by pointing to some other harms of alcohol. (A) would not be a good response for Clyde since he is concerned with Gerry's welfare. The fact that other people get drunk when Gerry does not is hardly a reason for Gerry to stop drinking. (B) is also incorrect. That other people do or do not get drunk is not going to strengthen Clyde's argument against Gerry. He needs an argument which will impress Clyde, who apparently does not get drunk. (D) is perhaps the second best answer, but the explicit wording of the paragraph makes it unacceptable. Gerry has been drinking the same quantity for 15 years. Now, admittedly, it is possible he will begin to drink more heavily, but that *possibility* would not be nearly so strong a point in Clyde's favor as the *present* existence of harm (other than inebriation). Finally, (E) is irrelevant, since it is white wine which Gerry does drink.

29. **(B)** The point of the passage is that a meaningful comparison between the two systems is going to be difficult since the one is cheap in the short run but expensive in the long run, while the other is expensive in the short run and cheap in the long run. The only appropriate way of doing the cost comparison is by taking account of both costs— which is what (B) does. To take just the long-run

costs would be to ignore the short-run costs involved, so (A) is wrong; and taking the short-run costs while ignoring the long-run costs is no better, so (C) is wrong. If (A) is wrong, then (D) also has to be wrong, and the more so because it is not even projecting operating costs. Finally, (E) is a distraction—the connection between diesel fuel and air pollution is irrelevant in a paragraph which is concerned with a cost comparison.

30. **(B)** One way of "making more money" other than raising the price of a product is to lower the size or quality of the product. This is what Vendo must have done. By doing so, they accomplished the equivalent of a price increase without actually raising the price. (C) contradicts the paragraph which states that Vendo did not violate the letter of the instructions—that is, the literal meaning—though they did violate the intention. (D) also contradicts the paragraph. Had Vendo forfeited the franchise, that would have been within the letter of the "either-or" wording of the instructions. (A) and (E) require much speculation beyond the information given, and you should not indulge yourself in imaginative thinking when there is an obvious answer such as (B) available.

31. **(D)** The author's argument seems fairly weak. He introduces the example of the second university without explaining why we should consider that case similar to the one we are arguing about (except for size). This shows that the author is introducing an analogy—though not a very strong one. (A) is perhaps the second best answer. But it would be correct only if there were a *contention* that the author had introduced new evidence in support of the argument. He does not articulate a contention and then adduce evidence for it. (B) is wrong because the author really has no solution to the problem—he wants to argue the problem does not exist. Finally, (C) and (E) must be wrong because the author never mentions a logical contradiction nor does he point to any ambiguity in his opponent's argument.

32. **(E)** Careful reading of the ad shows that all three propositions could be true even if the ad is correct. First, another deodorant might also give all-day protection. The ad claims that White Bear is the only deodorant which gives you *both* protection and scent—a vacuous enough claim since White Bear is probably the only deodorant with

the White Bear scent. Of course, III is not affected by this point, since the White Bear Company may put its unique scent into many of its products. Finally, II is also not inconsistent with the ad—that another product is more popular does not say that it has the features the ad claims for the White Bear deodorant.

33. **(D)** The easiest way to set this problem up is to draw a relational line:

```
        PE      IP      EL      BE
Dislikes————————————————————→ Likes
```

We note that Clara likes Basic Economics better than anything else, which means she must like it better than Advanced Calculus. So even though Advanced Calculus does not appear on our line, since we know that Basic Economics is the maximum, Clara must like Advanced Calculus less than Basic Economics. So (C) can be inferred. But we do not know where World History ranks on the preference line, and since Introductory Physics is not a maximal or a minimal value, we can make no judgment regarding it and an unplaced course. Quick reference to the line will show that (A), (B), and (E) are inferable.

34. **(B)** We have seen examples before of the form of argument Holmes has in mind: "P or Q; not-P; therefore, Q." Here, however, the first premise of Holmes' argument is more complex: "P or Q or R . . . S," with as many possibilities as he can conceive. He eliminates them one by one until no single possibility is left. The logic of the argument is perfect, but the weakness in the form is that it is impossible to guarantee that all contingencies have been taken into account. Maybe one was overlooked. Thus, (B) is the correct answer. (A), (C), and (E) are wrong for the same reason. Holmes' method is designed to answer a particular question—in this case, "Where did the body come from?" Perhaps the next step is to apply the method to the question of the identity of the murderer, as (E) suggests, but at this juncture he is concerned with the preliminary matter of how the murder was committed. In any event, it would be wrong to assail the logic of Holmes' deduction by complaining that it does not prove enough. Since (A) and (C) are even more removed from the particular question raised, they, too, must be wrong. Finally, (D) is nothing more than a reiteration of Watson's original comment, and Holmes has already responded to it.

35. **(C)** Notice that the student responds to the professor's comment by saying, "That can't be true," and then uses the Duchess of Warburton as a counter-example. The Duchess would only be a counter-example to the professor's statement had the professor said that women cannot inherit the estates of their families. Thus, (C) must capture the student's misinterpretation of the professor's statement. What has misled the student is that he has attributed too much to the professor. The professor has cited the general rule of primogeniture——the eldest male child inherits——but he has not discussed the special problems which arise when no male child is born. In those cases, presumably a non-male child will have to inherit. (E) incorrectly refers to inheriting from a mother in discussing a case in which the woman inherited her father's estate. (D) is wrong, for the student specifically mentions the conditions which make a child legitimate: born to the wife of her father. (A) was inserted as a bit of levity: Of course, only men can *father* children of either sex. Finally, first-born or not, a daughter cannot inherit as long as there is any male child to inherit, so (B) must be incorrect.